Contemporary Developments in Mathematical Psychology

VOLUME I

Contemporary Developments
in Mathematical Psychology

VOLUME I

Learning,
Memory,
and
Thinking

EDITED BY

DAVID H. KRANTZ
THE UNIVERSITY OF MICHIGAN

RICHARD C. ATKINSON
STANFORD UNIVERSITY

R. DUNCAN LUCE
UNIVERSITY OF CALIFORNIA, IRVINE

PATRICK SUPPES
STANFORD UNIVERSITY

W. H. FREEMAN AND COMPANY
San Francisco

Library of Congress Cataloging in Publication Data
Main entry under title:

Contemporary developments in mathematical psychology.

Includes bibliographies.
CONTENTS: v. 1. Learning, memory, and thinking.
1. Human behavior—Mathematical models—Collected
works. 2. Psychometrics—Collected works. I. Krantz,
David H., 1938–   ed. [DNLM: 1. Psychometrics.
BF39 C761]
BF39.C59   150'.1'84   73-21887
ISBN 0-7167-0848-5 (v. 1)

Printed in the United States of America.

9 8 7 6 5 4 3 2 1

Contents

Introduction

The two volumes of this symposium are an attempt by the editors to define the concept of progress in mathematical psychology. The definition is ostensive, by means of a series of exemplars; this preface attempts to define the same concept briefly by means of attributes and to note and to account for possible discrepancies between the two definitions.

A necessary feature of progress in science is its cumulative nature. We interpret this quite strictly: no experiment or theory, however clever, sophisticated, or compelling, fits our concept of progress unless it forms part of a growing chain or lattice of development. Thus, our criteria for excellence in mathematical psychology need not be the same as those for progress or development. It is considerably easier to judge excellence; that is what we usually do when refereeing articles. Excellent work may not lead to progress, for any of a variety of reasons: it may fall outside the mainstream of development, or it may reveal clearly why a particular approach is a blind alley, or it may be ahead of its time. On the other hand, it is quite possible that work that contains glaring flaws may nevertheless provide a key element on which all later work in the same field will depend.

It is easy to point to excellent work in mathematical psychology, past and present. But in retrospect, cumulative progress is less easy to find. Psychology is full of beginnings, and in the past two decades mathematical psychology has contributed no small part of these. One need not be apologetic about the sinking of many pillars that support little superstructure. Historically, cumulative progress is the exception rather than the rule in the search for knowledge. Nevertheless, without apologizing for the past, we do need to ask ourselves whether we can do better in the coming decades. Is it possible that the lack of cumulative progress is partly due to that goal being subordinated to others, such as originality or technical mastery? If so, then that goal needs to be formulated more directly, and seeking it needs to be encouraged.

Our conception, in this project, was to identify a series of areas in which mathematical methods (broadly defined) have played an integral role in the recent cumulative development of psychological knowledge. Our goal is to influence the scientific judgments of mathematical psychologists, both in respect to choice of problem area and in respect to standards of accomplishment. We are not trying to influence the level of technical excellence, nor to emphasize creativity, but rather to direct attention to the criterion of cumulative substantive progress. We wrote to potential authors as follows:

> The purpose of this project is to survey research areas in which mathematical methods have led, in recent years, to advances in psychological knowledge that seem relatively permanent. The majority of the contributions will exposit research in which the use of formal models and/or quantitative methods has produced substantive knowledge that is known, or ought to be known, by all workers in the given field, regardless of their mathematical orientation. Other contributions—though a minority—will exposit advances in mathematical methodology that seem to have wide applicability.
>
> The volume should constitute a set of paradigms for Mathematical Psychology, in two senses. First, it may influence mathematically oriented graduate students and fellow scientists to enter an area in which real progress has been made; their work will be likely to extend the progress. Second, it should set a standard of quality of achievement, influencing thereby the goals of psychologists in all fields of research.

Naturally, perturbations have occurred along the way. We were undoubtedly wrong in a good many of our decisions, both for inclusion and for exclusion of particular areas. Moreover, some chapters did not turn out exactly as we expected, and three or four that we invited and very much wanted to include were not forthcoming. Since these remarks, though perfectly truthful, sound like a hedge against criticism of our final product, it may be well for us to discuss more fully a few specific inclusions and exclusions.

Perhaps the most striking exclusion is the entire area of preferential choice. There is no lack whatever of technically excellent papers in this area, but they give no sense of any real cumulation of knowledge. What are the established laws of preferential choice behavior? (Since three of the editors have worked in this area, our attitude may reflect some measure of our own frustration.)

Perhaps the most striking inclusion is the strong emphasis on sensory mechanisms in Volume II. There is a chapter on vision and one on hearing (another chapter on vision was invited but was not written), and sensory mechanisms comprise the background and part of the substance of the three chapters on psychophysics as well as the chapter on brain function. The sensory emphasis may seem disproportionate when compared with the set of publications in mathematical psychology, but we think it is a natural consequence of our criterion of cumulative progress. Nowhere in psychology is there as much cumulative knowledge, much of it in quantitative form, as in the sensory area; so it is natural that new theoretical contributions should continue to build on the established paradigms.

Originally, we planned to include six chapters on methodological advances that we felt are so important that they are bound to have lasting value in psychology. They were: one chapter on the use of normative models, one on stochastic processes, and four on measurement and scaling. The chapter on normative models was not written; the one on stochastic processes turned out to be largely substantive (though we feel that perhaps its greatest contribution is in illustrating the advantage, and even the necessity, of translating vague verbal theories into precise models that have definite predictions); and one author, produced instead of a methodological piece, a new and integrative psychophysical theory. The latter is not in the least an exemplar of our original concept (though it could become one in time), but it is an interesting nonexemplar. In the end, we no longer tried to separate sharply the methodological from the substantive contributions. The chapter on covariance models is perhaps the most obviously methodological one, but even in it the examples illustrate important substantive developments in test theory.

During the summer of 1972, some of the authors and the editors met in Ann Arbor for three days presenting and discussing drafts of these chapters. On some issues there was surprising convergence—for example, no one seemed to take a reductionist position on the nature of truth in mathematical theorizing. On others, there was broad disagreement—for example, the future of learning theory, and the very criteria of cumulative progress. The areas of memory and thinking are beset with conflicting approaches; one critique is offered in the comments by an invited discussant.

The preparation of these two volumes and the 1972 summer conference were supported by funds from the Mathematical Social Science Board, which supervises a National Science Foundation grant administered through the Center for Advanced Study in the Behavioral Sciences. The editors wish to acknowledge the administrative contributions of the University of Michigan and of the Institute for Mathematical Studies in the Social Sciences, Stanford University. More specifically, we wish to mention the contributions of Amy Horowitz in the processing of manuscripts and organization of the summer conference and of Lillian O'Toole for copy editing and following up problems in the final manuscripts.

April 1974   *The Editors*

Contemporary Developments in Mathematical Psychology

VOLUME I

Representation of Learning as Discrete Transition in a Finite State Space

James G. Greeno

THE UNIVERSITY OF MICHIGAN

INTRODUCTION

Sometimes an important scientific development involves application of a very simple mathematical idea. The concept of a finite Markov chain is a simple mathematical idea, and it has been used in a large number of recent contributions to the psychological theories of memory, learning, and problem solving. In all these areas, analyses using finite Markov models have led to new substantive ideas and have also provided powerful new methods of analysis.

The impact of the idea of finite Markov chains in the psychology of learning has at least three aspects. First, the use of Markov chains with few states to represent learning has encouraged the development of ideas about learning processes involving relatively discrete changes in a learner's state of knowledge. Second, finite Markov chains have provided the basis of a rigorous methodology for investigating stages in the process of learning, both in the sense of separate accomplishments involved in a learning task, and in the sense of processing that occurs at different levels of a learning system. A third kind of impact involves the convenience achieved by representing a complex process as a homogeneous collection of elementary processes.

Discrete Changes in Learning

The idea that learning occurs as a discrete change usually has appeared in analyses given by Gestalt psychologists. The kind of learning discussed by Wertheimer (1959) is an example. In his well-known analysis of learning about the area of a parallelogram, the important learning event occurs when a child realizes that a triangle can be removed from one end of the parallelogram and placed at the other end, thus forming a rectangle whose area is the product of its two dimensions. This achievement gives a new understanding of what a parallelogram is—it corresponds to a change in the learner's cognitive structure. Similar emphasis on development of new cognitive organization in learning was given by Katona (1940), who illustrated the idea in experiments involving a kind of card trick. When Katona gave subjects a general procedure for tricks used in training, more subjects remembered the solutions to those tricks and transferred to new problems than was the case for subjects who learned only the specific solutions to the training tricks. The difference between the two groups does not seem to have resulted from some response that had higher strength in one group than the other. Rather, the difference probably occurred because of the presence of a cognitive structure corresponding to the general procedure in one group of subjects and the absence of that structure in the other group.

The occurrence of learning as a change in cognitive structure may occur suddenly, with the learner responding "Aha" when new insight is achieved; or the components of a new structure may be added one at a time, leading to a new understanding that is achieved without any dramatic feeling of discovery. Of course, discovery is fun, both for learners and for those who study the ways in which learning occurs. And some of the most widely known cases used to illustrate the idea of structural learning apparently have involved sudden and dramatic change in understanding. Köhler's (1927) observation of a chimpanzee who apparently realized in a flash of insight that two sticks could be put together to construct an object long enough to reach a banana in front of his cage has been used often as an illustration of nonhuman intellectual function. Another kind of learning involving discrete and sudden changes was considered by Lashley (1928), who assumed that learning in a situation involving many stimulus attributes or cues involves sudden shifts in attention; the learner will respond to one cue for a time, then attention will shift and he will respond to another cue. Achievement of successful performance eventually occurs when the subject (often a laboratory rat) finds a cue that is relevant in the sense of providing a basis for correct response.

In contrast to ideas of sudden change in cognitive structure, learning can also be conceptualized as a gradual change in some hypothetical quantity. Gradual change was assumed in early versions of association theory (see

Boring, 1950), where the strength of associative connection between ideas was assumed to increase each time the ideas are experienced together. A similar idea was used by Pavlov (1927), who assumed that a conditioned reflex gains strength each time the conditioned response is produced in the presence of the conditioning stimulus.

Conceptualizations of learning as gradual change in association or conditioned connection have been the basis of most theoretical analysis carried out during the twentieth century. Reasons for the greater popularity of gradualist ideas rather than structural conceptions were partly conceptual and philosophical. Many psychologists were much concerned with the ontological status of terms used in theory, and they were troubled by difficulties in dualistic views of the mind-body problem. Ideas like insightful discovery of relationships or shifts in attention seemed mentalistic and therefore out of tune with major methodological commitments of many theorists. A second set of reasons for the dominance of gradualist views about learning were probably experimental and technical. The kinds of situations needed to produce learning according to association theory or reflex theory are easy to assemble and are amenable to systematic control; by contrast, experimental study of insight and attention during learning has been more difficult.

But in addition to these reasons involving conceptualization and experimental procedures, there was a third reason for the dominance of learning theories that assume gradual changes in strength, and this reason involves mathematics. The mathematical training of psychologists, like that of most scientists, was centered around geometry and calculus. This training provided a natural basis for formalization of the idea of learning as a process of gradually increasing strength.[1] The major effort in developing a rigorous theory of learning during the 1940s and 1950s was carried out by Hull (1943, 1952) and Spence (1956). The Hull-Spence theory used the idea of a continuum of response strength represented by the real numbers, with learning processes producing changes in strength according to an exponential process. In the 1950s, a number of important analyses were given by Estes and others (see Estes, 1959), by Bush and Mosteller (1955), and by Luce (1959), treating response probability rather than response strength as the variable in which gradual changes occur during learning.

I cannot improve on the language used by Estes (1962, p. 111) in describing the importance of finite Markov chains against this background.

---

[1] Not only is serious analysis of discrete processes omitted in the standard mathematical curriculum, it is positively degraded. Continuous functions are 'well behaved,' while step functions have derivatives that 'vanish' or 'do not exist' at certain critical values. The kinds of functional relationships characteristic of discrete changes often count as one kind of 'pathological' behavior. Careful study might reveal that finite mathematicians, like other members of minority groups, suffer discrimination rooted in the very language we use to express our ideas.

. . . scientific theory in any area reflects the current state of formal as well as experimental methodology. The ideas which can be most fully elaborated and tested are those that can be expressed in terms of the mathematical apparatus available to the theorist. And the classical sequence of mathematical courses built around the calculus (from which most psychologists, like other scientists, draw their formal training) leads to familiarity almost exclusively with methods appropriate for dealing with changes in continuous variables. . . .

Only during the very last few years has the grip of the classical mathematical curriculum on the formal armamentarium of learning theorists been broken. It is hardly an exaggeration to say that some of the most important recent books in psychology have been written by mathematicians. The first, and perhaps most important of these, was Feller's (1950) classic presentation of probability theory for discrete sample spaces (i.e., for finite collections of events). With this volume, supplemented by the useful introductory treatments of finite mathematics by Kemeny and Snell and their associates (1957, 1960), psychologists have had placed in their hands the simple but powerful methods of finite Markov chains. Popularization of these techniques led almost immediately to a drastic change in the manner of operating with . . . theory.

(It may be added that many teachers of mathematical psychology now yearn for students prepared in the mathematics found in Feller, 1950, and in Kemeny, Snell & Thompson, 1957.)

One aspect of the change in manner of operating has been that psychologists have looked with increasing energy for changes of a discrete kind. Several changes that have been found in considerable number and in some variety are discussed in this chapter.

Investigation of Stages

A second aspect of the impact of finite Markov chains on the psychology of learning has been in providing a rigorous methodology for investigation of stages in the process of learning. The study of stages has had two forms. First, the process of learning may involve two or more accomplishments that are relatively discrete and that occur in a sequence. Use of a Markov model enables the investigator to estimate the number of such stages that are involved in a learning system and to estimate the difficulty of each stage. Effects of experimental manipulations can be examined. Sometimes an experimental treatment results in a change in the state of the system prior to other experimental procedures, and analysis focuses on the initial location of the system in its state space. Other kinds of experimental manipulation can retard or accelerate transition in various parts of the chain. By noting the pattern of change in the parameters of a Markov model, the investigator can make relatively strong inferences about the nature of psychological processes involved in learning.

Second, in addition to supporting analysis of stages in the learning process, Markov models have been useful in analysis of details of the process of learning as it occurs in real time. Here, the idea of a state refers roughly to the level at which an item has been processed by the learner. Thus, an item may be held for a brief time in short-term memory, whether or not it has been processed sufficiently to have achieved a permanent representation in the learner's long-term memory. Conceptualization of various levels of processing as states in a Markov chain has led to valuable investigation of relationships between transient effects that can occur during learning and processes that involve relatively more permanent changes in the learner's knowledge or understanding.

Analytic Convenience

The third aspect of the impact of Markov models in the psychology of learning involves the convenience achieved by representing a complex process as a homogeneous collection of elementary processes. In many situations where learning occurs gradually, it has been possible to conceptualize the total learning process as an aggregation of elementary learning events, each involving some aspect of the situation or 'stimulus element.' Applying the usual simplifying assumptions of homogeneity, analyses have been carried out of several important problems, including effects of similarity between different learning conditions, effects of frequency of experience with various components of stimuli, and effects of dependencies between frequency of reinforcement for response and choices made by subjects. In these analyses the Markov assumption is applied to hypothetical elements of the situation, and performance of a learner in the situation is assumed to depend on an aggregation of elements.

In this chapter I focus attention on the first and second kinds of impact on psychology of learning mentioned earlier. Thus, I will sketch some of the results that have been obtained in which new discoveries of discrete processes have been made, and where analyses of stages in learning and in processing have been carried out. Some instances of the third kind of impact, involving analyses of hypothetical Markovian components, will be involved in the discussion but I do not concentrate on those, partly because the kind of analysis carried out there is less distinctive of psychology (the general technique is used in physics, genetics, and economics, among other fields). The examples that I use to illustrate applications of finite Markov models come from two areas: the theory of memorizing and the theory of conditioning. A third important area in which finite Markov chains have been applied with great benefit is the theory of problem solving, especially concept identification. I have not included these applications in this chapter, but another contribution to this volume (Millward & Wickens, 1974) gives an excellent presentation of work on concept identification.

THEORY OF MEMORIZING

All-or-None Processes

Recognition memorizing.   Basic properties of human memory have been studied in a variety of experimental situations. In one kind of experiment, some items such as nonsense syllables or letters are presented, one at a time, each for a brief period; then a series of tests are given. On each test an item is shown and the subject says whether he recognizes that item as part of the list he saw at the beginning. In the tests, the subject is shown each of the items from the list, but he also is shown other items of the same general kind called distractor items. After a series of tests, the subject is again shown all the items in the list, then another series of tests is given, and so on until the subject gives correct responses on all tests.

One theory about this experiment is that a subject stores representations of the items in his memory system. In order for the stored representations to be useful to the learner they must be distinctive, so that test items from the list will not be confused with distractor items. The stored representations must also be stable, so they will not be lost from memory nor degraded by interference from efforts to store new representations during the experiment. The process of storing representations might be simple or complex. The simplest would be an all-or-none process, where each time the subject studies an item, there is some probability a that he will store a stable, distinctive representation of it in memory. If he succeeds, he will then give the correct response for that item in the tests that follow. If he fails, he will be uncertain whether the item was in the list, and he will be correct with some probability p when that item is tested.

Under these assumptions, the process of learning to recognize each item can be represented as a simple absorbing Markov chain with two states. Items begin in state U, where a representation has not yet been stored; learning corresponds to a transition to the other state S, where a stable and distinctive representation has been stored. The transition matrix is

$$P = \begin{array}{c} \\ S \\ U \end{array} \begin{array}{cc} S & U \\ \hline 1 & 0 \\ a & 1-a \end{array},$$

and this operator is applied to each item each time it is studied.

States S and U do not correspond directly to the responses made by subjects, because sometimes a correct response is given while an item is still in state U. The conditional probabilities of response given the states of learning are

$$P = \begin{array}{c|cc} & \text{Correct} & \text{Error} \\ \hline S & 1 & 0 \\ U & p & 1-p \end{array}.$$

Since the data are obtained only on test trials, it is convenient to represent the system in a way that combines assumptions about learning and performance. This representation has three states: S, where a representation has been stored and correct response occurs; UC, where the item is not stored but correct response is given; and UE, where the item is not stored and the response is incorrect. The initial and transition probabilities of this chain are

$$P(S(1), UC(1), UE(1)) = (a, (1 - a)p, (1 - a)(1 - p)),$$

$$P = \begin{array}{c|ccc} & S(n+1) & UC(n+1) & UE(n+1) \\ \hline S(n) & 1 & 0 & 0 \\ UC(n) & a & (1-a)p & (1-a)(1-p) \\ UE(n) & a & (1-a)p & (1-a)(1-p) \end{array} \qquad (1)$$

Because the all-or-none assumption has a simple mathematical representation, it is easy to derive theorems that can be used as the basis for empirical tests of the assumption. For example, consider the number of errors made by a subject on a single item. Each error corresponds to an occurrence of state UE in Equation 1. Eventually, the system will absorb in state L, so the number of occurrences of UE (the number of errors) will be finite. Also, for any number x, there is a definite probability that exactly x errors will occur before the system absorbs. Let X be a random variable equal to the number of errors occurring before absorption. The probability distribution of X is

$$P(X = x) = (1 - \alpha)^x \alpha, \qquad (2)$$

where α is a shorthand notation for the quantity $a/(1 - p + ap)$. Techniques for deriving theorems based on Markov chains are available in numerous sources, including Atkinson, Bower, and Crothers (1965); Kemeny and Snell (1960); Levine and Burke (1972); and Restle and Greeno (1970).

Use of a formula like Equation 2 in testing the all-or-none assumption depends on substituting a numerical value for the parameter α. This involves estimation of parameters, a problem in statistics that is quite easy to solve for simple Markov models (see Atkinson, Bower & Crothers, 1965, Ch. 9; Restle & Greeno, 1970, Ch. 9). As one example, consider the theoretical mean number of errors before learning, the expected value of X. From Equation 2, it can be shown that

$$\mu_x = (1 - \alpha)/\alpha;$$

therefore,

$$\alpha = 1/(1 + \mu_x).$$

Then to obtain a numerical estimate of α, one can substitute the observed mean number of errors $\bar{x}$, for the theoretical mean μ_x, obtaining the estimate

$$\hat{\alpha} = 1/(1 + \bar{x}). \tag{3}$$

With a numerical value for α, Equation 2 gives a set of theoretical proportions that can be compared with proportions obtained in the experimental results. The extent of agreement or disagreement can be evaluated using standard statistical techniques, such as the chi-square test for goodness of fit.

A large number of theorems like Equation 2 can be derived and used to test the empirical adequacy of a Markov model. For example, the trial number of the last error is a random variable, and its distribution can be derived easily. Conditional statistics, such as the probability of an error on trials before the last error, can also be derived and compared with data, as can the distribution of the length of runs of consecutive errors and other sequential properties.

Although any theorem in which a testable prediction is made about observable statistics can be used to test the model, some theorems relate to critical assumptions of the model in ways that seem intuitively direct. Theorems about the distributions of errors and trial of last error have that property, since they follow directly from the assumptions of parameter constancy that are at the core of the all-or-none assumption. In the geometric distribution, the theoretical proportion of items having n errors is a constant fraction α of the set of items having more than $n - 1$ errors. That is,

$$P(X > n - 1) = (1 - \alpha)^n,$$
$$P(X = n) = (1 - \alpha)^n \alpha = \alpha P(X > n - 1).$$

If learning did not occur in an all-or-none fashion, then the probability of achieving criterion should change during trials when partial learning was occurring. This could correspond to a system in which parameters like a and p changed over trials, and the distribution of statistics like the number of errors could be quite different from the geometric distribution in a system with changing transition probabilities.

Good agreement between predictions like Equation 2 and the empirical distributions seen in data has been obtained in at least one set of experiments on recognition learning (Kintsch & Morris, 1965). An important feature of such a test is that information is obtained regarding the complete distribution of scores. In much experimental work, the mean score in each experimental condition is used, but the rest of the information in the distribution of scores is not considered as useful information. In fact, variability is often considered as a positive nuisance, and experimenters hope for small variance that permits significant effects with few subjects. However, with a quantitative model that specifies a stochastic process generating subjects' performance, the variability between subjects and items is usable as data and provides information about the process that is being studied.

Paired-associate memorizing.   A second kind of learning system that is approximated by an all-or-none hypothesis is simple paired-associate memorizing with a small number of responses. In paired-associate memorizing, a list of stimuli (words, nonsense syllables, or some such) is presented, with each stimulus paired with a response of some sort, such as a word or a number. On a test the subject is shown a stimulus and tries to remember which response was paired with it. There may be a different response for each stimulus, or there may only be two or three responses, with several stimuli having the same response.

When the number of responses is small and stimuli are distinctive, data of paired-associate memorizing agree quite well with predictions derived from the all-or-none model. In an early study, Bower (1961) had subjects memorize lists where the response for each item was either the numeral '1' or '2.' Bower compared data with a large number of theorems, including distributions of the number of errors, trial of last error, and trial of first correct response, as well as several conditional statistics and sequential properties of subjects' performance. Agreement between these detailed quantitative predictions and the observed properties of data was virtually exact.

When more than two responses are used, but the number is still small, there are discrepancies from predictions of the all-or-none hypothesis. However, these discrepancies generally have been detected by special experimental procedures. For example, Binford and Gettys (1965) used three and six response alternatives, stopping subjects after each error and asking them to give their next guess about which response was correct. Performance on these second guesses was above chance, which indicated that subjects had information about at least some items that had not yet resulted in complete learning. On the other hand, in experiments run using the standard procedure for paired-associate memorizing with up to five or six responses, predictions about distributions and other statistical properties have generally been accurate enough that discrepancies are not detected by standard statistical techniques (Greeno & Scandura, 1966; Polson, Restle, & Polson, 1965). A reasonable conclusion from the present evidence would be that with distinctive stimuli and a small number of responses the process of memorizing an association is approximately equivalent to the process of learning to recognize a single item. A possible reason is that the process is mainly storage of a stable representation of the item, with only a small amount of information having to be retrieved for performance on a test to be correct.

Transfer of training.   One use of the all-or-none model has been the analysis of transfer or generalization of association. Generalization refers to the occurrence of response to a stimulus different from, though similar to, the stimulus paired with the response during training. In conditioning theory, stimuli are assumed to have locations in a mental space, with greater differences between stimuli corresponding to greater distances between locations in the space. In this view, an associative connection from a stimulus to a response generates an induced or generalized connection from other stimuli, near the first one, to the response. On the view that strength of stimulus-response connection is a point on a continuum, it is natural to expect that generalized stimulus-response connection should also be a continuous function, depending on the similarity between stimuli used in training and in the generalization test.

The view of generalized strength as a continuous function of similarity does not fit well with the idea that learning can be represented as a two-state system, with items residing either in a state where they are known or not known. This two-state view of learning seems to require a two-state view of generalization. If there are only two states of learning—learned and un-learned—then, if a new stimulus is presented after training on another stimulus that is similar, the subject should be in one of two states. Either the similarity is recognized and the new association is known, or the item is functionally new for the subject, who is in the unlearned state.

If stimulus-response association varies along the continuum, then similarity between stimuli should be related to generalized strength of response by a continuous function. But if stimulus-response association is discrete, being either unlearned or learned, then similarity between stimuli can determine probability of generalized association, so that generalization will occur for a larger proportion of similar than dissimilar stimuli. If learning can be described as a transition between states, as given in Equation 1, then the effect of generalization should be seen in the probability of a new item being in state S. In the discrete-state view, learning of a response r to stimulus x, similar to y, leads to a probability that association between y and r will occupy state S, rather than state U, at the beginning of practice on the y-r pair.

One experiment that tests this view begins with training on a set of associations. Then a new list of paired-associate items is presented, with items in the second list varying in similarity to items in the first list. The subject is asked to give a response to each stimulus in the second list as a preliminary test, then the pair is shown, thus informing the subject of the correct response. The complete list is shown, then shown again, and repeated until the subject can give the correct response on all tests.

Analysis in terms of occupancy of discrete states says that if learning is all or none, then items in the second list may start in the learned state, on the basis of transfer from similar items in the first list. The process is represented by a Markov chain with an initial vector allowing for such transfer:

$$P(S(1),\ UC(1),\ UE(1)) = (t, (1 - t)p, (1 - t)(1 - p)),\qquad (4)$$

where t is the probability that a new item is known at the beginning. The transition probabilities are the same as the original model, Equation 1. An important possibility is that differences between items in the second list could be due entirely to differences in the value of t, with no differences in the transition parameters. This would indicate that similarity between items affects probability of state occupancy at the beginning of a transfer task, but does not affect probability of transition between states during the transfer task.

One experimental test that has been conducted (Greeno & Scandura, 1966) used short transfer lists containing six stimuli and three responses, with the responses being easy nonsense syllables shown to the subject at all times. In a training list, subjects had memorized seven associations, with one, two, and four items in three categories. One version of the lists used is shown in Table 1. The four words paired with "Pel" in List 1 are similar in referring to things that are small, the two words paired with "Mur" refer to white things, and the word "Knuckle," paired with "Dix," is in the category of round things. (The attribution of category membership is based on associations given by subjects asked to give a sense impression they associate with each word in a long list. For example, a few subjects say that "Freckle" reminds them of "Small." See Underwood & Richardson, 1956.) The six items in List 2 include one new stimulus word in each of the three categories, paired with the same response that went with the corresponding words in the first list, and three control words each paired with one of the responses.

TABLE 1
Items used in transfer experiment

List 1		List 2	
Stimulus	Response	Stimulus	Response
Freckle	Pel	Atom	Pel
Earthworm	Pel	Sulphur*	Pel
Tweezer	Pel	Ivory	Mur
Grasshopper	Pel	Alley*	Mur
Paste	Mur	Globe	Dix
Sheep	Mur	Beak*	Dix
Knuckle	Dix		

* Control words, unrelated to the category concepts, which in these lists were small (Pel), white (Mur), and round (Dix).

The similarity between items in List 1 and List 2 was varied in two ways in the experiment. The main difference was between experimental and control items. No transfer should occur for the control words, but some amount of transfer was expected for the items in List 2 taken from the same categories as their List 1 counterparts. The other manipulation of similarity was based on the degree to which the category relationships were obvious. The association "White" is given by many subjects to words such as "Ivory" or "Linen" or "Snow." "White" is given much less frequently to words such as "Paste" or "Sheep." Items for which common membership in a category is obvious should have greater functional similarity; that is, more transfer should occur when words have a more obvious relationship of similarity. The degree of obviousness was varied in both List 1 and List 2, giving four experimental conditions (high degree of relationship in both, high in 1 and low in 2, low in 1 and high in 2, and low in both). In addition to varying the amount of transfer by degree of similarity between individual items, amount of transfer should also depend on the number of items from a category in List 1, since learning a larger number of items from a category should increase the probability that the subject will think of the category while learning List 1, and thus make it more probable that he has the category in mind when the items of List 2 are presented.

The major question asked in this study was whether the idea of transfer based on occupancy of discrete states agreed with the experimental results. In terms of the Markov model, the question is whether learning of the transfer items differed from control items mainly in the value of t, the probability of being in the learned state as soon as List 2 items were presented, with little or no difference in values of a and p, the probabilities of learning items that were not known at the beginning and of giving the correct response on an item not yet learned. The strongest test of this idea came from comparison between all the control items and all the experimental items, since this brought the largest amount of information to bear on the question. The result supported the discrete-state interpretation. A large difference was obtained between experimental and control items in the value of t; the average for the experimental items was 0.38, while the value of t for control items was not significantly different from zero. However, the transition parameters a and p had values that were not significantly different between transfer and control items.

The difference between transfer and control items can be examined in another way that uses frequency distributions of observed statistics rather than estimates of parameters and statistical tests. The relevant statistics are obtained by considering only items for which one or more errors occurred. Some control items should have no errors, since subjects have a chance of guessing correctly on the first trial and learning the item before an error is made. For the transfer items, there should be some cases in which transfer occurred, producing an item with zero errors, and in addition some nontransferred items should have no errors because of correct guessing and learning before an error. Thus, transfer and control items should have different proportions of items with zero errors. However, if the all-or-none idea is correct, the remaining items—those with one or more errors—should all be learned with equal difficulty. That is, if an error occurred on a transfer item, then it can be inferred that transfer did not occur on that item, and by the all-or-none hypothesis that item should be learned with the same parameters as control items. When comparison was made between transfer and control items that had one or more errors, no difference between the two conditional distributions was observed.

Learning conceptual categories. If the basic conclusion is accepted that learning and transfer are both occurring on the basis of transitions in a discrete state space, then that idea can be used to give an analysis of the process by which subjects learn the rules under which items are grouped into categories. This analysis involves an extension of the basic all-or-none learning theory. In addition to describing the learning of individual items, we wish to represent the process of discovering the relationships among items.

In experiments involving category relationships, the additional process is just one of finding the category in which related items belong. This suggests that whenever a subject learns a new item, there are two possibilities. He may learn the item in a way that does not involve the relationship it has to other items. Or his representation of the item may involve the property through which that item is similar to other items in the experiment.

A Markov model for the learning of items in one of the categories in a list has $k + 2$ states, where k is the number of items in the category. The subject starts in state S_0, where nothing is known. Each time an item from the category is presented, there is probability a that it will be learned, just as in the basic all-or-none theory. But if the item is learned, there are two possibilities. Either the subject moves from state S_0 to state S_1, where he simply has acquired a single stimulus-response association, or the subject moves from state S_0 to state C, where his representation of the item provides a basis for relating it to other members of the same category. If the subject is in state S_1 where one item has been learned, then presentations of other items in the category give opportunities to move either into state S_2, where two unrelated associations are known, or to state C. A transition matrix for the process is

$$T = \begin{array}{c} \\ C \\ S_k \\ S_{k-1} \\ \vdots \\ S_1 \\ S_0 \end{array} \begin{array}{c} C \\ \hline 1 \\ 0 \\ ac \\ \vdots \\ ac \\ ac \end{array} \begin{array}{c} S_k \\ 0 \\ 1 \\ a(1-c) \\ \vdots \\ 0 \\ 0 \end{array} \begin{array}{c} S_{k-1} \\ 0 \\ 0 \\ 1-a \\ \vdots \\ 0 \\ 0 \end{array} \begin{array}{c} \cdots \\ \cdots \\ \cdots \\ \\ \\ \cdots \\ \cdots \end{array} \begin{array}{c} S_2 \\ 0 \\ 0 \\ 0 \\ \vdots \\ a(1-c) \\ 0 \end{array} \begin{array}{c} S_1 \\ 0 \\ 0 \\ 0 \\ \vdots \\ 1-a \\ a(1-c) \end{array} \begin{array}{c} S_0 \\ 0 \\ 0 \\ 0 \\ \vdots \\ 0 \\ 1-a \end{array} \qquad (5)$$

where c is the conditional probability of acquiring the category, given that learning of an item occurs. It is easy to see that if learning is continued until all k of the items have been learned, one way or the other, the probability of the subject's having acquired the category is

$$P(\text{absorb in } C) = 1 - (1 - c)^k. \tag{6}$$

Equation 5 extends the learning theory in a straightforward way to allow for learning of category relationships. The other extension needed is an assumption about what happens when a transfer item is presented following training on a list with k examples of a categorical concept. The assumption used is that if the category was not acquired in List 1 (that is, if the system absorbed in state S_k rather than C) no transfer can occur. However, if the category was acquired, the new item will be correctly classified with some probability, denoted d. That is,

$$P(\text{transfer} \mid \text{absorb in } C) = d,$$
$$P(\text{transfer} \mid \text{absorb in } S_k) = 0. \tag{7}$$

Combining Equations 6 and 7, we obtain the value of the parameter t:

$$P(\text{transfer}) = t = [1 - (1 - c)^k]d. \tag{8}$$

Equation 6 was applied to the results obtained by Greeno and Scandura (1966), with c assumed to depend on the obviousness of the category relationships in List 1, and d assumed to depend on the obviousness of category membership of transfer items in List 2. Of course, k was set at the number of items in the category. The values of c obtained for obvious and not-so-obvious categories were 0.39 and 0.15; the respective values of d were 1.0 and 0.60. These estimated values of c and d give theoretical values of the transfer parameter t in all the conditions of the experiment where the obviousness of examples and the number of training examples varied. With values of t, a prediction can be made about the proportion of items in each condition that should have zero errors. The empirical proportions of errorless items were sufficiently consistent with the predicted proportions so that a chi-square statistic was not significant.

The analysis of learning conceptual categories illustrates an important use of Markov models in learning. Learning is not a unidimensional process, capable of representation as a change in value of a single variable. Rather, learning probably involves achievements and discoveries occurring at several levels, with events that occur at one level (such as coming to understand some general principle) affecting performance and influencing learning at other levels (such as learning individual items or solving specific problems). A model like that of Equation 5 does not begin to capture the complexity of many learning situations that we would like to understand, but it does show that, at least in simple cases, the principle of multilevel learning can be captured in a straightforward analysis that is easy to understand and work with.

The idea involved in this analysis is that learning at both of the levels involved is a discrete process, occurring in its simplest form in an all-or-none fashion. Greeno and Scandura's (1966) experiment gave information particularly relevant to the way in which knowledge at a more general level influences learning of individual items. Apparently that influence was all or none; if the category was acquired and the individual item was recognized as a member of the category, the response for the item was known; otherwise the item had to be learned as a new item. Greeno and Scandura's evidence about acquisition of the category concepts was not strong, consisting only in a successful analysis of the amount of transfer obtained in various conditions.

Much stronger evidence about the process of acquiring category concepts has been given by Batchelder (1971) and Polson (1972). Batchelder (1970) gave a careful analysis of the process of learning individual associations and acquiring a category concept when each category contains two items with similar stimuli and the same response. The two items in a category are distinguished in the analysis, so the system has five states: UU, where nothing is known; SU, where the first item has been learned as an individual association, but the second item is still unlearned; US, where the second, but not the first, item has been learned as an individual; SS, where both items are learned as individual associations; and C, where the category concept has been acquired. The purpose of this analysis is to represent a process in which general learning, affecting both items in a category, can occur when either of the individual items is studied. Two operators are distinguished; one applies when the first item is presented and the other applies when the second item is presented.

$$
P_1 =
\begin{array}{c|ccccc}
 & C & SS & US & SU & UU \\
\hline
C & 1 & 0 & 0 & 0 & 0 \\
SS & c_2 & 1 - c_2 & 0 & 0 & 0 \\
US & ac_1 & a(1 - c_1) & 1 - a & 0 & 0 \\
SU & c_2 & 0 & 0 & 1 - c_2 & 0 \\
UU & ac_1 & 0 & 0 & a(1 - c_1) & 1 - a
\end{array}
$$

$$
P_2 =
\begin{array}{c|ccccc}
 & C & SS & US & SU & UU \\
\hline
C & 1 & 0 & 0 & 0 & 0 \\
SS & c_2 & 1 - c_2 & 0 & 0 & 0 \\
US & c_2 & 0 & 1 - c_2 & 0 & 0 \\
SU & ac_1 & a(1 - c_1) & 0 & 1 - a & 0 \\
UU & ac_1 & 0 & a(1 - c_1) & 0 & 1 - a
\end{array}
$$

(9)

As before, a is the probability of storing an association; c_1 is the conditional probability of acquiring the category concept given that an association is stored at a certain trial, and c_2 is the probability that the category concept will be acquired when an item is shown for which the subject already has stored an individual association.

Batchelder (1971) applied the model of Equation 9 to five experiments in which related items (similar stimuli and the same response) were included in lists of associations that subjects memorized. Most of Batchelder's experiments used a procedure where just one of the related items was presented between tests of the entire list, so the tests gave considerable information about the way in which presentation of one item affected performance on the other. The model was tested by comparing predictions and data for performance on the individual items and the occurrence of double errors (tests when a subject gave incorrect response to both items in a category). Tests involving individual items compared theoretical and observed distributions of the number of errors and the trial of last error, as discussed earlier on pp. 7–8. (Of course, formulas for these distributions are different when categorical rules are being learned.) Predictions about the number of double errors relate directly to the special feature of Batchelder's experiment and the analysis we are considering, because the number of double errors reflects the interdependence between performance on the two similar items. A theory could give a correct analysis of the learning of individual items but be wrong about the way in which learning of categorical rules influenced performance on the individual items—that is, be wrong about the way in which learning of individual items was interrelated. We could hope to detect a mistake about the dependence between items by examining a statistic like the distribution of the number of double errors, which reflects the correlation between performance on related items. Batchelder's data were in good agreement with predictions derived from the model. Batchelder also found that an assumption of $c_2 > 0$ was supported better than $c_2 = 0$. (The assumption used and found to be consistent with data was $c_2 = ac_1$.)

The analysis given by Polson (1972) also considered acquisition of a concept category in detail. Polson analyzed the method of teaching concepts originally used by Hull (1920), in which a list is given that contains one stimulus item from each concept category to be taught, with each stimulus item paired with a different response. When this first list has been learned, a new list is given, containing a second example from each concept category paired with the same response as the example of that category in the first list. In any one list, the subject only has one item per category, and the category relationships occur between items in the successive lists.

The ideas used by Polson are similar to those presented above. Each time a subject learns an item in one of the lists, there is probability c that it will be learned in a way that can transfer to items from the same category in later lists. Whether transfer occurs depends on recognition of the new example; recognition occurs with probability d, given that the category concept has been acquired. Polson assumed that if a subject failed to recognize a category member in one list the category would be on another list and would have to be reacquired on a later list for transfer to occur again.

A model for the learning of items in the mth list has states C (category learned), S (individual association stored), and U (unlearned), with initial and transition probabilities

$$P_m(C_1, S_1, U_1) = (t_m, 0, 1 - t_m),$$

$$P = \begin{array}{c|ccc} & C & S & U \\ \hline C & 1 & 0 & 0 \\ S & 0 & 1 & 0 \\ U & ac & a(1-c) & 1-a \end{array} \qquad (10)$$

where t_m is the probability of ending the preceding list in state C and recognizing the new item, and where P applies each time an item is presented in the mth list. The learning of individual items is thus expected to be an all-or-none process, with the value of t_m measuring the amount of learning about category concepts that has taken place. Assuming that P is constant across all lists, the value of t_m is

$$t_m = \frac{cd}{1 - d + cd}[1 - (d - cd)^{m-1}], \qquad (11)$$

since learning the item from a category in each list provides an opportunity for the concept to be learned.

Polson applied the model of Equation 10 to experimental results, and some of the findings were impressively supportive. The main positive finding was that the effect of learning the categories was entirely a change in the value of t_m, with a, the probability of learning individual items, unrelated to the acquisition of category concepts. This finding is the same as the one obtained by Greeno and Scandura, described earlier, in which the difference between transfer and control items was entirely a difference in the initial probability of being in the learned state, with virtually no difference in transition parameters. The value of a was not constant over lists, but the same changes in a occurred for subjects who learned lists of unrelated words as for subjects who learned lists with category concepts. In this simple all-or-none system, the fact that the groups differed only in the initial parameters of each list means that in data the proportions of errorless items were greater for the lists with categorical relationships; however, if only items with one or more errors are considered, then the conditional distributions of errors were the same for transfer and control items. The conclusion of this finding is that to a good approximation, each item in the transfer lists either was known at the beginning of training on its list or had to be learned as an individual item with no benefit from the earlier training on related items. In other words, transfer occurred in an all-or-none fashion.

In addition to this positive finding regarding all-or-none transfer, Polson also obtained an important negative finding. In the theory derived from Equation 10, the probability of transfer t_m is a negatively accelerated function, as expressed in Equation 11. However, when t_m was estimated from the data, the values increased relatively slowly over the first two or three lists, in disagreement with the theory. Polson also observed strong dependency within the data of individual subjects. For example, several subjects showed essentially no transfer on the second and third lists, then apparently transferred on several of the items in the fourth list.

To adjust the model in light of this fact, Polson proposed that a certain proportion of subjects begin the experiment with an incorrect or incomplete understanding of the situation. This means that the value of c will be lower for some subjects than for others at the beginning of the experiment. The reason is that subjects who understand the nature of the relationships among items will be considering possibilities of the right kind, while subjects without that understanding will be less likely to find relationships among items because they are not looking for them. On the other hand, Polson proposed that when a subject with the lower initial value of c learned a concept happening by chance on a relationship that was present in the task, the subject thereby moved to the state in which the higher value of c applied. This two-stage theory of concept acquisition predicts values of t_m that increase more slowly on early lists, in agreement with Polson's empirical results.

Polson's analysis extends the use of Markov models to a system in which learning occurs at three interacting levels. Individual associations are memorized, there is learning of category concepts that involve relationships among the individual items, and there is discovery of a general learning strategy that influences the learning of the various category concepts. The conditions used in Polson's analysis are rather special, since the change in strategy always occurs when the first concept is learned. But the potential use of discrete-system analyses in the understanding of more general learning systems having several interacting levels seems most promising.

Stages of Learning

Learning occurs in an all-or-none fashion only under rather special circumstances. In cases where long lists of items are learned, especially when many response alternatives are used, or where stimuli are similar to each other, predictions derived from an all-or-none model are rejected in data. This means that in these situations learning is a more complex process than a single all-or-none transition. One reaction in research has been to investigate a model that is minimally more complex than the all-or-none model. The next simplest system beyond the all-or-none is a system with two stages of learning, each occurring in an all-or-none fashion. Then there are three states; denote them U, S, and R. A transition from U to S corresponds to the first stage of learning; transition into state R occurs when learning is complete. Transition probabilities can be denoted

$$P = \begin{array}{c} \\ R \\ S \\ U \end{array} \begin{array}{|ccc} R & S & U \\ \hline 1 & 0 & 0 \\ b_2 & 1 - b_2 & 0 \\ ab_1 & a(1 - b_1) & 1 - a \end{array} \qquad (12)$$

The value of a gives the probability of accomplishing the first stage of learning; b_1 and b_2 are probabilities of completing the learning process. Note that b_1 and b_2 are distinguished to allow for the possibility that the second stage is less likely to be accomplished on the trial when the system leaves state U than it is on later trials. For example, if the system always passed through state S on the way from U to R, then b_1 would be zero. In practice, b_1 and b_2 are therefore treated as separate parameters. However, in this discussion I will generally talk about the value of b, a single parameter, in referring to the probability of transition into state R. (Often data are consistent with the assumption $b_1 = b_2 = b$. In any case, b can be regarded as an average of b_1 and b_2.)

A decision that some learning system has two stages rather than just one can be made by examining the data obtained in a single experimental condition. In an all-or-none system, many statistics have distributions in the form of the geometric, as discussed earlier on pp. 7–8. When learning has two stages, statistics like the number of errors have more complex formulas and different forms that generally can be distinguished in data from the geometric. To derive the distribution it is necessary to make assumptions about initial probabilities and performance in the three states. If we assume

$$P(U_1, S_1, R_1) = (1 - a, a(1 - b), ab),$$

$$P = \begin{array}{c} \\ R \\ S \\ U \end{array} \begin{array}{|cc} \text{Correct} & \text{Error} \\ \hline 1 & 0 \\ p & 1 - p \\ 0 & 1 \end{array} \quad,$$

with $a \neq \beta$, then the distribution of the number of errors is

$$P(X = x) = [(1 - a)^{x+1} - (1 - \beta)^{x+1}] \frac{a\beta}{\beta - a}, \qquad (13)$$

where $\beta = b/(1 - p + bp)$. Equation 13 is the convolution of two distributions, each having the form of Equation 2, the distribution for a system with a single stage. One symptom of the difference between all-or-none learning and learning with two stages can appear in the mode of the distributions of errors and other statistics. Equation 2, for all-or-none learning, has its mode at zero. (With different assumptions about the initial probabilities, the mode may be at one.) Equation 13, for two-stage learning, has a mode greater than one for many parameter values, and generally has more density displaced away from zero toward the median of the distribution than does Equation 2. Data are frequently obtained in which distributions have a form like that of Equation 13, and where the geometric or almost geometric form required by the all-or-none hypothesis can be clearly rejected.

Although the results obtained in a single experimental condition can lead to the conclusion that learning involves two stages, that conclusion is not very rich in psychological content. A more satisfactory analysis specifies what happens at each stage of learning, and empirical tests of such specific hypotheses require some experimental manipulations. I will discuss three kinds of experimental investigation that have been carried out to study the nature of stages in memorizing.

Two of the kinds of empirical study are directly related to the idea that learning stages involve discrete transitions in a finite state space. The first kind uses an experimental treatment to manipulate probabilities of being in the various states at the beginning of a learning task. Manipulation of state occupancy influencing initial probabilities involves the same kind of logic as the analysis of category-concept acquisition described earlier. In the case of two-stage learning, if an experimental treatment can be found that places all items in state S or state R at the beginning of ordinary training, then we can infer that the process involved in the first stage of ordinary learning has been accomplished by the preliminary training. The kind of training that is effective in this way can be informative about the nature of the first learning stage.

A second kind of empirical study uses the idea that in the intermediate state of learning, after the first stage has been accomplished, performance should reflect whatever it is that constitutes the first stage of learning. In many situations, this change in performance can only be measured as a quantitative change in the probability of correct response, but some experiments have been developed in which transition to state S involves complete elimination of certain kinds of errors. In these experiments the ability to identify the kind of error made after completing the first stage of learning tells us a good deal about just what process is involved in the second stage of learning.

The third kind of empirical study that I will illustrate uses a property of the discrete-state representation that is more technical. On the assumption that the two stages of learning are both discrete transitions of an all-or-none kind, estimates of the probabilities of transition can be obtained. In the theory, the value of a determines the distribution of the number of trials spent in the unlearned state U, and the value of b determines the distribution of the number of trials spent in the intermediate state S. We cannot observe the transition from U to S directly, nor can we observe the transition into state R directly. Because only errors occur in state U, and only correct responses in state R, we do know that once a correct response occurs the item must have escaped state U, and if an error occurs the item must not yet be in state R. This means that if there are many trials before the first error, then the item probably had a long residence in state U; if there are many trials between the first correct response and the last error, then the item must have had many trials in state S, the intermediate state. However, these observable statistics in data are imperfectly correlated with the actual numbers of trials spent in the various states, and cannot be used in any simple way to estimate parameter values. The procedures that are appropriate for estimating a and b are somewhat more elaborate, involving computational methods. (Details are given by Greeno, 1968.)

A major purpose of extracting estimates of the parameters of the model is to be able to make inferences about the relative difficulty of the two stages of learning. If a turns out to be a large probability and b a small probability in some situation, then we can infer that the first stage of learning is quite easy in that situation, and that it is the second stage that causes most of the difficulty in learning. The kind of empirical study that exploits this property of enabling measurement of difficulty uses experimental variables that are known to influence overall difficulty of learning. When learning is compared in several situations, we can determine which experimental factors influence difficulty of the first stage, which influence difficulty of the second stage, and which influence difficulty in both stages. By noting what kinds of experimental variables produce changes in the difficulty in each stage of learning, we can draw inferences about what kind of process is involved at each stage.

Manipulation of state occupancy. The method of manipulating state occupancy was used in a study by Kintsch and Morris (1965). The experimental task involved studying a list of trigrams. One group of subjects memorized a list by the method of free recall, which involves studying all the items, then recalling as many as possible in any order, then studying the list again, and so on. The data were consistent with predictions derived from the two-stage model, such as Equation 13, and predictions such as Equation 2, derived from the all-or-none model, were rejected by the data. A second group had to learn to recognize the items in a list. Data of recognition learning were consistent with predictions derived from the all-or-none model.

It was suggested earlier that learning to recognize an item may involve an all-or-none process of storing a stable and distinctive representation of the item in memory. Kintsch and Morris' experiment was concerned with this possibility, and the all-or-none character of the result in recognition learning supports that idea. An additional possibility is that the first stage of learning in free recall memorizing is also a process of storing a representation of the item in memory. According to this idea, after an item is stored in memory there may be some further learning needed to enable the subject to recall the item reliably, but the first stage of recall learning should correspond to the kind of learning that occurs when a subject learns to recognize items.

Kintsch and Morris tested this idea by training one group of subjects to recognize a list of items, then having the subjects study the items in the method of free recall. If the first stage of free recall learning corresponds to a process that is accomplished when subjects learn to recognize, then the learning in free recall memorizing after recognition pretraining should be an all-or-none process. This expectation was confirmed. Recall that data from free recall memorizing had the properties of two-stage rather than all-or-none learning. (For example, the distribution of number of errors resembled the form of Equation 13, rather than Equation 2.) However, when subjects had to learn to recall items that they already had learned to recognize, data showed the more variable distributions and other properties of all-or-none learning. Since recognition training resulted in a situation where the remaining learning needed to recall items was apparently all or none, it is reasonable to conclude that, in free recall memorizing with no pretraining, the first stage of learning is closely related to the process of learning to recognize.

Diagnosis of stages by characteristic errors. The method of identifying characteristic errors in the intermediate stage was used by Polson, Restle, and Polson (1965), who studied the experimental task of paired-associate memorizing. The experiment was based on an idea developed by Restle (1964), who hypothesized that the first stage of paired-associate memorizing is the formation of an associative connection between stimulus and response, and that later stages involve learning to discriminate between similar stimuli and responses. Polson, Restle, and Polson's experiment used five distinctive responses and 16 stimuli. Eight of the stimuli were distinctive, and the other eight included four pairs that were very similar to each other. (For example, two stimuli were pictures of leaves, similar except for a small part of their outlines.) The expectation was that learning of the distinctive items should be all or none, because once the associative connection has been learned, the subject should be able to perform successfully on an item with a stimulus that will not be confused with other stimuli. However, the twinned items should have a two-stage learning process, because a process of learning to discriminate is needed in addition to learning of the stimulus-response connections. Further, the errors occurring in the twinned item after the first stage should be confined to the response that is correct for its twin.

The experimental result agreed with the expectation. Data from the distinctive items agreed with predictions from the all-or-none model, while for the twinned items distributions of statistics such as number of errors showed that more than one stage was involved in the learning process. On the other hand, the process of learning stimulus-response association was assumed to be all or none, and when that process has been accomplished errors different from the confusions between twinned items should no longer occur. This means that if confusions between twinned items are ignored the data for twinned items should agree with predictions from the all-or-none model. and this result was obtained to a good approximation. The result is consistent with the idea that the only errors that occurred in the intermediate state were confusions between similar items, and thus the result supported the idea that discrimination between similar items occurs during the second stage of learning.

Measuring effects of experimental variables on parameter values. The method of measuring effects of experimental variables on difficulty of the two stages has been used in two studies. Recall that this method involves obtaining estimates of learning parameters (a and b from Equation 12) in order to tell whether the first stage, the second stage, or both stages are affected by certain experimental variables. In a study conducted by Humphreys (Humphreys & Greeno, 1970) there was variation in difficulty of remembering differences between stimuli, with one set of stimuli being the numbers 1 through 8, and the other set being two-digit numbers 11, 12, 13, 21, 22, 23, 31, and 32. Another variable was difficulty of response, where responses in one set were pronounceable, such as HAZ, while responses in the other set were non-pronounceable, such as HPF. Response and stimulus difficulty were combined in the four possible ways, giving one condition with hard stimuli and hard responses, one with hard stimuli and easy responses, one with easy stimuli and hard responses, and one with easy stimuli and easy responses.

The difficulty of learning in each stage was measured in all four conditions, estimating parameters a and b. The main question is whether difficulty of stimuli and difficulty of response affect probability of learning in the respective stages. The standard statistical method of holding a parameter constant across conditions as a null hypothesis permits a well-defined test of the question whether a variable has substantial effect. For example, we consider whether response difficulty affected the first stage of learning. We can take two groups differing in response difficulty (for example, the groups having easy stimuli, one with easy responses and the other with hard responses) and fit the model to the data using the same value of the parameter a for both groups. (The method of fitting the model involves finding the value of a that gives the best fit.) We compare the agreement between the model and the data when a single value of a is used for both groups with the agreement when different values of a are used. If significant improvement is achieved by using different values of a, we conclude that response difficulty had an effect on difficulty of learning in the first stage.

The outcomes of the statistical test in Humphreys' data showed that response difficulty had an effect on learning in the first stage, but not in the second stage. Effects of stimulus similarity were significant in both the first and second stages of learning. The fact that difficulty in the second stage depended mainly on stimulus similarity agrees with Polson, Restle, and Polson's (1965) conclusion that learning to discriminate between similar items is the main process involved in the second stage of learning. The fact that the first stage depended on characteristics of both stimuli and responses suggests that the first stage is a process in which a representation of the stimulus-response pair is stored in memory. This evidence seems to go against a view, developed by Underwood and Schulz (1960) and held by many investigators, that the first stage of paired-associate memorizing is mainly a process of response learning and that stimulus-response association occurs mainly in the second stage. Underwood and Schulz's idea would lead us to expect that stimuli would have little effect in the first stage of learning, and that the second stage could easily depend on both stimuli and responses, in contrast to the result that was obtained.

The results obtained by Kintsch and Morris (1965), by Polson, Restle, and Polson (1965), and by Humphreys and Greeno (1970) all fit into a consistent interpretation of the psychological processes involved in the two stages of memorizing hypothesized in a model like that of Equation 12. The first stage of learning, transition out of state U, is a process of storing a stable representation of an item in memory. This process enables the subject to recognize the item, as in Kintsch and Morris' study, and its difficulty depends on characteristics of both the stimuli and responses used in the task, as found by Humphreys and Greeno. An additional stage of learning is needed if storage of a representation does not provide a reliable way of retrieving the item on a test. Learning to retrieve requires an additional stage if the subject has to recall items, as in Kintsch and Morris' study, probably because the subject needs an organized system of relationships among the items to be able to give all the responses. In paired-associate memorizing such as that studied by Polson, Restle, and Polson and by Humphreys and Greeno, difficulty in retrieval is closely related to similarity between stimuli, since the stimulus terms constitute the information given to the subjects on tests.

The general interpretation of two-stage learning involving storage and learning to retrieve was given further support in analysis of results involving negative transfer of training in memorizing. A number of experimental comparisons made by James and Greeno (1970) used two conditions often studied in investigations of paired-associate transfer. In one condition, called A-B, C-B, an initial list of stimulus-response pairs is followed by a transfer list having the same response terms but new stimuli. A second condition, called A-B, A-Br, has a transfer list containing the same stimulus and response terms as the initial list, but the items are repaired, giving a new set of stimulus-response associations. This experimental comparison shows greater difficulty in learning the A-Br list than the C-B list, showing that there is negative transfer of some kind due to memorizing the first list of associations.

Results obtained in measuring the difficulty of learning in the two stages have shown consistently large differences between C-B and A-Br in the parameters involved in the second stage, but small and usually nonsignificant differences in the first-stage parameter (Greeno, 1970; Greeno, James, & DaPolito, 1971). The result is consistent with the idea of two-stage learning having storage of a pair in the first stage and learning to retrieve in the second stage. The difference between C-B and A-Br is that in A-Br the stimuli used to retrieve items in the first list are still used, and the subject must develop a new system of retrieval for the second-list associations. The result seems inconsistent with another view, originated by Melton and Irwin (1940), in which a major source of negative transfer is the requirement of unlearning first-list associations. That view would lead us to expect most of the difference between C-B and A-Br to occur in the first stage of learning, contrary to the obtained finding.

Stages of Processing

The third kind of impact of the idea of a discrete system in the theory of memory has been its providing a way to represent the status of information at various stages of processing during study. The main contribution here has been the idea of a short-term memory system, capable of holding a few items at a time and generally holding any single item for only a brief interval. While an item is in the short-term memory system, processing occurs that strengthens the item's representation in more permanent memory, making it more likely that the subject can retrieve the item on a later test. The theory thus represents the process of memorizing as a series of discrete or partially discrete subprocesses, operating in real time.

Retention through brief intervals.   We are all familiar with the fact that a relatively small amount of information can be recalled a few seconds after it is received by a person, even if it is not learned in any permanent way. You may ask a friend, "What is so-and-so's phone number?" Then your friend speaks seven numbers. You say, "Thank you," step to the telephone, and pick up the receiver. This may take a few seconds of time. Usually you are able to recall the seven-digit number to dial it correctly. However, your ability to recall the number after a brief interval by no means indicates that permanent learning has necessarily occurred.

In an experimental procedure developed by Brown (1958) and Peterson and Peterson (1959) for studying short-term retention, a few letters or words are presented in a brief period and the subject must carry out some task that prevents continued rehearsal of the presented material. For example, the material to be remembered may be a trigram of three words, presented for 2 sec, and the rehearsal-preventing task may be to count backward by threes, starting with a number shown by the experimenter. A typical finding is that retention of the trigram occurs in only 0.15 to 0.20 of the cases if the retention interval is as long as 20 to 30 sec, but the trigram is retained with quite a high probability if the retention interval is brief—say, 2 sec or 5 sec.

Models of the kind discussed in the preceding section only specify states of learning; they give no explanation of transient phenomena such as those observed when retention is tested after an interval of only a few seconds. Theories that are concerned with differing stages of processing, occurring at differing levels of the memory system, have been based partly on analyses of transient phenomena that are observed in experiments dealing with learning and memory.

One major analysis of memory processing at different stages or levels was given by Norman and Rumelhart (1970). Their analysis used a theory of perceptual processing developed by Rumelhart (1970), in which items are recognized on the basis of features extracted from the presented stimulus. Feature extraction for a given item occurs at a rate dependent on the number of items for which processing is needed. When a certain criterion number of features has been received, the item is recognized. In Norman and Rumelhart's theory, once recognition takes place a vector of attributes for the item is placed in short-term memory. This memory vector is found in a dictionary of items held in long-term memory, which is accessed when the process of recognition succeeds. Once an item is stored in short-term memory, a process of transfer occurs by which attributes in long-term memory are tagged to indicate their presence in the situation. The process of transfer or tagging goes on with respect to all the attributes of items stored in short-term memory, with the probability of tagging any one attribute proportional to that attribute's clarity in short-term memory at the time. Clarity decreases over time, so the longer an item has been in short-term memory, the less processing is occurring for its attributes. Also, the process of transfer or tagging is limited in capacity, so if many items are in short-term memory there will be less transfer of information per item than if there are only one or two items in short-term memory.

Theories similar to that of Norman and Rumelhart's in various ways have been given by a number of workers. Reitman (1970) gave an analysis, based partly on a suggestion by Bower (1967), in which short-term memory is analyzed using queuing theory. In Reitman's analysis, entry into short-term memory depends on a process of serving items that are in the short-term sensory store, and entry into more permanent working memory depends on a process of serving items that are in short-term memory. Each server is limited in the rate at which it can process items, so items tend to queue up in the short-term sensory store waiting to be perceived if they are presented too rapidly for entry into short-term memory, and items tend to queue up in short-term memory waiting to be processed into working memory if they are presented too rapidly for memory processing. Items that are queued in short-term memory may be lost due to decay or bumped out by newly entered items if they have to wait too long before being processed.

A model of short-term memory that has been developed in detail and used to analyze many experimental results is that of Atkinson and Shiffrin (1968), who assumed that the short-term memory system consists of a buffer with some fixed number of positions for holding items in temporary storage. Entry into the buffer depends on a decision by the subject. If the buffer is full when an item is entered, one of the items presently in the buffer is replaced by the new item. As long as an item resides in the buffer, information about the item is transferred to long-term memory at a fixed rate. Thus, the longer an item resides in short-term memory, the more information about it will be transferred to long-term memory, and the more likely it is that the item can be recalled later in a test.

Serial position effects in memorizing.   In addition to providing analyses of retention that occurs through very brief retention intervals, the idea of a short-term memory system has also provided explanations of the effects of serial position in lists that are memorized in experiments. When a list of items is presented and a subject tries to remember all the items, the items presented near the beginning and near the end of the list tend to be remembered better than those that are in the middle. According to an explanation based on the idea of a short-term memory system, items at the beginning of the list have an advantage because they arrive when the short-term memory is uncrowded, so they receive more processing than items that arrive later. The advantage of the late items is explained by the idea that the last few items remain in short-term memory long enough to be easily retrieved in the test. While a representation of short-term memory as a discrete system is not strictly necessary to explain many effects of this kind (see Bernbach, 1969; Laughery, 1969), this kind of representation has been used frequently and very productively in analyzing many aspects of memory processing in real time.

Although many theorists have represented short-term memory as a discrete state of processing, none of the detailed analyses that have been given are consistent with the idea that storage of information about an item in long-term or working memory is an all-or-none process. An important question is what relationship the representations of learning as a Markov process have to models that consider the process of learning in more detail. One way in which a Markov model could relate to a more detailed theory would be as an approximation. The process of learning described in a more specific theory might generate performance similar to that expected on the basis of a Markov model. The Markov model could then be applied to experimental data with positive results, and the more specific theory might still be a good description of the learning process. Such a situation could be helpful to research and understanding in two ways. First, a Markov model generally gives a simpler description than more specific alternatives, so the Markov description can be used as a kind of abbreviation for more complex processes. Second, as described earlier, analysis using the Markov model can provide useful information regarding what kinds of experimental manipulation influence state occupancy and transition probabilities, and can lead to inference about the kinds of process that are involved at different stages of learning.

A study that directly investigated relationships between a Markov analysis and a more detailed descriptive theory was conducted by Heine (1970). Information useful in analyzing the role of short-term memory is obtained by serial position effects, comparing retention of items presented at different positions of a list. Information used in testing and estimating parameters of a Markov model involves sequential information obtained over a series of trials. Heine's study of free recall memorizing was developed to provide both kinds of information. A list was presented several times, with a test following each presentation, until the subject could give all the responses. But several items were always presented in the same general part of the list—beginning, middle, or end—so that performance over a series of trials could be observed for items that always occupied about the same position in the list.

Heine carried out a Markov analysis of the items that appeared in the various positions and found that the two-stage model gave a good description of the data. A major empirical finding was obtained when the parameters of the model were compared for items in various positions. The parameters relating to performance and learning in the second stage were constant across serial positions, with the exception that items from the end of the list had very high performance before learning, due to their recency at the time of testing. The effect of serial position on difficulty of learning, with items near the beginning of the list learned most easily, was entirely an effect on the difficulty of the first stage of learning. This result suggests that the first stage of learning could be closely related to the process of information storage described in the various models of short-term memory, since the mechanism of short-term memory produces a strong serial position effect. This idea is also consistent with the general interpretation mentioned earlier, which involves storage of information in the first stage of learning, and learning to retrieve items in the second stage.

Heine developed a theory of learning, based on Atkinson and Shiffrin's (1968) version of the short-term memory analysis, assuming that storage of information about an item occurs during the first stage of learning in proportion to the length of time the item resides in short-term memory. The first stage of learning is complete when a certain criterion or threshold amount of information has been stored, after which the second stage of learning can occur. The second stage has probability b of occurring on each trial. To test the theory, Heine carried out simulated learning using a computer, and compared the results with those obtained in the experiments. Each 'subject' simulated by the computer learned a list of words like the lists learned by the human subjects in Heine's experiment, but the process of learning and the probability of recall for each word was determined by a program that followed the assumptions of Heine's theory. The 'data' generated by this simulation were analyzed using the same statistical methods that had been applied in analyzing the data from the human subjects. That is, distributions of various statistics such as the number of errors, the trial of last error, and proportion of errors on trials before the last error, were examined and compared with predictions from the Markov model.

The result was that the various statistical properties of the 'data' obtained by simulation of learning agreed with predictions derived from the Markov model about as well as the experimental data. One conclusion is that the Markov model gave quite a good abbreviation of an underlying process of learning that was somewhat more complicated than the simple two-stage system that the model describes. It seems likely that the process of memorizing the items did involve something like the quantitative storage of information described in the more detailed model. At least that assumption gives an explanation for the difference in learning rates at the different serial positions, a fact that is described but not explained by the differences found in the Markov parameters. At the same time, the measurements obtained using the Markov model provided important guidance in the development of the more detailed theory about the learning process, and the Markov model gave a relatively powerful way of comparing the statistical properties of data simulated by the more detailed theory with the data obtained from human subjects.

Short-term retention during memorizing. Another use of discrete systems in approximating the role of short-term memory in learning has been the representation of short-term memory as a single state in a Markov chain. Let T denote a state in which a representation of an item is temporarily stored, and let S be a state involving more permanent storage of a representation. U is a state involving no stored representation, as before. A representation of the role of short-term memory that allows fairly general transition probabilities is given in Equations 14 and 15.

$$
P_1 = \begin{array}{c} \\ S \\ T \\ U \end{array}
\begin{array}{c}
S \quad\quad T \quad\quad U \\
\hline
\begin{array}{ccc}
1 & 0 & 0 \\
a_2 & 1 - a_2 & 0 \\
sa_1 & s(1 - a_1) & 1 - s
\end{array}
\end{array}
\quad (14)
$$

$$
P_2 = \begin{array}{c} \\ S \\ T \\ U \end{array}
\begin{array}{c}
S \quad\quad\quad T \quad\quad\quad U \\
\hline
\begin{array}{ccc}
1 & 0 & 0 \\
(1 - f)r & (1 - f)(1 - r) & f \\
0 & 0 & 1
\end{array}
\end{array}
\quad (15)
$$

Note that P_1, given in Equation 14, shows transitions that can occur when an item is presented for study. If an item is in state U when it is presented, it may not be studied at all (probability $= 1 - s$). If it is studied, there is probability a_1 that a permanent representation of the item is stored. Otherwise, a representation is stored in temporary memory. If the item is already in temporary memory when it is presented, the probability of storing a relatively permanent representation is a_2. The operator P_2, given in Equation 15, shows transitions that can occur during intervals when other items are presented. If the item is in temporary memory, its temporary representation is lost with probability f. If the representation is not lost, there is probability r that the representation is stored in more permanent memory; otherwise the item remains in state T.

Various versions of this model have been used by a number of investigators. Atkinson and Crothers (1964) showed that the model agreed with data from a variety of paired-associate memorizing experiments, although for a few experiments a significant improvement was obtained by adding an intermediate state U' in which the subject always processes presented items and Kintsch (1966) found that data of multitrial recognition memorizing agreed with the model. One use of the model has been the analysis of an effect produced by varying the interval between presentations of an item. If an item receives two presentations close together, its performance will be improved less than if two presentations are given with several other items intervening. In connection with Equations 14 and 15, this fact can be explained in two ways (Greeno, 1967). One explanation says that a_2 is small or zero. That is, when an item's second presentation occurs quickly, it is likely that the item is still in state T, and it is assumed that the subject is less likely to try hard to process the item if it is presented while it is still in temporary memory. The other explanation is that r is nonzero, so that transition to state S often occurs during intervals between an item's presentations. This explains the disadvantage of having presentations too close together because only in the intervals following the second presentation does the item receive its ordinary benefit of postpresentation rehearsal and consolidation. At this writing, experimental evidence for both kinds of explanation has been obtained, and it seems most likely that both kinds of process occur and influence the learning process. The Markov model representing short-term memory as a discrete state has been useful in describing these various possibilities in a clear way, and also has served as a baseline for analyses of other temporal effects in memorizing, some of which have led to more detailed and alternative hypotheses (Bjork, 1966; Izawa, 1971; Rumelhart, 1967; Young, 1971).

Another important use of the model given in Equations 14 and 15 involved an application to a problem of optimization of conditions for learning. Atkinson (1972) studied the process of learning German vocabulary words. The subjects were Stanford undergraduate students. Each subject studied a set of 84 German words with their English cognates. The 84 words were divided into seven lists of 12 each, of approximately equal difficulty. On each trial of the experiment one of the 12-item lists was displayed to the subject. One of the 12 items was selected; the subject was tested on that item, and the correct English translation of the word was shown.

Four experimental groups were run, differing in the way in which an item was selected from the list of 12 items shown on each trial. A baseline control group had an item selected randomly. A second group of subjects selected their own items. In the remaining two groups, the item selected for test on each trial was picked on the basis of calculations based on the model of Equations 14 and 15. Values of the parameters f, s, a_1, and a_2 were estimated from results of a pilot experiment. In addition, an initial parameter t, the probability of starting in the learned state, was also estimated from pilot data. In this application r was assumed to be zero. With numerical values of the parameters, a probability can be calculated for each item, giving the likelihood of that item going into state S if it is studied on the trial. This probability will differ depending on the subject's past performance on the item. If the subject made an error on the last occurrence of the item, then it is known that the item was in state U at that time. If the item was studied j trials ago, then the probability that the item is still unlearned and will become learned if it is studied now is

P_U(learn now)

$$= (1 - s)sa_1 + s(1 - a_1)[1 - (1 - f)^j]sa_1 + s(1 - a_1)(1 - f)^j a_2.$$

If the item was given correctly on its preceding trial, then it may have been in temporary memory at that time. If it was, then its probability of being learned if studied now is

$$P_T(\text{learn now}) = (1 - a_2)[1 - (1 - f)^j]sa_1 + (1 - a_2)(1 - f)^j a_2.$$

The actual probability of learning an item that was given correctly on its last trial is really some fraction of P_T(learn now), the fraction being the likelihood that the item was actually in state T rather than state S when the correct response was given. This probability can be computed from the subject's history of presentations and responses on that item during the training session.

In the two groups where selection was based on the model, on each trial the probability of learning was calculated for all 12 of the items in the list shown on that trial, and the item selected for test and study was the one with the highest probability of becoming learned. In one of these groups, a single set of parameters was used for all the items. In the other group, a separate set of parameters was estimated for each of the 84 items studied in the experiment, and the parameters for each individual item were used in calculating its probability of becoming learned.

In Atkinson's experiment, 30 subjects were run in each of the four groups. Each subject had a 2-hour training session which included 336 trials (an average of 4 trials per item). A test was given seven or eight days after the training session. In the test the proportion of correct responses was 0.38 following training with random selection of items. When subjects had selected their own items for study the proportion correct on the test was 0.58, which was about equal to the performance achieved by subjects who received items selected using the model with a single set of parameters; their proportion correct was 0.54. However, by far the best performance (0.79 correct) was achieved by subjects who had items selected on the basis of the model with different parameters for the different items.

THEORY OF CONDITIONING

A major source of experimental data in the psychology of learning has been the study of conditioning of several kinds. Much of the work done in mathematical learning theory during the 1950s was concerned with conditioning experiments (for example, Bush & Estes, 1959; Bush & Mosteller, 1955; Estes, 1950). However, most of the quantitative theorizing about learning done since 1960 has dealt with human verbal learning, of the kind discussed in the preceding section, or with simple problem solving. But although there are fewer examples of rigorous theory about conditioning than about verbal learning and problem solving using discrete representations, there are some notable examples, and these illustrate the same kinds of impact of the mathematical representation on psychological theory as those described earlier.

Aversive Conditioning

In one kind of conditioning experiment, an animal is trained to perform some response to escape or avoid some painful stimulation, usually electric shock. In a series of studies, Theios and Brelsford have provided rigorous experimental and theoretical analyses, leading to a new interpretation of one kind of aversive conditioning.

In one study, Theios (1965) trained rats in a T maze where the stem and one arm of the maze were electrified and the rat had to learn to go to the safe arm to get away from the shock. The rat was placed in the maze and kept there until he reached the safe arm, then placed in the start box of the maze again, and so on, with trials repeated every 30 sec until the rat learned which arm to choose. Then the situation was reversed with the opposite arm made safe and the rat had to learn to choose that arm. Statistical properties of the experimental data were consistent with predictions of the two-stage Markov model, and parameters of the model were related to experimental variables. One variable was the number of correct trials given by the subject before the reversal occurred. The main effect of this variable was on the probability of accomplishing the first stage of learning—the parameter a in Equation 12—with greater amounts of overtraining of the first response leading to slower learning in the first stage after reversal, appearing in the results as a smaller value of a when there were more prereversal trials. A second variable that was manipulated was the number of reversals that a subject had experienced. It was found that previous experience with reversals increased the value of a nearly to one, and also led to an increased probability of accomplishing the second stage of learning at the same trial as the first stage—that is, an increase in the value of b_1 in Equation 12.

In a different kind of experiment, rats are given a signal before a shock is turned on and are allowed to make a response by which they can avoid shock. Theios (1963) found that performance in this situation also gave data with statistical properties consistent with predictions from the two-stage Markov model. Then a study was conducted by Theios and Brelsford (1966b) in which the effect of an experimental manipulation was measured to infer the nature of the stages involved in learning.

A widely held view is that avoidance conditioning consists of two subprocesses. One subprocess is the conditioning of an emotional reaction to the stimulus used as a signal. When the animal fails to avoid shock, it experiences pain, and this happens while the signal is present. After this happens a few times, the animal becomes aroused and fearful when the signal occurs. The other subprocess is that the animal learns what to do when it becomes aroused. The appropriate response in the experiment is to run out of the compartment the animal is in. When the animal has acquired an emotional response to the signal and has learned to run when it becomes aroused emotionally, it will give the correct response and avoid shock consistently.

In most discussions of avoidance conditioning it has been assumed that emotional conditioning precedes conditioning of the running response. Theios and Brelsford tested this idea by using a manipulation that should affect the ease of learning the running response. One group of animals was trained in a situation where the running response was permitted on all trials. If the animal ran within 5 sec of the beginning of the signal it avoided shock. And if the animal failed to avoid the shock it could get away from the shock by running out of the compartment after the shock was turned on. A second group was run with a trapping procedure that did not allow the running response as an escape from shock. If an animal in the trapped group did not avoid the shock, the door out of the compartment was closed and the shock was left on for 0.85 sec—the average time that it took animals in the un-trapped group to escape the shock.

The trapping procedure should affect the rate of learning the running response. The untrapped group could perform the response in order to get away from the shock, and could thereby connect the response with the emotional experience of the shock directly. The trapped group was only allowed to run before the shock was turned on, so had fewer opportunities to connect the response of running with the emotional reaction. If conditioning of the running response occurred in the second stage of learning, after emotional conditioning occurred, then the trapped and untrapped groups should differ in the second stage of learning.

Just the opposite effect was found. The trapped and untrapped groups showed no difference in the parameters of learning in the second stage, but the value of a—the probability of accomplishing the first stage—was much lower for the trapped group than for the untrapped group. This result led Theios and Brelsford to a new interpretation of avoidance conditioning. The first stage of the learning process involves learning to run if there is an event that causes emotional arousal. The first stage also involves forming at least a temporary connection between the warning signal and the emotional reaction. But the second stage of learning involves acquiring the connection between the stimulus signal and the emotional reaction in a permanent way, so the animal always remembers the significance of the signal.

Theios and Brelsford's interpretation can be shown in relation to the states and transition probabilities given in Equation 16.
State U applies at the beginning of training, where nothing has been conditioned. Since the trapping procedure influenced the value of a, it was inferred that the system leaves state U when the running response has been learned. Then learning is completed when a permanent association between the warning signal and emotional arousal is stored. Until that happens there

$$
P = \begin{array}{c} \\ S \\ T \\ F \\ U \end{array}
\begin{array}{cccc}
S & T & F & U \\
\hline
1 & 0 & 0 & 0 \\
b_3 & (1 - b_3)(1 - f) & (1 - b_3)f & 0 \\
b_2 & (1 - b_2)(1 - f) & (1 - b_2)f & 0 \\
ab_1 & a(1 - b_1)(1 - f) & a(1 - b_1)f & 1 - a
\end{array} \tag{16}
$$

is probability $1 - f$ that the connection will be held in temporary memory (state T) on any given trial. If the system is in state T an avoidance response will occur. But if the connection is lost from temporary memory the system will be in state F, and an error will occur.

A series of studies was conducted by Brelsford (1967) to test and extend the interpretation of avoidance conditioning represented by Equation 16. In one study Brelsford gave a strong test of the idea that once the first stage of learning has been accomplished the system moves back and forth between states T and F, but it does not return to the initial state U where nothing has been conditioned. The experiment used the property that no avoidance response occurs until the system has moved at least to state T. After the animal's first avoidance response the shock was turned off, giving extinction trials for the avoidance response. Some of the animals should not make errors after their first avoidance; other animals will make their first avoidance in state T and return to state F. When shock is not given in state F, the animal should remain in state F until shock is again given. In the extinction condition, shock was not given until the animal had given ten consecutive failures of the avoidance response. Then shock was resumed until the animal's next avoidance response, when it was turned off again, continuing until the animal gave a criterion run of ten consecutive avoidance responses on trials when the shock was turned off. The data consisted of the proportion of animals absorbing in state S and therefore having no more errors after each successive avoidance response. The proportions were quite close to those predicted on the basis of performance by a group trained in the ordinary way, with a shock after every failure to avoid.

In a second experiment Brelsford used a preconditioning procedure in which pairings of the warning signal and inescapable shock were given before avoidance training was begun. The intent was to provide a permanent connection between the signal and emotional arousal before avoidance training, thus completing the second stage of learning before the first was accomplished. According to Theios and Brelsford's hypothesis, this manipulation should lead to performance in which no errors occurred once an animal had given its first avoidance response. This result was obtained, although it also appeared that learning in the first stage was made more rapid by the preconditioning.

The third experiment conducted by Brelsford tested the interpretation in a particularly subtle way. According to the hypothesis, failures to avoid occurring after the first correct response are due to forgetting the connection between the signal and an emotional reaction. In the experiment, an attempt was made to reinstate that connection by presentation of a brief (0.1 sec) shock simultaneously with the onset of the warning signal. If the manipulation had its intended effect, there should be no errors on trials when the brief shock was given. One group received the brief shock on all trials following the first successful avoidance, and 65 of 70 animals made no errors on those trials. A second group was given brief shocks only after the first avoidance had been followed by a failure to avoid. Nineteen of 20 animals in this one-error group performed in accordance with the hypothesis, making no errors on trials when the brief shock occurred. In a third group, brief shocks were given only after a run of ten failures to avoid followed the first avoidance response. Even with this long run of responses with the connection out of temporary memory, the brief shocks succeeded in reinstating the connection for about one-half of the animals, and 7 of the 13 animals who gave the needed ten failures to respond showed an immediate recovery of avoidance response as soon as brief shocks were introduced.

Reflex Conditioning

Another kind of conditioning experiment uses a stimulus that already produces some reflex response when it is presented. A reflex frequently used is the eyeblink response, with the unconditioned stimulus of a puff of air blown at the subject's eye. When some new stimulus such as a red light is presented many times, followed briefly by the puff of air, subjects eventually come to blink their eyes when the red light goes on. A response is counted if the subject blinks his eye after the red light has gone on, but before the air puff.

Results of this kind of experiment have been analyzed with the two-stage Markov model with some success when the subjects were rabbits (Theios & Brelsford, 1966a). However, with human subjects the process seems to be slightly more complicated. Assume that a subject begins with some probability P_0 of blinking his eye during a brief interval. The probability remains at that level until trial K, a trial where learning begins. After trial K, probability of response increases toward an asymptotic value P_∞, in a gradual manner. The probability of response at trial n is

$$P_n = \begin{cases} P_0, & n < K, \\ P_\infty - (P_\infty - P_0)(1 - \theta)^{n-K}, & n \geq K, \end{cases} \tag{17}$$

where θ is a number between zero and one, representing the rate of learning, once learning begins.

The idea of analyzing learning as a two-phase process, one discrete and the other continuous, was developed by Norman (1964). It has been used by

Prokasy and his associates in several experiments involving eyeblink conditioning. The model has proved useful in identifying the aspects of the learning process that are affected by certain experimental variables. For example, change in the intensity of the air puff influenced K, the number of trials before learning begins, and P_∞, the asymptotic level of performance, but did not influence the rate at which learning proceeds during the gradual phase (Prokasy & Harsanyi, 1968). A different pattern of parameter effects was obtained when comparison was made between subjects whose responses are of a type that suggest they tried to anticipate the air puff and other subjects who apparently gave only involuntary eyeblinks. There were no significant differences in K between voluntary and involuntary responders, but voluntary responders had higher values of θ and P_∞ (Prokasy & Kumpfer, 1969).

CONCLUSIONS

In this article I have described some applications of the mathematical idea of a discrete-state system to the analysis of learning. Applications in the theory of memorizing have been dealt with primarily, but other problems have been analyzed with the same techniques, and I have included a brief description of some applications in the theory of conditioning. I have included examples to illustrate three kinds of influence on scientific work. First, the availability of a tractable representation for a discrete system has stimulated investigation to determine whether certain learning systems may in fact be approximately discrete in nature. In early stages of work on a problem, considerable energy may be given to this question, especially since most psychologists (like most other people) are accustomed to thinking about learning as a process of gradual growth. If evidence is obtained that makes a discrete-state representation plausible, then powerful analytical tools are available for investigating the kinds of processes that occur at various stages of learning. In one kind of investigation, experimental operations are used to manipulate the probabilities of occupying the various states of the system prior to learning. This method was illustrated in Greeno and Scandura's (1966) study of transfer based on category concepts, by Kintsch and Morris' (1965) study of free recall memorizing following recognition pretraining, and by Brelsford's (1967) study of avoidance conditioning following preconditioning trials where the warning signal was paired with inescapable shock. A second kind of study uses a hypothesis about the subject's state during a certain stage of learning, and identifies characteristic performance in that state or manipulates performance in accordance with the hypothesis. One example is Polson, Restle, and Polson's (1965) identification of confusion errors in the intermediate state of paired-associate memorizing. Another example is Brelsford's (1967) use of brief shocks to reinstate an emotional reaction hypothesized to be lost from temporary memory during the intermediate stage of learning. And a third kind of experimental study measures the effect of an empirical variable on transition parameters of a model, showing which aspect or stage of the learning process is influenced by various aspects of the learning situation. Many illustrations of this method have been given; they include Humphreys and Greeno's (1970) finding that the first stage of paired-associate memorizing is influenced by both stimulus and response variables, while the second stage depends on stimulus variables but not on response difficulty. A second example is Heine's (1970) finding that serial position effects on learning are entirely in the first stage of the learning process. A third example is Theios and Brelsford's (1966b) finding that a procedure of trapping used in avoidance conditioning has its effect on the first stage of learning. One more example is Prokasy and Harsanyi's (1968) result showing that intensity of the air puff in eyeblink conditioning influences the duration of the initial period of stationary performance, but not the rate of change in performance once change begins to occur.

The major goal of scientific investigation is the development of more accurate and deeper understanding of the processes being studied. Two kinds of development have been illustrated in this chapter. One kind involves the use of experimental results and measurements obtained with quantitative models to draw inferences about the kind of psychological process that occurs at various stages of learning. One example is the conclusion that, in memorizing, an initial stage is the storage of information, and a second stage involves learning to retrieve the stored information reliably. Another example is the inference that in avoidance conditioning the first stage involves learning what to do when frightened, and the second stage is learning to remember that the warning signal is dangerous.

The other kind of theoretical development occurs when a process is analyzed into components, operating at different levels, and relationships between these components are clarified by the analysis. One example is the analysis of memorizing processes with short-term and long-term components, and the investigation of the role played by short-term processes in the long-term storage of information. Another example is the analysis of relationships between learning of individual items, of category concepts that involve relationships between items, and of general strategies relating to the subject's understanding of the kind of relationships that are involved in a situation

In closing, it should be said by way of qualification that most psychologists remain quite conservative on the question of whether learning really involves discrete changes at the most elementary level. One reason is that tests of the theory usually consist of comparison between data and predictions, with support for the theory coming from acceptance of the null hypothesis. It is well understood that inference in such a case is uncertain; evidence can lead to definite rejection of a null hypothesis, but the best one can say for a null hypothesis is that the data failed to reject it. A second reason is that even when the null hypothesis is accepted in data there are many differing processes that could generate the data obtained. The change that is characterized as a discrete-state transition in a Markov model may actually be an event in which some continuously variable quantity such as response strength first exceeds a threshold. Restle (1965) showed that a learning system in which response strength gradually increases over trials is empirically equivalent to an all-or-none system if the gradual system has a threshold and an appropriate distribution of varying initial strengths of response. Heine's (1970) study of free recall memorizing showed that the observable properties of a two-stage Markov model correspond closely to the observable properties of data generated by a system in which varying amounts of information are stored about different items as a function of their time of residence in short-term memory, and a process of making stored items retrievable occurs after a threshold amount of information has been stored. And Theios (1972) has pointed out that the model used by Prokasy (1972; Prokasy & Harsanyi, 1968; Prokasy & Kumpfer, 1969), postulating a discrete event of initial change in response probability, can be interpreted as an approximation to a gradual process of learning like that hypothesized by Hull (1943, 1952) in which response probability remains constant until response strength exceeds a threshold, and then increases to some limit. In any case, the use of theoretical representations that characterize learning as a discrete transition has served and will continue to serve as a productive means of furthering our understanding of learning processes, and as a fruitful basis for development of solutions for applied problems regarding learning.

ACKNOWLEDGMENT

Preparation of this chapter was supported by National Science Foundation grant GB-31045.

REFERENCES

Atkinson, R. C. Optimizing learning a second vocabulary. *Journal of Experimental Psychology*, 1972, **96**, 124–129.
Atkinson, R. C., Bower, G. H., & Crothers, E. J. *An introduction to mathematical learning theory.* New York: Wiley, 1965.
Atkinson, R. C., & Crothers, E. J. A comparison of paired-associate learning models having different acquisition and retention axioms. *Journal of Mathematical Psychology*, 1964, **1**, 285–315.
Atkinson, R. C., & Shiffrin, R. M. Human memory: A proposed system and its control processes. In G. H. Bower and J. T. Spence (Eds.), *The psychology of*

learning and motivation: Advances in research and theory. Vol. 2. New York: Academic Press, 1968.

Batchelder, W. H. An all-or-none theory for learning on both the paired-associate and concept levels. *Journal of Mathematical Psychology*, 1970, **7**, 97–117.

Batchelder, W. H. A theoretical and empirical comparison of the all-or-none multi-level theory and the mixed model. *Journal of Mathematical Psychology*, 1971, **8**, 82–108.

Bernbach, H. A. Replication processes in human memory and learning. In J. T. Spence and G. H. Bower (Eds.), *The psychology of learning and motivation: Advances in research and theory.* Vol. 3. New York: Academic Press, 1969.

Binford, J. R., & Gettys, C. Nonstationarity in paired-associate learning as indicated by a second-guess procedure. *Journal of Mathematical Psychology*, 1965, **2**, 190–195.

Bjork, R. A. *Learning and short-term retention of paired-associates in relation to specific sequences of interpresentation intervals.* Technical Report No. 106. Stanford: Institute for Mathematical Studies in the Social Sciences, Stanford University, 1966.

Boring, E. G. *A history of experimental psychology.* New York: Appleton-Century-Crofts, 1950.

Bower, G. H. Application of a model to paired-associate learning. *Psychometrika*, 1961, **26**, 255–280.

Bower, G. H. A descriptive theory of memory. In D. P. Kimble (Ed.), *Proceedings of the second conference on learning, remembering, and forgetting.* New York: New York Academy of Sciences, 1967.

Brelsford, J. W., Jr. Experimental manipulation of state occupancy in a Markov model for avoidance conditioning. *Journal of Mathematical Psychology*, 1967, **4**, 21–47.

Brown, J. Some tests of the decay theory of immediate memory. *Quarterly Journal of Experimental Psychology*, 1958, **10**, 12–21.

Bush, R. R., & Estes, W. K. (Eds.) *Studies in mathematical learning theory.* Stanford: Stanford University Press, 1959.

Bush, R. R., & Mosteller, F. *Stochastic models for learning.* New York: Wiley, 1955.

Estes, W. K. Toward a statistical theory of learning. *Psychological Review*, 1950, **57**, 94–107.

Estes, W. K. The statistical approach to learning theory. In S. Koch (Ed.), *Psychology: A study of a science, Vol. 2, General systematic formulations, learning, and special processes.* New York: McGraw-Hill, 1959.

Estes, W. K. Learning theory. In P. R. Farnsworth, O. McNemar, and Q. McNemar (Eds.), *Annual review of psychology.* Vol. 13. Palo Alto, Calif.: Annual Reviews, Inc., 1962.

Feller, W. *An introduction to probability theory and its applications.* Vol. 1. (2nd ed.) New York: Wiley, 1950.

Greeno, J. G. Paired-associate learning with short term retention: Mathematical analysis and data regarding identification of parameters. *Journal of Mathematical Psychology*, 1967, **4**, 430–472.

Greeno, J. G. Identifiability and statistical properties of two-stage learning with no successes in the initial stage. *Psychometrika*, 1968, **33**, 173–215.

Greeno, J. G. How associations are memorized. In D. A. Norman (Ed.), *Models of human memory.* New York: Academic Press, 1970.

Greeno, J. G., James, C. T., & DaPolito, F. J. A cognitive interpretation of negative transfer and forgetting of paired associates. *Journal of Verbal Learning and Verbal Behavior,* 1971, **10,** 331–345.

Greeno, J. G., & Scandura, J. M. All-or-none transfer based on verbally mediated concepts. *Journal of Mathematical Psychology,* 1966, **3,** 388–411.

Heine, R. T. *Quantitative analysis of multitrial free recall learning.* Michigan Mathematical Psychology Program Report MMPP 70-12. Ann Arbor: The University of Michigan, 1970.

Hull, C. L. Quantitative aspects of the evolution of concepts. *Psychological Monographs,* 1920, **28,** Whole No. 123.

Hull, C. L. *Principles of behavior: An introduction to behavior theory.* New York: Appleton-Century-Crofts, 1943.

Hull, C. L. *A behavior system.* New Haven: Yale University Press, 1952.

Humphreys, M. S., & Greeno, J. G. Interpretation of the two-stage analysis of paired-associate memorizing. *Journal of Mathematical Psychology,* 1970, **7,** 275–292.

Izawa, C. The test trial potentiating model. *Journal of Mathematical Psychology,* 1971, **8,** 200–224.

James, C. T., & Greeno, J. G. Effect of A-B overtraining in A-Br. *Journal of Experimental Psychology,* 1970, **83,** 107–111.

Katona, G. *Organizing and memorizing.* New York: Columbia Univ. Press, 1940.

Kemeny, J. G., & Snell, J. L. *Finite Markov chains.* Princeton: Van Nostrand, 1960.

Kemeny, J. G., Snell, J. L., & Thompson, G. L. *Introduction to finite mathematics.* Englewood Cliffs, N.J.: Prentice-Hall, 1957.

Kintsch, W. Recognition learning as a function of the length of the retention interval and changes in the retention interval. *Journal of Mathematical Psychology,* 1966, **3,** 412–433.

Kintsch, W., & Morris, C. J. Application of a Markov model to free recall and recognition. *Journal of Experimental Psychology,* 1965, **69,** 200–206.

Köhler, W. *The mentality of apes.* New York: Harcourt Brace, 1927.

Lashley, K. S. *Brain mechanisms and behavior.* Chicago: University of Chicago Press, 1928.

Laughery, K. R. Computer simulation of short-term memory: A component-decay model. In G. H. Bower and J. T. Spence (Eds.), *The psychology of learning and motivation: Advances in research and theory.* Vol. 3. New York: Academic Press, 1969.

Levine, G., & Burke, C. J. *Mathematical model techniques for learning theories.* New York: Academic Press, 1972.

Luce, R. D. *Individual choice behavior: A theoretical analysis.* New York: Wiley, 1959.

Melton, A. W., & Irwin, J. M. The influence of degree of interpolated learning on retroactive inhibition and the overt transfer of specific responses. *American Journal of Psychology,* 1940, **53,** 173–203.

Millward, R. B., & Wickens, T. D. Concept-identification models. This volume.

Norman, D. A., & Rumelhart, D. E. A system for perception and memory. In

D. A. Norman (Ed.), *Models of human memory*. New York: Academic Press, 1970.

Norman, M. F. A two-phase model and an application to verbal discrimination learning. In R. C. Atkinson (Ed.), *Studies in mathematical psychology*. Stanford: Stanford University Press, 1964.

Pavlov, I. P. *Conditioned reflexes* (trans. by G. V. Anrep). Oxford: Oxford University Press, 1927.

Peterson, L. R., & Peterson, M. J. Short-term retention of individual verbal items. *Journal of Experimental Psychology*, 1959, **58**, 193–198.

Polson, M. C., Restle, F., & Polson, P. G. Association and discrimination in paired-associates learning. *Journal of Experimental Psychology*, 1965, **69**, 47–55.

Polson, P. G. A quantitative analysis of the conceptual processes in the Hull paradigm. *Journal of Mathematical Psychology*, 1972, **9**, 141–167.

Prokasy, W. F. Developments with the two-phase model applied to human eyelid conditioning. In A. H. Black and W. F. Prokasy (Eds.), *Classical conditioning II: Current theory and research*. New York: Appleton-Century-Crofts, 1972.

Prokasy, W. F., & Harsanyi, M. A. Two-phase model for human classical conditioning. *Journal of Experimental Psychology*, 1968, **78**, 359–368.

Prokasy, W. F., & Kumpfer, K. One- and two-operator versions of a two-phase model applied to the performances of Vs and Cs in human eyelid conditioning. *Journal of Experimental Psychology*, 1969, **80**, 231–236.

Reitman, J. S. Computer simulation of an information-processing model of short-term memory. In D. A. Norman (Ed.), *Models of human memory*. New York: Academic Press, 1970.

Restle, F. Sources of difficulty in learning paired associates. In R. C. Atkinson (Ed.), *Studies in mathematical psychology*. Stanford: Stanford University Press, 1964.

Restle, F. The significance of all-or-none learning. *Psychological Bulletin*, 1965, **62**, 313–324.

Restle, F. & Greeno, J. G. *Introduction to mathematical psychology*. Reading, Mass.: Addison-Wesley, 1970.

Rumelhart, D. E. *The effects of interpresentation intervals on performance in a continuous paired-associate task. Technical Report No. 116*. Stanford: Institute for Mathematical Studies in the Social Sciences, Stanford University, 1967.

Rumelhart, D. E. A multicomponent theory of the perception of briefly exposed visual displays. *Journal of Mathematical Psychology*, 1970, **7**, 191–218.

Spence, K. W. *Behavior theory and conditioning*. New Haven: Yale University Press, 1956.

Theios, J. Simple conditioning as two-stage all-or-none learning. *Psychological Review*, 1963, **70**, 403–417.

Theios, J. The mathematical structure of reversal learning in a shock-escape T-maze: Overtraining and successive reversals. *Journal of Mathematical Psychology*, 1965, **2**, 26–52.

Theios, J. Formalization of Spence's dual-process model for eyelid conditioning. In A. H. Black and W. F. Prokasy (Eds.), *Classical conditioning II: Current theory and research*. New York: Appleton-Century-Crofts, 1972.

Theios, J., & Brelsford, J. W., Jr. A Markov model for classical conditioning: Application to eyeblink conditioning in rabbits. *Psychological Review*, 1966, **73,** 393–408. (a)

Theios, J., & Brelsford, J. W., Jr. Theoretical interpretations of a Markov model for avoidance conditioning. *Journal of Mathematical Psychology*, 1966, **3,** 140–162. (b)

Underwood, B. J., & Richardson, J. Some verbal materials for the study of concept formation. *Psychological Bulletin*, 1956, **53,** 84–95.

Underwood, B. J., & Schulz, R. W. *Meaningfulness and verbal learning.* New York: Lippincott, 1960.

Wertheimer, M. *Productive thinking.* New York: Harper & Row, 1959.

Young, J. L. Reinforcement-test intervals in paired-associate learning. *Journal of Mathematical Psychology*, 1971, **8,** 58–81.

Concept-Identification Models

Richard B. Millward
BROWN UNIVERSITY

Thomas D. Wickens
UNIVERSITY OF CALIFORNIA, LOS ANGELES

SCOPE

In most learning situations, what is to be learned is fairly explicitly defined as an overt response to a specific stimulus. In concept learning, on the other hand, we can only *infer* that a subject has learned a concept when he makes appropriate responses. Psychologists have only a partial understanding of how concepts are learned—partial in the sense that the definition of the term 'concept' is incomplete, and that even within this limited definition, only a partial statement of the learning process has been made.

The problem of defining a concept has been avoided to some extent by dividing the problem of concept learning into a number of subproblems to which relatively refined analyses can be applied. This chapter will focus primarily on one of these subproblems, that which is generally designated *concept identification*, and for which relatively successful mathematical analyses have been developed. Earlier reviews (Bourne, 1966; Hunt, 1962; Millward, 1971) provide an introduction to other aspects of the problem and make clear many distinctions pertinent to current analyses of concept learning. Our discussion will concentrate on mathematical theories of concept identification to the exclusion of much experimental work and nonmathematical theories. These other results will appear here mainly as they are reflected in the models, and the reader is again referred to the review papers just cited for details. Before turning to the development of these theories, however, we shall briefly review the definition of a concept and the basic paradigms that have been used in analyzing how concepts are learned.

Concept Definition

Hovland (1952) argued that an analysis of how subjects learn a concept requires an understanding of how the subject describes the objects involved in the concept. He described the stimuli to his subjects so that he and they would agree on their description. Bruner, Goodnow, and Austin (1956) also adopted Hovland's argument, and Hunt (1962) formalized Hovland's description of a set of stimulus objects. Because Hunt's formalism has become the basis of the definition used by most researchers, it is the one adopted here.

A *concept* is any rule by which a subset of a set of stimulus objects can be selected from a universe of stimulus objects, O. The rule is the concept; the subset of selected objects is the denotation of the concept. The set O is contained within the *descriptive space* (D), which is defined as the cross product of a series of sets known as *dimensions* or *attributes*, $O \subseteq D = D_1 \times D_2 \times \cdots \times D_d$. Each dimension is defined by a source of variation among the stimulus objects, so that any characteristic that could distinguish at least one pair of stimuli is a potential dimension. Each dimension, D_i, consists of a set of values, $d_{i1}, d_{i2}, \cdots$, which may be either finite or infinite (continuous); however, since subjects cannot make infinitely fine discriminations, an infinite dimension must be partitioned into a finite set of equivalence classes. A *stimulus object* is a d-tuple of values, one from each dimension. The complete set of stimulus objects is contained in D, but because the dimensions need not be independent of each other and because certain values on different dimensions may be incompatible with each other, D may contain impossible or unreal objects. The set of dimensions can be expanded or restricted, depending on the degree of refinement desired in a description of stimulus objects: if every object in O has a unique description, the descriptive space is *complete*; if not, it is *incomplete*. In other words, an incomplete space has at least one point that contains more than one stimulus object, whereas a complete space has at most one stimulus object per point in the descriptive space. However, objects may not be defined for all points.

The conceptual rule partitions D into a number of subsets labeled by members of the set of feedback events, E. Frequently, $E = \{\text{true, false}\}$, and the sets of the partition are the *exemplars* or the *denotation* of the concept and the *nonexemplars* of the concept, respectively. However, any set of two or more names can be used for the categories of the partition. For example, $E = \{0, 1, \cdots, e\}$, $E = \{\alpha, \beta\}$, or $E = \{\text{TUZ, HEG}\}$. A subject is said to know a concept if he classifies each stimulus object in **O** into the appropriate category. The set of behavioral responses available to the subject is designated **B**. The set **B** may be the same as the set **E** but may vary in name as long as the behavior is consistent with the partition imposed on **D** by the conceptual rule. Often, for theoretical reasons, the behavior of greatest interest is not the actual response of the subject but a derived measure indicating the correctness of the response. If the response is correct, it is coded as C; if the response is erroneous, it is coded as E. Most of the models to be developed attempt to describe the sequences of Cs and Es generated by a subject as he learns to classify a set of stimuli into the appropriate categories (see the following section on Procedures).

A trivial classification rule is simply a list of the exemplars, but a conceptual rule is usually a statement based on a subset called the set of *relevant* dimensions. Rules may be categorized according to the number of relevant dimensions involved and their logical relationships. The *simple affirmative* rule is based on only one dimension, $\mathbf{D}\rho$. This rule is essentially a projection of **D** onto $\mathbf{D}\rho$ with those stimuli that take certain *focal values* of $\mathbf{D}\rho$ being exemplars and the remainder nonexemplars. When two or more relevant dimensions are involved, the rules can be expressed with the logical connectives of the sentential calculus (Suppes, 1957). For example, if $\mathbf{D}_1$ and $\mathbf{D}_2$ are both relevant and $d_{1f} \in \mathbf{D}_1$ and $d_{2g} \in \mathbf{D}_2$ are members of the focal set, then any logical connective,—'and' $(d_{1f} \wedge d_{2g})$, 'or' $(d_{1f} \vee d_{2g})$, 'conditional' $(d_{1f} \Rightarrow d_{2g})$, etc. —defines a conceptual rule. Each rule has associated with it a *complementary* rule, which makes all exemplars nonexemplars and vice versa. When **B** consists of arbitrary names rather than {true, false}, a rule and its complement are equivalent. Although this method of defining a concept cannot be applied to all situations where conceptual behavior seems to be involved, the definition is extremely flexible in its generality.

The scheme has been extended in several ways. One extension is to rules involving three or more relevant dimensions (Shepard, Hovland, & Jenkins, 1961). Under a second extension, the conceptual classification is not into exemplars and nonexemplars, but into three or more sets; the same sorts of logical analysis can be applied here, but multiple focal values are selected. Although several models have been proposed for this extension (Bower & Trabasso, 1964; Bourne & Restle, 1959; Trabasso & Bower, 1964), they have received little attention until recently (Chumbley, 1972). Another variation involves presenting single words representing instances of a concept. For example, the concepts *green, red*, and *round* might be represented as follows: green by grass, go, and unripe; red by stop, beets, and blood; round by ball, circle, and saucer. The subject classifies each word by associating to it a nonsense syllable standing for the concept to be discovered. Polson (1972) assumed that this task involves two processes: paired-associate learning and concept learning. Concept learning occurs in two ways: in the discovery of the common characteristic of each concept, and in the insight that there is a rule behind the way responses are associated to stimuli. Finally, the conceptual classification, as it has been defined here, is deterministic. A stimulus object either is or is not an example of a concept. It is possible to overlay this scheme with a probability measure and produce probabilistic concepts, but such extensions have not been examined in a way particularly relevant to this chapter (see Estes, 1972; Millward, 1968; Peterson, Hammond, & Summers, 1965).

Procedures

Like other psychological processes, concept learning has been studied by a number of different procedures. In the *selection* procedure, introduced by Bruner, Goodnow, and Austin (1956), a set of stimuli is shown to the subject, and a positive example of the concept is selected by the experimenter and shown to the subject. Subsequent stimulus instances are selected and classified by the subject. After each instance is classified, the subject is told the correct classification, and sometimes he is asked to state the rule he used in making his classification. The subject's strategy can then be inferred from his sequence of choices and his statements about the rules he used. This procedure is analogous to the experimental method in which hypotheses are formulated and tested by explicit experiments.

In contrast, in the *reception* procedure, the sequence of stimuli is not under the control of the subject. The experimenter presents stimuli to the subject, usually in random order, and the subject classifies them into one of **b** responses. Following each classification response, the subject is informed of the correct classification. The experimenter's control of the stimulus sequence reduces considerably the range of strategies available to the subject. Historically, the reception procedure is introduced as a simple extension of the paired-associate learning paradigm. The major changes are a reduction in the number of responses and the introduction of a rule. The reception procedure relates to an extensive literature on choice behavior, including the area of discrimination learning. Certainly the bulk of the experiments reported during the past 20 years have used the reception procedure. Because the reception procedure has proved amenable to quantitative analysis, the models constructed for concept identification have been limited almost exclusively to that procedure; we shall consider only such models in this chapter.

The data from a concept-learning experiment using the reception procedure are very limited in extent, consisting only of the correctness of the responses, and perhaps their latencies, without direct information about strategies. In an attempt to overcome this limitation, two variant procedures have been developed. The first of these injects a series of 'blank' trials on which no feedback is given. Assuming that these blank trials have no effect on the learning, they serve well as a probe of the subject's current hypothesis. The second variant procedure involves asking the subject to select the set of stimulus attributes that he wants to see. The values requested are supplied from the usual randomly chosen stimuli. Presumably the subject's current strategy is reflected in the information he requires and hence in the attributes he requests. These variant procedures have contributed primarily to the experimental information about concept learning and only indirectly to mathematical theories, so they will not be explicitly discussed here. Levine (1969) summarizes the extensive results of the blank-trial procedure; preliminary results from the stimulus-attribute selection task can be found in Millward and Spoehr (1973).

THEORY

In the following discussion of theoretical models, we consider only the *concept-identification* (CI) paradigm, in which a simple affirmative rule is identified using a reception procedure. The subject's task is simply to determine which stimulus attribute is correlated with the correct classification. Many of the models which describe more complicated tasks, such as those involving conjunctive rules, are extensions of the affirmative CI models (e.g., Nahinsky, 1970; Williams, 1971).

Models of CI can be divided into two classes on the basis of the type of learning assumed to be taking place. Associational models generally assume gradual increase in strength between the relevant cue and the correct response to that cue. On the other hand, hypothesis models assume that the subject learns suddenly (all-or-none learning) when he discovers the rule governing the classification of the stimuli. Although certain models contain both incremental and all-or-none processes (e.g., Falmagne, 1970), it appears from recent work, both theoretical and experimental, that even if not completely correct, the all-or-none hypothesis-testing models are more solidly supported. Accordingly, we devote the major portion of this review to them and treat the incremental-associational position only briefly in the following section.

Association Models

Association models generally treat each value on each dimension as a set of cues and assign a saliency measure to these cues. Cues associated with the relevant dimension are always consistent with reinforcement, while the irrelevant dimension cues are consistent only on some proportion of the trials, usually one-half when strict random stimulus presentation occurs. Restle's (1955) model of discrimination learning has been applied to this situation by

Bourne and Restle (1959). In their model, the conditioning and adaptation of cues are described by incremental and decremental linear operators, such as $C_{n+1} = (1 - \theta)C_n + \theta$ and $C_{n+1} = (1 - \theta)C_n$. Relevant cues are consistently associated with the same classification outcome, and C_n, the probability of their being conditioned on trial n, increases by repeated applications of the acquisition operator to give $C_n = 1 - (1 - C_1)(1 - \theta)^{n-1}$. Because irrelevant cues are associated with the correct response on half of the trials and with the incorrect response on the other half, no net change in their response strength takes place and $C_n = \frac{1}{2}$. Besides receiving no net conditioning, irrelevant cues are adapted so that they no longer contribute to the determination of the response probabilities. A similar linear model is applied to the probability that an irrelevant cue is adapted, $A_n : A_n = 1 - (1 - A_1)(1 - \theta)^{n-1}$. The same rate parameter, θ, is used here for both C_n and A_n (see Bourne & Restle, 1959, for an explanation of this assumption). Relevant cues, on the other hand, do not adapt. On each trial, the probability of a correct response, P_n, is determined by the proportion of nonadapted cues conditioned to the correct response,

$$P_n = \frac{\sum C_n(1 - A_n)}{\sum (1 - A_n)},$$

where the sums are over the set of cues, here unindexed.

There are many supplementary predictions of this theory, but they are too detailed for this review. It should be noted, however, that learning occurs gradually. The state of each cue or set of cues changes slowly over trials, either by being adapted or by being conditioned; i.e., concept learning is interpreted as an extension of simple learning.

Before turning from this brief discussion of conditioning theories to hypothesis-testing theories, we should at least mention another related set of theories excluded from this review. Because the simple affirmative problem is an example of discrimination learning, one might expect models for this task to be included. However, these models are probably most appropriate for animals, and perhaps for young children, but they do not seem to apply to older children and adults. Thus the work of Zeaman and House (1963), Lovejoy's (1968) two-phase model plus much other theoretical work on discrimination learning (Sutherland & MackIntosh, 1971) are excluded. Norman has discussed some of these models in his chapter in this volume.

Hypothesis Models

During the past ten years, the trend in theorizing has been away from gradual learning through associations and toward the idea that subjects solve concept problems more abruptly by explicitly testing hypotheses (e.g., Bower

& Trabasso, 1964; Falmagne, 1970; Gregg & Simon, 1967; Restle, 1962; Wickens & Millward, 1971). A considerable body of empirical support for this position has been collected and a general hypothesis-testing theory seems to provide a more accurate picture of the subject's behavior in CI tasks than does an associationist theory. However, until recently, published models were designed to describe behavior of naive subjects in a single quite restricted situation. Yet it seems obvious that no single model within the hypothesis-testing framework can accurately represent all CI behavior, because subjects differ in their overall problem-solving abilities, and situations differ in the strategies required of the subjects (Wickens & Millward, 1971). The diversity of CI behavior that should be covered is so great that no single set of axioms can encompass all the properties of all behaviors. The predictions of such a general model would be so weak as to provide little insight into the psychological basis of the particular CI behavior of interest. Furthermore, in order to make precise predictions in specific situations, additional axioms or principles would be necessary. What is needed is a collection of axioms to illustrate the way in which the hypothesis-testing theory can be applied in a variety of situations for subjects of various abilities. The axioms presented in this chapter are an attempt to meet this need. The approach taken is to give alternative forms to many of the axioms, allowing different specific models to be selected for use in different situations. The resulting models can have different implications and, as will be seen, can lead to quite different mathematical representations.

The general theory, then, is the total collection of axioms; selecting a correct model for a specific situation is a matter of selecting the correct subset of axioms as well as 'fitting' the parameters of the model to the data. Although we have tried to formulate these axioms to include both models currently in favor and models of historical interest, we have made no attempt to be exhaustive. Thus, we present one possible integration of the extant mathematical models of CI behavior in the hope that it will help to organize theoretical work and serve as a guide to further integrative efforts.

Hypothesis-testing theory, as it is developed here, contains a number of primitive notions and structural aspects that are to be assumed when the collection of axioms is presented. A brief overview of the theory should make these explicit. If a subject is to test hypotheses, there must be a set of hypotheses for him to consider. This set is called **H** and is partitioned into three subsets on the basis of the attentional status of hypotheses. Subset **A** contains hypotheses to which the subject is not attending but to which he might attend on subsequent trials. Subset **S** contains hypotheses of active interest to the subject. Subset **U** represents hypotheses previously considered but rejected as not being solutions to the problem. Figure 1 presents a schematic representation of these three subsets. The flow of hypotheses is from **A** to **S** when a subject samples, from **S** to **U** when he eliminates inconsistent hypotheses, and

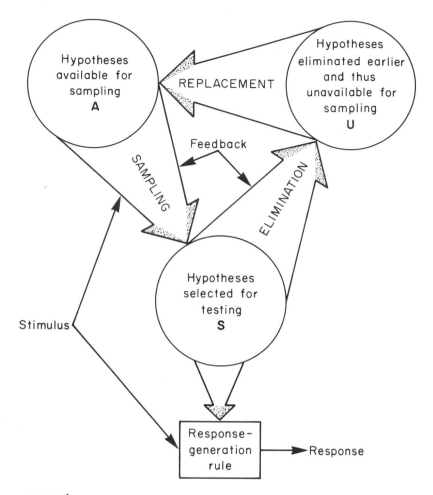

FIGURE 1.
Schematic diagram of the structure of the general hypothesis-sampling theory.

from **U** back to **A** when he replaces hypotheses previously eliminated. The *sampling*, the *elimination*, and the *replacement* processes all require specification in detail if a model is to be explicitly realized. The subject's classification response is assumed to be based on his comparison of the set of active hypotheses with the presented stimulus. A *response-generation rule* is required for this process. Finally, the subject must begin testing hypotheses without previous feedback and assumptions must be made about the *initial state* of the system. A second illustration of these processes is contained in Figure 2, which diagrams the events that take place during the first two trials of a CI problem. The diagram is not as general as that given in Figure 1—it depends

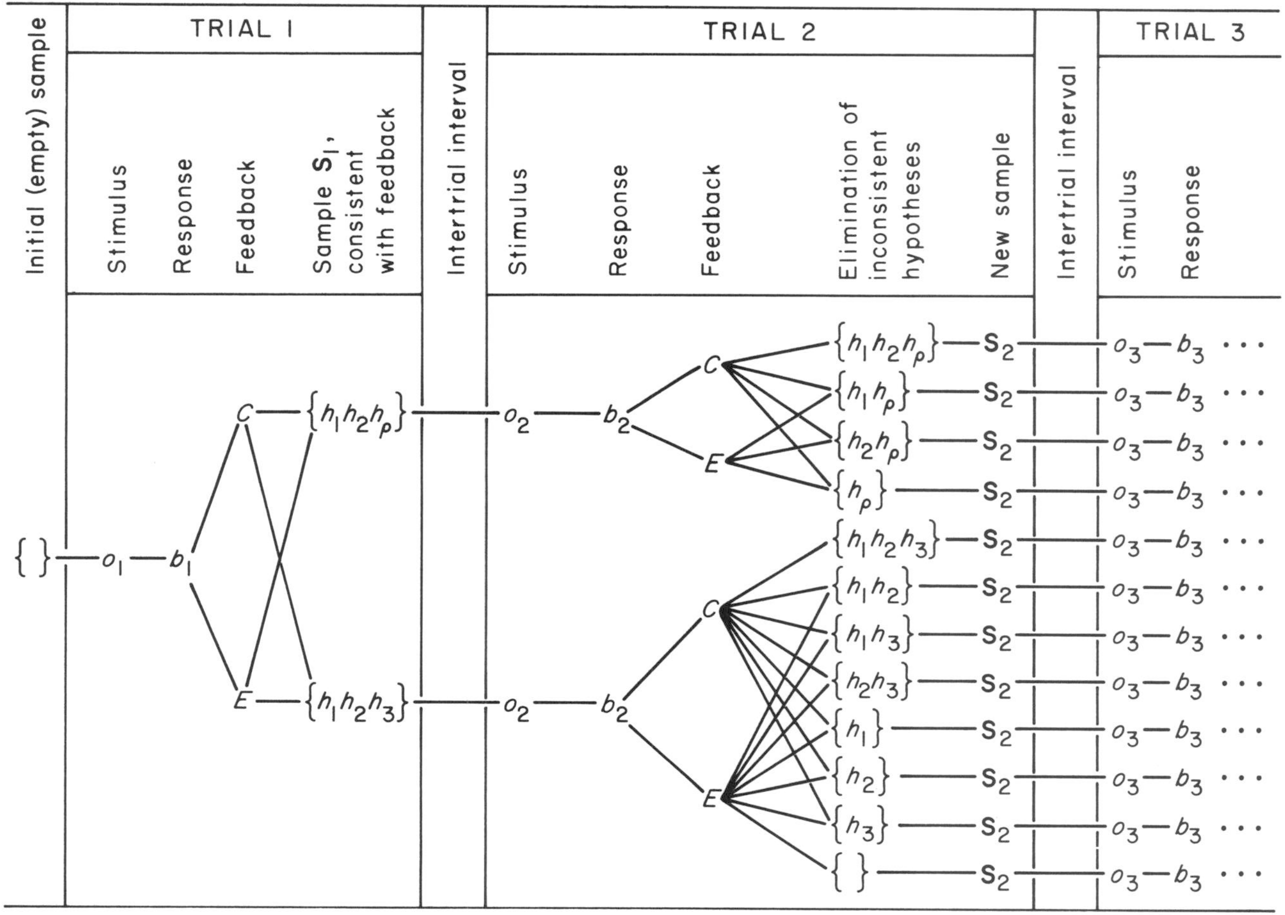

FIGURE 2.
Tree diagram of events during trials 1 and 2 of a CI experiment. A model with Axioms S2b, E1b, and I1c is assumed, and $\sigma = 3$. Hypotheses h_1, h_2, and h_3 are irrelevant and h_p is relevant.

on several specific choices among the axioms that we will present—but it illustrates the approximate sequence of events and the decisions that must be made at each point. The details of Figure 2 and its relation to the axioms will be amplified as the theory is presented.

The definitions and assumptions of the theory are grouped into sections indicated by capital letters corresponding to the processes just described. Within each section, individual assumptions are indicated by numbers and alternative forms of the same assumption by lowercase letters. No strict distinction is made between axioms, assumptions, and definitions. The first section includes the structural and definitional assumptions of the system. The second contains the axioms concerning sampling hypotheses from **A** for **S**, and the third contains axioms for eliminating hypotheses from **S** and their eventual replacement in **A**. The next two sections treat the assumptions about response generation and the initial state of the system. The assumptions in these sections are presented as deterministic mechanisms for concept identification. Although the data of CI experiments usually appear highly variable, the approach here assumes that this variability is due to the mixing of a variety of deterministic mechanisms. Possible additional probabilistic assumptions are discussed in the section on errors in processing. These assumptions take the form of allowing errors in the deterministic assumptions to occur with some specified probability. A final section discusses the definition of a trial sequence during the experiment. We feel this is necessary because our definition of states in the Markov chains relies critically on a correct formulation of what information is included in each state definition.

The inclusion of alternative assumptions allows a great many models to be constructed, although not every combination of alternative axioms represents a viable CI model. Some sets of axioms produce rather absurd models while others contain internal contradictions. However, the bulk of the models are at least plausible and the inadmissible ones are usually obvious. The alternative axioms also help to point out the empirical questions that must be answered about performance in CI experiments.

Structure.   In this section, we present the structural assumptions and basic definitions of hypothesis-testing theory. These differ from the other groups of assumptions in that they make no mention of process. In essence, they formalize the structural features of the theory already outlined.

The exact definition of a hypothesis depends on the details of the experimental situation. Instructions, practice, and the logical rule(s) involved are the critical determiners of **H**, the total set of hypotheses. In a poorly formulated situation, a subject's hypotheses tend to be diffuse, unrelated to the appropriate dimensions, and perhaps even logically wrong, while a highly practiced and well-instructed subject begins with a limited and specific set of hypotheses. Included here is the notion of a hypothesis generator—any inductive process that adds hypotheses to **H** as the experiment progresses. In the most reduced case, the subject's hypotheses are identical to the attributes of the stimulus and the value-response association is not specified until the particular value occurs with classificatory feedback. In the following definitions, each $h \in \mathbf{H}$ is a function that maps **D** onto the response set, **B**. Each definition specifies a set of such functions. The examples are based on a descriptive space defined by the dimensions of size, color, and shape and $\mathbf{B} = \{1, 2\}$.

D1:   Hypothesis definitions.
   (a)   **H** consists of hypotheses (or functions) that are poorly specified and may not be related systematically to the attribute structure.

For example: "Every other stimulus is a 1," or "Red stimuli following blue are 1 while blue following red are 2."

   (b)   **H** consists of all hypotheses based on the values of the attributes and all possible logical connections.

For example: "All red and square stimuli are 1," "All (large or red) and (square or green) stimuli are 1," or "If red, then square stimuli are 1."

   (c)   **H** consists of one hypothesis for each value on each dimension.

For example: "Red is 1," "Green is 2," or "Blue is 1."

   (d)   **H** consists of one hypothesis for each dimension.

For example: "Red is 1," "Square is 1," "Large is 1," etc. Each hypothesis is selected in the presence of feedback; i.e., "Red is 1" is selected when a red stimulus is classified as a 1. As with D1c, this class of hypotheses is appropriate only for the simple affirmative rule, although analogous definitions can be formulated for more complex rules. Unlike D1c, it is also appropriate only with Sampling Axiom S2b, below.

D2:   Partitioning of **H**.
   At any point in the learning process, **H** may be partitioned into three sets: **A**, **S**, and **U**.

Of these three sets, **S** must be finite; hence **U**, containing a finite number of rejected samples, will also be finite. The set **H** and therefore the set **A** may or may not be finite, depending on the definition of a hypothesis that is chosen. The size of the sets **H**, **A**, **S**, and **U** is denoted by lowercase boldface letters, **h**, **a**, **s**, and **u**, respectively. When we use **h** or **a**, we assume that **H** or **A** is of finite size.

   S is assumed to have a structural upper bound, σ.

D3:   Maximum size of **S**.
   There is an integer σ such that $\mathbf{s} \leq \sigma$ at all times.

Hypothesis sampling.   The selection of hypotheses from **A** for active testing in **S** raises three issues. Two of these issues concern the time when sampling takes place: first, the initiating event; and second, the particular point in a trial when the actual sample is made. The third issue concerns the order of selection of hypotheses from **A** and the effect of the selection on **A**.

When hypotheses are removed from **S**, they must eventually be replaced by new hypotheses from **A** unless **S** already contains the relevant hypothesis. The simplest assumption is that sampling is initiated only when all the old hypotheses in **S** have been eliminated. This assumption provides the mathematically most tractable models and seems to be the procedure adopted by the less sophisticated subjects. A more efficient procedure, although a more difficult one from the subject's point of view, is to assume that any decrease in **S** from σ initiates sampling so that hypotheses are continually sampled.

S1:   Initiating sampling.
   (a)   Whenever $\mathbf{s} = 0$, σ hypotheses are sampled from **A** to form **S** (if $\mathbf{a} < \sigma$, then all **a** are sampled and $\mathbf{s} = \mathbf{a}$).
   (b)   Whenever $\mathbf{s} < \sigma$, $\sigma - \mathbf{s}$ hypotheses are sampled from **A** and entered in **S** (if $\mathbf{a} < \sigma - \mathbf{s}$, then all **a** are sampled).

In the following discussion S1b will be the fundamental assumption of one of the models treated in detail, the *continuous-sampling model*.

Within a trial, sampling can take place either in the presence of the feedback just before the intertrial interval or when the stimulus is presented at the beginning of the trial. The time of sampling can determine the nature of the hypotheses selected and is closely related to the definition of a hypothesis; i.e., D1c and D1d become equivalent under S2b.

S2:   Time of sampling.
   (a)   Sampling occurs at the start of a trial with the presentation of a stimulus.
   (b)   Sampling takes place at the end of a trial, and hypotheses selected are consistent with the current feedback.

When S2b holds, the selection of hypotheses is said to show *local consistency* (Gregg & Simon, 1967). Empirically, it appears that S2b holds when post-feedback intervals are sufficiently long (Bourne, Guy, Dodd, & Justesen, 1965). Figure 2 has been drawn assuming the S2b Axiom, since the sampling operation takes place immediately after the feedback and before the intertrial interval. If S2a were adopted, this sampling would take place immediately following the presentation of the stimuli, o_1, o_2, o_3, etc.

If **H** contains more than σ hypotheses, some rule must be given for the order of their selection in forming **S**. The simplest such rule, when **H** is finite, is to make the sampling probabilities equal for all hypotheses. Equal probabilities are unlikely when naive subjects solve their first problem, but are more likely when selection is from a small population of hypotheses well known to the subjects. More generally, weights or saliencies can be assigned to different hypotheses, and selection can be based on probabilities defined by these weights. In the treatment of Axiom S3b, weights remain constant throughout the problem, although more elaborate axiomatizations could include the possibility of their change (see the section on Hypothesis Elimination and Falmagne, 1970). Finally, with practice, subjects show evidence of developing a fixed order in which to sample hypotheses; Axiom S3c defines fixed-order sampling.

S3:　Sampling probabilities.
　　(a)　Hypotheses are sampled randomly from **A** for **S**. For $h_i \in$ **A**, $P(h_i$ sampled$) = 1/$**a**.
　　(b)　Hypotheses in **A** are sampled for **S** according to a set of weights. For each $h_i \in$ **H**, there is an $\omega_i > 0$, such that if $h_i \in$ **A**,

$$P(h_i \text{ sampled}) = \frac{\omega_i}{\sum\limits_{h_i \in A} \omega_j}.$$

　　(c)　Hypotheses are selected for **S** according to a fixed ordering of **H**.

Hypotheses can be allowed either a single or a multiple representation in **S**. Multiple representation has been used in at least one model (Trabasso & Bower, 1968), although it seems somewhat out of the spirit of hypothesis-testing theory as presented here. For this reason, Axiom S4a rather than S4b has been used in the models discussed in detail in this chapter.

S4:　Sampling replacement.
　　(a)　If $h \in$ **A** is sampled for **S**, it is removed from **A**.
　　(b)　**A** remains unchanged by sampling.

Hypothesis elimination and replacement.   Elimination of some hypotheses from **S** takes place whenever a hypothesis makes a prediction that is inconsistent with the observed classification of a stimulus. Early models (Restle, 1962; Bower & Trabasso, 1964) contained the assumption that the full sample was eliminated whenever an overt error was made. This assumption greatly simplifies the mathematics, but is not consistent with all data (e.g., Wickens & Millward, 1971; Falmagne, 1970; Levine, 1969; Millward & Spoehr, 1973). With practiced subjects it is much more appropriate to assume that sampling takes place without regard to the overt responses, Axiom E1b.

E1:　Eliminating hypotheses from **S**.
　　(a)　Whenever an overt error is made, all hypotheses in **S** are eliminated from **S** and entered in **U**. Whenever a correct response

is made, any hypotheses in **S** that are inconsistent with the observed feedback are eliminated from **S** and are entered in **U**.

(b)   Whenever a hypothesis is inconsistent with the observed feedback, it is eliminated from **S** and entered in **U**.

E1a is the assumption commonly called *resampling on errors*. Two further comments should be made about Axiom E1. In E1a, an error empties **S**; E1a in conjunction with S1 requires another sample to be taken. However, for a number of reasons, one may wish to assume that sampling does not necessarily occur when **S** is empty. Falmagne (1970) considered the possibility that **S** remained empty for one trial (see the section on the Initial State). The second point relates to the question of probabilistic mechanisms. The E1 Axiom represents one of the more likely places for deterministic processing to break down, so a probabilistic version of E1 will be introduced later. The elimination process illustrated in Figure 2 is that of E1b. If E1a were assumed, all branches from the error feedback would go to the completely eliminated sample, denoted by empty braces, { }.

Two memory mechanisms are assumed in hypothesis-testing theory: The active set of hypotheses, **S**, is obviously a kind of short-term memory. The memory for information not in **S** can be referred to as long-term memory (Atkinson & Wickens, 1971). There are also two ways in which information is stored. One is a memory for specific stimuli presented on earlier trials, while the second is for specific hypotheses. Although stimulus memory may be important in some contexts, it seems inefficient and unnecessary for the affirmative problem; Coltheart (1971) makes a strong case against its use. Williams (1971) assumed a stimulus memory in her model, which was designed primarily to describe behavior in a conjunctive concept-learning task. However, only hypothesis memory is allowed by the hypothesis-sampling model.

Once a hypothesis is eliminated, it is placed in **U** and remains unavailable while there, being remembered by the subject as unsatisfactory. However, the learning rates observed in many subjects are not sufficiently great to permit **U** to be a permanent storage for tested hypotheses. Instead, these hypotheses must be allowed to return to **A** after a number of trials have passed. Some simple models have eliminated **U** altogether, assuming replacement directly from **S** into **A** (Bower & Trabasso, 1964; Restle, 1962). On the other hand, with practiced subjects, permanent elimination or *global nonreplacement* (Gregg & Simon, 1967) can take place. These two extreme cases are represented by Axioms E2a and E2b below. The remaining axioms represent intermediate positions in which the time in **U** is temporary, although each includes E2a and E2b as special cases.

E2:   Hypothesis elimination.

(a)   **u** = 0: Hypotheses eliminated from **S** are replaced immediately in **A** (sampling with replacement).

(b) $\mathbf{u} \geq \mathbf{h} - \sigma$: Hypotheses eliminated from **S** are never returned to **A**.

(c) If $\mathbf{u} > \lambda\sigma$, the oldest hypothesis in **U** is removed to **A**. The parameter λ is a small integer.

(d) Each hypothesis eliminated from **S** remains in **U** for κ trials.

Axiom E2c represents the size of **U** as a fixed number of samples, and is paired logically with Sampling Axiom S1a. One interpretation of this scheme is that the stimuli consist of a number of clusters of attributes that the subject naturally treats together. Thus, **U** represents a memory for λ clusters rather than for λ hypotheses.

Response generation.   On each trial, the subject must make an overt response as well as process the sampled hypotheses. It is certainly reasonable to assume that the response rule involves using the sampled hypotheses in conjunction with the presented stimulus to determine the response, but this assumption is not necessary. Of course, from the experimenter's point of view, if the subject is to solve the problem, he must make a criterion run of correct responses, and this is accomplished most easily by responding according to the relevant hypothesis. Axiom R1a provides for complete independence of the response from the stimulus and is probably unrealistic; R1b through R1e provide for responses based on the hypotheses in **S**.

R1:   Response generation.

(a)   The stimulus classification is based on rules unrelated to the presented stimulus.

(b)   A hypothesis is selected from **S**, and responses are generated by it so long as it remains uneliminated. The selection of the response-determining hypothesis can be made in one of three ways: random with equal probabilities, by weights as in Axiom S3b except restricted to the set **S**, or by selecting the oldest hypothesis in **S**.

(c)   On each trial a hypothesis in **S** is selected at random or by weights and is used to generate the response for that trial.

(d)   If x_i hypotheses in **S** imply the response b_i, then $P(b_i) = x_i \mathbf{s}$.

(e)   If x_1 hypotheses in **S** imply the response b_1 and x_2 hypotheses imply the response b_2, then the response will be b_1 if $x_1 > x_2$, b_2 if $x_2 > x_1$, and either b_1 or b_2 with probability $\frac{1}{2}$ if $x_1 = x_2$.

A special axiom is sometimes needed to generate a response at the start of the experiment before any sample has been selected if the subject is forced to respond at a time when $\mathbf{s} = 0$ (Falmagne, 1970).

R2:   Response generation when $\mathbf{S} = \varnothing$.

A response based on an empty sample, $\mathbf{S} = \varnothing$, is a random selection of one of the response alternatives with equal probabilities for each.

Initial state.   Three initial-state assumptions have been used.

I1:   Initial state.
   (a)   Initially, **S** contains only incorrect hypotheses.
   (b)   Initially, **S** contains a sample of σ hypotheses from **H**, selected according to Axiom S3.
   (c)   Initially, $\mathbf{S} = \varnothing$.

The choice of the Initial-state Axiom is closely related to the choice of the Time-of-Sampling Axiom, S2. Axiom I1c is most appropriate when sampling is locally consistent (S2b) and when the initial response is explicitly included as the first trial. This is the situation diagrammed in Figure 2. Since no feedback exists before the first trial, no hypotheses can be formed, $\mathbf{S} = \varnothing$, and R2 is used to generate the first response (see Millward, 1968, for a variant of these assumptions). This guess allows the subject to defer sampling until the first stimulus and feedback are available. Axiom I1b is appropriate in the same situation if the first trial is dropped from the analysis and the process starts with the second response. In Figure 2, this corresponds to deleting the portion of the figure to the left of the first sample. With either axiom the first response is a guess and will be correct with a probability denoted by γ. With Axiom I1a, at least one error will occur; in Figure 2 this corresponds to the portion of the figure originating with the sample $\mathbf{S}_1 = \{h_1 h_2 h_3\}$, which does not contain the relevant hypothesis, h_ρ. Bower and Trabasso (1964) used this to generate a prediction of at least one error. Its most reasonable application is to transfer experiments where the error is forced by the design. Under S2a, Axiom I1c seems no longer appropriate, but either I1a or I1b may be selected.

Errors in processing.   Models based on the preceding axioms describe the subject as processing information perfectly, at least up to capacity restrictions. The facts that only a limited number of hypotheses are tested at once, that eliminated hypotheses may reappear in **A**, and that new hypotheses are not checked against past stimuli are all manifestations of finite mental capacity; but aside from these limitations, the performance based on the above axioms is without error. Clearly, as we mentioned earlier, these are not completely realistic assumptions. Nevertheless, the models generated by the given axioms are important because they state ideals of performance. Even though they are not always followed exactly, they show most clearly the structure that the subject imposes on the problem. The introduction of probabilistic assumptions to take account of processing errors in the models tends to hide this structure. Although the introduction of stochastic processes may allow an accurate description, an even finer analysis of behavior might provide an explanation for the processing errors.

The large number of ways in which processing errors can take place provides a second reason why the analysis of error-free models is important. Almost any of the nonstructural axioms above can be modified to include errors. Such a plethora of possibilities leads to weak models in which parameter estimation either is impossible or yields results so variable as to be meaningless. It seems best to proceed, not by developing a general stochastic model and attempting to fit data to it, but by establishing the correct structural form of the model and then determining what variables lead to processing errors. The introduction of processing errors is intuitively more natural in some places than in others. The most important modifications of the collection of axioms are considered in the following paragraphs. It should be noted that none of these probabilistic changes alters the basic Markovian nature of the models. The revised axioms can be analyzed by the procedures discussed in later sections.

The processes that would seem to be most subject to error are those that involve the transfer of hypotheses from one set to another, that is, those represented in the sampling Axiom S1 and the elimination Axioms E1 and E2. The first modification is to allow elimination to occur on a probabilistic basis.

E′1:   Probabilistic hypothesis elimination.
  (a)   Let rejecting S be the process of eliminating all hypotheses in S and taking a new sample of size σ from A as in E1a. Then S is rejected with probability ϵ_e on an error response and with probability ϵ_c on a correct response. If S is not rejected, then Axiom E′1b applies.
  (b)   Inconsistent hypotheses in S are eliminated from S with probability δ_i and are kept in S with probability $1 - \delta_i$. Consistent hypotheses are eliminated with probability δ_c and are kept with probability $1 - \delta_c$.

Axiom E′1b allows for elimination to fail to take place with inconsistent hypotheses and for consistent hypotheses to be incorrectly eliminated. The error-free Axioms E1a and E1b are equivalent to these if $\epsilon_e = \delta_i = 1$ and $\epsilon_c = \delta_c = 0$. At this time, Axiom E′1b seems intuitively reasonable, but E′1a does not. One would expect these parameters to deviate from values defining the deterministic model when, for example, the intertrial interval is short or the size of S is excessively large.

There are at least three ways of treating the return of rejected hypotheses probabilistically. The first seems wrong since it destroys the organization of the stimulus by the subject and, more importantly, it is hard to think that a subject would not remember more recently eliminated hypotheses better than those eliminated earlier. The second is mathematically intractable. The third adds a probabilistic return process to the end of Axiom E2d and provides for perfect memory of recently rejected hypotheses.

E′2:   Probabilistic return of eliminated hypotheses.
   (a)   For each $h_i \in H$ there is an $\eta_i > 0$ such that for every trial in which $h_i \in U$, h_i is transferred from U to A with probability η_i.
   (b) U is empty and hypotheses eliminated from S are replaced in A with lower weights. On each subsequent trial the weights increase, until they reach their original value.
   (c)   Each attribute eliminated from S remains in U for κ trials, after which Axiom E′2a holds.

Axiom E′2b requires the sampling-by-weights assumption S3b and is a probabilistic statement of E2a.

The probabilistic version of the sampling axiom is best found, not by replacing Axiom S1, but by introducing an additional axiom, here called S′5, to define what is meant by a sampled hypothesis in S1.

S′5:   Probabilistic sampling.
   (a)   If $t \leq \sigma$ hypotheses are sampled on any trial, then with probability β, all fail to enter S and remain in A, and with probability $1 - \beta$ they all enter S.
   (b)   If $t \leq \sigma$ hypotheses are sampled on any trial, j fail to enter S and stay in A with probability $\binom{t}{j} \beta^j (1 - \beta)^{t-j}$.

Under the S1a assumption, S′5a could easily leave a null sample, which would require a special response-generating rule, e.g., R2. Distracting events might occasion S′5a, while S′5b is more likely a substantial psychological assumption—subjects may simply vary their sample size from trial to trial.

The same general procedures used to revise E1, E2, and S1 Axioms can be followed to introduce random properties to several other axioms, but this will not be done here. The above axioms have introduced at least three and as many as six new parameters that would have to be estimated; further modification of the axioms would only increase this number. It is to be emphasized that insofar as the models must be tested against data from multiple problems, it is difficult to distinguish between probabilistic assumptions and the average of varying deterministic ones. Thus, in the absence of specific experiments to distinguish among the alternatives, a catalogue of possibilities provides few further insights of psychological importance.

State definitions.   In the remainder of this chapter various Markov chains will be defined by specifying their states, transition probabilities, and initial vectors. Since the state definitions can become fairly complex and since their specification is important to the definition of the transition probabilities, we make a preliminary statement about them at this point. The division between trials that we use is illustrated in Figure 2. Here a natural division at the intertrial interval has been made, combining a response with the sample that is created following it. It would also have been possible to place the break so as to combine in a trial a sample and the response that is based on it. This definition is more natural under Axiom S2a, when the sampling takes place after the intertrial interval and before the response, but either choice of S2 can be analyzed with either type of trial. Because we assume S2b in the models we discuss, however, there is a strong argument for the choice we have made. The correctness of a response is determined by the feedback, so that to specify the correctness of a response, one must specify the feedback and this, under S2b, determines the next sample. If the trial separation is placed between the sampling and the feedback, the information about the feedback is not available when the results of sampling are completed and conditional probabilities of transitions must be introduced. Extra states are also required to take account of the fact that when an error occurs at least one hypothesis must be eliminated. Although the two definitions lead to equivalent processes, the introduction of the extra states and conditional probabilities is cumbersome.

Our definition suffers from one disadvantage. In it, states of the model contain information about the response on trial n and the sample used to generate the $(n + 1)$st response. This makes definition of transition probabilities very natural, but means that if we are interested in the relation between responses and the samples that generate them we must look back a trial. In Figure 2, for example, the response b_2 is based on S_1, not on whichever of the S_2 samples at the end of trial 2 is eventually selected. In interpreting the models in the remainder of this chapter, the reader should keep this fact in mind.

DEVELOPMENT OF SPECIFIC MODELS

In this section, three specific models of concept identification will be developed in some detail. They differ in the sophistication that they assume on the part of the subject, and more particularly, in the basic structure of the sampling and elimination processes as specified in Axioms S1 and E1. The first and simplest model assumes that resampling occurs when and only when an error is made (S1a and E1a). The second model represents what appears to be a good approximation of how practiced subjects solve problems, i.e., resampling occurs only when the sample, S, is empty. If an error is made that does not empty S, the remaining hypotheses in S are carried on to the next trial (S1a and E1b). The third model represents highly sophisticated problem-solving behavior. Resampling occurs whenever any attribute is eliminated from **S** so that **S** is kept at some fixed size, σ (S1b and E1b).

Models with Resampling on Errors

Because almost all hypothesis-testing models have assumed resampling on errors and because they are well developed elsewhere, we only summarize the earlier work. Two specific developments seem worthy of mention, however. One is the ability to predict results for specific sequences of stimulus presentation, and the second is the change in the sample size during runs of consecutive correct responses.

The first hypothesis-sampling model.   Restle's (1962) original hypothesis-sampling model defines hypotheses abstractly, as correct, wrong, or irrelevant (D1a). Single hypotheses have equal sampling probability (S3a), but the three types have different frequencies, and hypotheses of each type are treated as equivalent. Selection occurs at the time of stimulus presentation (S2a), responses are made according to a proportional rule (R1d), and if the response is correct, inconsistent hypotheses are eliminated (E1a). On an error trial, the current sample is abandoned (S1a and E1a) and resampling occurs with replacement (E2a). Restle proved a central property of this model, i.e., that the recurrence of errors is independent of σ, the size of **S**. More generally, his proof begins by assuming a finite set of **H** hypotheses, divided into correct, error, and irrelevant hypotheses with frequencies N_c, N_w, and N_i, respectively. In a sample of size σ, assuming that each hypothesis has the same probability of being sampled, the distribution of the number of each type of hypothesis n_c, n_w, and n_i is given by a hypergeometric distribution,

$$P(n_c, n_w, n_i) = \frac{\binom{N_c}{n_c} \binom{N_w}{n_w} \binom{N_i}{n_i}}{\binom{N}{\sigma}}.$$

Let F_j be the event that the first error occurs on the *j*th trial following the acquisition of a new sample. For F_j to take place, the subject must select either a correct hypothesis or one of the irrelevant hypotheses that happened to be correct on the first $j - 1$ trials; then on the *j*th trial he must select either a wrong hypothesis (possible only if $j = 1$) or an irrelevant hypothesis that happens to be wrong. Since the hypotheses are of equal sampling probabilities, the conditional probability that the first error occurs on trial *j* given n_c, n_w, and n_i is

$$P(F_j \mid n_c, n_w, n_i) = \begin{cases} \dfrac{n_w + \frac{1}{2}n_i}{\sigma}, & j = 1, \\ \dfrac{n_i}{\sigma}\left(\dfrac{1}{2}\right)^j, & j > 1. \end{cases}$$

Since, for example, $E(n_i) = \dfrac{\sigma N_i}{N}$, the unconditional probability is

$$
P(F_j) = \begin{cases} \dfrac{N_w + \frac{1}{2}N_i}{N}, & j = 1, \\[2ex] \dfrac{N_i}{N}\left(\dfrac{1}{2}\right)^i, & j > 1. \end{cases}
$$

This result is independent of σ, establishing Restle's basic property of the model. Furthermore, results that can be expressed in terms of $P(F_j)$, such as the distribution of the number of errors (TNE) and the trial of the last error (TLE), will also be independent of σ.

Bower and Trabasso (1964) altered Restle's model by adopting a more restricted definition of a hypothesis (D1c) by assuming that sampling occurs at the end of the trial (S2b) and by explicitly setting $\sigma = 1$. They assumed that the initial sample contained only incorrect hypotheses (I1a) and that the first trial was a guess (R2), which was correct with probability γ and incorrect with probability $1 - \gamma$. These restrictions on sampling and elimination are strong ones and make their model quite tractable. Their formulation can be expressed as a three-state Markov chain with transition matrix

$$
T = \begin{array}{c} \\ \\ \text{state} \\ \text{on} \\ \text{trial } n \end{array} \begin{array}{c} \\ \\ L \\ C \\ E \end{array} \overset{\displaystyle \begin{array}{ccc} \multicolumn{3}{c}{\text{state on trial } n + 1} \\ L & C & E \end{array}}{\left[\begin{array}{ccc} 1 & 0 & 0 \\ 0 & \pi & 1 - \pi \\ \theta & \pi(1 - \theta) & (1 - \pi)(1 - \theta) \end{array}\right]} \tag{1}
$$

and initial vector

$$
V_1 = (0, \pi, 1 - \pi).
$$

The parameter π is the probability of a correct response, and $1 - \pi$ the probability of an error response based on the sampled hypothesis. The learning parameter θ is the probability of sampling the relevant hypothesis. When the process is in state L, the relevant hypothesis has been sampled, while in states C and E an irrelevant hypothesis has been sampled. State C is used when the hypothesis is consistent with the current feedback so as to produce a correct response and state E is used when the hypothesis is inconsistent. Notice that the initial-state Axiom I1a requires at least one error before entering L. If I1b were used, the possibility would exist that the initial hypothesis is the relevant one, and the initial vector would look like the transition probabilities from E:

$$
V_1 = (\theta, \pi(1 - \theta), (1 - \pi)(1 - \theta)).
$$

If I1c were adopted, the initial response would be a guess, correct with probability γ, and

$$V_1 = (\gamma\theta, \gamma(1 - \theta), 1 - \gamma).$$

If V_n is the state probability vector on trial n, then, $V_{n+1} = V_n T$ and, by simple recursion, $V_n = V_1 T^{n-1}$. A great many statistics related to the learning process have been fully developed for the resampling-on-error model by Bower and Trabasso (1964), as well as by a number of secondary sources (e.g., Atkinson, Bower, & Crothers, 1965). Therefore, only three derivations will be considered here. The first increases the precision of the model so that predictions can be made for individual stimulus sequences. The second expresses the general model as a Markov chain and looks at the generality of Restle's proof that the probability of a recurrent error is independent of σ. The third adds sample size as a new dependent variable of the model.

Predictions for specific sequences of stimuli. The assumptions of the model specified by the transition matrix in Equation 1 allow for stronger predictions than those just mentioned. All stimuli are not equivalent by this model but depend for their effectiveness on the extent to which they differ from the previously presented stimulus. For example, if the stimulus on trial $n + 1$ differed from that on trial n on every dimension except the relevant one, it would force an error unless the relevant hypothesis had been selected. On the other hand, if the stimulus on trial $n + 1$ differed on no dimensions from the relevant one, then a correct response would be made with probability 1. More generally, the set $\mathbf{H}' = \mathbf{H} - \{h_\rho\}$, formed by excluding the relevant hypothesis h_ρ from $\mathbf{H}$, can be partitioned in 2^{h-1} ways into two disjoint sets, $\mathbf{H} = \mathbf{H}_c \cup \mathbf{H}_e$, where $\mathbf{H}_c$ is the set of hypotheses that are consistent with the classification on trials n and $n + 1$, and $\mathbf{H}_e$ is the set of hypotheses that are inconsistent with the classification on the two trials. As all possible pairs of stimuli on trials n and $n + 1$ are varied, all 2^{h-1} possible partitions of $\mathbf{H}'$ are generated. Or alternatively, over all consecutive pairs of trials, all possible pairs of stimulus combinations will occur if the stimuli are randomly presented. Let the partition produced on trial n by the stimuli on trials n and $n + 1$ be denoted by Γ_n, and let θ_i represent the probability that hypothesis h_i is selected, with θ_ρ the probability of selecting the relevant hypothesis. Then the transition matrix for trial n, T_{Γ_n}, is

$$T_{\Gamma_n} = \begin{array}{c} \\ L \\ C \\ E \end{array} \begin{array}{c} \overset{L}{} \\ \left| \begin{array}{c} 1 \\ 0 \\ \theta_\rho \end{array} \right. \end{array} \begin{array}{c} \overset{C}{} \\ \begin{array}{c} 0 \\ \dfrac{1}{1 - \theta_\rho} \sum\limits_{h_i \in \mathbf{H}_c} \theta_i \\ \sum\limits_{h_i \in \mathbf{H}_e} \theta_i \end{array} \end{array} \begin{array}{c} \overset{E}{} \\ \begin{array}{c} 0 \\ \dfrac{1}{1 - \theta_\rho} \sum\limits_{h_i \in \mathbf{H}_e} \theta_i \\ \sum\limits_{h_i \in \mathbf{H}_e} \theta_i \end{array} \end{array} \cdot$$

Here, the state probabilities are given by

$$V_n = V_1 T_{\Gamma_1} T_{\Gamma_2} \ldots T_{\Gamma_{n-1}},$$

where $\Gamma_1, \Gamma_2, \ldots, \Gamma_{n-1}$ are the partitions of $\mathbf{H}'$ generated by successive pairs of stimuli and V_n is the state vector on the nth trial. Note that Γ_i is not necessarily different from Γ_j for any pair of subscripts i and j. In this form the model makes specific predictions about the sequence of responses that will be made to a particular sequence of stimuli. These predictions are considered by Cotton (1971) and Falmagne (1970). Cotton has also shown that $E(V_n) = V\bar{T}^{n-1}$, where

$$\bar{T} = \frac{\sum_{\Gamma} T_{\Gamma}}{2^{h-1}},$$

and the sum is over all 2^{h-1} partitions of $\mathbf{H}'$. This result reduces the transition matrix based on the specific sequence of stimuli so that it is the same form as the transition matrix represented by Equation 1.

Representation of the general model as a Markov chain. The assumption of resampling on errors is a powerful one, and variants of this model that result from changes of other assumptions produce only minor differences from the formulation already considered. If the sample size is increased to $\sigma > 1$, the predictions change little even though a model with more states is required. Although Restle's derivation proving that the learning rate is independent of the sample size was performed in the special case of equal sampling probabilities (S3a) and the proportional response rule (R1d), it also can be derived from other assumptions. Let θ' represent the probability that no more errors follow an error. If $\sigma = 1$, $\theta' = \theta$, whereas if $\sigma > 1$, θ' is given by

$$\theta' = \sum_{\mathbf{S'} \subset \mathbf{H'}} P(\mathbf{S} = \mathbf{S'} \cup \{h_\rho\}) P(\text{no error} \mid \mathbf{S} = \mathbf{S'} \cup \{h_\rho\}), \qquad (2)$$

where the sum is over the $\binom{h-1}{\sigma-1}$ possible sets of $\sigma - 1$ irrelevant hypotheses from $\mathbf{H}$. When equal weights are assumed (Axiom S3a), all response rules R1b–R1e imply that

$$P(\text{no error} \mid h_\rho \in \mathbf{S}) = \frac{1}{\sigma}$$

does not depend on the contents of $\mathbf{S}'$. Because of the equal weights assumption,

$$\sum_{\mathbf{S'} \subset \mathbf{H'}} P(\mathbf{S} = \mathbf{S'} \cup \{h_\rho\}) = P(h_\rho \in \mathbf{S}) = \frac{\sigma}{h}.$$

Thus, Equation 2 reduces to $\theta' = \frac{1}{h}$, so that as long as Axiom S3a is kept, the independence of θ' and σ holds. When weights are unequal as in Axiom S3b, independence no longer holds and the value of θ' depends on the size of the sample. Response Axiom R1b has a special characteristic in that, regardless of the sample size, it reduces to the model expressed in Equation 1. This reduction takes place because the hypothesis selected from S according to R1b plays the same role as the single hypothesis selected from H when $\sigma = 1$. However, if weights are unequal, the learning rate may still change with the sample size. A detailed discussion of this relatively minor point concerning the independence of θ' and σ is not in order here, although further work would be required to determine how the learning rate changes with σ when the S3b Axiom is assumed.

The above discussion has shown that, when the S3a Axiom is assumed, the sequence of correct and error responses does not depend systematically on σ. However, the model does contain information not embodied in this response sequence. Measures such as the latency of the response, confidence judgments about the correctness of the response, and the trial on which a subject can state with certainty that the solution has been found should depend on the size and contents of the sample. Similarly, results relating to reversal problems in which the concept rule is changed before the subject reaches criterion or to relevant-redundant cue problems in which two or more dimensions are simultaneously relevant depend on the contents of the sample to an extent not measured simply by the overt sequences of correct and error responses (see Trabasso & Bower, 1966; 1968). Accordingly, a further result will be developed involving the way the size of the sample changes over trials. The specific model to be considered is based on Axioms D1, D2, D3, S1a, S2b, S3a, S4a, E1a, E2a, R1b, R2, and all three versions of I1. The selection of R1b instead of R1c or R1d is somewhat specific, but a model with R1c or R1d can be analyzed by the same techniques as those used here.

The model may be represented as a Markov chain with $2\sigma + 1$ states. Errors always cause resampling in the same way; hence they can be represented in a single state, E. On the other hand, the transitions following a correct response differ depending on how many hypotheses there are in S and on whether or not S contains the relevant hypothesis. Let I_i be the state that does not contain the relevant hypothesis but does contain i irrelevant hypotheses, $i = 1, 2, \ldots, \sigma$. Let R_i be the state where S contains the relevant hypothesis and $i - 1$ irrelevant hypotheses. Since resampling occurs only after an error, and since the relevant hypothesis cannot be eliminated, there are no direct transitions between the I_i and the R_i states. In later derivations it will be convenient to refer to sets of states, so let $\mathbf{R} = \{R_1, R_2, \ldots, R_\sigma\}$, $\mathbf{I} = \{I_1, I_2, \ldots, I_\sigma\}$, and $\mathbf{C} = \mathbf{R} \cup \mathbf{I}$, the set of states in which a correct response is made. The state X refers to some unspecified state such as E, I_i, or R_i, and the set $\mathbf{X}$ to one of the sets $\mathbf{R}$, $\mathbf{I}$, or $\mathbf{C}$. The notation $\mathbf{X}(k)$, $\mathbf{R}(k)$, etc., is used to indicate that the process is in one of the states in the $\mathbf{X}$, $\mathbf{R}$, etc., set of states on trial k, while $E(k)$, $I_i(k)$, etc., similarly indicates states E, I_i, etc., on trial k. The Markov chain model can then be expressed by a transition matrix, T:

$$T = \begin{array}{c} \\ \mathbf{R} \\ \mathbf{I} \\ \mathbf{E} \end{array} \begin{array}{|ccc} \mathbf{R} & \mathbf{I} & \mathbf{E} \\ \hline Q_{RR} & 0 & Q_{RE} \\ 0 & Q_{II} & Q_{IE} \\ Q_{ER} & Q_{EI} & Q_{EE} \end{array} , \tag{3}$$

where Q_{XY} represents a submatrix of transitions from state(s) X to state(s) Y. The transitions from each of the three rows of T must be defined.

1. Transitions from $\mathbf{I}$. Regardless of the number of irrelevant hypotheses remaining in $\mathbf{S}$, the probability of an error is $1 - \pi$; thus:

$$P(I_i \longrightarrow E) = 1 - \pi, \qquad i = 1, 2, \ldots, \sigma.$$

As long as one or more of the hypotheses is consistent, the transitions from an $\mathbf{I}$ state can be to another $\mathbf{I}$ state. Of the i hypotheses in $\mathbf{S}$, when in state I_i, the number that are consistent will be distributed binomially with parameters i and π. If j hypotheses are consistent, then the probability that no error is made, hence that the process remains in $\mathbf{I}$ and passes to I_j, is j/i by any of the three Response Axioms R1b, R1c, or R1d. Thus,

$$P(\mathbf{I}_i \longrightarrow I_j) = \frac{j}{i} \binom{i}{j} \pi^j (1 - \pi)^{i-j}$$

$$= \binom{i-1}{j-1} \pi^j (1 - \pi)^{i-j}.$$

2. Transitions from $\mathbf{R}$. Since states in $\mathbf{R}$ contain the relevant hypothesis, which can never be inconsistent and eliminated, the R_1 state is absorbing:

$$P(R_1 \longrightarrow R_1) = 1.0.$$

The transitions within $\mathbf{R}$ are similar to those within $\mathbf{I}$ but depend only on the $i - 1$ irrelevant hypotheses in $\mathbf{S}$. Hence, if $j - 1$ irrelevant hypotheses are consistent, the probability of a correct response is j/i and

$$P(R_i \longrightarrow R_j) = \frac{j}{i} \binom{i-1}{j-1} \pi^{i-1} (1 - \pi)^{i-j}.$$

For $i \neq 1$, R_i can lead to an error with probability $\dfrac{i - j}{i}$. Each possible value of $j < i - 1$ yields a probability of an error. The total probability is the weighted sum over all j values:

$$\sum_{j=1}^{i-1} \frac{i-1}{i} \binom{i-1}{j-1} \pi^{i-i} (1 - \pi)^{i-1} = \frac{i-1}{i} (1 - \pi).$$

Thus,

$$P(R_i \longrightarrow E) = \begin{cases} 0, & i = 1; \\ \dfrac{i-1}{i}(1-\pi), & 1 < i \le \sigma. \end{cases}$$

3. Transitions from E. When an error is made, state E is entered and a full sample of size σ is taken. Let θ be the probability that this sample contains the relevant hypothesis and $1 - \theta$ the probability that it does not. In state E the sample **S** is identical to the sample in state R_σ with probability θ and is identical to the sample in state I_σ with probability $1 - \theta$. Transitions from E have the same dynamics as transitions from R_σ and I_σ:

$$P(E \longrightarrow I_j) = (1 - \theta)P(I_\sigma \longrightarrow I_j)$$
$$= (1 - \theta)(\tbinom{\sigma-1}{j-1})\pi^i(1 - \pi)^{\sigma-i};$$
$$P(E \longrightarrow R_j) = \theta P(R_\sigma \longrightarrow R_j)$$
$$= \theta\,\frac{j}{\sigma}\,(\tbinom{\sigma-1}{j-1})\pi^{i-1}(1 - \pi)^{\sigma-i};$$
$$P(E \longrightarrow E) = \left(1 - \frac{\theta}{\sigma}\right)(1 - \pi).$$

4. The initial vector. If IIa is selected, the initial sample must contain only irrelevant hypotheses, so the initial vector contains only the normalized transitions from I_σ. If IIb is chosen, the sample is just like any sample after an error, and the initial vector will look like the transitions from state E. If IIc is used (appropriate when the subject guesses on the first trial and this trial is included), then a new state G is defined with the same transitions as those from state E and $P(X \longrightarrow G) = 0$ for all states X. The new state G is entered on the first trial with probability γ, the probability of a correct response, and state E is entered with probability $1 - \gamma$, the probability of an error. Although this adds an extra state to the transition matrix, the state is only entered on the first trial and leads to little difficulty in analysis. The solution here including the first trial and Axiom IIc can be compared with the solution with IIa in Equation 1.

Sample-size statistics.   In determining the size of the sample that produces the response on a particular trial, three cases must be distinguished. These three sample-size statistics are determined by the sequence of events following an error on trial n of the experiment. They are random variables denoting the sample size on trial $n + k + 1$ of the experiment when the response on trial n is an error and the responses on trials $n + 1, n + 2, \ldots , n + k$ are correct. In general, they will be written as $\mathcal{S}(k + 1)$. The first case concerns the run of correct responses that terminates the experiment. The typical experimental procedure specifies that the experiment should run until a criterion of c consecutive correct responses occurs. This criterion event will be symbolized by cr and its complement, failure to make c correct responses after an error, by $\overline{cr}$. The first statistic, the random variable S_{cr}, applies to all sequences that meet criterion. Thus $S_{cr}(1)$ is the sample size on the first trial of a criterion run, while $S_{cr}(c)$ is the sample size on trial $n + c$, the final trial of the experiment (Table 1). The remaining two random variables concern

TABLE 1
Description of sample-size statistics

Statistic					Sequence				
Trial number	n	$n+1$	$n+2$	$\cdots$	$n+i$	$\cdots$	$n+c-2$	$n+c-1$	$n+c$
Run length, k		0	1	$\cdots$	$i-1$	$\cdots$	$c-3$	$c-2$	$c-1$
Criterion run statistic: $S_{cr}(n+k+1)$	E	$\underline{C}^*$	$\underline{C}$	$\cdots$	$\underline{C}$	$\cdots$	$\underline{C}$	$\underline{C}$	$\underline{C}$
		$S_{cr}(1)$	$S_{cr}(2)$	$\cdots$	$S_{cr}(i)$	$\cdots$	$S_{cr}(c-2)$	$S_{cr}(c-1)$	$S_{cr}(c)$
Precriterion run statistic:	E	$\underline{C}$	E						
	E	$\underline{C}$	$\underline{C}$	$\cdots$	E				
	E	$\underline{C}$	$\underline{C}$	$\cdots$	$\underline{C}$	$\cdots$	E		
	E	$\underline{C}$	$\underline{C}$	$\cdots$	$\underline{C}$	$\cdots$	$\underline{C}$	E	
$S_{\overline{cr}}(n+k+1)$	E	$\underline{C}$	$\underline{C}$	$\cdots$	$\underline{C}$	$\cdots$	$\underline{C}$	$\underline{C}$	E
		$S_{\overline{cr}}(1)$	$S_{\overline{cr}}(2)$	$\cdots$	$S_{\overline{cr}}(i)$	$\cdots$	$S_{\overline{cr}}(c-2)$	$S_{\overline{cr}}(c-1)$	
Precriterion run statistic:	E	$\underline{E}$	E						
	E	C	$\underline{E}$						
	E	C	C	$\cdots$	$\underline{E}$				
	E	C	C	$\cdots$	C	$\cdots$	$\underline{E}$		
	E	C	C	$\cdots$	C	$\cdots$	C	$\underline{E}$	
$S_e(n+k+1)$	E	C	C	$\cdots$	C	$\cdots$	C	C	$\underline{E}$
	$S_e(1)$	$S_e(2)$		$\cdots$	$S_e(i)$	$\cdots$	$S_e(c-2)$	$S_e(c-1)$	$S_e(c)$

* The statistics are defined for all underlined responses.

the precriterion runs, $\overline{cr}$. The first precriterion statistic, $S_{\overline{cr}}$, measures the sample size on the correct responses of the run; i.e., the sample size on trial $n + k + 1$ for $k = 0, 1, \ldots, c - 2$, where trials $n + 1$ through $n + k + 1$ are correct and an error occurs on at least one of the trials $n + k + 2$ to $n + c$. Notice that $S_{\overline{cr}}(k + 1)$ involves averaging over sequences with the terminating errors on trials $n + k + 2$ to $n + c$. The third statistic, S_e, measures the sample size on the error trial $n + k + 1$ that terminates a run of $0 \leq k < c$ correct responses. In each of the three statistics there will be more than one state that can lead to a particular response sequence and these states will generally not have the same sample sizes. Thus, our goal will be to derive the probability distribution of sample sizes for each of the three random variables for each trial on which they are defined. The expected sample size can then be determined.

As noted above and in Table 1, the sample size on trial $n + 1$ depends on the state on trial n, because the state definition includes the response on trial n and the sample for trial $n + 1$. Thus, for all three statistics, when the run length $k = 0$, the sample size corresponds to a full sample of size σ taken on the error trial. To derive the statistics for $k \geq 1$, we must know the probability of occupying the **C** states on trials $n + 1$ to $n + c - 1$. Since an error is a transient recurrent event, these probabilities do not depend on the trial number n, but only on the number of trials since the last error. So, except for $n = 1$, when the initial vector is involved, the value of n is irrelevant and can be dropped from the following discussion. An error requires starting the process in state E, while the sequence of consecutive correct responses requires that, once an error occurs, the sequence be dropped from further consideration. The probability of being in a state in **C** on trial $j + 1$ is expressed by the jth power of T and sequences with intervening errors are prevented by making E absorbing: When E is entered, no further correct states are possible. Let T' be the transition matrix in Equation 3 with E absorbing, i.e., $P(E \longrightarrow E) = 1$;

$$T' = \begin{array}{c} \\ \mathbf{R} \\ \mathbf{I} \\ E \end{array} \begin{array}{|ccc} \mathbf{R} & \mathbf{I} & E \\ \hline Q_{\mathbf{RR}} & 0 & Q_{\mathbf{R}E} \\ 0 & Q_{\mathbf{II}} & Q_{\mathbf{I}E} \\ 0 & 0 & 1 \end{array}.$$

The kth power of T' is easily found to be

$$T'^k = \begin{array}{c} \\ \mathbf{R} \\ \mathbf{I} \\ E \end{array} \begin{array}{|ccc} \mathbf{R} & \mathbf{I} & E \\ \hline Q_{\mathbf{RR}}^k & 0 & Q_{\mathbf{R}E}^{(k)} \\ 0 & Q_{\mathbf{II}}^k & Q_{\mathbf{I}E}^{(k)} \\ 0 & 0 & 1 \end{array},$$

where the submatrices within T'^k are:

$$Q_{\mathbf{RR}}^k = \left[\frac{j}{i} \binom{i-1}{j-1} \pi^{k(j-1)} (1 - \pi^k)^{i-j} \right], \qquad \begin{array}{l} i = 1, 2, \ldots, \sigma, \\ j = 1, 2, \ldots, i; \end{array}$$

$$Q_{\mathbf{II}}^k = \left[\binom{i-1}{j-1} \pi^{kj} (1 - \pi^k)^{i-j} \right], \qquad \begin{array}{l} i = 1, 2, \ldots, \sigma, \\ j = 1, 2, \ldots, i; \end{array}$$

where the unspecified entries are zero. The powers of $Q_{\mathbf{RR}}$ and $Q_{\mathbf{II}}$ can be verified by induction, while the transitions to E are one minus the sum of the rows excluding E itself:

$$Q_{RE}^{(k)} = \left[\frac{(i-1)(1-\pi^k)}{i}\right], \qquad i = 1, 2, \ldots, \sigma;$$

$$Q_{IE}^{(k)} = [1 - \pi^k].$$

In the following derivations, the state in which the process starts a run of correct responses will be needed; hence, the probability of transitions from E to the various correct states, conditional on entry to the $\mathbf{C}$ states, will be derived. The unconditional probabilities of entering the sets of states $\mathbf{I}$ and $\mathbf{R}$ are

$$P(E \longrightarrow \mathbf{I}) = \sum_{j=1}^{\sigma} P(E \longrightarrow I_j)$$

$$= (1 - \theta)\pi;$$

$$P(E \longrightarrow \mathbf{R}) = \sum_{j=1}^{\sigma} P(E \longrightarrow R_j)$$

$$= \theta\left(\pi + \frac{1-\pi}{\sigma}\right).$$

The unconditional probability of entering any correct response state is the sum $P(E \longrightarrow \mathbf{I}) + P(E \longrightarrow \mathbf{R})$,

$$P(E \longrightarrow \mathbf{C}) = \pi + \frac{\theta(1-\pi)}{\sigma}.$$

These can be used to conditionalize the entry probabilities, giving

$$P(E \longrightarrow R_j \mid E \longrightarrow \mathbf{C}) = \frac{P(E \longrightarrow R_j)}{P(E \longrightarrow \mathbf{C})}$$

$$= \frac{j\theta\binom{\sigma-1}{j-1}\pi^{i-1}(1-\pi)^{\sigma-i}}{\pi\sigma + (1-\pi)\theta}.$$

Similarly,

$$P(E \longrightarrow I_j \mid E \longrightarrow \mathbf{C}) = \frac{(1-\theta)\sigma\binom{\sigma-1}{j-1}\pi^i(1-\pi)^{\sigma-i}}{\pi\sigma + (1-\pi)\theta}.$$

It will be convenient to represent these probabilities in a row vector $P_\mathbf{C}$, with the $P(E \longrightarrow R_j \mid E \longrightarrow \mathbf{C})$ probabilities as the first σ entries, $P(E \longrightarrow I_j \mid E \longrightarrow \mathbf{C})$ as the second σ entries, and 0 in the last place, corresponding to $P(E \longrightarrow E \mid E \longrightarrow \mathbf{C})$. This vector gives the state probabilities for the first trial in a run of correct responses following an error.

1. Criterion-run statistic, $\mathcal{S}_{cr}$. For a criterion run of c correct responses to take place, i.e., the event $cr = \mathbf{C}(1) \wedge \mathbf{C}(2) \wedge \cdots \wedge \mathbf{C}(c)$, the subject must enter $\mathbf{C}$ following an error and remain in $\mathbf{C}$ for the next $c - 1$ transitions. This means that on trial c the process is still in $\mathbf{C}$. The probability of this event is

$$P(cr) = P_C T'^{c-1} C_C. \tag{4}$$

Here C_C is a column vector containing ones at the location of states in C and zeros elsewhere (the state E) and serves to sum the probabilities in the cells associated with correct states in the vector $P_C T'^{c-1}$. Because T' rather than T is used, there will be no returns from E to C. Since E is only a single state, Equation 4 equals $1 - P(E(c))$, suggesting that the results could be found without the final summation. The method given here is general, however, and would apply to models, such as those to be considered later, in which there is more than a single error state.

To determine the sample size for trials 2 through c, we need the state probabilities for $k = 1, 2, \ldots, c - 1$. The probability that the process is in state $X \in C$ on trial k and that a criterion run is to be made (the event $X(k) \wedge cr$) can be found by inserting into Equation 4 a matrix M_X that selects only those paths passing through the state X on trial k. The matrix M_X contains zeros except for a one in the diagonal position corresponding to state X. Then

$$P(X(k) \wedge cr) = P_C T'^{k-1} M_X T'^{c-k} C_C, \quad k = 1, 2, \ldots, c - 1. \tag{5}$$

The conditional probability of being in a state X given a criterion run is found by combining Equations 4 and 5:

$$P(X(k) \mid cr) = \frac{P_C T'^{k-1} M_X T'^{c-k} C_C}{P_C T'^{c-1} C_C}, \quad k = 1, 2, \ldots, c - 1. \tag{6}$$

The same technique can be used to restrict the process to multiple paths through a set of states X, using a matrix M_X containing ones in the diagonal positions corresponding to all states in X and zeros elsewhere.

As already mentioned, Equation 6 gives the state probabilities for each trial $k = 1, 2, \ldots, c - 1$, but it does not give the sample size directly. To obtain the probability of a specific sample size z on trial $k + 1$, one must substitute for M_X a matrix M_Z that selects all correct response states with a sample of size z. The set Z contains all states in which S has size z. To obtain the expected sample size over all possible sample sizes on trial $k + 1$, we replace M_X in Equation 6 by another matrix, M_C'. In M_C' the diagonal elements corresponding to the states in C are the corresponding sample sizes of these states and the element corresponding to state E is zero. Such a matrix both selects correct states on trial k and weights their probabilities by their sample sizes for trial $k + 1$. Thus, the expected sample size for the criterion-run statistic on trial $k + 1$ is

$$E(S_{cr}(k + 1)) = \begin{cases} \sigma, & k = 0, \\ \dfrac{P_C T'^{k-1} M_C' T'^{c-k} C_C}{P_C T'^{c-1} C_C}, & k = 1, 2, \ldots, c - 1. \end{cases} \tag{7}$$

Evaluating the matrix product in Equation 7 is straightforward although somewhat tedious. Because transitions between $\mathbf{I}$ and $\mathbf{R}$ are impossible, the numerator for $k > 0$ can be broken into two parts:

$$P_\mathbf{C} T'^{k-1} M_\mathbf{C}' T'^{c-k} C_\mathbf{C} = P_\mathbf{R} Q_\mathbf{RR}^{k-1} M_\mathbf{R}' Q_\mathbf{RR}^{c-k} C_\mathbf{R} + P_\mathbf{I} Q_\mathbf{II}^{k-1} M_\mathbf{I}' Q_\mathbf{II}^{c-k} C_\mathbf{I},$$

where $P_\mathbf{R}$ and $P_\mathbf{I}$ are σ-element subvectors of $P_\mathbf{C}$ giving the starting probabilities for the sets $\mathbf{R}$ and $\mathbf{I}$, $M_\mathbf{R}'$ and $M_\mathbf{I}'$ are $\sigma \times \sigma$ matrices with m_{ii} equal to the size of $\mathbf{S}$ in the ith state of $\mathbf{R}$ or $\mathbf{I}$, all other entries zero, and $C_\mathbf{R}$ and $C_\mathbf{I}$ are σ-element column vectors containing all ones. In evaluating these terms it is helpful to evaluate the two vectors $P_\mathbf{X} Q_\mathbf{XX}^{k-1}$ and $Q_\mathbf{XX}^{c-k} C_\mathbf{X}$ first, then the full sum. For example,

$$P_\mathbf{R} Q_\mathbf{RR}^{k-1} M_\mathbf{R}' Q_\mathbf{RR}^{c-k} C_\mathbf{R}$$

$$= \sum_{i=1}^{\sigma} \left\{ \frac{\theta i}{\sigma \pi + \theta(1-\pi)} \binom{\sigma-1}{i-1} \pi^{k(i-1)}(1-\pi^k)^{\sigma-1} \right\} \{i\} \left\{ \frac{(i-1)\pi^{c-k}+1}{i} \right\},$$

where the terms in braces come, respectively, from the first vector, $M_\mathbf{R}'$, and the second vector. Evaluating this sum, the corresponding one involving $\mathbf{I}$, and the denominator of Equation 7 yields

$$E(\mathcal{S}_{cr}(k+1)) = \frac{(\sigma-1)(\sigma-2\theta)\pi^{c+k} + (\sigma - 2\theta + \theta\sigma)\pi^c + \theta(\sigma-1)\pi^k + \theta}{(\sigma-\theta)\pi^c + \theta}.$$

Note that if c is large, $\pi^c \approx 0$, so $E(\mathcal{S}_{cr}(k+1)) \approx 1 + (\sigma-1)\pi^k$ for large c.

2. Precriterion-run statistic, $\mathcal{S}_{\overline{cr}}$. Here the statistic of interest is the sample size on trial $k+1$ after a run of $k = 1, 2, \ldots, c-1$ correct responses, given that E is entered on some later trial. The derivation is similar to that of $\mathcal{S}_{cr}$ except the conditionalization is different; $\overline{cr}$ is the event $C(1) \wedge (E(2) \vee E(3) \vee \cdots \vee E(c))$ so the run must end with an error. The joint probability of a correct state on trial k and a later error is

$$P(\mathbf{C}(k) \wedge \overline{cr}) = P_\mathbf{C} T'^{k-1} M_\mathbf{C} T'^{c-k} C_E,$$

where C_E contains a one in the position corresponding to state E and zeros elsewhere and selects those sequences that have produced an error by the end of the criterion run. The probability of interest is that of being in state $X(k) \in \mathbf{C}$ conditional on an error on one of the next $c - k$ trials:

$$P(X(k) \mid \overline{cr}) = \frac{P_\mathbf{C} T'^{k-1} M_X T'^{c-k} C_E}{P_\mathbf{C} T'^{k-1} M_\mathbf{C} T'^{c-k} C_E}.$$

As in the criterion-run statistic, this equation can be modified by changing M_X to M_Z to obtain the probability of being in a state with $\mathbf{S}$ of size z, and to $M_\mathbf{C}'$ to obtain the expected sample size on trial $k+1$. The expectation of $\mathcal{S}_{\overline{cr}}(k+1)$ becomes

$$E(\mathcal{S}_{\overline{cr}}(k+1)) = \begin{cases} \sigma & k = 0, \\ \dfrac{P_C T'^{k-1} M'_C T'^{c-k} C_E}{P_C T'^{k-1} M_C T'^{c-k} C_E} & k = 1, 2, \ldots, c-2, \end{cases} \tag{8}$$

and reduces to

$$E(\mathcal{S}_{\overline{cr}}(k+1)) = \frac{(\sigma - 1)(\sigma - 2\theta)\pi^k + \theta\sigma + \sigma - 2\theta}{\sigma - \theta},$$

a result that is independent of the criterion-run length, c.

3. Precriterion-run statistic, $\mathcal{S}_e$. When one error follows another on the next trial ($E(1)$), the sample size is σ. For errors on trial $k + 1$ following k consecutive correct responses, the sample size for the error trial depends on the correct response state just before the error. Here, the joint probability of a correct state on trial k and an error on trial $k + 1$ is

$$\begin{aligned} P(C(k) \wedge E(k+1)) &= \sum_{X \in C} P(X(k) \wedge E(k+1)) \\ &= \sum_{X \in C} P(E(k+1) \mid X(k)) P(X(k)) \\ &= P_C T'^{k-1} M_C T' C_E. \end{aligned}$$

For a particular correct response state, $X(k)$, the conditional probability is

$$\begin{aligned} P(X(k) \mid C(k) \wedge E(k+1)) &= \frac{P(X(k) \wedge E(k+1))}{P(C(k) \wedge E(k+1))} \\ &= \frac{P_C T'^{k-1} M_X T' C_E}{P_C T'^{k-1} M_C T' C_E}, \quad k = 1, 2, \ldots, c-1. \end{aligned}$$

As before, to obtain the probability of a fixed sample size z, the M_X matrix is replaced by the M_Z matrix, and the expected sample size on trial $k + 1$ is

$$E(\mathcal{S}_e(k+1)) = \begin{cases} \sigma, & k = 0, \\ \dfrac{P_C T'^{k-1} M'_C T' C_E}{P_C T'^{k-1} M_C T' C_E}, & k = 1, 2, \ldots, c-1. \end{cases} \tag{9}$$

The resulting expression has the same form as Equation 8 except that $c - k$ in Equation 8 is replaced by one in Equation 9. Therefore, Equation 9 should have the same value if c is set to $k + 1$. Since the result of Equation 8 was independent of c, the value of c makes no difference and $E(\mathcal{S}_{\overline{cr}}(k+1)) = E(\mathcal{S}_e(k+1))$, $k = 0, 1, \ldots, c-1$. This result is a consequence of the fact that the error process is identical for all states in the chain.

The implication of these equations is that the sample size on precriterion runs should be greater than the sample size on criterion runs. These expected

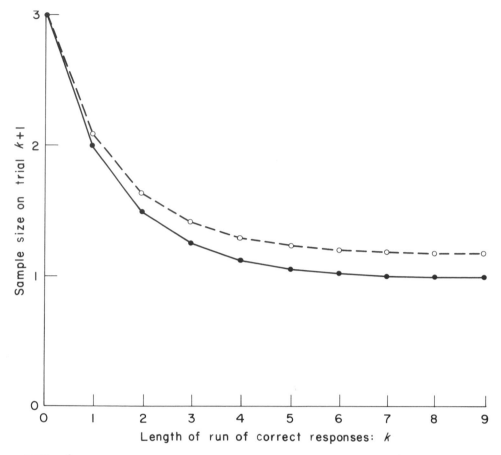

FIGURE 3.
Expected sample size for the resampling-on-errors model with $\sigma = 3$, $\theta = 0.25$, $\pi = 0.5$, and c large. The solid line represents $E(\mathcal{S}_{cr}(k))$, and the dashed line represents $E(\mathcal{S}_{\overline{cr}}(k))$ and $E(\mathcal{S}_e(k))$.

sample sizes are plotted in Figure 3 for the particular case of $\sigma = 3$, $\theta = \frac{1}{4}$, and $\mathbf{h} = 12$. The criterion, c, is taken to be large.

Another related model. The hypothesis-manipulation model of Chumbley (1969, 1972) is closely related to the resampling-on-error model. Chumbley assumes that all hypotheses are tested at once, requiring $\sigma = \mathbf{h}$. He also assumes that after an error the subject is capable of recovering the hypotheses that are still consistent with probability α and fails to recover them with probability $1 - \alpha$. This assumption represents a modification of our Axiom Ela to E'la, setting $\epsilon_e = 1 - \alpha$ and $\epsilon_c = 0$ and in E'lb $\delta_i = 1$ and $\delta_c = 0$. The resulting model stands between the one discussed in this section and those presented below. The representation in the form of a Markov chain is easily accomplished using the development just presented. An error does not automatically lead to state E; rather, it does so with probability $1 - \alpha$. With probability α, the transition is to a new error state that retains all the consistent hypotheses and eliminates the inconsistent ones. When the sample does not contain the relevant hypothesis, possible only if $\sigma < \mathbf{h}$ and not considered by Chumbley, it is possible by these assumptions to produce an empty sample, which could be treated as a null sample or which could force resampling.

Summary.   The salient feature of the resampling-on-error model is the fact that an error is a recurrent event. It overpowers the effect of larger samples with the S3a Axiom and no doubt weakens any sample-size effect even with the S3b Axiom, although that has not been mathematically demonstrated here. Because of the possibility of eliminating the relevant hypothesis on an error, it makes the introduction of memory for eliminated hypotheses (E2b, E2c, and E2d) ineffective. The resampling limits the maximum rate of acquisition to that of the simple model with $\sigma = 1$. It can be demonstrated that this limit is too low and that, at least with practiced subjects, the effect of errors must be less drastic (Wickens & Millward, 1971). Models without the resampling-on-error assumption are considered in the next two sections.

Models with Resampling When S Is Empty

The model presented in this section is essentially the one developed by Wickens and Millward (1971). Its assumptions are similar to those of the resampling-on-error model, but with the fundamental change in the elimination axiom from E1a to E1b and the memory axiom from E2a to E2c. The E1b assumption requires that elimination take place without regard to errors until S is empty, instead of eliminating the whole sample on each error as E1a requires. An important result of this change in axioms is that errors no longer represent uncertain recurrent events, and the basis of analysis cannot be the occurrence of each error response. However, a different unit of analysis is available, which leaves the mathematics reasonably simple. Since processing of a sample by the subject continues after an error, the predictions of the model depend on the size of the samples, and since it is not possible to arbitrarily eliminate the relevant hypothesis on an error, it is now reasonable to introduce a memory for hypotheses that have been rejected by replacing E2a with E2c. With E2c the set U is an active part of the process, and unlike the slow learning of the resampling-on-error model, rather rapid learning rates are possible. Axiom R1b in which a single hypothesis is selected and used until inconsistent has been chosen to determine the response. Axiom R1b is simpler to work with than Axioms R1c or R1d and does not alter the final results in any significant way. The complete model is defined by any of the hypothesis definitions D1b through D1d, D2, D3, S1a, S2b, any of S3a through S3c, S4a, E1b, E2c, R1b, R2, and any of the Initial-State Axioms, I1a–I1c. The important parameters of this model are σ, the maximum size of S, and λ, which restricts the maximum size of U to $\sigma\lambda$ hypotheses.

Mathematical analysis.   The processing of a single sample set S is the appropriate unit of analysis for the model considered here. A distinction must be made between samples that contain the relevant hypothesis, called *terminal* samples, and samples that contain only irrelevant hypotheses, called *nonterminal* samples, since selection of the former will necessarily solve the problem, while selection of the latter cannot. The sequence of operations that a subject uses to process any sample is independent of that required to eliminate any previous sample. This means that statistics that can be expressed as the sum of events occurring in each sample are equivalent to the sum of independent random variables,

$$\mathfrak{N}_1 + \mathfrak{N}_2 + \mathfrak{N}_3 + \cdots + \mathfrak{N}_{\mathcal{K}} + \mathfrak{I}, \tag{10}$$

when $\mathcal{K} + 1$ samples are required for solution. The $\mathfrak{N}_i$ are identically distributed random variables associated with nonterminal samples; $\mathfrak{I}$ is a random variable associated with the final, terminal sample; and $\mathcal{K}$ is a random variable giving the number of nonterminal samples required to draw a terminal sample. Both the trial-of-last-error (TLE) and the total-number-of-errors (TNE) statistics fall into this category, although the sequential statistics do not. Sequential properties of the model and statistics concerning sample size can be determined by converting the process to a Markov chain and using methods such as those presented above or those to be discussed in conjunction with the continuous-resampling model.

The problem of calculating statistics conforming to the additive logic of Equation 10 reduces to several simpler subproblems: (1) the determination of the distribution of the random variable $\mathfrak{I}$, (2) the determination of the distribution of $\mathfrak{N}$, (3) the determination of the distribution of $\mathcal{K}$, and (4) a final mixture of the sums in Equation 10 according to the distribution of $\mathcal{K}$. The special case of the model when $\sigma = 2$ will be considered and the statistic TLE specifically derived. The logic for other sample sizes and other statistics is identical to that used here. Both the TLE and the TNE for sample sizes of four or less are considered in more detail by Wickens and Millward, 1971.

1.   Distribution of $\mathfrak{I}$.   A terminal sample of $\sigma = 2$ hypotheses will contain one relevant and one irrelevant hypothesis. By the Response Axiom

R1b, one of these is chosen as a response base. If it is the relevant hypothesis, no errors will be made in eliminating the other attribute, and $\mathfrak{Z} = 0$. If the irrelevant hypothesis is chosen, one error will be made as the irrelevant hypothesis is disconfirmed and then the relevant hypothesis will be used to determine the response and no more errors will be made. Let θ_2 be the probability of selecting the relevant hypothesis from a set of two hypotheses. Also let π' be the probability that the irrelevant hypothesis is consistent given that it is selected, i.e., the probability of a correct response given that the irrelevant hypothesis is selected. Then

$$P(\mathfrak{Z} = t) = \begin{cases} \theta_2, & t = 0, \\ (1 - \theta_2)(1 - \pi')\pi'^{t-1}, & t > 0, \end{cases}$$

where the expression for $t > 0$ results from a geometrically distributed series of correct responses preceding the error.

2.   Distribution of $\mathfrak{N}$.   The presence of two irrelevant hypotheses in a nonterminal sample makes the analysis slightly more complicated. If only the TLE is of interest, a simple derivation is possible. If π is the probability that a hypothesis is not disconfirmed on a given trial, then $1 - \pi^t$ is the probability that on or by trial t the hypothesis is disconfirmed, $(1 - \pi^t)^2$ is the probability that on or by trial t, both have been disconfirmed, and $(1 - \pi^t)^2 - (1 - \pi^{t-1})^2$ is the probability that the final disconfirmation and error come on trial t. This simple calculation has only limited application to statistics other than the TLE, so a more general procedure will be used. Let S_S represent the state where **S** contains s hypotheses at the start of a trial and let S_0 indicate that **S** is empty and resampling will take place on that trial. The transitions between these states, the probabilities of these transitions, and the responses associated with the transitions are given in Figure 4.

The transition probabilities are expressed in terms of the probability that the hypothesis determining the response is consistent and a correct response is made, π', and that a hypothesis not determining the response is consistent, π. Generally, for a two-choice task, $\pi' = \pi = \frac{1}{2}$. In order to eliminate a sample the process must go from S_2 to S_0. This can be done by either of two paths: $S_2 \longrightarrow S_1 \longrightarrow S_0$ or $S_2 \longrightarrow S_0$. The relative probabilities of taking these two paths are given by the ratios of exit probabilities from S_2:

$$P(S_2 \longrightarrow S_1 \longrightarrow S_0) = P(S_2 \longrightarrow S_1)$$
$$= \frac{(1 - \pi')\pi + (1 - \pi)\pi'}{1 - \pi\pi'};$$

$$P(S_2 \longrightarrow S_0) = \frac{(1 - \pi')(1 - \pi)}{1 - \pi\pi'}.$$

The distribution of $\mathfrak{N}$ will be a mixture of two distributions conditional on these path probabilities:

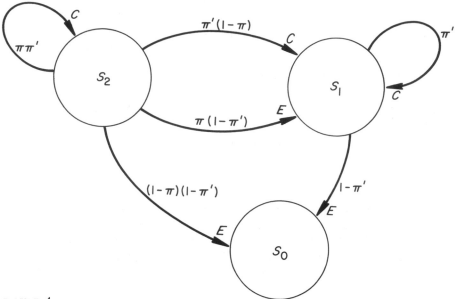

FIGURE 4.
State transition diagram for nonterminal samples of size $\sigma = 2$ in the resampling-on-empty-samples model.

$$P(\mathfrak{N} = t) = P(\mathfrak{N} = t \mid S_2 \longrightarrow S_0)P(S_2 \longrightarrow S_0)$$
$$+ P(\mathfrak{N} = t \mid S_2 \longrightarrow S_1 \longrightarrow S_0)P(S_2 \longrightarrow S_1 \longrightarrow S_0).$$

The first conditional distribution, $P(\mathfrak{N} = t \mid S_2 \longrightarrow S_0)$ is simply the distribution of the number of trials to leave S_2, since the last error will be made with the exit from S_2. This is a simple geometric distribution—call it the random variable $\mathfrak{N}_2$:

$$P(\mathfrak{N}_2 = t) = (1 - \pi\pi')(\pi\pi')^{t-1}.$$

On the path from S_2 to S_0 via S_1, trials will be spent in both S_2 and S_1, so the total number of trials is the sum of those in S_2 and those in S_1, or $\mathfrak{N}_2 + \mathfrak{N}_1$, where $\mathfrak{N}_1$ is the number of trials to leave S_1. At this point, direct calculation of the probability distributions becomes rather complicated, and it is simpler to work with their generating functions (GFs) (see, e.g., Feller, 1968). The GF of a geometric distribution, ab^{i-1}, $i = 1, 2, \ldots$, is $\dfrac{a\zeta}{1 - b\zeta}$, so

$$\Phi_{\mathfrak{N}_2}(\zeta) = \frac{(1 - \pi\pi')\zeta}{1 - \pi\pi'\zeta},$$

and by a similar argument,

$$\Phi_{\mathfrak{N}_1}(\zeta) = \frac{(1 - \pi')\zeta}{1 - \pi'\zeta}.$$

The GF of a sum of random variables is just the product of the individual GFs, so the GF for $P(\mathfrak{N} = t \mid S_2 \longrightarrow S_1 \longrightarrow S_0)$ is just $\Phi_{\mathfrak{N}_2}(\zeta)\Phi_{\mathfrak{N}_1}(\zeta)$, and

$$\Phi_{\mathfrak{N}}(\zeta) = \Phi_{\mathfrak{N}_2}(\zeta)P(S_2 \longrightarrow S_1) + \Phi_{\mathfrak{N}_2}(\zeta)\Phi_{\mathfrak{N}_1}(\zeta)P(S_2 \longrightarrow S_1 \longrightarrow S_0),$$

because the GF of a mixture of random variables is the same mixture of GFs. So,

$$\Phi_{\mathfrak{N}}(\zeta) = \frac{(1 - \pi')[1 - \pi + (1 - \pi')\pi\zeta]\zeta}{(1 - \pi\pi'\zeta)(1 - \pi\zeta)}$$

after appropriate substitution and simplification.

3. Distribution of the number of nonterminal samples, $\mathcal{K}$. The number of nonterminal samples obtained before a terminal sample is selected depends on the size of **S**, the extent of the subject's memory for past samples, and the initial state assumptions. In the following discussion, all nonterminal samples will be assumed to be equivalent and the necessary corrections for the initial state will be introduced later. The memory assumption adopted here, E2c, keeps the λ most recently eliminated samples in **U** while earlier samples return to **A**. Thus, **U** has a maximum size $u = \lambda\sigma$. The fact that previously eliminated samples return to **A** means that the probability of selecting a terminal sample from **A** is not constant but changes as **U** fills up. Let r_i be the probability that a sample from **A** is terminal when **U** contains i samples (or $i\sigma$ hypotheses), $0 \le i \le \lambda$. The r_i probabilities are difficult to calculate exactly if hypotheses do not have equal weights (Axiom S3b). The probability of a terminal sample will decline slightly immediately after the λth sample as the irrelevant hypotheses from the early samples, which tend to have higher weights, reenter **A**. However, if r_λ, the probability of sampling the terminal sample from **A** when λ samples have been removed from **A**, is assumed to be constant, then

$$P(\mathcal{K} = k) = \begin{cases} \left[\displaystyle\prod_{j=0}^{k-1} (1 - r_j)\right] r_k, & k < \lambda, \\[4mm] \left[\displaystyle\prod_{j=0}^{\lambda-1} (1 - r_j)\right](1 - r_\lambda)^{k-\lambda} r_\lambda, & k \ge \lambda. \end{cases} \tag{11}$$

If the assumption of equal hypothesis weights (S3a) is made, the approximation for r_λ becomes correct, and moreover,

$$r_j = \frac{\sigma}{(\mathbf{h} - j\sigma)},$$

which implies that

$$\prod_{j=0}^{k-1} (1 - r_j)r_k = r_0$$

for any k. This reduces Equation 11 to the simple form

$$P(\mathcal{K} = k) = \begin{cases} r_0, & k < \lambda, \\ r_0(1 - r_\lambda)^{k-\lambda}, & k \geq \lambda. \end{cases} \tag{12}$$

a distribution having the GF

$$\Phi_\mathcal{K}(\zeta) = r_0 \frac{1 - \zeta^\lambda}{1 - \zeta} + \frac{r_0\zeta^\lambda}{1 - (1 - r_\lambda)\zeta}. \tag{13}$$

If $\lambda(\sigma - 1) > h$, the correct hypothesis will be identified before U overflows because A is exhausted first, and the distribution takes the even simpler form

$$P(\mathcal{K} = k) = \begin{cases} \dfrac{\sigma}{h}, & k \leq m, \\ \dfrac{h - m\sigma}{h}, & k = m + 1, \end{cases} \tag{14}$$

where m is the greatest integer less than or equal to h/σ.

Equations 12 and 13 are correct if Initial Axiom I1c is adopted and if the recording of responses starts with the first nonguess trial (usually trial 2). The other initial axioms lead to slight modifications of these equations. If Axiom I1a is selected, the first sample is necessarily nonterminal and the distribution of $\mathcal{K}$ becomes

$$P(\mathcal{K} = k) = \begin{cases} 0, & k = 1, \\ \dfrac{r_0}{1 - r_0}, & 1 < k < \lambda, \\ \dfrac{r_0}{1 - r_0}(1 - r_\lambda)^{k-\lambda}, & k \geq \lambda, \end{cases}$$

with GF

$$\Phi_\mathcal{K}(\zeta) = \frac{r_0\zeta}{1 - r_0} \frac{1 - \zeta^{\lambda-1}}{1 - \zeta} + \frac{r_0\zeta^\lambda}{(1 - r_0)[1 - (1 - r_\lambda)\zeta]}.$$

If I1b is used, the random response assignments made before the first stimulus is presented have only probability $\frac{1}{2}r_0$ of forming a nonterminal sample, since they are not correlated with the correct stimulus assignment. Then,

$$P(\mathcal{K} = k) = \begin{cases} \frac{1}{2}r_0, & k = 1, \\[2mm] \dfrac{r_0}{1 - \frac{1}{2}r_0}, & 1 < k < \lambda, \\[3mm] \dfrac{r_0}{1 - \frac{1}{2}r_0}\,(1 - r_\lambda)^{k-\lambda}, & k \geq \lambda, \end{cases}$$

and

$$\Phi_{\mathcal{K}}(\zeta) = \tfrac{1}{2}r_0\zeta + \frac{r_0\zeta}{1 - \frac{1}{2}r_0}\,\frac{1 - \zeta^{\lambda-1}}{1 - \zeta} + \frac{r_0\zeta^\lambda}{(1 - \frac{1}{2}r_0)[1 - (1 - r_\lambda)\zeta]}.$$

4. Combination of $\mathfrak{N}$, $\mathfrak{J}$, and $\mathcal{K}$ to form TLE. For a particular value of $\mathcal{K} = k$ the GF of the sum, Equation 10, will be just $[\Phi_{\mathfrak{N}}(\zeta)]^k\Phi_{\mathfrak{J}}(\zeta)$. The GF of the final distribution of the TLE, $\Psi(\zeta)$, is a linear combination of these GFs, weighted by the probabilities of $\mathcal{K}$, representing a mixture of the distributions of Equation 10. Thus,

$$\begin{aligned} \Psi(\zeta) &= \sum_{k=0}^{\infty} P(\mathcal{K} = k)[\Phi_{\mathfrak{N}}(\zeta)]^k\Phi_{\mathfrak{J}}(\zeta) \\ &= \Phi_{\mathcal{K}}[\Phi_{\mathfrak{N}}(\zeta)]\Phi_{\mathfrak{J}}(\zeta). \end{aligned} \tag{15}$$

When IIc is adopted, Equation 15 is correct if the first response is ignored. The first trial is a guess, which we assume to be correct with probability γ and unrelated to later responses. The simplest way to treat the first trial is to drop it from the analysis altogether, but if it is to be included, Equation 15 must be modified. The modification consists of adding a one to all TLE values except a proportion γ of the cases when TLE = 0. The GF $\Psi(\zeta)$ is replaced by

$$\gamma\Psi(0) + \zeta[\Psi(\zeta) + (1 - \gamma)\Psi(0)].$$

The GFs produced here are the ratio of polynomials and can be decomposed by partial fractions into terms from which the TLE distribution can be recovered by elementary, but frequently tedious, calculations. Of course, it is not necessary to calculate $\Psi(\zeta)$ if only the moments of the distribution are desired, since the ith moment can be found by taking the ith derivative of $\Psi(\zeta)$ with respect to ζ and setting $\zeta = 1$. From Equation 15, then,

$$\begin{aligned} E(\text{TLE}) &= \frac{\partial \Psi(\zeta)}{\partial \zeta}\,(1) \\ &= \mu_{\mathcal{K}}\mu_{\mathfrak{N}} + \mu_{\mathfrak{J}}, \end{aligned}$$

where the $\mu_{\mathcal{K}}$, $\mu_{\mathfrak{N}}$, and $\mu_{\mathfrak{J}}$ are the means of the $\mathcal{K}$, $\mathfrak{N}$, and $\mathfrak{J}$ distributions. These can be found by differentiating the appropriate GFs, or by direct calculations from the distributions. Similar methods can be applied to find the variance; thus,

$$\text{Var (TLE)} = \mu_{\mathcal{K}}\,\text{Var}\,(\mathfrak{N}) + \text{Var}\,(\mathfrak{J}).$$

Modifications of the model.   Changes in the sampling and/or response axioms are the most appropriate modifications for the model with resampling when **S** is empty. If the ordered-sampling assumption (S3c) is made, the relevant hypothesis will certainly be drawn within the first h/σ samples, although in which particular sample will not be known. Eliminated hypotheses do not reenter the sampling order before the problem is solved, which amounts to making λ sufficiently large so that replacement never occurs. Equation 14 gives the distribution of the number of nonterminal samples and the resulting model is identical to the one just discussed.

Changes in the response axiom have no net effect on nonterminal samples and make but minor changes in the terminal samples. The only major differences come when the 'Majority Rule' Response Axiom R1e is used. In Figure 5 state diagrams corresponding to the elimination of terminal samples of size $\sigma = 3$ under Axioms R1b–R1e are shown. Statistics can be derived from these in the manner shown above. For example, when $\theta_3 = \frac{1}{3}$ and $\theta_2 = \frac{1}{2}$, the distribution of the total number of errors (TNE) is

$$P(\text{TNE} = t) = \begin{cases} \dfrac{1}{3}, & t = 0, \\[2mm] \dfrac{2 + \pi}{3(1 + \pi)}, & t = 1, \\[2mm] \dfrac{\pi}{3(1 + \pi)}, & t = 2, \end{cases}$$

for Axioms R1b–R1d, but is

$$P(\text{TNE} = t) = \begin{cases} \dfrac{\pi}{1 + \pi}, & t = 0, \\[2mm] \dfrac{1}{1 + \pi}, & t = 1, \end{cases}$$

for Axiom R1e. This example points up the small effect of the choice of response rule: The difference between the mean TNE under these rules would be $(3\pi - 1)/3(\pi + 1)$, or $\frac{1}{9}$ when $\pi = \frac{1}{2}$. Such a difference might be detected in a large experiment, but at this time experimental technique is not sufficiently precise to do so.

Summary.   The model based on resampling only when **S** is empty is much more realistic for many CI experiments than the model based on resampling on every error. It assumes that the subject's memory and information-processing capacity are relatively efficient. Furthermore, there is an effect of an increase in the maximum sample size, σ, which appears more in accord with recent experimental results. One unique feature of the model is the

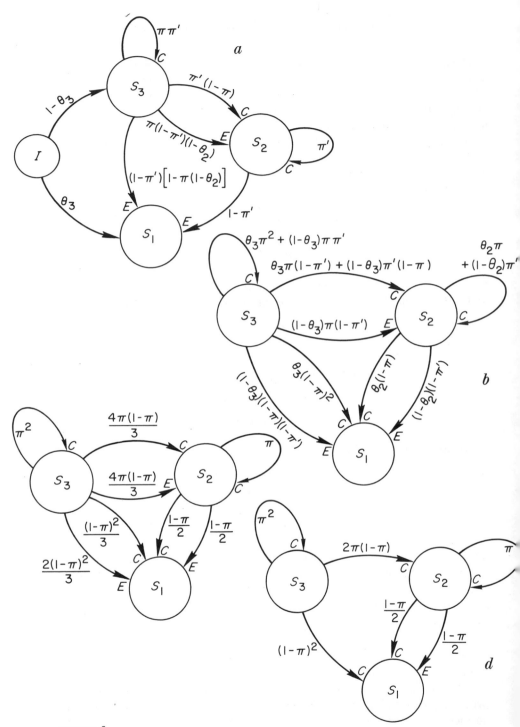

FIGURE 5.
State transition diagrams for terminal samples of size $\sigma = 3$ in the resampling-on-empty-samples model under various response axioms. In these diagrams, θ_s is the probability of selecting the relevant hypothesis from S. (a) Axiom R1b. State I is an initial state associated with selection of the response-determining hypothesis and does not generate a response. (b) Axiom R1c. (c) Axiom R1d. In this and in Axiom R1e, no single hypothesis determines the response, so π is the probability of an inconsistency and π' is not used. (d) Axiom R1e.

assumption that memory for eliminated hypotheses is in terms of groups of hypotheses and not in terms of individual hypotheses. Although probably not universally applicable, it does appear reasonable for hypotheses that are sampled together to be replaced together. Certainly when hypotheses form natural groups, for example, hypotheses based on visual dimensions in physical proximity, this assumption has advantages over those that treat each hypothesis independently. Another feature of the memory characteristics of the model is that eliminated hypotheses remain unavailable for a time measured in psychological units: Replacement occurs after λ samples have been eliminated. Thus, it is some limitation on storage for past activities that is involved here and not an arbitrary number of trials or length of time. If the correct replacement process is really random in terms of trials or time, this model may still be relatively accurate, since it replaces hypotheses stochastically with respect to trial number. Further work comparing the E2c replacement axiom with other assumptions such as those in E'2 is needed.

One aspect of the processing of hypotheses relates directly to the next model we shall consider, the continuous-resampling model. On many of the trials of the experiment, a subject following the rule to resample only when **S** is empty, will be examining less than a full sample of size σ. It would be more efficient if he resampled every time a hypothesis was eliminated, so that **S** would always be full. It should be remembered, however, that the more frequent resampling that this would require further burdens the subject and might, in fact, lead to errors in processing hypotheses in **S**, discounting the advantages of a full sample. A subject may prefer a larger σ with fewer occasions when sampling must occur to a smaller σ with frequent sampling. Our observations (Millward & Spoehr, 1973; Wickens & Millward, 1971) have indicated that subjects differ in their choice of strategy here, some using a decreasing sample-size strategy of the sort discussed in this section and others using the constant sample-size strategy discussed in the next.

Models with Continuous Resampling

The resampling-on-error model places few processing demands on the subject and most suitably describes the behavior of relatively naive subjects. The model that assumes resampling only when **S** is empty and a memory for eliminated hypotheses represents the sort of behavior observed in many relatively well-practiced subjects. The continuous-resampling model, described in this section, matches the behavior of the most capable and highly practiced subjects. The first two models differ in the choice of the elimination axiom E1; the third model takes the same form of this axiom (E1b) as the second model. The continuous-resampling model contrasts the S1a sampling-hypothesis axiom of the first two models with S1b in which sampling is continuous so as to maintain $s = \sigma$ at the start of every trial. The choice of the response axiom in the continuous-resampling model is crucial. When the sample size is greater than one, the subject will continue to test and eliminate hypotheses even after the relevant hypothesis is sampled. If one of the response axioms R1a, R1b, R1d, or R1e is chosen, errors can be made until all hypotheses have been eliminated. The selection of a single hypothesis to be used until proved irrelevant (R1b) is more appropriate than R1d or R1e for this efficient model. Furthermore, in the analysis here, the most refined variant of R1b is adopted; that is, the subject bases his response on the oldest attribute in S.

With these assumptions of the continuous-resampling model in effect, a subject will test a sequence of hypotheses one after the other until he eventually arrives at the relevant one. In such a model, the rate of learning is governed by the number of hypotheses that are sampled and eliminated before the relevant hypothesis is used to generate the response. Here it seems realistic to pair the sophisticated handling of samples with a sophisticated sampling order and assume that the hypotheses are tested according to a fixed order (S3c). Such an assumption subsumes the idea of memory for tested hypotheses, since no hypothesis will be examined more than once. The complete model is now defined by Axioms D1d, D2, D3, S1b, S2b, S3c, E1b, E2b, the strong version of R1b, R2, and either I1b or I1c. It describes a highly structured process with relatively few random aspects. Indeed, the only probabilistic characteristics arise from the random choice of stimuli and from the experimenter's uncertainty about the subject's actual sampling order.

The continuous-resampling process gives the model properties unlike those of either model considered thus far and makes it less easy to analyze. The model lacks repeatable units that can be applied for more than a single trial and is no longer amenable to the analysis involving GFs. It can be specified as a Markov chain, but in a detailed description of the model a different chain is obtained for each value of σ, for each number of potential hypotheses, **h**, and, more seriously, for each position of the relevant hypothesis in the sampling order. For small values of σ and a small number of hypotheses in **H**, the Markov chains are easy to treat analytically. However, for large values of **h** or σ, the chains become extremely large and analytically tedious. Therefore, it is easier to derive predictions using numerical techniques such as those developed by Millward (1969) and available as a computer program (Millward, Wickens, & Waters, forthcoming).

Three levels of representation will be presented, each characterizing the continuous-resampling model as a Markov chain of a different degree of precision. Each level is obtained as a reduction of the lower level. In most detail, level one, the states of the Markov chain are defined by the exact set of hypotheses in S on trial $n + 1$ and the correctness of the response on trial *n*. After the first reduction, the level-two Markov chain contains states that specify the number of hypotheses that remain to be eliminated before the relevant hypothesis and the number to be eliminated after the relevant hypothesis. This representation still includes the process of eliminating irrelevant hypotheses after the relevant hypothesis has assumed the role of response generator, i.e., it specifies the testing behavior even after the TLE. After the second reduction, the level-three Markov chain details only the elimination of hypotheses before the relevant hypothesis becomes the response generator, thus ignoring the process after the TLE. Although the level-one analysis is generally far more refined than is necessary for most theoretical and empirical work, its presentation will help clarify the assumptions and the definition of states. In particular, the error and correct response states are more clearly understood at this level. The three levels can be illustrated most simply by an example. In the example, $H = \{h_1, h_2, h_3, h_4, h_5, h_6\}$, where the subscript indicates the order of sampling. The relevant hypothesis in position ρ will be h_4, so $\rho = 4$. The sample S is of size $\sigma = 2$ and is written in parentheses rather than braces to indicate that it is an ordered 2-tuple, $S = (h_i, h_j)$, with the first entry, h_i, determining the response.

Level one.   The subject begins with the first two hypotheses, $S = (h_1, h_2)$. Since both are irrelevant, h_1, h_2, neither hypothesis nor both hypotheses may be eliminated with probabilities $\pi(1 - \pi)$, $(1 - \pi)\pi$, π^2, and $(1 - \pi)^2$, respectively. As each hypothesis is eliminated, another is sampled according to the sampling order. Thus, if h_1 is consistent and h_2 inconsistent, $S = (h_1, h_2)$ changes to $S = (h_1, h_3)$. Since h_4 is relevant, once it has been sampled, only one hypothesis can be eliminated on each trial. Eventually, when all hypotheses have been eliminated and $S = (h_4, —)$, the process is complete.

The above discussion ignores the overt responses. These are introduced by defining a correct and an error response for each sample. The states of the Markov chain are denoted XS to indicate that response X (either C or E) is made on trial n and is followed by elimination and resampling processes to produce the new sample S. For example, the possible transitions from state $X(h_1, h_2)$ and the probabilities of these transitions are

$$P(X(h_1, h_2) \longrightarrow C(h_1, h_2)) = \pi^2,$$
$$P(X(h_1, h_2) \longrightarrow C(h_1, h_3)) = \pi(1 - \pi),$$
$$P(X(h_1, h_2) \longrightarrow E(h_2, h_3)) = (1 - \pi)\pi,$$
$$P(X(h_1, h_2) \longrightarrow E(h_3, h_4)) = (1 - \pi)^2.$$

Notice that the transitions from trial n to trial $n + 1$ depend only on the sample on trial n and are independent of the response, here denoted X, on that trial. The transition matrix for the example we are considering becomes:

	$C(h_4, —)$	$C(h_4, h_6)$	$C(h_4, h_5)$	$E(h_4, h_5)$	$C(h_3, h_4)$	$E(h_3, h_4)$	$C(h_2, h_4)$	$C(h_2, h_3)$	$E(h_2, h_3)$	$C(h_1, h_4)$	$C(h_1, h_3)$	$C(h_1, h_2)$	$E(h_1, h_2)$
$C(h_4, —)$	1	0	0	0	0	0	0	0	0	0	0	0	0
$C(h_4, h_6)$	*	π	0	0	0	0	0	0	0	0	0	0	0
$C(h_4, h_5)$	0	*	π	0	0	0	0	0	0	0	0	0	0
$E(h_4, h_5)$	0	*	π	0	0	0	0	0	0	0	0	0	0
$C(h_3, h_4)$	0	0	0	*	π	0	0	0	0	0	0	0	0
$E(h_3, h_4)$	0	0	0	*	π	0	0	0	0	0	0	0	0
$C(h_2, h_4)$	0	0	0	*	0	0	π	0	0	0	0	0	0
$C(h_2, h_3)$	0	0	0	$*^2$	0	$\pi*$	$\pi*$	π^2	0	0	0	0	0
$E(h_2, h_3)$	0	0	0	$*^2$	0	$\pi*$	$\pi*$	π^2	0	0	0	0	0
$C(h_1, h_4)$	0	0	0	*	0	0	0	0	0	π	0	0	0
$C(h_1, h_3)$	0	0	0	$*^2$	0	$\pi*$	0	0	0	$\pi*$	π^2	0	0
$C(h_1, h_2)$	0	0	0	0	0	$*^2$	0	0	$\pi*$	0	$\pi*$	π^2	0
$E(h_1, h_2)$	0	0	0	0	0	$*^2$	0	0	$\pi*$	0	$\pi*$	π^2	0

where $*$ represents the expression $(1 - \pi)$. The state $E(h_1, h_2)$ is associated only with an initial incorrect guess under Axioms I1c and R2. Thus, with I1c the initial vector is

$$(0, 0, 0, 0, 0, 0, 0, 0, 0, 0, 0, 0, \gamma, 1 - \gamma),$$

where γ is the probability of a correct guess on the first trial. On the other hand, with Axiom I1b, $E(h_1, h_2)$ is never entered and can be removed. With Axiom I1b the initial vector becomes the same as the $C(h_1, h_2)$ row vector.

A complete analysis of the $\sigma = 2$ model with six hypotheses would require five more such matrices, one for each position of the relevant hypothesis. If the sampling order is not known only average results can be obtained, i.e., a uniform mixture of the properties of the six chains. Unfortunately, each of these matrices is complicated, making analytic solution very difficult and generalization almost impossible. Therefore, a simplification of the process seems appropriate.

Level two. Unless the actual sampling order is known or measurable, several of the states in the level-one description have equivalent properties. In both state $C(h_1, h_3)$ and state $C(h_2, h_3)$, one of the first two hypotheses has been eliminated, while the other remains. Similarly, $C(h_1, h_4)$, $C(h_2, h_4)$, and $C(h_3, h_4)$ are equivalent, with one irrelevant hypothesis determining the response and the relevant hypothesis sampled. The transition probabilities from these states to other states are identical, so the states are lumpable (Burke & Rosenblatt, 1958) forming a new ten-state Markov chain. The saving in states is not large here, but becomes more important as σ or h become larger. For example, when $\sigma = 3$, $h = 8$, and $\rho = 5$, the reduction is from 45 states at level one to 19 states at level two. The determining variable for the states at level two is the number of hypotheses that remain uneliminated before and after the relevant hypothesis. Let $X_{i,j}$ be the state where response X (either C or E) is made and where, after elimination, i hypotheses remain before h_ρ in the sampling order and j hypotheses remain after h_ρ. In the example with $\rho = 4$ the state $C_{2,2}$ combines the old states of level one, $C(h_1, h_3)$ and $C(h_2, h_3)$, while state $E(h_3, h_4)$ is now called $E_{1,2}$. The transition matrix of the new chain is

	$C_{0,0}$	$C_{0,1}$	$C_{0,2}$	$E_{0,2}$	$C_{1,2}$	$E_{1,2}$	$C_{2,2}$	$E_{2,2}$	$C_{3,2}$	$E_{3,2}$	
$C_{0,0}$	1	0	0	0	0	0	0	0	0	0	
$C_{0,1}$	$*$	π	0	0	0	0	0	0	0	0	
$C_{0,2}$	0	$*$	π	0	0	0	0	0	0	0	
$E_{0,2}$	0	$*$	π	0	0	0	0	0	0	0	(16)
$C_{1,2}$	0	0	0	$*$	π	0	0	0	0	0	
$E_{1,2}$	0	0	0	$*$	π	0	0	0	0	0	
$C_{2,2}$	0	0	0	$*^2$	$\pi*$	$\pi*$	π^2	0	0	0	
$E_{2,2}$	0	0	0	$*^2$	$\pi*$	$\pi*$	π^2	0	0	0	
$C_{3,2}$	0	0	0	0	0	$*^2$	$\pi*$	$\pi*$	π^2	0	
$E_{3,2}$	0	0	0	0	0	$*^2$	$\pi*$	$\pi*$	π^2	0	

with starting vector for Axiom IIc

$$(0, 0, 0, 0, 0, 0, 0, 0, \gamma, 1 - \gamma).$$

For Axiom IIb, state $E_{3,2}$ is removed from the matrix and the initial vector is the same as the $C_{3,2}$ row. This is only one of h such chains (here 6) that must be considered since there is one for each position of the relevant hypothesis in the sampling order.

For other values of σ and h, the level-two Markov chain can always be obtained as a reduction from the level-one Markov chain, but as the number of states gets large this quickly becomes prohibitively difficult. Accordingly, it is important to be able to obtain the level-two Markov chain directly. Consider an h-hypothesis problem with the relevant hypothesis appearing in position ρ of the sampling order. The level-two transition probabilities take their form from the binomial elimination of hypotheses from S. Three cases must be distinguished. The first two depend on whether h_ρ is in S or not, and thus on whether only $S - \{h_\rho\}$ or all of S is vulnerable to elimination. The third case occurs when all hypotheses before h_ρ have been eliminated. Then, since h_ρ is determining the response, no further errors will occur. The transition probabilities are

Case 1: $h_\rho \not\subset S : i = \sigma, \sigma - 1, \ldots, \rho - 1.$

$$P(X_{i,h-\rho} \longrightarrow C_{i-k,h-\rho}) = \binom{\sigma-1}{k}(1 - \pi)^k \pi^{\sigma-k}, \quad k = 0, 1, \ldots, \sigma - 1; \quad (17a)$$

$$P(X_{i,h-\rho} \longrightarrow E_{i-k,h-\rho}) = \binom{\sigma-1}{k-1}(1 - \pi)^k \pi^{\sigma-k}, \quad k = 1, 2, \ldots, \sigma. \quad (17b)$$

Case 2: $h_\rho \in S : i = 1, 2, \ldots, \sigma - 1; j = 0, 1, \ldots, h - \rho.$

$$P(X_{i,j} \longrightarrow C_{i-k,j-\ell}) = \binom{i-1}{k}\binom{m}{\ell}(1 - \pi)^{k+\ell}\pi^{i+m-k-\ell},$$
$$k = 0, 1, \ldots, i - 1, \quad (17c)$$
$$\ell = 0, 1, \ldots, m;$$

$$P(X_{i,j} \longrightarrow E_{i-k,j-\ell}) = \binom{i-1}{k-1}\binom{m}{\ell}(1 - \pi)^{k+\ell}\pi^{i+m-k-\ell},$$
$$k = 1, 2, \ldots, i, \quad (17d)$$
$$\ell = 0, 1, \ldots, m;$$

where $m = \min(j, \sigma - i - 1)$ is the number of hypotheses following h_ρ in S.

Case 3: $h_\rho \in S : j = 0, 1, \ldots, h - \rho.$

$$P(X_{0,j} \longrightarrow C_{0,j-\ell}) = \binom{m}{\ell}(1 - \pi)\,\pi^{m-1}, \quad \ell = 0, 1, \ldots, m; \quad (17e)$$

where $m = \min(j, \sigma - 1)$.

A simple algorithm will generate all states of a chain for given values of σ and h. By starting with states $C_{\rho-1,h-\rho}$ and $E_{\rho-1,h-\rho}$ all other states reached from them are defined by the permissible transitions of Equation 17, which are then applied recursively to the newly generated states. If Axiom IIb is used instead of IIc, the $E_{\rho-1,h-\rho}$ state can be dropped from the matrix as indicated in earlier examples.

Level three.   The level-two analysis is useful if statistics based on the contents of S are of interest. In particular, if the sample-size statistics developed for the resampling-on-error model are of interest, the level-two Markov chain has to be used, since there is no change in the sample size until all the hypotheses have been sampled and because level-three states do not code sample size. If only statistics based on the correct and error responses are important, a further simplification is possible. Level-two states that differ only in the number of hypotheses following the relevant hypothesis have the same implications regarding the sequences of correct and error responses and thus can be lumped together. In the previous example, Equation 16, states $C_{0,0}$, $C_{0,1}$, and $C_{0,2}$ can be combined to form a single absorbing state, C_0. The second subscript on all states becomes redundant and can be dropped. An additional benefit to this reduction is that, once the chain is entered, the transitions are independent of the position of the relevant hypothesis in the sampling order and depend only on the number of hypotheses that must be eliminated in order to reach it. Since the absorbing state C_0 is the same for all positions of the relevant hypothesis, the **h** separate matrices of the first- and second-level analyses can be incorporated into a single matrix.

Under Axiom IIc, when h_ρ is the relevant hypothesis, the general matrix is entered at states $C_{\rho-1}$ or $E_{\rho-1}$ with probabilities γ and $1 - \gamma$, respectively. Under Axiom IIb, the entry probabilities are identical to row $C_{\rho-1}$, and under IIc an extra guessing state must be added. The process never backtracks to lower states but progresses upward to the absorbing state. For example, with **h** = 6 and σ = 2, the full matrix is

	C_0	E_0	C_1	E_1	C_2	E_2	C_3	E_3	C_4	E_4	C_5	E_5	
C_0	1	0	0	0	0	0	0	0	0	0	0	0	
E_0	1	0	0	0	0	0	0	0	0	0	0	0	
C_1	0	$*$	π	0	0	0	0	0	0	0	0	0	
E_1	0	$*$	π	0	0	0	0	0	0	0	0	0	
C_2	0	$*^2$	$\pi*$	$\pi*$	π^2	0	0	0	0	0	0	0	
E_2	0	$*^2$	$\pi*$	$\pi*$	π^2	0	0	0	0	0	0	0	(18)
C_3	0	0	0	$*^2$	$\pi*$	$\pi*$	π^2	0	0	0	0	0	
E_3	0	0	0	$*^2$	$\pi*$	$\pi*$	π^2	0	0	0	0	0	
C_4	0	0	0	0	0	$*^2$	$\pi*$	$\pi*$	π^2	0	0	0	
E_4	0	0	0	0	0	$*^2$	$\pi*$	$\pi*$	π^2	$0\cdot$	0	0	
C_5	0	0	0	0	0	0	0	$*^2$	$\pi*$	$\pi*$	π^2	0	
E_5	0	0	0	0	0	0	0	$*^2$	$\pi*$	$\pi*$	π^2	0	

The starting vector under Axiom IIc is

$$\tfrac{1}{6}(\gamma, 1 - \gamma, \gamma, 1 - \gamma, \gamma, 1 - \gamma, \gamma, 1 - \gamma, \gamma, 1 - \gamma, \gamma, 1 - \gamma),$$

which is the simplest vector to deal with at this level of analysis. More generally, the transition probabilities for a general **h** and σ are:

$$P(X_i \longrightarrow C_{i-k}) = \binom{m-1}{k}(1 - \pi)^k \pi^{m-k}, \qquad k = 0, 1, \ldots, m - 1;$$
$$P(X_i \longrightarrow E_{i-k}) = \binom{m-1}{k-1}(1 - \pi)^k \pi^{m-k}, \qquad k = 1, 2, \ldots, m; \tag{19}$$

for $i \neq 0$ and $m = \min(i, \sigma)$, and $P(X_0 \longrightarrow C_0) = 1$. The maximum value of i is **h** − 1, and the initial vector has odd entries $\gamma/\mathbf{h}$ and even entries $(1 - \gamma)/\mathbf{h}$.

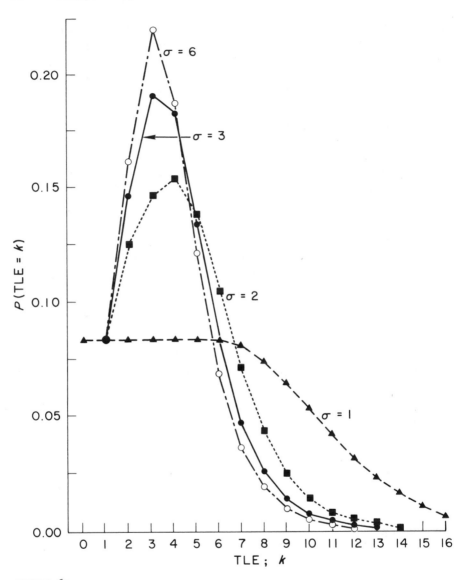

FIGURE 6a.
Distribution of the TLE for the continuous-resampling model with the sampling position of the relevant hypothesis distributed uniformly over all **h** positions: **h** = 6; σ = 1, 2, 3, and 6.

To illustrate some results from the continuous-resampling model, the chain represented by Equation 19 has been numerically evaluated to determine the distribution of the TLE for **h** = 6, σ = 1, 2, 3, 6, and for **h** = 12, σ = 1, 2, 3, 6, 12 (see Millward, 1969, for the relevant formulas). These results are presented in Figure 6. Both of these sets of curves show a flat TLE distribution associated with small values of σ and the more peaked distribution for larger values of σ. Such a shift in the shape of the TLE function with σ is a characteristic not only of this model, but also of the model with resampling when **S**

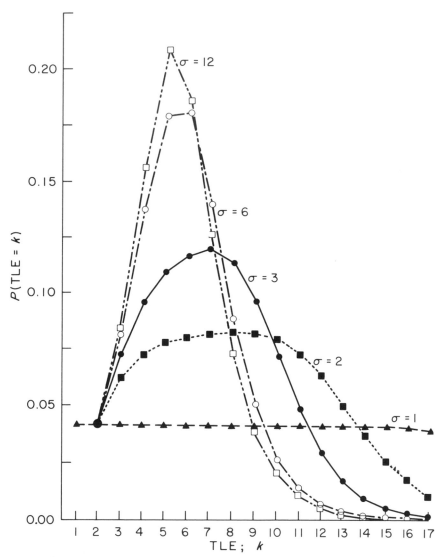

FIGURE 6b.
Distribution of the TLE for the continuous-resampling model with the sampling position of the relevant hypothesis distributed uniformly over all **h** positions: **h** = 12; σ = 1, 2, 3, 6, and 12.

is empty (Wickens & Millward, 1971), and represents one way to approximate the size of the sample that the subject is using. The curves when $\sigma = \mathbf{h}$ represent optimum performance, in that all the variance of the distribution of the TLE is due to the probabilistic structure of stimulus generation and none to the subject. Note that the predictions when $\sigma = \mathbf{h}$ are identical to those of the model in which resampling occurs only when $\mathbf{S}$ is empty, with $\sigma = \mathbf{h}$.

Summary

The continuous-resampling model, as presented, attributes a very high standard of information processing to the subject since use is made of every opportunity to test a sampled hypothesis. Clearly, few subjects could attain this standard with anything but very small values of σ. Fortunately, modification of the model to take errors into account can easily be made. Axiom E'1b could be substituted for E1b fairly directly as long as the probability of eliminating a consistent hypothesis was zero, i.e., $\delta_c = 0$. The probability of elimination is simply decreased and Equations 17 and 19 are rewritten with $1 - \pi$ replaced by $(1 - \pi)\delta_i$ and π by $1 - (1 - \pi)\delta_i$. Modification of the sample size by S'5b is more difficult because the sample size will then depend on the number of hypotheses eliminated on the previous trial, necessitating a substantial increase in the number of states in the model. It might be possible to approximate the S'5b Axiom, however, by creating an uncontingent distribution of sample sizes. If T_σ is the transition matrix of the form of Equation 17 or 19 for a particular value of σ and if $\mathbf{S}$ is the random variable denoting the distribution of sample sizes, then the total process can be represented by the matrix

$$T = \sum_\sigma P(\mathbf{S} = \sigma)T_\sigma.$$

This matrix can be analyzed by the same numerical methods as were used to produce the results in Figure 6. Because of a lack of detailed data, we have not investigated these modifications further.

Whereas the second model emphasizes memory for groups of hypotheses and provides a mechanism for handling the organization of hypotheses into groups, the continuous-resampling model provides a list structure for the organization of hypotheses. An advantage of lists over groups is that with a list of hypotheses to check no memory storage for eliminated hypotheses is required. The subject simply keeps track of the last hypothesis sampled, information available from the sample $\mathbf{S}$. However, the subject must organize his set of hypotheses into a list and that takes some processing effort. Because hypotheses do not come organized into lists, this model is probably only appropriate after some practice during which the subject structures the list or when he has time to organize the list before testing begins. Obviously the degree to which the problem is structured beforehand is related to how soon a subject begins testing hypotheses according to a fixed order.

SUMMARY

We have attempted to do two things in this chapter. First, we constructed an organized set of axioms for hypothesis-testing models of CI. In our axiomatization we have not attempted to be complete, in the sense that we have not given axioms for all CI models that could be proposed. Such a listing would be too extensive to be of much use and probably would be impossible to accomplish. What we have attempted to do instead is to lay out, in our lettered and numbered organization, the processes that are important in defining hypothesis-testing models of CI. Thus, we hope that a worker attempting to develop new models could use our set of axioms as an initial pool of ideas from which to sample.

Second, we described several representative models in some detail. It is important to realize that the 'correct' model is the very general one schematized in Figure 1, that is, the general hypothesis-testing formulation. The various axioms within each set provide for many different specific models, but no one model is more correct than any other. As we have tried to emphasize, the model appropriate to a particular set of data will depend on such things as the timing of the stimulus presentation, the set of stimuli and responses, and the population of subjects. Accordingly, in the second section of the chapter, we developed three versions of the hypothesis-testing model in detail, in order to represent different degrees of sophistication on the part of the subject and to illustrate different characteristics of their mathematical analysis. All are plausible models under appropriate circumstances.

There are three areas of interest in CI that we have more or less slighted in this chapter. First, we have made no attempt to evaluate any empirical evidence, either to determine goodness of fit to the models or to delimit, more than roughly, which versions of the model are most appropriate for which situations. Second, we have not considered the processing error assumptions in the sort of detail that they deserve. There are, as we noted, many problems associated with parameter estimation, but nevertheless more specific conclusions are possible. Finally, we have confined our models only to the simple affirmative CI task. In particular, we have ignored models of other logical problems—conjunctive, disjunctive, etc.—that have been proposed. These models will certainly require a more extensive set of assumptions and a more elaborate analysis than those given here. We believe, however, that the axiomatization we have developed will provide an organization from which to begin investigation of these problems.

ACKNOWLEDGMENTS

This work was supported in part by National Institutes of Mental Health grant MH-11255 and National Science Foundation grant GB-34122A to Richard Millward, and by National Institutes of Mental Health grant MH-19099-01 and a grant from the University of California to Thomas Wickens.

REFERENCES

Atkinson, R. C., Bower, G. H., & Crothers, E. J. *An introduction to mathematical learning theory*. New York: Wiley, 1965.

Atkinson, R. C., & Wickens, T. D. Human memory and the concept of reinforcement. In R. Glaser (Ed.), *The nature of reinforcement*. New York: Academic Press, 1971.

Bourne, L. E., Jr. *Human conceptual behavior*. Boston: Allyn and Bacon, 1966.

Bourne, L. E., Jr., Guy, D. E., Dodd, D. H., & Justesen, D. R. The effects of varying length and informational components of the intertrial interval. *Journal of Experimental Psychology*, 1965, **69**, 624–629.

Bourne, L. E., Jr., & Restle, F. Mathematical theory of concept learning. *Psychological Review*, 1959, **66**, 278–296.

Bower, G. H., & Trabasso, T. R. Concept identification. In R. C. Atkinson (Ed.), *Studies in mathematical psychology*. Stanford: Stanford University Press, 1964.

Bruner, J. S., Goodnow, J. J., & Austin, G. A. *A study of thinking*. New York: Wiley, 1956.

Burke, C. J., & Rosenblatt, M. A Markovian function of a Markov chain. *Annals of Mathematical Statistics*, 1958, **29**, 1112–1122.

Chumbley, J. Hypothesis memory in concept learning. *Journal of Mathematical Psychology*, 1969, **6**, 528–540.

Chumbley, J. A duoprocess theory of concept learning. *Journal of Mathematical Psychology*, 1972, **9**, 17–35.

Coltheart, V. Memory for stimuli and memory for hypotheses in concept identification. *Journal of Experimental Psychology*, 1971, **89**, 102–108.

Cotton, J. W. A sequence-specific concept identification model: Infra-structure for the Bower and Trabasso theory. *Journal of Mathematical Psychology*, 1971, **8**, 333–369.

Estes, W. K. Elements and patterns in diagnostic discrimination learning. *Transactions of the New York Academy of Sciences*, 1972, **34**, 84–95.

Falmagne, R. Construction of a hypothesis model for concept identification. *Journal of Mathematical Psychology*, 1970, **7**, 60–96.

Feller, W. *An introduction to probability theory and its application*, Vol. 1. (3rd ed.) New York: Wiley, 1968.

Gregg, L. W., & Simon, H. A. Process models and stochastic theories of simple concept formation. *Journal of Mathematical Psychology*, 1967, **4**, 246–276.

Hovland, C. I. A "communication analysis" of concept learning. *Psychological Review*, 1952, **59**, 461–472.

Hunt, E. B. *Concept learning*. New York: Wiley, 1962.

Levine, M. Neo-noncontinuity theory. In G. H. Bower and J. T. Spence (Eds.), *The psychology of learning and motivation: Advances in research and theory*. Vol. 3. New York: Academic Press, 1969.

Lovejoy, E. *Attention in discrimination learning: A point of view and a theory*. San Francisco: Holden-Day, 1968.

Millward, R. B. Probabilistic reinforcement of reversal and dimensional shifts. *Journal of Mathematical Psychology*, 1968, **5**, 196–223.

Millward, R. B. Derivations of learning statistics from absorbing Markov chains. *Psychometrika*, 1969, **34**, 215–232.

Millward, R. B. Theoretical and experimental approaches to human learning. In J. W. Kling, L. A. Riggs & seventeen contributors, *Woodworth & Schlosberg's experimental psychology*. (Rev. ed.) New York: Holt, Rinehart & Winston, 1971.

Millward, R. B., & Spoehr, K. T. Direct measurement of hypothesis-sampling strategies. *Cognitive Psychology*, 1973, **4**, 1–38.

Millward, R. B., Wickens, T. D., & Waters, R. THE MODELLER: A program for estimating parameters and generating statistics for absorbing Markov chain models of learning. (Forthcoming)

Nahinsky, I. D. A hypothesis sampling model for conjunctive concept identification. *Journal of Mathematical Psychology*, 1970, **7**, 293–316.

Peterson, C. R., Hammond, K. R., & Summers, D. A. Optimal responding in multiple-cue probability learning. *Journal of Experimental Psychology*, 1965, **70**, 270–276.

Polson, P. G. A quantitative theory of the concept identification processes in the Hull paradigm. *Journal of Mathematical Psychology*, 1972, **9**, 141–167.

Restle, F. A theory of discrimination learning. *Psychological Review*, 1955, **62**, 11–19.

Restle, F. The selection of strategies in cue learning. *Psychological Review*, 1962, **69**, 329–343.

Shepard, R. N., Hovland, C. I., & Jenkins, H. M. Learning and memorization of classifications. *Psychological Monographs: General and Applied*, 1961, Whole No. 517.

Suppes, P. *Introduction to logic*. Princeton, New Jersey: Van Nostrand, 1957.

Sutherland, N. S., & Mackintosh, N. J. *Mechanisms of animal discrimination learning*. New York: Academic Press, 1971.

Trabasso, T., & Bower, G. H. Component learning in the four-category concept problem. *Journal of Mathematical Psychology*, 1964, **1**, 143–169.

Trabasso, T., & Bower, G. H. Presolution dimensional shifts in concept identification: A test of the sampling with replacement axiom in all-or-none models. *Journal of Mathematical Psychology*, 1966, **3**, 163–173.

Trabasso, T., & Bower, G. H. *Attention in learning: Theory and research*. New York: Wiley, 1968.

Wickens, T. D., & Millward, R. B. Attribute elimination strategies for concept identification with practiced subjects. *Journal of Mathematical Psychology*, 1971, **8,** 453–480.

Williams, G. F. A model of memory in concept learning. *Cognitive Psychology*, 1971, **2,** 158–184.

Zeaman, D., & House, B. J. The role of attention in retardate discrimination learning. In N. R. Ellis (Ed.), *Handbook of mental deficiency*. New York: McGraw-Hill, 1963.

Thinking Processes

Herbert A. Simon
Allen Newell
CARNEGIE-MELLON UNIVERSITY

This chapter deals with formal theories of human thinking, and in particular, with examination of those theories that are formulated in information-processing languages. Since this formalism—information-processing languages—is somewhat remote from classical mathematics, the initial section provides a brief characterization of these languages, shows how they can be used to construct psychological theories, and compares them with stochastic learning theory in application to a specific task environment in concept formation. Subsequent sections survey the current state of information-processing theory as applied to human problem solving, to verbal learning and some related perceptual processes, and to human discovery of serial patterns. These are perhaps the three principal aspects of human thinking for which information-processing theories of human thinking have been constructed and tested.

INFORMATION-PROCESSING LANGUAGES

In pure mathematics, information-processing languages are one of several formalisms used in the subject that is variously known as Turing machine theory, recursive function theory, and automaton theory. As tools of applied mathematics, information-processing languages are employed in linguistics, computer science (particularly theory of programming and artificial intelligence), and cognitive psychology. Our strategy in this chapter is not to provide a formal treatment of information-processing languages, as might be appropriate if our interests were in pure mathematics, but to show how these languages have been used for theory building and theory testing in cognitive psychology, and to indicate what they have added to our knowledge of the human mind and brain.

Information-processing languages are formalisms designed to describe information-processing systems, and to permit the properties of such systems to be inferred.[1] An information-processing system (IPS) consists of a memory containing symbol structures, a processor, effectors, and receptors. Hence, it incorporates: (a) a set of elements, called *symbols;* (b) *symbol structures*, consisting of instances of symbols connected by *relations;* (c) *memories* capable of storing and retaining symbol structures; (d) *information processes* that take symbol structures as inputs and outputs; (e) a processor that includes a set of *elementary information processes* (eips), a *short-term memory* that holds the inputs of the eips, and an *interpreter* that determines the order in which the eips will be executed; and (f) *input* and *output* channels.

A computer is a now familiar example of an IPS. The work described in this chapter derives from the conjecture that a thinking human being is also an IPS. This, of course, is an empirical hypothesis that, like all such hypotheses, is to be tested by confronting it continually with data relating to a wide range of thinking tasks.

List Processing

The particular information-processing languages that have been most widely used for building theories of human cognitive processes are *list-processing languages*. In a list-processing system, the fundamental symbol structure is the *list*, an ordered set of symbols. The ordering relation, *next*, connects each symbol with its immediate successor on the list. A stimulus-response association, for example, can be represented by a list of two elements, where the *next* relation stands for the association between the first element, the stimulus, and the second element, the response.

In addition to the successor relation, list-processing languages usually also provide for the naming of an indefinite number of other binary relations called *descriptors* or *properties*. Thus, COLOR(APPLE, RED) describes a relation between APPLE and RED, whose property or descriptor is COLOR.

---

[1] For a more complete introduction to information-processing systems and languages, see Newell and Simon (1972, Ch. 2). The description here is based on that chapter.

With each symbol structure in the IPS may be associated, in this way, a list (*description list* or *property list*) of relations that collectively describe the symbol structure. From a psychological standpoint, descriptions may be identified with the 'directed associations' introduced by the Wurzburg school as an essential addendum to simple associations. As we shall see, an associatively organized memory can be represented in a simple and direct way by means of symbol structures, lists, and descriptions.

Goals of Formalization

Psychological theories can be formalized by expressing them in information-processing languages. The goals of formalization are the same here as in any other application of mathematics to empirical science: to permit the theory to be stated rigorously, and to permit the use of formal reasoning to draw out the implications of the postulates of the theory. Among its other contributions, formal rigor assures that all assumptions are made explicit. If certain mechanisms are being postulated to explain some phenomena, formalization reveals whether the mechanisms are, indeed, sufficient to produce the phenomena. Hence, formal statement of a theory permits *sufficiency tests* to be applied to the theory.

The enhanced inferential power provided by formalization contributes to the *parsimony* of theories, for it permits relatively large sets of phenomena to be derived from relatively small sets of assumptions. It discloses the interconnectedness of things. One serious barrier to parsimony in psychology has been the difficulty of comparing complex stimuli of various kinds used in different experiments. To formalize theories, stimuli have had to be scaled, but the scales derived with most scaling techniques are each specific to rather narrow ranges of stimuli. In many cases, however, stimuli can be described rather directly in information-processing languages, and hence they can be introduced into the theoretical development without an intermediate scaling step.

Consider, for example, the three letter sequences, ABMCDM . . . , 56A67A . . . , and DEFGEFGH. . . . On a common-sense basis, the first two resemble each other more than either resembles the third. In a formalization of a theory on effects of similarity, using classical mathematics, this intuitive notion of similarity would have to be replaced by a measure of judged similarity, or by some other scaling procedure. In a formalization using an information-processing language, this measurement step can be omitted by encoding the stimuli into strings of symbols isomorphic to them, and by simply observing how the IPS processes them (see Simon & Kotovsky, 1963; Simon, 1972). This can certainly be done in any case where the stimuli are symbol structures.

Dynamic Theories

The most powerful formalisms of theoretical physics and chemistry are dynamic theories—that is to say, theories that deal with the time paths of systems. Such theories are generally formalized by sets of differential equations or difference equations. A physical system is hypothesized to be describable in terms of its *state* at each moment of time. Its path through time is then a path through the space of possible states, or *state space*. The differential equations express the position of the system in state space at each particular moment in time (say, $t + \Delta t$) as a function of its position at the 'immediately' preceding moment in time (say, t). With differential equations, the system moves continuously through time; with difference equations, it moves by discrete increments of time.

In formalizing a theory in an information-processing language, the function of the differential or difference equations is performed by a *program*. Formally, a program is simply a set of difference equations, for it determines the state of a system (e.g., a computer) at each moment in time as a function of its state at the preceding moment (at the previous instruction cycle). The time path of a computer through its state space under the control of a program can be interpreted directly as a model of the time path of a system through its state space under the control of dynamic laws isomorphic to the program. Thus the program of an IPS, written in an information-processing language, is a dynamic theory of the system's behavior.

Concept Formation: An Illustrative Application

The dynamic models with which we are perhaps most familiar in psychology are the stochastic models that have been used to theorize about learning and concept attainment. It is instructive to compare theories of human performance that have been formalized in two different ways for the same task: in stochastic terms and in information-processing terms, respectively. (This section is based on Gregg & Simon, 1967a.)

In one standard paradigm for concept-attainment experiments, the subject is presented with N-dimensional stimuli having two possible values on each dimension, and is asked to classify the stimuli according to the presence or absence of a particular value on one dimension, specified by the experimenter but unknown to the subject. On each trial, the subject responds to the stimulus with 'Positive' or 'Negative,' and is reinforced by 'Right' or 'Wrong' as appropriate.

A stochastic model. Bower and Trabasso (1964) built a stochastic model of this situation on the assumptions that (a) stimuli are generated at random; (b) the subject, on a given trial either knows the correct concept, and therefore responds correctly, or does not know it, and then responds with a probability p of making an error; (c) after an error, the subject shifts from the state of not knowing the concept to the state of knowing it with a fixed probability π.

These assumptions can be translated into a three-state Markov process by considering the state of the subject just after he has made a response. He is in one of three possible states: (a) he has already learned the concept and has made a right response (LR); (b) the concept is unlearned, but he has made a right response by chance (UR); or (c) the concept is unlearned, and he has made a wrong response (UW). If he is in state LR, he remains in that state with probability 1; if he is in state UR, he remains in U, hence on the next trial finds himself in state UW with probability p, and in UR with probability $(1 - p)$; if he is in state UW, he has a probability π of shifting to LR (learning the concept on that trial), and probability $(1 - \pi)(1 - p)$ and $(1 - \pi)p$ of shifting to states UR and UW, respectively.

Hence the entire model can be described by the matrix of transition probabilities.

$$
\begin{array}{cc}
 & \text{To State:} \\
\end{array}
$$

$$
\begin{array}{c}
\text{From} \\
\text{State:}
\end{array}
\quad
\begin{array}{c}
LR \\
UR \\
UW
\end{array}
\begin{array}{ccc}
LR & UR & UW \\
\left[\begin{array}{ccc}
1 & 0 & 0 \\
0 & (1 - p) & p \\
\pi & (1 - \pi)(1 - p) & (1 - \pi)p
\end{array}\right]
\end{array}
$$

The psychological content of this model is quite modest. The strong assumptions incorporated in it are the hypotheses that the two parameters p and π are constants, remaining unchanged over successive trials. The subject either knows the concept (L), or he does not (U), and if he does not, there is a fixed chance of his getting the right answer (UR) or the wrong answer (UW), respectively. The assumption of the constancy of p is usually referred to as the one-trial learning hypothesis—the subject's performance does not improve at all until he acquires the concept, at which time it becomes perfect. The constancy of p—which can be tested by estimating it trial by trial over a group of subjects, or for successive blocks of trials for a single subject—has been verified empirically over a considerable range of experimental conditions.

The constancy of π is very difficult to test. From data on trial of last error for a group of subjects, an estimate can be made of π for each trial. However, this estimate will have a very large variance compared with the estimate of p, and moreover, it rests on the almost certainly incorrect assumption that π is the same for all subjects. If that assumption is false, subjects with larger π

will, on average, learn the concept more quickly than subjects with smaller π, and these intersubject differences will be confounded with intrasubject changes in π.

For experiments with simple concepts, the essential constancy of p is almost guaranteed by the structure of the stimuli and their random presentation. By virtue of this structure, there is no partial knowledge of the correct concept (e.g., it is *not x*) that would improve the subject's response score. Hence, even if the three-state Markov process fits the empirical data well, as it often does, it is not clear that it says much of psychological interest about the subject's behavior.

An information-processing model.   The basic limitation of the Markov process as a psychological theory stems from its failure to postulate anything about the subject's learning process. The transition from the unlearned to the learned state is, in this theory, a random event lacking in an underlying mechanism. Additional psychological content can be introduced, without completely eliminating the stochastic character of the theory, by making assumptions about the way in which the subject generates concepts to be tested. The subject's hypothesized process for generating concepts may retain a random element in it, and in the simplest cases, the process model may still be describable as a Markov process, but the structure of the theory is more transparent if it is formalized in information-processing terms.

Let us consider the simplest possibility. First, we define a number of symbols and symbol structures that are assumed to be stored in the memory of the subject or of the experimenter, displayed by the experimenter to the subject, or communicated by the subject to the experimenter.

Instance: Its value is a description list containing a value (e.g., 'large,' 'square') for each of N attributes (e.g., 'size,' 'shape'). Instances may be generated by the experimenter and displayed to the subject (stimuli), or may be stored in the subject's memory.

Attribute-structure: Its value is a list of pairs of values (e.g., 'red-blue') for each of N attributes. This structure is used by the experimenter to generate instances. In most forms of the concept-attainment experiment, it is also stored in the memory of the subject.

Counterinstance: An instance formed from another instance by taking the alternate value in the attribute-structure for each of the attributes. It may be generated by the subject and stored in memory.

Correct-response: Its value is one of the two constants: 'Positive,' 'Negative.' It is generated by the experimenter and stored in his memory.

Correct-hypothesis: Its value is one of the $2N$ attribute values in the attribute-structure. It is initially stored in the experimenter's memory.

Current-hypothesis: Its value is one of the $2N$ attribute values in the attribute structure. It is held in the subject's memory.

Response: Its value is one of the two constants: 'Positive,' 'Negative.' It is generated by the subject and communicated to the experimenter.

Reinforcement: Its value is one of the two constants: 'Right,' 'Wrong.' It is generated by the experimenter and communicated to the subject.

New-hypothesis: Its value is one of the $2N$ attribute values in the attribute-structure. It is generated by the subject.

Possible-hypotheses: Its initial value is the list of $2N$ attribute values in the attribute-structure. It is held in the memory of the subject.

Tally: Its value is a positive integer. It is held in the experimenter's memory.

Constants: 'Positive,' 'Negative,' 'Right,' 'Wrong,' the integers, K, and the symbols for the $2N$ attribute values.

Processes: **Set-equal-to** (denoted by ⟵), **Test-if-instance** (denoted by ∈), **Test-if-equal** (denoted by =), **Do, Generate, Name** (denoted by ⟹), **Delete, Reverse, Goto, Branch.**

$X \longleftarrow Y$ sets the symbol structure X equal to the symbol structure Y. $X \in Y$ tests if the symbol structure X belongs to the list Y. $X = Y$ tests if two symbol structures are equal. **Do** X executes the process named X. **Generate** selects items from a list and provides them as arguments to a process. There are in fact several variants of this process, which will all be denoted by the generic name 'generate,' qualified by indications of their special characteristics. $(\Rightarrow X)$ assigns the name X to the list structure that has been output by the previously executed process. **Delete** X **from** Y deletes the symbol structure X from the list Y. **Reverse** X replaces each value on instance X with the alternative member of its pair on attribute-structure—that is, it converts instance X into its counterinstance. **Goto** x transfers control to instruction x. **Branch** is of the following form: **If** T **then** x **else** y. If test T is satisfied, then x is executed; if not, y is executed.

We now define a simple process theory for the concept-attainment experiment, which incorporates a hypothesis about how the subject goes about discovering the correct concept. The theory is a program making use of the representation and processes just introduced:

E1:   Do E3; then do E4.

S1:   If current-hypothesis ∈ instance,
        then response ⟵ 'Positive',
        else response ⟵ 'Negative'.

E2:   If response = correct-response,
        then reinforcement ⟵ 'Right',
        else reinforcement ⟵ 'Wrong'.

S2:   If reinforcement = 'Wrong',
        then current-hypothesis ⟵ S5.

E3:   Generate instance (sampling randomly from each pair on attribute-structure) ($\Rightarrow$ generated-instance)
       instance $\longleftarrow$ generated-instance.

E4:   If correct-hypothesis $\subset$ instance,
       then correct-response $\longleftarrow$ 'Positive',
       else correct-response $\longleftarrow$ 'Negative'.

S5:   Generate hypothesis (sampling randomly from possible-hypotheses) ($\Rightarrow$ new-hypothesis)
       current-hypothesis $\longleftarrow$ new-hypothesis.

E0:   Do E1, do S1, do E2,

       If reinforcement = 'Right',
       then tally $\longleftarrow$ tally $+$ 1
       else tally $\longleftarrow$ 0, do E0.

       If tally = K,
       then halt,
       else do S2, goto E0.

In this program, the processes prefixed 'E' are experimenter processes, those prefixed 'S' are subject processes. (No such factorization is possible in the three-state Markov process.) E processes take inputs only from E's memories or from S's responses, and communicate only to E's memories or to structures readable by S; S processes take inputs only from S's memories or E's communications, and output only to S's memories or to structures readable by E.

The theory does not postulate completely determinate behavior for S, retaining a stochastic component in S5, the process whereby S selects new hypotheses for testing. Nevertheless, it is considerably stronger than the three-state Markov process, for it allows a no-parameter estimate to be made of the expected number of trials (or total errors) to concept attainment. This prediction rests, however, on the assumption of equal saliency of all stimulus dimensions (random sampling with equal probability from possible-hypotheses). If differences in cue saliency are important, additional parameters would have to be introduced into the sampling process (or the sampling process replaced by some other) to allow for this.

Comparison with the Markov process.   The program is sufficiently simple that it can be translated into a Markov process, but with a larger state space than the three-state process. Number the hypotheses on possible-hypotheses from 1 to $2N$, assigning 1 to correct-hypothesis, and 2 to its complement on attribute-structure. Then, if current-hypothesis is i, and the subject has made a correct response, we will say the system is in state iR; if he has made a wrong response, we will say it is in state iW. There are then $4N - 1$ states (two

To State:

From State:	1R ···	iR ···	jR ···	2W ···	iW ···	jW ···
1R	1 ···	0 ···	0 ···	0 ···	0 ···	0 ···
⋮	· ···	· ···	· ···	· ···	· ···	· ···
	· ···	· ···	· ···	· ···	· ···	· ···
iR	0 ···	$\frac{1}{2}$ ···	0 ···	0 ···	$\frac{1}{2}$ ···	0 ···
⋮	· ···	· ···	· ···	· ···	· ···	· ···
	· ···	· ···	· ···	· ···	· ···	· ···
jR	0 ···	0 ···	$\frac{1}{2}$ ···	0 ···	0 ···	$\frac{1}{2}$ ···
⋮	· ···	· ···	· ···	· ···	· ···	· ···
	· ···	· ···	· ···	· ···	· ···	· ···
2W	$\frac{1}{2N}$ ···	$\frac{1}{4N}$ ···	$\frac{1}{4N}$ ···	$\frac{1}{2N}$ ···	$\frac{1}{4N}$ ···	$\frac{1}{4N}$ ···
⋮	· ···	· ···	· ···	· ···	· ···	· ···
	· ···	· ···	· ···	· ···	· ···	· ···
iW	$\frac{1}{2N}$ ···	$\frac{1}{4N}$ ···	$\frac{1}{4N}$ ···	$\frac{1}{2N}$ ···	$\frac{1}{4N}$ ···	$\frac{1}{4N}$ ···
⋮	· ···	· ···	· ···	· ···	· ···	· ···
	· ···	· ···	· ···	· ···	· ···	· ···
jW	$\frac{1}{2N}$ ···	$\frac{1}{4N}$ ···	$\frac{1}{4N}$ ···	$\frac{1}{2N}$ ···	$\frac{1}{4N}$ ···	$\frac{1}{4N}$ ···

FIGURE 1.
Matrix of transition probabilities for information-processing model of concept attainment (from Gregg & Simon, 1967a).

for each member of possible-hypotheses, except for hypothesis 1, since $1W$ is impossible). The matrix of the Markov process is shown in Figure 1.

Suppose we now modify the experimental procedure so that the subject, on each trial, responds not only 'Positive' or 'Negative,' but also states his current-hypothesis. We accommodate this change in the theory by modifying S1 to read

S1∗:   If current-hypothesis is ∈ instance,
              then response ⟵ 'Positive' ⟨current-hypothesis⟩,
              else response ⟵ 'Negative' ⟨current-hypothesis⟩.

With this change, we are able to test S1 directly, since we can now observe whether the response is jointly consistent with instance and current-hypothesis. We are also able to observe directly which state the subject is in after his response and can therefore determine whether he changes his current-hypothesis when and only when his response is wrong, as postulated by S2.

With the original S1, having only the response 'Positive' or 'Negative,' we cannot observe directly the successive states of the process. However, we can aggregate the state space into a smaller space whose elements are observable and correspond, respectively, to the elements in the three-state space of the

Markov process postulated by Bower and Trabasso. We observe that, for each state, iR, $i \neq 1$, there is a probability of $\frac{1}{2}$ of a transition to some iR state, and a probability of $\frac{1}{2}$ of a transition to some iW state. We define an aggregate state AR, and say that the system is in AR if it is in any of the states iR, $i \neq 1$. We define an aggregate state W, and say that the system is in W if it is in any of the states iW, $i = 2, \ldots, 2N$. Then we can see readily that the probability of a transition from W to $1R$ is $\frac{1}{2}N$, from W to AR is $(N - 1)/2N$, and from W to W, $\frac{1}{2}$.

$$
\begin{array}{c}
\text{To State:} \\
\begin{array}{cc}
 & \begin{array}{ccc} 1R & AR & W \end{array} \\
\begin{array}{c} 1R \\ \text{From } AR \\ \text{State:} \quad W \end{array} &
\left[\begin{array}{ccc}
1 & 0 & 0 \\
0 & \frac{1}{2} & \frac{1}{2} \\
\dfrac{1}{2N} & \dfrac{(N-1)}{2N} & \frac{1}{2}
\end{array} \right]
\end{array}
\end{array}
$$

The new matrix differs from the matrix for the original three-state process in two respects: first, it requires that $p = \frac{1}{2}$ and $\pi = \frac{1}{2}N$; second, there is a very small difference between the transition probabilities for row W in the two matrices. The value $p = \frac{1}{2}$ derives primarily from the structure of the experiment and the random presentation of the stimuli, and has little psychological significance; the value $\pi = \frac{1}{2}N$ depends, as noted earlier, upon the assumption of equal saliency of attribute values, which, in turn, is implicit in the very simple hypothesis-generating process, S5.

Aggregation of the process model into a three-state stochastic process is only possible because of the extremely simple structure of the matrix of the disaggregated system. In general, no exact aggregate will exist in the smaller space. Hence, if we wish to complicate our model to obtain a better fit to the experimental data, we must rely on the process model as our formalism, and derive predictions of the behavior of the system by simulating it on a computer.

Elaboration of the process model. There are a number of directions in which we might want to elaborate the process model. We have already mentioned the matter of attribute saliency. We might attempt to account for this by eliminating the stochastic element entirely from S5. For example, attribute values might be arranged on possible-hypotheses in order of saliency as estimated from other data (e.g., judged saliency). Then a modified S5 could be:

S5*:   Generate new-hypothesis in order of occurrence on possible-
       hypotheses ($\Rightarrow$ new-hypothesis)
       current-hypothesis $\longleftarrow$ new-hypothesis.

A weaker model would retain the stochastic element in S5, but would sample with unequal probabilities from possible-hypotheses, on the basis of independent data on saliency. A possibly more veridical theory would make saliency on a particular trial depend on the specific sequence of stimuli that had been presented. For example, saliency of an attribute value that changed frequently might increase relative to the saliency of an attribute value that remained constant. Such a possibility could readily be accommodated in S5 by inserting an additional process, e.g.,

S5+: Generate each pair on attribute-structure
        If attribute-value of current-insurance = attribute-value of prior-
          instance,
          then move value down one place on possible-hypotheses.

      Generate new-hypothesis in order of occurrence on possible-
        hypotheses ($\Rightarrow$ new-hypothesis)
      current-hypothesis $\longleftarrow$ new-hypothesis.

Note that this new version of S5 will be operable only if the subject re-members both the current-instance and prior-instance. Hence there is implicit in this version a changed assumption about the short-term memory capacity and memory strategy of the subject.

Assumptions about what the subject remembers about previous stimuli and about hypotheses he has entertained previously represent a major direction of exploration for such process models. Consider the following variants on S5:

S51: Generate hypothesis (sampling randomly from possible-hypothe-
        ses) ($\Rightarrow$ new-hypothesis)
      If new-hypothesis = current-hypothesis goto S51,
        else current-hypothesis $\longleftarrow$ new-hypothesis.

S52: If response = 'Negative',
        reverse current-instance

      Generate hypothesis (sampling randomly from possible-hypothe-
        ses) ($\Rightarrow$ new-hypothesis)
      if new-hypothesis $\in$ current-instance
        then sample again,
        else current-hypothesis $\longleftarrow$ new-hypothesis.

S53: If response = 'Negative',
        reverse current-instance

      Generate values from instance ($\Rightarrow$ wrong-value)
        Delete wrong-value from possible-hypotheses

Generate hypothesis (sampling randomly from possible-hypotheses) ($\Rightarrow$ new-hypothesis)
current-hypothesis $\longleftarrow$ new-hypothesis.

Process S51 differs from S5 in sampling from possible-hypotheses without replacement instead of with replacement. It assumes, therefore, that the subject, in adopting a new hypothesis, remembers what hypothesis he has just rejected. Process S52 assumes a still greater retention and use of prior information. It assumes that the subject retains the information about the current-instance, and rejects hypotheses that are inconsistent with that instance. Process S53 assumes an optimal use of prior information—all hypotheses that are incompatible with any stimulus that has been presented are removed permanently from the list of possible-hypotheses. Note that with S53, π, the probability of learning on a given trial, is no longer constant.

Table 1 shows the predictions of total errors prior to concept attainment that would be made for models, otherwise identical, that incorporate S5, S51,

TABLE 1
Prediction of total errors: four models and six experiments

Subjects' Hypothesis Generator	Experiment No.								
	1	2	3		4		5		6
			C	R&N	C	R&N	C	R&N	
S5	10 ✓	6	8	8	12 ✓	12 ✓	10 ✓	10 ✓	10
S51	9 ✓	5	7	7	11 ✓	11 ✓	9 ✓	9 ✓	10
S52	5	3	4	5	6	7	5?	5?	∞ ✓
S53	2.1	1.4	2	2	2.3	2.3	2.1	2.1	∞ ✓
Actual Errors	12.2	13.4	19.1	18.7	12.9	14.5	8	7.8	48–∞

Note: Reprinted from Gregg and Simon (1967a, Table 2). The entries in the table are the average number of errors per subject predicted by each model for each experiment. The numbers followed by a check mark (✓) are reasonably compatible with the actual data shown in the last line; the numbers followed by a question mark are conceivably consistent with the data; the remaining entries are incompatible with the data.

S52, and S53, respectively, on the assumption that all attribute values are equally salient: the table compares these predictions with the values actually observed for a number of experiments reported by Bower and Trabasso. The values for models P0 and P1 are very close to each other, but all the other models are clearly distinguishable from each other. In the table, checks (✓)

designate predictions that are close to the observed values, while question marks (?) designate two predictions that may be regarded as 'tolerable.' Since the data from all of these experiments, except number 6, were fit very successfully by the three-state Markov model, we see that the additional assumptions introduced into the process models provide a great deal of additional discriminability. Moreover, if data are gathered directly on the successive hypotheses held by the subjects (as defined in S1∗ above), it becomes a straightforward matter to determine in exactly what respects the behavior differs from that postulated in the formal process model.

This example shows that information-processing languages permit us to enrich the psychological content of theories of concept attainment beyond the limits that are feasible with stochastic models, and without losing our power to test empirically the new assumptions that are added. The information-processing models enable us to associate specific aspects of the experimental data with particular assumptions about the subjects' information-processing strategies. For a principal factor in determining the outcomes of these experiments (and particularly the speed of concept attainment) is the subjects' strategies of using information to choose hypotheses (process S5 and its variants). Which strategies will be selected depends on (a) how much information subjects can keep in short-term memory, (b) what auxiliary external memories are provided to subjects to enable them to keep additional information, and (c) what experience and previous training they have had in efficient strategies for using information in this kind of task. The structure of the information-processing models warns us that it is futile to expect consistent outcomes of our experiments unless we exercise control over these variables (something that has not typically been done). Thus the formalism provides important guidance to the design of experiments.

Concept attainment provides an example of the role of information-processing theories as tools for critical analysis of a task area and of experimental paradigms. The theories have served us also as an introduction to the information-processing formalism. We turn next to the task area where the largest amount of research using information-processing theories has been carried out: human problem solving.

PROBLEM SOLVING

The experience with even the simple concept-attainment task shows that the processes used by subjects may vary widely from one individual to another, or from one task to an apparently innocuous variant of the same task. Traditionally, psychology has usually dealt with individual differences in experimental situations by averaging over subjects (although the traditions of psychophysics and operant conditioning diverge from the general mores).

Statistical invariants have been sought amidst the individual variation, with a consequent loss of most of the fine structure in the data.

When information-processing formalisms are used, two paths are open. One is to proceed from the data on the behavior of individual subjects performing specific tasks and to construct detailed process models of the behavior. The other is to construct 'representative' models that capture the most important characteristics of human performance in the task environments in question. Both paths have been followed in the study of human problem solving. We examine one example of each approach: a simulation of the behavior of a single subject in a cryptarithmetic task; and the General Problem Solver, a program aimed at simulating the main features of human problem-solving behavior over a range of task environments.

Cryptarithmetic

The theory of problem solving that has emerged from information-processing models is an elaboration of four basic propositions—perhaps they should be called 'metapropositions.'

(1) Only a few, gross characteristics of the human IPS are invariant over task and problem solver.

(2) These characteristics are sufficiently strong to determine that an IPS represents its task environment as a problem space, and that its problem solving takes place in the problem space.

(3) The structure of the task environment places limits—generally narrow ones—on the possible forms of the problem space.

(4) The structure of the problem space places corresponding limits on the possible programs that can be used for problem solving.

We have already seen these propositions illustrated in the case of simple concept attainment. The task environment was defined by the instructions and structure of the stimuli. The problem space had, as its main elements (a) instances, (b) hypotheses, and (c) a few simple processes for generating hypotheses, testing them against instances, and storing information. The programs were alternative organizations of these processes. The characteristics and richness of the problem space were determined jointly by the task environment and by limits on the subjects' memory—particularly short-term memory.

In the task now to be considered, the following display is presented to a subject:

$$
\begin{array}{ll}
\text{DONALD} & \text{D} \leftarrow 5 \\
\text{+GERALD} & \\
\hline
\text{ROBERT} & \\
\end{array}
$$

The subject then is instructed: "Each letter represents a digit (0, 1, . . . , 9). In particular, D represents the digit 5. Each letter represents a distinct digit, and each digit a distinct letter. For example, no letter other than D may equal 5, nor may any digit other than 5 correspond to D. What digits should be assigned to the letters so that, when the letters are replaced by their corresponding digits, the sum above is satisfied?"

To describe the task environment and problem space formally, we use the notation known as BNF (Backus Normal Form).[2] In BNF, the elements contained in a simple problem space for these task instructions can be described as in Figure 2.

⟨letter⟩ :: = A | B | D | E | G | L | N | O | R | T
⟨digit⟩ :: = 0 | 1 | 2 | 3 | 4 | 5 | 6 | 7 | 8 | 9
⟨expression⟩ :: = ⟨letter⟩ ⟵ ⟨digit⟩
⟨knowledge-state⟩ :: = ∅ | ⟨expression⟩ |
　　　　⟨expression⟩, ⟨knowledge-state⟩
U: set (⟨knowledge-state⟩)
⟨operator⟩ :: = Add [⟨expression⟩]
Q: set (⟨operator⟩)

FIGURE 2.
BNF definition of basic problem space for cryptarithmetic task (adapted from Newell & Simon, 1972, Fig. 5.1).

The first line in this figure can be translated as "A letter is an A or a B or . . . or a T." The third line as "An expression is a letter followed by a left arrow (⟵) followed by a digit." The fourth line as "A knowledge state is the null state, or an expression, or a knowledge state followed by an expression (i.e., a string of expressions)." The fifth line as "U is the set of knowledge states." The sixth line as "An operator consists of the term 'Add' followed by a left bracket ([) followed by an expression followed by a right bracket (]).'' The second and seventh lines are read similarly.

Now the problem space (basic problem space) we wish to consider is simply U, the set of knowledge states. The subject begins in the state consisting of (D ⟵ 5). As he discovers, or believes that he has discovered, the appropriate digit to assign to some letter, he creates an expression for that assignment (e.g., E ⟵ 9). Using the operator 'Add,' he annexes this new expression to his knowledge state. When he has solved the problem, his knowledge state will consist of the expressions stating the full set of assignments of digits to letters.

It is possible to trace a subject's progress through this problem space. One way is to place the DONALD + GERALD display on a blackboard and instruct the subject, whenever he wishes to make or change an assignment, to ask the experimenter to enter it on the display. From the sequence of assignments and changes, we can construct a problem-behavior graph (PBG)

---

[2] For further discussion of human behavior in this task environment, see Newell and Simon (1972, Chs. 5–7).

that represents the successive stages of the subject's information (see Fig. 3). Each node on the PBG represents a specific state of information. Application of the Add operator leads to a new node. If the subject abandons one or more assignments, he retreats to a prior node. Time runs to the right, then down; thus the graph is linearly ordered by time of generation.

Given the PBG of a subject, we must explain why his behavior took this particular course through the problem space—what processes guided it. In terms of the strategy being examined here, the explanation will finally take the form of a program written in an information-processing language. PBG constitutes a set of behavior points against which the trace of the program can be compared. However, the test of the theory can be strengthened to the extent that the density of data points can be increased. Such an increase can be accomplished by securing additional data from the subject during the course of his problem-solving efforts—in particular, by recording a thinking-aloud protocol, and/or by recording his eye movements.

Figure 4 shows the first portion of the more complete PBG, inferred from the verbal protocol, corresponding to the first line (through the node B47) of the previous figure. As before, each node in the PBG represents a knowledge state of the subject, but the increased number of nodes corresponds to an enlargement of the problem space to account not only for the subject's explicit assignments of digits to letters, but also to other kinds of information about the assignments that he amasses along the way. This additional information includes information about carries (e.g., 'c2 = 1,' which is to be read "1 is carried into column 2"), and about properties of the assignments (e.g., 'R odd,' read "R is to be assigned an odd digit"). In this augmented problem space, a move is the application of an operator that generates some new item of knowledge. The PBG includes a specification not only of the knowledge states at the nodes, but also of the specific operators that produce a transition from one node to another. A BNF description of the augmented problem space is shown in Figure 5.

The problem-behavior graph in the augmented problem space is constructed by 'shallow' interpretation of the protocol—that is, by detecting all information the subject mentions explicitly, together with other information he was clearly aware of, as inferred from the language of the protocol. Thus 'R odd' in B22.1 was inferred from the protocol statement, "which will mean that R has to be an odd number." A few moments earlier, the subject has said, "and this R . . . three Rs . . ." This statement, in its context, is taken to imply that the subject is pursuing the goal of obtaining more information about R.

The interpretation of a protocol in order to construct a problem-behavior graph is not completely free from subjectivity, although experience in carrying out such analyses suggests that the leeway for the interpreter is not great in most cases. Recently, Newell and Waterman have written a computer

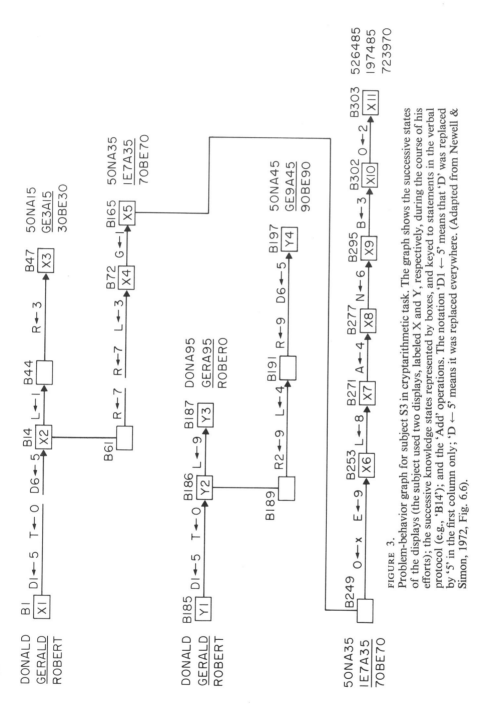

FIGURE 3.
Problem-behavior graph for subject S3 in cryptarithmetic task. The graph shows the successive states of the displays (the subject used two displays, labeled X and Y, respectively, during the course of his efforts); the successive knowledge states represented by boxes, and keyed to statements in the verbal protocol (e.g., 'B14'); and the 'Add' operations. The notation 'D1 ← 5' means that 'D' was replaced by '5' in the first column only; 'D ← 5' means it was replaced everywhere. (Adapted from Newell & Simon, 1972, Fig. 6.6).

118

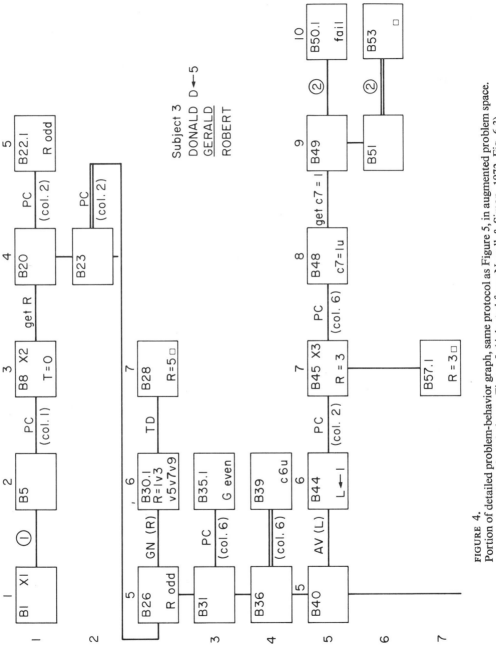

FIGURE 4.
Portion of detailed problem-behavior graph, same protocol as Figure 5, in augmented problem space.
For interpretation of symbols, see Figure 5. (Adapted from Newell & Simon, 1972, Fig. 6.3).

⟨digit⟩ :: = 0 | 1 | 2 | 3 | 4 | 5 | 6 | 7 | 8 | 9
⟨digit-variable⟩ :: = x | y
⟨general-digit⟩ :: = ⟨digit⟩ | ⟨digit-variable⟩
⟨digit-set⟩ :: = ⟨general-digit⟩ ∨ ⟨general-digit⟩ | ⟨general-digit⟩ ∨ ⟨digit-set⟩
⟨letter⟩ :: = A | B | D | E | G | L | N | O | R | T
⟨letter-set⟩ :: = ⟨letter⟩ | ⟨letter⟩ ⟨letter-set⟩
⟨carry⟩ :: = c⟨column-number⟩
⟨variable⟩ :: = ⟨letter⟩ | ⟨carry⟩
⟨column⟩ :: = column.⟨column-number⟩
⟨column-number⟩ :: = 1 | 2 | 3 | 4 | 5 | 6 | 7
⟨column-set⟩ :: = ⟨column⟩ | ⟨column⟩ ⟨column-set⟩
⟨assignment-expression⟩ :: = ⟨variable⟩ ⟵ ⟨general-digit⟩ |
      ⟨variable⟩ = ⟨general-digit⟩
⟨constraint-expression⟩ :: = ⟨variable⟩ ⟨parity⟩ | ⟨variable⟩ = ⟨digit-set⟩ |
      ⟨variable⟩ ⟨inequality⟩ ⟨general-digit⟩ | ⟨variable⟩ ⟨qualifier⟩
⟨parity⟩ :: = even | odd
⟨inequality⟩ :: = > | <
⟨qualifier⟩ :: = free | last
⟨expression⟩ :: = ⟨variable⟩ | ⟨assignment-expression⟩ | ⟨constraint-expression⟩
⟨state-expression⟩ :: = ⟨expression⟩ | ⟨expression⟩ ⟨tag⟩
⟨tag⟩ :: = new | □ | unclear | unknown | note
⟨knowledge-state⟩ :: = ⟨state-expression⟩ | ⟨state-expression⟩ ⟨knowledge-state⟩
⟨operator⟩ :: = PC[⟨column⟩] | GN | AV | TD
⟨goal⟩ :: = get⟨expression⟩ | get⟨letter-set⟩
      check⟨expression⟩ | check⟨column-set⟩
Particular sets:
    all-letters, free-letters
    all-digits, free-digits
    all-columns

FIGURE 5.
BNF definition of augmented problem space for cryptarithmetic task (adapted from Newell & Simon, 1972, Fig. 6.1).

program that is able to carry through the entire protocol analysis and construction of the problem-behavior graph automatically. The program is still in the testing and development stage, but it has successfully constructed graphs in several test instances.

The successful construction of a problem-behavior graph from a protocol provides evidence that (a) the subject's problem solving proceeded through the states of knowledge shown in the graph; (b) a specified set of operators took him from one state of knowledge to another, accounting for the transitions; and (c) the operators, along with a set of processes for selecting operators, evaluating states of knowledge for termination, and selecting prior nodes to which to return, constitute a sufficient set of processes for explaining the subject's behavior at the level of detail considered.

As a next step toward explaining the behavior, a program can be hypothesized to explain the path through the problem-behavior graph. Such a program, for the protocol we are discussing, is shown in Figure 6. It consists

P1:   ⟨assignment-expression⟩ new ⟶
        FC(variable of expression) (⟹ column); PC[column]

P2:   get ⟨variable⟩ | get ⟨variable⟩ = ⟨general-digit⟩ ⟶
        FC(variable) (⟹ column); PC[columns for variable]

P3:   get ⟨letter.1⟩ ⟶ FA(letter.1) (⟹ column);
        AV(letter.2 of column); PC[column for letter.1]

P4:   get ⟨variable⟩ and (⟨constraint-expression⟩ new) with variable ⟶
        GN(variable) (⟹ digit-set); size (digit-set) = small ⟶
        AV(variable)

P5:   check ⟨column-set⟩ ⟶ GNC(column-set) (⟹ column); PC[column]

P6:   ⟨expression⟩ unknown ⟶ (get expression)

P7:   ⟨expression⟩ ☐ ⟶ (get variable of expression)

P8:   check ⟨expression⟩ new ⟶ (get expression)

P9:   get ⟨letter-set⟩ ⟶ FL(letter-set) (⟹ letter); (get letter)

P10:   ⟨expression⟩ note ⟶ (check expression)

P11:   ⟨letter⟩ = ⟨digit⟩ new | GN(⟨letter⟩) (⟹ ⟨digit⟩) ⟶
        TD(letter, digit)

P12:   ⟨expression.1⟩ ☐ ⟶ FA(expression.1) (⟹ expression.2);
        (expression.2 ☐)

P13:   ⟨operator⟩⟹ (⟨expression⟩ unclear) ⟶
        (get variable of expression); repeat operator(variable)

P14:   check ⟨expression⟩ ⟶ FP(expression) (⟹ production);
        (get expression); repeat production on expression

FIGURE 6.
Production system for cryptarithmetic task
(from Newell & Simon, 1972, Fig. 6.7).

of 14 processes, each one of them in the form of a *production*. A production is a process consisting of two parts: a *condition* (to the left of the right arrow) and an *action* (to the right of the right arrow). The process statement $C \longrightarrow A$ is to be read, "If condition C holds, then perform action A; else do nothing." The complete set of productions, together with a rule to determine when each will be executed, forms a *production system*. In the 'purest' form of a production system, the productions are simply scanned in sequence until one is found whose condition is satisfied. That production is then executed, and the scanning process is repeated.

We will not attempt to explain here the entire production system that is depicted in Figure 6. As an example of how the notation is to be read, we interpret the first production. The condition in this production is that there has just occurred ('new') the assignment of a digit to a letter. The action to be taken when this condition prevails is to find a column in DONALD + GERALD that contains the letter involved in the assignment expression (FC (variable of expression)) and then to process that column in an endeavor to extract new information from it (PC column). An example from the beginning of the protocol, just after the subject has been instructed that D = 5 (D = 5 new), is the passage: "Therefore, I can, looking at the two Ds . . .

each D is 5; therefore, T is zero" (Find column containing D ($\Rightarrow$ column.1) and process column.1).

The production system can now be programmed for a computer, the program can be given the DONALD + GERALD problem, and the trace of the program compared with the protocol. A more limited, but reasonably severe, test of the hypothesized system can also be performed without the computer. The protocol can be compared with the production system to determine whether productions were in fact executed when the system called for them to be executed. Such a comparison was carried out for the protocol at hand (see Fig. 7). The abscissa of the figure lists the productions in the order of frequency of their occurrence in the protocol. The ordinate indicates the number of occasions for application of productions. The figure shows that there were a total of 275 nodes to be explained. Eight of these involve statements by the subject that clearly lay outside the problem space. Of the

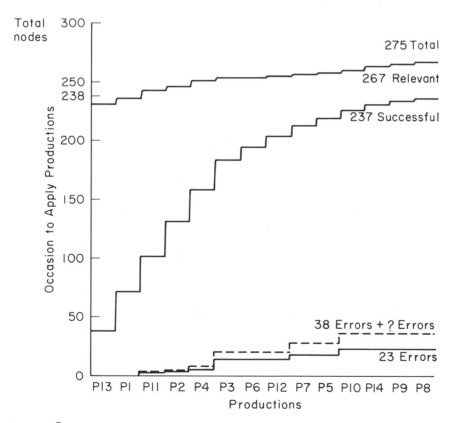

FIGURE 7.
Comparison of predicted with actual productions in a cryptarithmetic protocol (from Newell & Simon, 1972, Fig. 6.10).

remaining 267 relevant nodes, 237 were successfully explained by 1 of the 14 productions. There are several ways of counting errors, and more than one error may occur at a single node. The interpretation was erroneous or dubious at 38 of the 275 nodes, and there were 30 errors of omission and 23 errors of commission. An error of omission means failure to find a production to explain a node; an error of commission means that the wrong production—in terms of the postulated production system—was actually evoked. The figure indicates that, in the present state of the art, it is possible to explain 75 to 80 percent of the subject's movements through the problem space in a situation of this kind.

Analysis of protocols at this level of detail is immensely time consuming. More summary modes of analysis have been devised that enable us to define the problem spaces in which subjects operate, and the main outlines of their PBGs at a more summary level. Such analysis applied to the DONALD + GERALD task shows that most college-level subjects who have been studied use an augmented problem space very similar to the one described above. Subjects with little mathematical training, however, tend to use simpler problem spaces (e.g., the basic problem space described earlier) and production systems. A close relation can be shown between the nature of the problem space and production system used, and the quality of the problem-solving performance. This relation can be explained, moreover, in terms of the ways in which the richer information available in the more sophisticated problem spaces enables the subject to reduce the amount of trial-and-error search required to reach the solution.[3] Analysis in terms of production systems has been less successful in explaining certain kinds of errors (forgetting of information previously known), or the process of error recovery. Presumably, processes not yet understood at a more microscopic level than the productions are involved in these error phenomena.

The General Problem Solver

The kind of bottom-up theory construction process we have been describing is highly particularistic. That is, it begins by constructing a theory (production system or other program) to explain the behavior of a single subject solving a single problem. Because we would like to be able to generalize both across subjects and across tasks, we are faced with a difficult aggregation problem.

Generalization across subjects and tasks is only possible, of course, to the extent that there are actually invariants across subjects and tasks. Biologists

---

[3] The role that selective heuristics play in individual differences in problem-solving capability is perhaps most dramatically demonstrated by the chess-mating combination programs of Simon and Simon (1962) and Baylor and Simon (1966).

are faced with the same problem. It would be very nice to build a theory of 'organisms.' But organisms come in hundreds of thousands of kinds, and nothing is gained by pretending that they are all alike—that the differences do not exist. The aggregation problem in generalizing about human cognitive behavior is very much like the problem of generalizing about living systems.

One approach to generalization would be to observe and describe common features of the programs of different subjects on the same task. One example of this has already been provided, when we remarked that most subjects with some training in mathematics use the augmented problem space in solving the cryptarithmetic task. We also wish to be able to generalize across tasks. An important cross-task generalization is that much human problem solving appears to be describable in terms of selective search through a problem space.

A slightly different strategy of generalization, which offers some hope of making the generalizations more precise, is to write generalized problem-solving programs that purport to describe the main mechanisms appearing in the behavior of nearly all subjects ("all college sophomores of good intelligence," say) over some range of tasks. The General Problem Solver (GPS) is a program—or, more exactly, a family of closely related programs—that aims at this kind of generalization (see Ernst & Newell, 1969; Newell & Simon, 1972, Chs. 8–10).

GPS generalizes over tasks because the program itself contains no reference to any specific task environment. It is constructed entirely in terms of abstract objects, operators, and differences that take on concrete meanings only when they are associated with some particular task environment. Figure 8 shows the information that is given to GPS in order to define the problem space for a particular task, the Father and Sons Problem. The information consists of a set of declarations that classify certain objects (fathers, sons, sides, etc.) by type; a statement of the problem's final goal; a description of the initial and goal states (initial-obj and final-obj); a definition of the allowable moves; and a few other items whose character will become clear as we proceed.

The mechanisms that GPS uses to process this information in order to solve the problem are quite simple. The basic problem-solving heuristic it employs is means-ends analysis, which may be described roughly as in Figure 9.

To solve the problem of changing initial object I into goal object G, compare I with G to detect a difference, D; find in memory an operator, O, that is relevant to reducing differences of the type of D; apply the operator to produce new object I'; repeat with I' and G.

Thus the central processes in GPS are the procedure that matches two objects to discover differences between them, and the operators, each of which is associated with the difference or differences to which it is relevant. The table of connections between differences and operators may be thought of

A heavy father and two young sons have to cross a swift river in a deep wood. They find an abandoned boat, which can be rowed across, but which sinks if overloaded. Each young son is 100 pounds. A double-weight son is just as heavy as the father and more than that is too much for the boat. How do the father and the sons cross the river?

```
DECLARE      (
  BOAT = ATTRIBUTE
  D-L = FEATURE
  D-R = FEATURE
  FATHERS = ATTRIBUTE
  FINAL-OBJ = OBJECT-SCHEMA
  FROM-SIDE = LOC-PROG
  F-L = FEATURE
  F-R = FEATURE
  INITIAL-OBJ = OBJECT-SCHEMA
  SAIL = MOVE-OPERATOR
  SONS = ATTRIBUTE
  SIDES = SET
  S-L = FEATURE
  S-R = FEATURE
  TO-SIDE = LOC-PROG
  WEIGHT = EXPRES
  0-1 = SET
  0-1-2 = SET
  1-2 = SET
                  )
```

TASK-STRUCTURES
  TOP-GOAL = (TRANSFORM THE INITIAL-OBJ INTO THE FINAL-OBJ .)
  INITIAL-OBJ = (LEFT (SONS 2 FATHERS 1 BOAT BOAT)
                        RIGHT (SONS 0 FATHERS 0))
  FINAL-OBJ = (LEFT (SONS 0 FATHERS 0)
                     RIGHT (FATHERS 1 SONS 2 BOAT BOAT))
  WEIGHT = $(X + X + Y)$
  SAIL = S SAIL THE BOAT FROM THE FROM-SIDE TO THE TO-SIDE
         WITH X FATHERS AND Y SONS IN IT . S
         (CREATION-OPERATOR
           VAR-DOMAIN
           1. THE FROM-SIDE IS AN EXCLUSIVE-MEMBER OF THE
               SIDES .
           2. THE TO-SIDE IS AN EXCLUSIVE-MEMBER OF THE SIDES .
           3. X IS A CONSTRAINED-MEMBER OF 0-1 . THE CONSTRAINT
               IS THAT THE WEIGHT IS IN-THE-SET 1-2 .
           4. Y IS A CONSTRAINED-MEMBER OF 0-1-2 . THE
               CONSTRAINT IS THAT THE WEIGHT IS IN-THE-SET 1-2 .
           MOVES
           1. MOVE THE BOAT AT THE FROM-SIDE TO THE BOAT AT
               THE TO-SIDE .
           2. DECREASE BY THE AMOUNT X THE FATHERS AT THE
               FROM-SIDE AND ADD IT TO THE FATHERS AT THE TO-
               SIDE .

    3. DECREASE BY THE AMOUNT Y THE SONS AT THE FROM-
        SIDE AND ADD IT TO THE SONS AT THE TO-SIDE .)

```
SIDES = ( LEFT RIGHT )
0-1 = ( 0 1 )
0-1-2 = ( 0 1 2 )
1-2 = ( 1 2 )
S-L = ( THE SONS AT THE LEFT )
S-R = ( THE SONS AT THE RIGHT )
F-L = ( THE FATHERS AT THE LEFT )
F-R = ( THE FATHERS AT THE RIGHT )
D-L = ( THE BOAT AT THE LEFT )
D-R = ( THE BOAT AT THE RIGHT )
BASIC-MATCH = ( COMP-FEAT-LIST ( F-R S-R D-R ) )
COMP-OBJECTS = ( BASIC-MATCH )
DIFF-ORDERING = ( 1. ( F-L F-R )
                  2. ( S-L S-R )
                  3. ( D-L D-R ) )
TABLE-OF-CONNECTIONS = ( ( COMMON-DIFFERENCE SAIL ) )
LIST-OF-VAR = ( FROM-SIDE TO-SIDE X Y )
OBJ-ATTRIB = ( FATHERS SONS BOAT )
END
```

FIGURE 8.
Input required to specify father and sons task to GPS
(See Newell & Simon, 1972, Fig. 14.9).

as a set of S-R connections or, alternatively, as a production system depictable as $D_i \longrightarrow O_j$—read "if difference i is detected, then apply operator j."

For reasons that have already been made clear, a particular version of GPS cannot be expected to explain in detail the behavior of a whole range of subjects over a whole range of tasks. Rather, to take GPS as a theory of human problem-solving behavior might mean (a) that by making relatively minor adaptations in the program, it could be made to fit a range of behavior over tasks and subjects, or (b) that a large part of the contents of subjects' PBGs in problem-solving situations can be accounted for by GPS-like mechanisms—for example, applications of some form of means-ends analysis.

GPS(situation, goal-situation)
    difference new $\longrightarrow$
        find-operator(difference) ($\Longrightarrow$ operator new)
    operator new, situation $\longrightarrow$
        apply-operator(situation) ($\Longrightarrow$ situation new)
    situation new $\longrightarrow$
        find-difference(situation, goal-situation)
            ($\Longrightarrow$ difference new)

FIGURE 9.
Simplified description of GPS.

Both methods of application of GPS to empirical data have been attempted with some success.

The most extensive empirical testing of GPS has been in the environment of a task invented by O. K. Moore and Scarvia Anderson in which subjects 'recode' certain strings of symbols. The task is formally equivalent to the inductive task of discovering proofs for theorems in the logic of Whitehead and Russell. Several versions of GPS have been fitted successfully to segments of thinking-aloud protocols, and a more global analysis of protocols from seven different subjects on one problem shows that a large part of their behavior consists of means-ends analysis and other GPS-like processes. Finally, comparison of the search trees of these subjects with those of 64 other subjects who were working without thinking-aloud instructions showed that both sets of subjects explored essentially the same parts of the task environment in their searches for problem solutions. As in the case of the cryptarithmetic tasks, substantially all subjects worked in nearly the same problem space in the logic task; differences in their representation of the problem were sufficiently subtle to make difficult the explanation of differences in their success in solving the problems.

Summary

The account provided here of the cryptarithmetic and logic tasks gives a sampling of the present state of information-processing theory of these problem-solving phenomena (see Newell & Simon, 1972, Ch. 14). In summary, the evidence suggests that it is possible to describe the problem solver as working in a problem space; that the nature of the problem space can be determined from analysis of thinking-aloud protocols, problem-behavior graphs derived from them, and summaries of those graphs; that the problem spaces of subjects drawn from the same population are closely similar; that the programs of subjects solving these problems can be described as production systems; and that much of the behavior has a GPS-like character, with considerable prominence of means-ends analysis.

The behavior examined in the two previous sections was that of relatively naive subjects—none of the subjects had had any great previous familiarity with the task or any proficiency in it. In a third task that has been studied intensively—chess—there are enormous differences in previous experience among subjects (see Newell & Simon, 1972, Chs. 11–13; de Groot, 1965). Chess-playing behavior has been studied with subjects who range in skill and experience all the way from tyros to grandmasters, including some former world champions. The differences between the programs of skilled and unskilled players are enormous, but lie primarily in the chess-specific content of the productions available to them rather than in program organization. Expert chess players are able to detect a considerable number of features (equivalent to differences) when these occur in a position, and have stored a great deal of information as to what moves to consider when particular kinds of features are present. Using this information to guide their searches, they are able to find strong moves with about the same amount of search that weak players use to find poor moves.

From the evidence of chess, we see again that we must not expect program invariance over tasks or over individuals. The programs of chess masters differ vastly from the programs of ordinary players, and they differ specifically with respect to their chess content. If invariants are to be found, they must lie in broader characteristics of program organization, such as the means-ends analysis structure in GPS. This does not mean that our explanations of behavior must be limited to these invariants. On the contrary, we have seen that it is possible to write quite detailed programs to explain the behavior of individual subjects in specific task environments.

PERCEPTUAL AND LEARNING PROCESSES IN THINKING

The explanations of problem solving that have been achieved through protocol analysis, programs written in information-processing languages, and simulation are circumscribed in several important ways. First, they take the subject's problem space as a given, a boundary condition for the prediction of his behavior, and not as a datum to be explained. Very little is known as yet about how humans acquire the problem spaces they use to solve problems—either when they are operating in a novel task environment with the task instructions as their only initial source of information, or when they have gradually accumulated experience in the task environment over a period of hours, weeks, or years.

A second limitation of the theories is that they say only a little about the detail of the processing at the level of short-term memory organization or elementary perceptual processes. The operations postulated in the problem-solving models typically require several seconds for their execution—residence times in the observed knowledge states range from 2 to 8 secs in the protocols that have been analyzed. These are composite processes, themselves made up of more elementary processes. In this section we consider a second class of tasks where it has been possible to learn something about some of the more elementary processes that are implicated in thinking.

Elementary Perceiver and Memorizer (EPAM)

About 1958, Feigenbaum constructed an information-processing theory (EPAM) of the processes involved in learning in the standard laboratory verbal-learning paradigms: paired associate and serial learning of nonsense materials by the anticipation method. EPAM lies closer to the traditions of experimental psychology than does GPS, both because it constitutes a theory of a set of phenomena that have been studied extensively in innumerable psychological laboratories, and because it has been tested, for the most part, by numerical comparison with standard experimental data from groups of subjects rather than by the techniques of protocol analysis.[4]

Figures 10 through 13 give programs for EPAM and its main components. The executive program, which provides for the execution of the subject's processes in parallel with the experimenter's processes (the turning of the memory drum) is not shown, but corresponds to the normal laboratory procedure for verbal-learning experiments (in paired-associate or serial-anticipation paradigms, as the case may be).

The subject-strategy program (Fig. 10) is specific to the paired-associate paradigm, of course. A different strategy, making use of the same component processes, would have to be postulated for an experiment with the serial-anticipation paradigm. Moreover, variations might be anticipated in the subject-strategy program as a function of individual differences, or of experimental instructions that affected subjects' attentional strategies. The strategy shown here is the one that has been used in the successful simulation of a number of paired-associate experiments, to be described below.

```
paired-associate-executive (list-of-pairs)
        test drum-cycle-phase (⟹ phase)
        phase = stimulus-phase  ⟶
                respond (stimulus) (⟹ response)
                store response in STM  ⟶
        last-response ∈ STM  ⟶
                last-response = correct response  ⟶ exit
                learn (S-R), exit
        learn (response)*, exit
```

* 'learn (response)' means to familiarize or 'chunk' that response, not to learn its connection with the stimulus [which is 'learn (S-R)'].

FIGURE 10.
Paired-associate subject strategy for EPAM.

---

[4] This discussion of EPAM is based upon Feigenbaum (1961); Feigenbaum and Simon (1962); Simon and Feigenbaum (1964); and Gregg and Simon (1967b).

```
respond (stimulus)
      recognize (stimulus) (⟹ stimulus-image)
            not-recognized ⟶ learn (stimulus), exit.
      construct-pair (stimulus) (⟹ S-∗)
      recognize (S-∗) (⟹ S-∗-image)
            not-recognized ⟶ learn (S-∗), exit.
      find-second-element (S-∗-image) (⟹ response)
      externalize (response), exit.
```

FIGURE 11.
Response process for EPAM.

The subject strategy program uses several subprocesses, of which the principal two are *respond* and *learn*. The *respond* process is shown in Figure 11, and the *learn* process in Figure 12. Both of these make use of the *recognize* process, which is shown in Figure 13. *Recognize* operates on a structure, the

```
learn (structure)
      recognize (structure) (⟹ image)
            not-recognized ⟶ create-image, exit.
      image ∈ structure ⟶ add detail of
            structure to image, exit.
      list differences (image, structure) (⟹ differences)
      create-and-append-subnet (differences), exit.
```

FIGURE 12.
Learning process for EPAM.

EPAM net, which represents in the simulation the information stored in the subject's LTM. The EPAM net (Fig. 14) is a hierarchy of nodes connected by links. To each node is linked a *test*. Application of the test to a stimulus selects a particular link that leads to a next node down the hierarchy. Thus

```
recognize (word)
      find first-node (net) (⟹ node)
            fail ⟶ report not-recognized, exit.
1   find test (node)
            fail ⟶ report not-recognized, exit.
      apply test (node, word) (⟹ test-result)
      find node (test-result) (⟹ new node)
            fail ⟶ report not-recognized, exit.
      find terminal (new-node) (⟹ image)
            fail ⟶ node ⟵ new-node, goto 1
      report image, exit.
```

FIGURE 13.
Recognition process for EPAM.

the net can be represented as a description-list structure: with each node (object) is associated a number of other nodes (values), each by a distinct

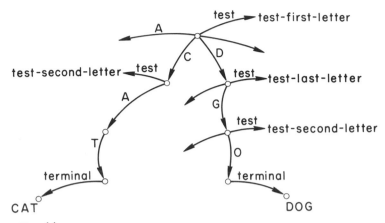

FIGURE 14.
Fragment of discrimination net (from Newell & Simon, 1972, Fig. 2.9).

link (attribute). The test at a node is also stored as the value of the attribute *test*.

With this mechanism, recognizing a stimulus consists in sorting it down this hierarchical structure by applying to it the series of tests stored at the nodes that are reached. (Apply the process of Fig. 13 to the net of Fig. 14.) At the end of this twenty-questions process, a terminal node is an image of the stimulus—that is, more or less complete information about its characteristics. (It may require only very incomplete information about the stimulus to sort it down to its terminal node.) If the image at a node is sufficiently complete, then it can be used by the *response* process (see Fig. 11) to produce a response.

EPAM learns new stimuli, and stimulus-response pairs, by 'growing' or expanding the net under control of the *learn* process. Learning a stimulus consists in (a) elaborating the net so that the test nodes will now discriminate between that stimulus and other stimuli, and (b) storing image information at the terminal node for the stimulus. Learning a stimulus-response pair consists in elaborating the net to discriminate between a pair with that particular stimulus and a pair with different stimuli, and in storing at the appropriate terminal node an image, more or less complete, of the stimulus-response pair. The details of these net-building processes ('add detail of structure to image' and 'create and append subnet') are not shown in the figures, but they are straightforward list-processing routines.

A survey of published experiments on verbal learning shows that a relatively small set of variables produce large effects on the rate of learning. The most powerful are the levels of meaningfulness and familiarity of the stimuli, and the amount of similarity among them. The EPAM theory has done a generally good job of accounting for the following phenomena.

1.   The effects of meaningfulness and similarity of stimulus and response syllables upon rate of learning (Simon & Feigenbaum, 1964). Maximum effects of about 2.5 to 1 in learning time can be obtained between hardest-to-learn and easiest-to-learn materials. EPAM predicts differences of this same magnitude (Table 2).

TABLE 2
Effects of familiarization and meaningfulness

Meaningfulness[c] (or familiarity)	Chenzoff's (1962) data[a]				EPAM[b]	
	(1) High meaning-fulness	(2) High familiar-ization	(3) Low meaning-fulness	(4) No familiar-ization	(5) No previous familiar-ization	(6) Previous familiar-ization
H-H or F-F	1.0	1.0	1.0	1.0	1.0	1.0
L-H or U-F	1.0	1.1	1.2	1.2	1.3	1.0
H-L or F-U	1.0	1.2	1.6	1.2	1.8	1.5
L-L or U-U	1.0	1.2	1.8	2.2	2.5	1.7

Note: From Simon and Feigenbaum (1964).
[a] Reciprocal of number of correct responses; H-H or F-F = 1.0.
[b] Relative number of errors to criterion; H-H or F-F = 1.0.
[c] H = High meaningful; L = Low meaningful; F = Familiar; U = Unfamiliar.

2.   The effects of intralist stimulus-item similarity and intralist response-item similarity (Simon & Feigenbaum, 1964). EPAM predicts the approximate magnitude of the observed effects, and predicts, correctly, a greater effect of similarity for materials of low than for materials of high familiarity or meaningfulness (Table 3).

TABLE 3
Comparison of EPAM with Underwood's (1953) data on intralist similarity

Data	Condition of stimulus and response similarity				
	L-L	L-M	M-L	L-H	H-L
Underwood	100	96	109	104	131
EPAM ("visual only")	100	88	141	91	146
EPAM ("aural only")	100	100	100	100	114
EPAM ("visual" and "aural" mixed, 1:1)	100	94	121	96	130
EPAM ("visual" and "aural" mixed, 1:2)	100	96	114	97	125

Note: From Simon and Feigenbaum (1964). Relative number of trials to criterion. L-L = 100.

3.   The conditions for one-trial learning versus the conditions for incremental learning (Gregg & Simon, 1967b). EPAM predicts correctly that one-trial learning will be observed principally when stimuli and responses are already highly familiarized, and when the drum-turn speed is low (Table 4).

TABLE 4
Comparison of EPAM learning rates with human rates

Rates	Experimental conditions							
	One-at-a-time				All-at-once			
	Fast		Slow		Fast		Slow	
	N	R	N	R	N	R	N	R
EPAM[a] (1/errors)	43	39	116	71	49	20[b]	84	44
EPAM[a] (1/trials)	50	38	114	69	69	19[b]	86	50
Human Ss[a]	69[c]	45	100[c]	67	69[c]	19	100[c]	32

Note: From Gregg and Simon (1967b).
[a] Entries in the EPAM rows are the reciprocals of the numbers of errors and numbers of trials, whereas the entries in the last row are numbers of correct responses on the tenth trial, both expressed as ratios to the average of the SNO and SNA conditions.
[b] List not learned in 11 trials. Learning rate estimated.
[c] In the N conditions, there was no difference in the learning rates of O and A Ss. The rates used here are those for the entire group of 20 Ss in each condition.

Under other conditions, learning will be incremental. The theory also shows how subject strategies can affect the extent of one-trial learning.

4.   The independence of learning time from memory-drum speed (Feigenbaum, 1961). EPAM predicts correctly that, within moderate ranges of variation of the stimulus and response exposure intervals, the number of trials to criterion will vary approximately inversely with exposure interval, and hence the total *time* to criterion will be nearly independent of exposure interval.

5.   An EPAM serial-anticipation strategy program predicts the shape of the serial position curve, with good quantitative agreement with experimental data (Feigenbaum & Simon, 1962). Since the program is a function of subject strategy, it also provides an explanation of the way in which manipulation of the experimental materials or instructions can produce the von Restorff effect or other modifications in the shape of the serial-position curve.

The dependence of the performance of EPAM on the subject-strategy program (see particularly points 3 and 5, above) has considerable methodological significance. It warns us that such commonly observed phenomena as the typical serial-position curve cannot be regarded as an invariant 'law of nature' (see Vitz & Todd, 1969), but rather as a consequence of the particular attentional strategies that subjects employ in performing the experimental task. Although these strategies may not be indefinitely malleable—or even consciously malleable—they are not necessarily the same in all subjects, nor fixed once and for all. Hence, the observation of a regularity like the serial-position curve is to be interpreted 'sociologically'—i.e., as a generalization about typical attention strategies among American college sophomores (or whatever is the population from which subjects have been drawn), and not necessarily as a physiological invariant. We have seen earlier that a similar caution must be observed in interpreting the findings of concept-attainment experiments, where the rates of learning typically depend on subject strategies for storing information.

Perception in Chess

As information-processing theories of cognitive process are extended to new task environments, we would expect and hope that a commonality of mechanisms would begin to emerge among these programs. It would be a suspicious circumstance if it proved necessary to invent as many new fundamental mechanisms as there were phenomena to be explained, and the explanations, under these circumstances, would be ad hoc and unconvincing. In this section, we sketch out a sequence of researches that has shown how mechanisms drawn from the previous work on problem solving and perception can be organized to explain a new range of phenomena of a perceptual kind in the task environment of chess.

Baylor and Simon (1966) constructed a special-purpose chess-playing program that was particularly powerful in discovering checkmating combinations. This program, which exists in a number of versions and whose generic name is MATER, organizes its problem solving as heuristic tree search. Like some earlier chess programs, particularly the Newell-Shaw-Simon (1958) program, MATER embodies 'perceptual' processes for discovering meaningful relations, of attack, defense, and so on, among the pieces on the board. The presence and locations of these relations were used to generate plausible moves, thence to guide the selective search, and were crucial to MATER's performance. Thus, MATER, presented with a chess position, notices and remembers which pieces attack which pieces, which pieces defend which pieces, and the like, and is therefore not limited to proceeding by blind search of all legal moves on the board.

Simon and Barenfeld (1969) used the mechanisms of MATER to explain and simulate the eye movements of an expert chess player when confronted with a position and instructed to find the best move. Their program (PERCEIVER) postulated that the player would fixate his eyes on important pieces on the board, would notice in peripheral vision the attack, defense, and other meaningful relations between the piece fixated and other pieces, and would shift his fixation by a saccade to one of the pieces so related. Thus, attention would be driven around the board in a succession of saccades by the perception of elementary chess relations between pieces. Simon and Barenfeld showed that a program of this kind would exhibit eye movements of the same kind as those observed in human subjects by Tichomirov and Poznyanskaya (1966) and other investigators.

Chase and Simon (1973), examining the remarkable ability of chess masters to reproduce correctly positions that they have seen for only 5 or 10 secs, provided evidence that the superior ability of the master was due, at least in considerable part, to the availability in his long-term memory of large numbers of familiar subpatterns of pieces that recur frequently in game positions. That is to say, the master could be supposed to have in long-term memory a large EPAM net of such subpatterns, which would be recognized when seen as components of an actual chess position, and which could be stored as chunks in short-term memory. If the beginner's short-term memory chunks were individual pieces, while the master's were constellations averaging four or five pieces each, then the master, with the same chunk limit on short-term memory as the beginner, would be able to remember and recall the locations of four or five times as many pieces.

Simon and Gilmartin (1973) tested this hypothesis by building a simulation program, MAPP, that combines the perceptual capabilities of the PER-CEIVER program with the learning and memory capabilities of EPAM (Fig. 15). They showed that this program, with a net of about 1,000 stored subpatterns, was slightly superior to a Class A player in ability to reproduce a briefly exposed position; and they estimated, by extrapolation, that a net of perhaps 50,000 patterns would bring the program up to a master's level of performance. This estimate is in agreement with estimates arrived at earlier by Simon and Barenfeld (1969).

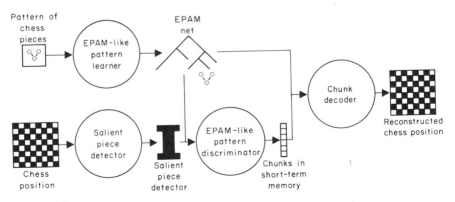

FIGURE 15.
Principal processes of MAPP. The learning component is shown in the upper half of the figure; the three parts of the performance component are in the lower half (from Simon & Gilmartin, 1973).

The sequence of programs running from the Newell-Shaw-Simon chess program and EPAM through MATER, PERCEIVER, and MAPP illustrates how the scope of an information-processing theory can be extended far beyond the initial domain of application, by making consistent use of a small number of basic perceptual, problem-solving, and attention-directing mechanisms.

RULE INDUCTION

In addition to the task environments discussed so far, one other kind of task has received considerable attention in terms of the information-processing languages and simulation techniques: the discovery and extrapolation of serial patterns. Here, more or less independent efforts by Feldman (1961), Glanzer and Clark (1962), Restle (1967), and Vitz and Todd (1969) in binary choice tasks, Laughery and Gregg (1962) in a multiple-switch-setting task, and Simon and Kotovsky (1963) studying the Thurstone Letter Series Completion Test converged on a common set of mechanisms to explain human capabilities in these tasks (Simon, 1972).

Sequence Extrapolation Tasks

The basic performance requirements for all these tasks are the abilities to detect and represent the relation of identity between symbols (e.g., to detect and remember that two Ms are the same), and to notice the successor relation between successive symbols on a well-learned list or 'alphabet' (e.g., to notice the successor relation between F and G in the English alphabet, or between 7 and 8 in the list of integers). Using a same and a next relation for identity and succession, respectively, the pattern implicit in each sequence can then be represented by a symbol structure in a space of patterns.

Consider, for example, how the sequence, ABMCDMEFM . . . , may be represented in such a pattern space. In the IPS, a working memory, call it w, contains the name of an alphabet and a pointer to a particular location of the alphabet. Using this idea, with E as the name of the English alphabet, s denoting 'same,' n denoting 'next,' and $*$ the iteration operator, we can notate the pattern of the sequence above by:

$$(w \longleftarrow E)(n(w)n(w)M)*,$$

which can be read: "Set the pointer in w to the name of the English alphabet, E. Move the pointer one place down the alphabet (i.e., to $n(E) = A$), then one more place (i.e., to $n(A) = B$; then produce the letter M; and repeat these three processes indefinitely."

Simon and Kotovsky (1963) wrote a pair of programs for an IPS, the first of which discovers, in the space of patterns, a pattern representing a given sequence, and the second of which uses the pattern to extrapolate the sequences. There is substantial empirical evidence that these programs simulate closely the information processes used by human subjects in the Thurstone Letter Series Completion task (Kotovsky & Simon, 1973), and that similar programs can account for performance in the other tasks mentioned above.

A Generalized Approach to Rule Induction

If we abstract from the specific content of the series extrapolation tasks, and view them from a slightly more general viewpoint, we see that they can be characterized in information-processing terms as follows: (a) there is a space of *instances*—the successive symbols of the sequence; (b) there is a second space of *rules*—of possible patterns to represent sequences; (c) the problem-solving task is to search in the space of rules for a particular rule that represents a given set of instances—a given sequence.

This way of describing matters generalizes the theory in two important directions. First, it equates the sequence-extrapolation task with other cognitive tasks that involve inducing a general rule or pattern from instances. In particular, the characterization of the task just given fits equally well the concept-attainment task analyzed in an earlier section of this chapter. The space of rules in that case was simply the space of possible concepts. The characterization also fits such tasks as inducing a grammar from a set of sentences and nonsentences in a language. Here, the space of rules is the space of possible grammars, and the space of instances is the space of strings classified as sentences or nonsentences.

At about the same level of generality as the General Problem Solver, we can describe an executive program for a General Rule Inducer (GRI) that is applicable over the whole range of rule-induction tasks. The program is given in Figure 16. It consists mainly of some generators and tests of sorts that are

General Rule Inducer:
1 Modify rules ($\Rightarrow$ rule);
2 generate instance ($\Rightarrow$ instance);
    predict status of instance ($\Rightarrow$ predicted-status)
    if predicted-status = actual-status,
       if finished, exit,
       goto 2;
    goto 1.

FIGURE 16.
Executive program for a general
rule inducer.

familiar from IPSs designed for problem-solving tasks: a rule generate (called 'modify rules' to indicate its possibly incremental character), an instance generator, and a two-part rule test comprised of a process for predicting instances from the rules, and a second process for checking the prediction.

Rule Induction and Problem Solving

This brings us to the second generalization: the close parallelism between rule-induction tasks and the kinds of tasks usually referred to as 'problem solving.' These have generally been treated quite separately in the psychological literature. Yet we see from the above account that rule induction can be described as problem solving that has two special earmarks. First, two problem spaces are involved (the spaces of rules and instances, respectively), the search taking place in one of these—the rule space—and the checking of the outcome in the other. Second, a process must be available that connects the objects in the two spaces—in particular that uses rules to generate instances or to classify purported instances as conforming or not conforming to the rule. Formalizing the theories of problem solving and of rule induction by expressing them as programs in an information-processing language reveals this mapping between the two domains.

Returning now to the program exhibited in Figure 16, we can state more specifically how it is specialized to particular classes of tasks like concept attainment, or sequence extrapolation. If we refer back to the concept-attainment program described earlier, we see that, with minor changes in organization, it can be mapped directly on the program of Figure 16. Process S2 (containing S5 as a subprocess) generates the rules, or hypotheses; process E1 (containing E3 and E4) generates the instances; process S1 uses the current hypothesis to predict whether the current instance does or does not fit the concept; while process E2 checks the prediction and informs the problem solver of the outcome. Notice (a common but not essential characteristic of rule induction processes) that the hypothesis generator may use the information from the instances to enhance its selectivity. In those forms of the concept-attainment experiment where the subject selects the instances, information may flow in the opposite direction as well: the particular instances constructed may depend on the current hypothesis that is held (Simon & Lea, unpublished).

The application of the program of Figure 16 to the sequence extrapolation task may be described as follows. The rule generator uses information obtained by comparing pairs of instances (pairs of symbols in the sequence) to detect possible relations for incorporation. In most forms of the task, the entire set of instances is generated once and for all by the experimenter, but instances are sometimes presented to the subject one by one, in analogy with the concept-attainment task. Rule components are used to predict other instances—subsequent symbols in the sequence—and an identity match between predicted and actual symbol tests the prediction.

Finally, the same executive has been used to organize a program for inducing grammars (Simon & Lea, unpublished). The problem solver gradually assembles a set of grammar rules (rule generator). He uses these to generate sentences (combined predictor and instance generator). A 'native informant'—the experimenter—states whether or not each sentence is grammatical (test of prediction).

We must mention an important difference between the GRI program described in Figure 16 and a general problem-solving program like GPS. The information that must be supplied to GPS to implement it for any particular task domain consists mostly of descriptions of the objects and operators involved. It is mostly in the form of data rather than program, although some program elements (e.g., a match process) must usually be provided. To implement GRI, on the other hand, specific subroutines, adapted to the task environment, must be provided to execute the processes (generate, test, etc.) named in the executive program. This difference between the two programs has wide implications for the nature of generality in cognitive performance, but we cannot pursue this topic here (see Newell & Simon, 1972, pp. 852–860).

INTERNAL REPRESENTATION AND SEMANTICS

From this brief survey of some extant information-processing theories and their associated computer programs it appears that the greatest progress has been made in accounting for problem solving in well-structured task environments, for simple concept attainment, for certain perceptual performances, and for pattern discovery. Other cognitive domains have been explored only to a modest extent. Among these are (a) problem solving in vaguely defined, poorly structured tasks; (b) the processes for acquiring a problem space and program when a new task is encountered; (c) the ways in which tasks are represented internally, in memory, for purposes of processing; in particular, the nature of visual imagery as a form of representation; and (d) the 'interface' between natural-language processing and other cognitive processing, and particularly, the ways in which meaning is extracted from information presented in natural language.

These four domains are closely related, one to the others. If we knew how problem spaces and programs were acquired in new tasks, we would at the same time know a great deal about the internal representations used for these problem spaces and programs. Moreover, dealing with a poorly defined problem very likely *is* simply a task of better defining that problem—i.e., acquiring a problem space and program for it. Further, problems are frequently specified for humans in whole or part in natural language. Hence, an initial problem in dealing with a new task is to extract meaning from the natural-language statement of the task. Finally, information about problems comes in the form of visual stimuli, and visual imagery is to be understood as an important special aspect of internal representation.

Human Simulations

Information-processing programs explicitly designed to simulate these aspects of human performance are still exceedingly rare. One exception is a program by Baylor (1971) dealing with a visual-processing task. A typical task is the following:

> One side of a 3-inch cube is painted blue. Two sides of the cube, opposite to each other but adjacent to the blue side, are painted red. The cube is now diced into 27 1-inch cubes. How many of the 1-inch cubes have exactly one blue and one red side?

Subjects uniformly report that they image the cube in order to solve the problem. Baylor constructed a simulation program to specify what this imaging consisted of, and compared the behavior of his program, with some success, with a human protocol.

Of course the programs for chess perception discussed earlier also have an internal representation of the chessboard, which may be regarded as a visual image. However, these chess programs were generally not concerned with the exact internal representation of the whole board, since an actual board (with or without pieces on it) was within range of the subject's vision during the tasks which these programs simulated. Baylor, on the other hand, had to face the problem of how the information was represented internally, since there was no external—even partial—representation available to the subject; the visual image had to be generated from the natural-language description of the problem.

We cannot describe the detail of Baylor's representation here, beyond noting that it was fabricated from list structures of the same kind that have been employed in the other programs we have discussed. These relational structures proved adequate, in this instance also, to account for the processing the subject was able to carry out on the internal image.

Another program that deals with internal representation is Quillian's (1968) hypothesized organization of long-term memory as an associational net. This program stores in an associate memory a set of dictionary definitions of words. The system's processes allow association from each word to its definition, to the terms occurring in that definition, to the definitions of those terms, and so on. Collins and Quillian (1969) showed that certain data on latencies in recall tasks could be explained by a net with this organization.

Other closely similar schemes for representation of long-term memory have been developed, or are in process of development, by Anderson (1972) and Rumelhart, Lindsay, and Norman (1972). All of these schemes are based on essentially the same fundamental list-processing mechanisms for assembling associational structures—that is to say, upon lists and description lists. A list is an ordered set; a description list (or property list) is a list of asymmetrical two-termed relations. The EPAM discrimination net depicted in Figure 14 is a typical example of a structure based on description lists. With each node is associated a list of attribute-value pairs. The first attribute of every node is 'test,' and its value is the name of the test to be performed at that node. The remaining attributes are the various possible outcomes of the test; their values are the names of the nodes associated with those outcomes.

The stimulus-response pair is a familiar example of a (two-element) list from stimulus-response psychology; descriptions first appeared in the psychological literature as the 'directed associations' of the Würzberg School. The main accomplishment of work on semantic memory organization to date has been the demonstration that memories assembled out of these elementary kinds of associational structures appear to have the general characteristics needed to account for the associational properties of human memory. (See also Newell & Simon, 1963; 1972, pp. 23–28.)

Artificial Intelligence

While detailed simulations of the psychology of representation and semantic processes are still uncommon, considerable progress has been made toward building artificial intelligence systems that handle a number of aspects of semantic meaning and natural-language processing. An early example was Lindsay's (1963) SAD-SAM program. A substantial number of more recent examples are collected by Minsky (1969) and Simon and Siklóssy (1972). Included among these examples are a program for doing algebra story problems (Bobrow), a program for everyday inference (Raphael), a program for doing figural analogies (Evans), a program for scene analysis (Guzman), a program that programs itself to take an intelligence test from worked-out examples of test items (D. Williams), a programming language for playing games which requires as its input a set of information approximately equivalent to that provided by Hoyle (T. Williams), a program for using semantic (visual) information to remove syntactic ambiguity from natural-language sentences (Coles), and a program that uses semantic (visual) information to learn a language (Siklóssy).

None of these programs was designed to simulate human performance; nevertheless, because their designers undoubtedly drew heavily upon their introspection and upon data from psychology for ideas about the heuristics that might be effective, it is not unreasonable to refer to the programs as sources of hypotheses about the corresponding human processing systems. The semantic information-processing programs provide a base for the next stage in psychological research on representation, meaning, natural-language processing, and image processing comparable to the basis provided a decade or two ago for research on human problem solving by the early artificial-intelligence heuristic problem-solving programs.

One highly interesting artificial intelligence program of this kind has been described recently by Winograd (1972). The 'world' on which this program operates is a simulated toy world consisting of a set of blocks upon a table. The program has capabilities for interpreting natural-language queries and commands relating to this world, and inference capabilities for drawing out the consequences of its information. It can, for example, be queried about the presence or absence of certain kinds of objects, or the number of them. It can also be commanded to move objects about its toy world. In performing these tasks, it parses natural-language input (using a systemic grammar), and solves subproblems that are raised in the course of trying to perform the tasks given it.

Thus the Winograd system gives us a coherent survey of the present state of the art of semantic processing, and shows how a variety of component processes and mechanisms that have been developed to handle more specialized tasks can be combined coherently into a relatively intelligent and powerful language-understanding and problem-solving system.

CONCLUSION

In this chapter we have sought to describe the techniques for expressing and testing psychological theories in information-processing languages, and the progress that has been made in explaining significant areas of cognitive behavior in these terms. We have compared the information-processing formalism with stochastic models in the task environment of simple concept attainment, and we have described briefly some of the principal information-processing theories that have been constructed to explain problem-solving processes (GPS), verbal-learning processes (EPAM), perceptual processes in chess (MATER, PERCEIVER, and MAPP), rule-induction processes, and a variety of other processes. We have sketched out and illustrated, also, the kinds of evidence that have been used to test these theories, and the techniques for acquiring and analyzing the evidence.

From the examples of programs provided here, the reader can obtain some feeling for the information-processing formalism. In one sense, it has a very 'informal' appearance about it. In a programming language that permits closed subroutines, any process, no matter how complex, can be given a name, and thenceforth can be called by any other process simply by mentioning that name. If the language allows a free choice of names, and if that choice is exercised by naming processes mnemonically, the resulting programs can be 'read' almost as if they were written in a natural language. This appearance should not deceive anyone about the formalism, for it *is* a formalism. By defining each process down to the level of the elementary information processes defined in the underlying programming language, the program is specified precisely so that it can be run on a digital computer, and used to simulate behavior in the task environment of interest. In the examples of the formalism provided in this chapter, we have not generally carried the definitions down to that level of detail, and to that extent the theories we have presented are only incompletely specified here. However, all of them have actually been programmed and run to test the completeness of the specification, and provide detailed data for comparison with the performance of human subjects in the same tasks.

The information-processing formalisms have permitted areas of complex human behavior to be explored at a level of rigor previously reserved for extremely simple processes. They have provided us with the technical means to create a 'mental chemistry' of cognitive processes, and they have already served to extend that mental chemistry to a significant range of task environments.

ACKNOWLEDGMENT

This study was supported by Public Health Service research grant MH-07722 from the National Institute of Mental Health.

REFERENCES

Anderson, J. R. FRAN: A simulation model of free recall. In G. H. Bower (Ed.), *The psychology of learning and motivation.* Vol. 5. New York: Academic Press, 1972.

Baylor, G. W., Jr. Program and protocol analysis on a mental imagery task. Second International Conference on Artificial Intelligence. *British Computer Society*, September 1971.

Baylor, G. W., Jr., & Simon, H. A. A chess mating combinations program. *AFIPS conference proceedings 1966 spring joint computer conference*. Washington, D.C.: Spartan Books, 1966.

Bower, G. H., & Trabasso, T. R. Concept identification. In R. C. Atkinson (Ed.), *Studies in mathematical psychology*. Stanford: Stanford University Press, 1964.

Chase, W. G., & Simon, H. A. The mind's eye in chess. In W. G. Chase (Ed.), *Visual information processing*. Proceedings of the Eighth Annual Carnegie Psychology Symposium. New York: Academic Press, 1973.

Chenzoff, A. P. The interaction of meaningfulness with S and R familiarization in paired-associate learning. Unpublished doctoral dissertation, Carnegie Institute of Technology, 1962.

Collins, A. M., & Quillian, M. R. Retrieval time from semantic memory. *Journal of Verbal Learning and Verbal Behavior*, 1969, **8**, 240–247.

de Groot, A. D. *Thought and choice in chess*. The Hague: Mouton, 1965.

Ernst, G. W., & Newell, A. *GPS: A case study in generality and problem solving*. New York: Academic Press, 1969.

Feigenbaum, E. A. The simulation of verbal learning behavior. *Proceedings of the Western Joint Computer Conference*, 1961, **19**, 121–132.

Feigenbaum, E. A., & Simon, H. A. A theory of the serial position effect. *British Journal of Psychology*, 1962, **53**, 307–320.

Feldman, J. Simulation of behavior in the binary choice experiment. *Proceedings of the Western Joint Computer Conference*, 1961, **19**, 133–144.

Glanzer, M. S., & Clark, H. H. Accuracy of perceptual recall: An analysis of organization. *Journal of Verbal Learning and Verbal Behavior*, 1962, **1**, 289–299.

Gregg, L. W., & Simon, H. A. Process models and stochastic theories of simple concept formation. *Journal of Mathematical Psychology*, 1967, **4**, 246–276. (a)

Gregg, L. W., & Simon, H. A. An information-processing explanation of one-trial and incremental learning. *Journal of Verbal Learning and Verbal Behavior*, 1967, **6**, 780–787. (b)

Kotovsky, K., & Simon, H. A. Empirical tests of a theory of human acquisition of concepts for sequential patterns. *Cognitive Psychology*, 1974, in press.

Laughery, K., & Gregg, L. W. Simulation of human problem solving behavior. *Psychometrica*, 1962, **27**, 265–282.

Lindsay, R. K. Inferential memory as the basis of machines which understand natural language. In E. A. Feigenbaum and J. Feldman (Eds.), *Computers and thought*. New York: McGraw-Hill, 1963.

Minsky, M. (Ed.). *Semantic information processing*. Cambridge, Mass.: M.I.T. Press, 1969.

Newell, A., Shaw, J. C., & Simon, H. A. Chess-playing programs and the problems of complexity. *IBM Journal of Research and Development*, 1958, **2**, 320–335.

Newell, A., & Simon, H. A. Computers in psychology. In R. D. Luce, R. R. Bush, and E. Galanter (Eds.), *Handbook of mathematical psychology*. Vol. 1. New York: Wiley, 1963.

Newell, A. & Simon, H. A. *Human problem solving*. Englewood Cliffs, N.J.: Prentice-Hall, 1972.

Quillian, M. R. Semantic memory. In M. Minsky (Ed.), *Semantic information processing*. Cambridge, Mass.: M.I.T. Press, 1968.

Restle, F. Grammatical analysis of the prediction of binary events. *Journal of Verbal Learning and Verbal Behavior*, 1967, **6**, 17–25.

Rumelhart, D. E., Lindsay, P. H., & Norman, D. A. A process model for long-term memory. In E. Tulving and W. Donaldson (Eds.), *Organization of memory*. New York: Academic Press, 1972.

Simon, H. A. Complexity and the representation of patterned sequences of symbols. *Psychological Review*, 1972, **79**, 369–382.

Simon, H. A., & Barenfeld, M. Information-processing analysis of perceptual processes in problem solving. *Psychological Review*, 1969, **76**, 473–483.

Simon, H. A., & Feigenbaum, E. A. An information-processing theory of some effects of similarity, familiarization, and meaningfulness in verbal learning. *Journal of Verbal Learning and Verbal Behavior*, 1964, **3**, 385–396.

Simon, H. A., & Gilmartin, K. A simulation of memory for chess positions. *Cognitive Psychology*, 1973, **5**, 29–46.

Simon, H. A., & Kotovsky, K. Human acquisition of concepts for sequential patterns. *Psychological Review*, 1963, **70**, 534–546.

Simon, H. A., & Siklóssy, L. (Eds.). *Representation and meaning*. Englewood Cliffs, N.J.: Prentice-Hall, 1972.

Simon, H. A., & Simon, P. A. Trial and error search in solving difficult problems: Evidence from the game of chess. *Behavioral Science*, 1962, **7**, 425–429.

Tichomirov, O. K., & Poznyanskaya, E. D. An investigation of visual search as a means of analyzing heuristics. *Soviet Psychology*, 1966, **5**, 2–15. (Translated from *Voprosy Pskihologii*, 1966, **2**, 39–53).

Underwood, B. J. Studies of distributed practice: VIII. Learning and retention of paired nonsense syllables as a function of intralist similarity. *Journal of Experimental Psychology*, 1953, **45**, 133–142.

Vitz, P. C., & Todd, R. C. A coded element model of the perceptual processing of sequential stimuli. *Psychological Review*, 1969, **76**, 433–449.

Winograd, T. Understanding natural language. *Cognitive Psychology*, 1972, **3**, 1–191.

Mathematical Psychology and Cognitive Phenomena: Comments on Preceding Chapters

Rachel Joffe Falmagne
CLARK UNIVERSITY

A number of issues have been raised at various times at the conference concerning this volume, regarding psychological relevance of findings, identity of mathematical psychology as a field, and strategical priorities between parsimony, generality of theories, and stress on explicitly derivable predictions. Such considerations are familiar to anyone working in the field, but their public emphasis in such a context is a relatively new and certainly significant social phenomenon. Concerns of this sort have also been expressed in a number of chapters in this volume and are central to the present comments, insofar as they relate to the various authors' arguments, to a current general set, and to my own concerns. This chapter has a nonlinear organization, as it deals with issues at various levels of specificity, at various distances from the authors' arguments, and at various degrees of subjectivity. Relevance and long-term strategies, however, are the central questions, especially in the context of the more 'cognitive' content area to which mathematical psychology has been applied.

TWO VIEWS ON RELEVANCE

Both Greeno (this vol.) and Simon and Newell (this vol.) emphasize the psychological relevance and suggestive power of the approaches they survey: Markov models and information-processing models, respectively. Two quite different routes to psychological relevance and fruitfulness are indicated by these authors, and it is interesting to contrast them, because these two conceptions represent polar options in some essential respects and relate to basic philosophical attitudes characterizing the two respective traditions. In fact, the two chapters together contain the material for a controversy that only the written format prevents from being overt.

The concern for psychological relevance—understood as focusing on complex intelligent achievements—has always, it seems to me, been active in the computer simulation field, and has been served by the flexibility of theoretical tools. It is more recent, as a major strategical concern, in the case of mathematical models, because early developments have subordinated it to other requirements whenever these were in conflict. The nature of the change can be grossly characterized by a political analogy. Mathematical psychology originated as a dissident party 20 years ago, as behaviorism had previously, with in fact a similar ultimate aim toward rigor—though with a different conception of what rigor is about. As with a new political party, its initial identity was gained through controversial positions and programs and a number of innovative accomplishments: parsimony is one of the issues around which the identity of the field was built; emphasis on explicitly derivable predictions is another; also, models were predominantly viewed as formal structures accounting for the data rather than characterizations of the 'true' mechanism. With increasing power and effective implements, the field has come to be identified, in public perception as well as in self-perception, not only with its tools and philosophy, but with its practical achievements evaluated, in this case, from a psychological standpoint. The content of many discussions at the conference is symptomatic of this reallocation of emphasis. So is Greeno's choice of organizing his review as an argument in favor of the psychological fruitfulness of Markov models for memory and verbal learning, rather than stressing more technical accomplishments of this line of research. Greeno outlines and presents examples of two strategical uses that can be made of formal models to enrich our psychological knowledge. One strategy relies on a psychological interpretation of the abstract states postulated by the model in order to analyze the effect of particular experimental conditions in theoretically meaningful terms. Different conditions of initial training, for example, can be found to produce transfer effects operating specifically on the stimulus encoding stage or, alternatively, on the response learning stage, and the author shows how some understanding of the nature of the initial training condition can be gained from such results.

Reversing the direction of inferences, a second strategy outlined by Greeno consists in seeking a psychological interpretation of the components of the originally formal model, by studying how these components are affected by intuitively meaningful variations in experimental conditions. Thus Greeno reports examples of this sort based on the differential effect of some experimental conditions on the various transition probabilities, that is, on the 'difficulty' of the corresponding stages, and shows how these results can be used to interpret the nature of the stages involved. Such a strategy could be qualified as second-order experimental psychology. That is, instead of inferring an underlying psychological process from the effects of intuitively meaningful experimental variations on behavioral indices, we infer it from estimated changes in the unobservable components of the model, i.e., from the effect of these variations on the behavior of the model itself.

Greeno's argument is interesting for a number of reasons, and some examples are convincing. A number of qualifications, however, seem appropriate about the strength of the results obtained in such an approach. Regarding the first strategy, it should be acknowledged that the characterization of the nature of experimental conditions is necessarily model-dependent: a condition found to exclusively affect the encoding stage in one model may be found to affect both encoding and response learning in a model involving different transition and response assumptions. The second strategy, on the other hand —second-order experimental psychology—is endowed with the same uncertainty as is the traditional experimental approach, because the conclusions rely on an a priori intuitive analysis of what the experimental variations consist of (and such an analysis can be quite arbitrary in some cases). This is not to deny its usefulness but to emphasize that its intuitionist character must be acknowledged in the qualification of the results obtained. Also, alternating both strategies in a line of research can be vulnerable to circularity.

The distinctive aspect of the approach described by Greeno in contrast with other strategies is that the models involved are formal models describing the phenomenon at a level of gross approximation. The effort towards psychological relevance rests on a utilization of simple formal models across a range of experimental situations, rather than on within-situation refinements of approximations to data. The models retain their simplicity in such an enterprise, so that psychological fruitfulness is in minimal conflict with parsimony requirements. Relevance is aimed at without altering the identity of the mathematical psychology approach.

This is particularly striking when contrasted with the developments in the concept-learning area, to which I turn later. It is also in direct conflict with Simon and Newell's perspective on psychological fruitfulness.

Simon and Newell make the polemical claim, recurrent in their writing, that information-processing theories are richer than stochastic models in psychological content and promise, and they question the relevance of Markov models in general, especially of simplified models of the sort surveyed by Greeno, to the psychological process. The sense in which they use the term 'information-processing models' is not made entirely clear: does it refer to the technology of computer simulation or to the theoretical notions involved, in whatever way they are implemented? Even in the latter sense, the opposition they emphasize is not clear, because Markov models are abstract processes and information processing is a language in which such processes can be and have been interpreted. But to come back to Simon and Newell's argumentation, they explicitly conceive of relevance as a product of the language used (". . . information-processing languages permit us to enrich the psychological content of theories of concept attainment beyond the limits that are feasible with stochastic models . . .") and of the level of detail at which the data are accounted for. The latter criterion is clearly related to the deterministic philosophy traditional in that field, and I come back to it later. Regarding the former, I do not see why the more 'psychological' formulation of theories would necessarily grant them psychological fruitfulness, any more than would commonsense descriptions of the phenomenon in introspective terms. The interest of Greeno's survey is to exemplify another strategy guided by the same psychological concerns, namely, the use of simple models to yield a unified picture of a given task domain, and to show that simplification can have its counterpart in interpretability.

Simon and Newell's argumentation is much more convincing regarding suggestive value. Suggestive value of theories is important, of course, since research must be mediated by the investigators' thinking. The suggestive value of the information-processing language is obvious because of the compatibility of the concepts involved with everyday psychology and because our thinking as investigators operates on an everyday psychology basis. In the case of Markov chains, the suggestive power of these models advocated by Greeno is less convincing; psychology has not needed Markov models to conceptualize paired-associate learning as stimulus encoding chained with response learning.

These different conceptions about psychological fruitfulness and routes to relevance clearly relate to differences in basic philosophical positions traditional in the two respective fields, especially with regard to the existential status of the constructs proposed. Whereas the stochastic tradition is one of conventionalism—models are seen as convenient approximations to data, and proving the equivalence of superficially different models is seen as a positive contribution—the simulation field appears to be guided by realist conceptions. Although existing models are recognized as imperfect, the ultimate aim appears to be to capture psychological reality. Such a spirit is consonant with, and perhaps in part generated by, the fact that the theories are couched in utterly concrete terms of computer functions and organs: the computer is another person and, to that extent, the approach could be qualified as a modern version of physiological reductionism transposed into the computer technology. It does indeed convey the same philosophical flavor and similar conceptions about the nature of explanation.

The different positions of the two traditional approaches with respect to 'truth' are reflected in the metatheoretical language used, in the subtle difference between the terms 'adjustment' and 'fit,' associated with the context of stochastic models, and the corresponding term of 'simulation.' The first terms convey a notion of alterity and approximation; the last term does not explicitly deny it, but carries a connotation of reproducibility of the real phenomena. The common effort at predicting data as accurately as possible has a different significance in these two conceptions: in the first case, it represents an aim towards a better approximation, and hence is optional and open to strategic choices; in the latter, it is an effort at accounting for the 'true' process.

Another, yet associated, difference involves the deterministic philosophy traditional in the computer simulation field. This is clearly a philosophically rather than a technically based discrepancy. Obviously, the deterministic vs. probabilistic character of a model is not an essential difference either formally (as the deterministic model is a limiting case of a probabilistic model) or technically (as random variables could be introduced at any decision node without altering the process in any essential way). However, when random elements are introduced in a simulation model it is likely to be done with reluctance and apology (cf. Feigenbaum, 1963, p. 305).

The stress on parsimony, traditional in the stochastic approach, in contrast with the priorities in the computer simulation work is closely related to these factors: if capturing the very nature of the phenomena is a hopeless objective, we might as well keep our theories at a manageable level of complexity, and find other paths to psychological fruitfulness.

CONCEPT IDENTIFICATION AND CONVERGENCE OF THE TWO TRADITIONS

Simon and Newell's claim has another facet to which I turn now. Aside from its evaluative methodological assertion discussed above, it also reflects the authors' perception of a fundamental difference between the information-processing formalism and concepts and the notions pertaining to the stochastic approach. This claim seems to me to be contradicted by the most recent developments from both traditions, and in particular by several chapters in this book. If the discussion is confined to those content areas on which both approaches overlap—excluding complex problem solving and chess playing, which are evidently at present outside the scope of stochastic models —there is a striking (and increasing) similarity between the respective sets of notions. The formulations appear to be highly similar theoretical accounts generated by two different traditions, rather than different substantive theories. In the case of memory models, this similarity is manifest in the notions of a buffer, transfer from short- to long-term memory, and scanning of a list of items in memory, which are used in the context of Markov models. Concept identification offers a particularly clear example of this convergence, and the entire development of the area is characterized by an increasing commitment of theories to cognitive notions and, in addition, an increasing focus on the details of the process. The biographical profile of the area is instructive in that respect.

Mathematical learning models were initially developed for simple learning situations with animals. Only later and very cautiously—I am tempted to say 'reluctantly'—did they come to be applied to concept-learning tasks. This is partly due to the greater complexity of the situation and hence the technical complexity of the models required. But another reason may lie in the introspective accessibility of the phenomenon studied: simplifying assumptions necessarily involved in model building that may seem legitimate when dealing with animal learning often seem to violate some psychological reality when applied to partially conscious processes in humans. Relatedly, the first applications used an impersonal abstract language without reference to the subject or his strategies. In Bourne and Restle's (1959) model, the subject was not making hypotheses: cues were being conditioned or adapted out. Clearly, cues and hypotheses are respectively the objective and subjective version of the same notion: a hypothesis consists in tentatively considering one or several cues as relevant, so that formally identical models can be developed using both languages. It is interesting, for what it is worth, to note the primacy (chronologically) of the nonsubjective language; this is what I meant by 'reluctantly.' Only later did the subject enter the scene, when models were reformulated in terms of hypothesis selection, or active attention to cues. Innocuous as it may seem, such a shift entails effective consequences, because of the surplus meaning involved and the suggestive power associated with it; for example, on-line confidence ratings about the various possible concepts appear to be an obvious response to ask from the subject if he is making hypotheses, but not if he is undergoing a cue-conditioning process. Other examples of the shift in language are the notions of focus of attention, active vs. passive states, and consistency checks, which have appeared in the more recent literature. As contended above, the language used in theories is not by itself a guarantee of their psychological relevance. It indicates, however, a change in perspective, away from the initial formalist attitude characteristic of earlier developments.

A concurrent shift concerns the structure of the models, the questions they serve to investigate, and the level of detail of the data considered relevant. A large part of the early literature focused on the all-or-none vs. incremental controversy, using the one-element model as a sophisticated statistical tool for that purpose and focusing on global statistics on the data, such as the precriterion mean-error curve. Likewise, the models of Restle and of Bower and Trabasso, which proposed formulations of the all-or-none assumption in terms of a 'psychological' hypothesis-testing process, essentially focused on the same kind of data, as their formal axioms were stated at an average level (with respect to the process informally invoked) under implicit conditions on the program of presentation of stimuli.

Frequent discrepancies of the data with respect to all-or-none characteristics have led to the introduction of memory assumptions of various types in more recent developments, so that the pool of hypotheses now has a (temporary) structure on every trial as a function of past events.

Concurrently with this, the data have come to be analyzed and considered for prediction in much finer detail, and the focus has shifted from mean statistics towards statistics conditioned upon past events. Although naturally associated with the theoretical focus on memory assumptions, this is not a trivial consequence of it. As contended variously by Cotton (1971), Falmagne (1970), and Gregg and Simon (1967), Bower and Trabasso's no-memory model could have been applicable to data of this type had its formal axioms been stated at that level. Symmetrically, more complex models involving a memory for past events could limit themselves to the prediction of mean statistics. Therefore, the point to be acknowledged here is not that the fits to the same data have been improved through memory assumptions, but that the data being considered have changed.

The increasingly detailed level at which data are accounted for, as well as the language in which models are formulated, render the most recent concept-learning studies stemming from the stochastic tradition quite close to the computer simulation approaches, as can be verified by comparing Millward and Wickens' chapter with Simon and Newell's account of concept learning. The essential difference between the two traditions appears to lie in their basic philosophical positions, rather than in theoretical constructs and language. Yet, even in terms of philosophical attitudes, one could say that the work in the concept identification area has converged towards the simulation tradition, in that it appears to ultimately aim—explicitly or not—at a deterministic account of fine-grain data, with a corresponding de-emphasis of parsimony and analytically derived predictions. In that respect, and in spite of their similar convergence towards the information-processing language, it appears that the respective areas of memory and concept identification have been guided by largely different strategical options in terms of allocation of efforts and use of models: as Greeno's review indicates, a substantial part of the efforts in memory studies has involved manipulation of situational variables, whereas concept-identification studies have predominantly aimed at refining predictions for a single situation.

CONCEPT IDENTIFICATION AND A THIRD VIEW ON RELEVANCE

Unfortunately, the increasing complexity of concept-identification models has not been accompanied either by a widening of their range of applicability, or by a comparable effort toward extensions of the experimental situation. In connection with the general concern for relevance, the concept-identification field appears to be at a choice point. One possible development is toward an increasingly accurate account of detailed data through increasingly complex memory and sampling assumptions. Such a development would in fact extend the proliferation of competing models reflected in the literature. I should like to propose that this is no longer the most fruitful perspective, although accurate prediction of performance in a tightly controlled situation may have been a rightful objective in the short run.

Two types of extensions are desirable if some generality and/or relevance is to be attained. The first type involves variation of the experimental paradigms used and, correspondingly, the development of learning models applying simultaneously to these situations. Aside from usual generality concerns, the anticipative situation offers the particular disadvantage of being meagerly informative about the learning process. One critical aspect is that the possibly complex memory process referred to by hypothesis models must be uninformatively lumped into an anticipative (usually binary) response. As a theoretical counterpart, this reduction must be accounted for by a complex hypothesis sampling and response mechanism. More informative responses and models involving a basic memory and reasoning mechanism applicable to this range of arbitrary performance indices would obviously be desirable. Attempts at extensions of this sort have been infrequent so far. On the theoretical side, Millward and Wickens (this vol.) present an attempt at integrating existing models and similar models into a general framework, with the aim of eventually accounting for the variations in strategies and memory processes as a function of prior experience and instructions. As another attempt to some generality, a model relating latency data, confidence ratings, and anticipative responses to a common memory process has been presented elsewhere (Falmagne, 1970; 1971; 1972). On the experimental side, attempts to manipulate salience, to introduce redundant relevant cues, or to analyze confidence ratings, latency data, and data from the selection paradigm must be acknowledged, but these are isolated attempts that do not reflect the main stream of the literature.

The other type of extension needed relates more crucially to the relevance of the experimental situation with respect to the everyday concept attainment of which it is deemed to be a restricted analogy and, correspondingly, to the relevance of the associated models for the process of original interest. I want to expand on this point, which to me seems critical.

In its most general form—that is, in the absence of direct social transmission—concept learning consists in discovering regularities in what initially was chaos. From a complex unspecified set of objects or situations encountered one at a time, a person eventually abstracts two classes, one for which a given response is suitable—the word 'dog,' 'epistemic,' or 'disclaim,' the appropriate opening in a bridge game, the appropriate behavior in interpersonal situations, or an idiosyncratic vocabulary term used by somebody else—and one to which the response does not apply. When transposed into the laboratory to become an object of study, the elements of the situation must be unequivocally specified for at least one person, the investigator. Hence the subject is presented geometric forms or other items for which the experimenter possesses a description system (shape, color, etc.), and whether a response to a given object is suitable or not is unambiguously signified to the subject. In the context of the experimental approach, such a codification of the everyday situation is legitimate—that is, restrictive but unavoidable— and preserves the analogy with the original situation, although it would be preferable to have a less stereotyped set of stimuli and concepts, so that the analogy would be with concept learning rather than concept identification. Much less legitimate, however, are additional restrictions that have been introduced in that situation and, more importantly, limitations in the theoretical developments that are associated with these restrictions.

Most current theories conceive of the subject as entertaining hypotheses about the concept, and learning is represented by the process ultimately leading to the exclusive application of the correct hypothesis. Within this general outlook, it is clear that the total learning process involves several components or stages, among which are the generation of a description of the environment and the generation of the hypotheses to be tested. However, the models have concentrated exclusively on the selection process operating on a set of prespecified hypotheses. Typically, the subject's universe of reasoning is assumed to be, for example, the set of unidimensional binary partitions on the set S of stimuli (referred to as the set of all unidimensional hypotheses); a given model then describes how the subject samples, retains, or discards specific hypotheses in that universe. In conjunction with the usual practice of presenting the stimuli sequentially, there could be a paradox associated with this type of model, since the subject cannot be assumed to know S (hence its power set), say on trial 1. This already indicates the regional character of these models, but what I want to point out first is that, in order for the assumption above to be meaningful, the instructions must specify S and its dimensions of variation, which is a first restriction on the situation. In order, furthermore, for the assumption to be realistic, the subject is usually told what the set of possible concepts or partitions is. The remoteness of the resulting experimental situation with regard to the phenomenon of original interest does not require further emphasis (whether this remoteness results in irrelevancy or whether it is a restriction of an optional nature, is a question that will only be answered after sufficiently general theories, applying to the whole range of situations, have been developed). What I wish to emphasize now is the partial scope of the associated models with respect to concept learning, and the way in which the hypothesis selection described articulates with other components of the process. The comments below are presented in order of increasing subjectivity and are deliberately confined within the very framework of hypothesis models. A radically different perspective on concept learning could perhaps be developed, but given that hypothesis models have proved useful for the limited situation, it is natural as a next step to retain and expand their basic notions.

Formally, a hypothesis can be defined as a function h mapping a set S of objects onto a set R of responses, and likewise for the concept c chosen by the experimenter. In most cases, the experimenter has an a priori encoding or description of the elements of S, so that each s in S is a point in a 'descriptive space' (to use Millward and Wickens' and other investigators' terminology) $\Omega = \Omega_1 \times \cdots \times \Omega_n$, where Ω_i denotes a particular attribute (color, shape, . . .) conventionally used by the experimenter to describe the elements of S. The concept is then a projection of S on Ω_i (or on $\Omega_i \times \cdots \times \Omega_j$), composed with a response assignment mapping Ω_i (or $\Omega_i \times \cdots \times \Omega_j$) onto R.

Similarly, the subject can be assumed to represent the stimuli in a descriptive space $\Omega' = \Omega_1' \times \cdots \times \Omega_m' \ldots$[1] If the subject knows that he has to discover a concept, we only need to consider hypotheses that consist of 'systematic' partitions of Ω'. A hypothesis h is then a projection of S on Ω_i' or on $\Omega_i' \times \cdots \times \Omega_j'$, composed with a response assignment. Learning consists in selection of the function h identical to c.

From the above formal account as well as on psychological grounds, it is clear that an intrinsic component of what the subject must do in a concept learning task, if hypothesis-testing notions are taken seriously, is to build up the appropriate descriptive space, or at least a descriptive space allowing for the appropriate projection of S.

This calls for two remarks. First, in the most general case, there is no reason why Ω should be identical to Ω'. An illustrative example is Hull's (1920) experiment using Chinese signs as stimuli, or in another context, Gibson and Gibson's (1955) scribble experiment. Implicit considerations of

---

[1] This is not a strong assumption. In particular, it is not committed to an encoding of the stimuli in terms of elementary features, since Ω_i' can be a compound dimension (from somebody else's point of view), and as a limiting case an encoding of the pattern as a whole.

this sort have led to the traditional restrictions in the experimental situation mentioned above. Their relevance here is to emphasize the theoretical limitations of the corresponding hypothesis models.

Second, even if the attributes Ω_i are culturally shared by the subject, the specific set of attributes that will eventuate in his descriptive space for S obviously depends on the whole set of stimuli presented, save in uninterestingly stereotyped cases. The same object will be described as a small circle when presented among geometrical forms, and as a lowercase letter 'o' when presented with letters. Such remarks, incidentally, also apply to models involving discrimination nets, such as EPAM, or to notions of distinctive encoding, as in Greeno's survey, a point to which I return later.

Turning now to more subjective remarks, the gradual construction of the descriptive space on the one hand, and the generation of hypotheses on the other, are perhaps the most interesting objects of study in concept learning, as contrasted with the ensuing testing and selection process, granting for the sake of exposition that these are separable subprocesses.

As regards the generation of the descriptive space, in the most general case of complex unfamiliar stimuli, the effective dimensions are likely to emerge as a result of contrast between consecutive stimuli (or between stimuli presented within the appropriate memory span), aside from a few salient or stereotyped categories that the subject may use when presented with the first stimulus. This argument can be pushed as far as one wants towards a Gibsonian view; however, for the sake of the present discussion, it is not necessary to push it further than the preexisting verbal categories of the subject. Concurrently, a process of elimination can conceivably develop whereby attributes that were included in the descriptive space at one point may be neutralized if their value is kept constant long enough. A subject may encode the first stimulus presented as a black square on a white background, but if the background is kept constant while size and shape are varied, the same object presented later on might be encoded as a large square. In the case of the Chinese signs used by Hull, or other unfamiliar material for which the subject does not have even a tentative initial encoding, the contention here is that the description of the items builds up in part as a consequence of initially unanalyzed perceptual contrast, although each resulting descriptive system will probably be couched in preexisting verbal categories.

The process of generation of hypotheses from a given descriptive space is equally bypassed by the current theoretical approaches with exclusive focus on hypothesis testing. The construction of hypotheses is the most intriguing part of the inferential process—what Watanabe (1969), in another context, refers to as "abduction," as opposed to the inductive process involved in Bayesian inference. Abduction, the generation of hypotheses, and the intuition of the counterexample in the mathematical context are probably the result of a largely unconscious process involving complex reorganizations, and for which incremental strength notions quite distinct from explicit strategies might have to be assumed. The 'cognitive' tradition in psychological theories with its emphasis on plans, explicit strategies, and well-formed hypotheses has been detrimental to the study of such obscure but fascinating phenomena. A notable exception is Piaget's account of the mechanism of cognitive development, which takes over such phenomena in its usual non-predictive but insightful way: new conceptual or logical structures emerge when the existing ones are felt to be unsuited to handling the data from the environment. Such transitions are generated by a feeling of incompleteness and inadequacy of existing schemes. At moderate levels of discrepancy between the environment-generated input and the conceptual system, the data are filtered, possibly distorted, to fit the existing conceptual structures. With repeated exposure to crucial experiences and/or with time, the discrepancy becomes patent and cognitive reorganization occurs. In some situations (e.g., conservation), reorganization may consist in enlarging the span of attention to include and integrate more aspects of the situation, because focusing on one aspect at a time is felt to lead to inconsistent judgments. Although not spelled out, an incremental notion is implicit in this account. Its relevance to the generation of hypotheses in the most general concept-learning case is obvious.

CREATIVITY

The discussion above relates to a more general issue about the creative vs. a priori character of the process formalized by the models. It seems fair to say that a widely shared feeling about human intelligence is that it is creative, so that allowing for creativity is an ultimate objective of theories about intelligent achievements. Failures to achieve this either are experienced as temporary limitations due to technical constraints, or, if felt to be unavoidable, are nevertheless regretted. The comments in the previous section could be reformulated by saying that concept-identification models and procedures short-circuit the creative part of the concept-learning process. The motivation for raising the issue of creativity more generally here is to reexamine some evaluative distinctions that are sometimes made and are not entirely justified. I think that questions similar to the ones raised above about the plugged-in descriptive system in concept-identification models and experiments can be raised in other areas as well, especially memory models and computer simulation approaches.

Creativity is an explicit concern in the information-processing-simulation field; claims that a program simulating problem solving is inventive are claims of success. Minsky (1968), for example, insists on the nontriviality of parsing programs by emphasizing that the programmer usually will be unable to predict the result of all inputs, even though he has instructed the machine about the legal principles for operating. Furthermore, the feeling is commonly expressed that computer simulation programs permit one to model creative achievements, which other techniques (Markov models or others) do not. The question of when a process is creative and when it is not is a subtle and probably insoluble one, and I have no pretension at even a loose acceptable definition here. Two broad alternatives, however, are worth evoking to try to understand what the simulation investigators' claim might mean. A straightforward behavioral definition of a creative accomplishment would be for an individual to produce a solution or an action that specifically meets the circumstances and that he has never exhibited before. The claim certainly holds in that sense, but it is a rather trivial one and, in its most general form, certainly is not exclusive to computer simulation models. Once one departs from this behavioristic definition, however, and tries to define creativity at the level of the process itself, in terms of novel operations or representations—which seems to be more in keeping with the connotations of that notion—difficulties appear. It is hard, for example, to understand the simulation investigators' claim in any way other than a loss of control—like Pygmalion—on the realizations that combinatorially result from the a priori components of the program. As another example, generative grammars are creative only in the limited sense of being recursive applications of a priori rules.

As Minsky (1968) indicates, the most important problem faced by computer simulation or artificial intelligence approaches is the representation of knowledge. Two broadly defined types of knowledge are, on the one hand, general problem-solving heuristics and, on the other hand, the intake of primitive information from the external world, namely, the encoding (description) of the stimulus in a learning task, of the premises in a logical task, etc. This is the type of knowledge that I am concerned with in connection with the previous discussion of concept-identification tasks. To only concentrate on that domain of application of information-processing models, which overlaps with the scope of current mathematical models, consider EPAM or Hintzman's (1968) probabilistic model, which involves closely related notions. The fact that the process grows its own discrimination net, i.e., its representation of the stimuli, is taken—explicitly in Hintzman's case—as a step towards taking over the naiveté of the subject who enters the situation, and it is indeed. However, at the more primitive level, the stimulus is 'perceived' through a predetermined input code. The investigator thereby imposes his (stereotyped) descriptive space on the organism in exactly the same way that the restricted concept-identification procedure does. That this feature is linked to technological irremovable constraints is a point about the technology involved and does not dismiss the present remark. Limitations of this sort are acknowledged by Simon and Newell (this vol.) regarding the plugged-in problem space in complex problem-solving tasks, but they apparently conceive of EPAM as overcoming this limitation.

The mathematical models for paired-associate learning surveyed by Greeno involve a similar limitation, though in a more indirect way, through the assumption that a distinctive representation of each item is stored on each trial with a constant probability. It is well known that the ease of memorizing an item—hence, supposedly, the ease of constructing a distinctive representation—is a function of the whole list and, in particular, of the interitem similarity. However, the subject does not know the list in advance when, say, the first item is presented. The dynamic process by which he constructs distinctive representations of individual items as a function of the context is thus analogous to the construction of the descriptive space in concept learning. In fact, it can be thought of as being exactly the same mechanism, though operating in conjunction with different additional task components. Assuming the probability of a distinctive encoding to be constant from trial 1, when context is inexistent, bypasses that creative process. The comment here concerns the implausibility of the assumption, whereas in concept-identification studies such a problem was disposed of by restrictive instructions.

Two qualifications are needed about these remarks. First, acknowledging such limitations does not detract from the interest of the findings obtained, but points at their local character, and should generate a constructive dissatisfaction. Second, focusing on cases where they are most obvious—i.e., concept identification, as contended above—should not eventuate in a specific criticism of the state of these areas, but rather should serve to sensitize us to analogous problems faced by other areas as well.

MATHEMATICAL PSYCHOLOGY AND COGNITIVE PHENOMENA

An earlier part of these remarks pointed at the increasing concern for psychological relevance in mathematical psychology. A related phenomenon seems to be a weakening in the initial identity of the field, and the need for its redefinition has been expressed at this conference and elsewhere. A number of converging reasons can account for this decrease in cohesiveness. One is the diversification of substantive interests and associated formal tools. This feature, together with the increased emphasis on genuinely psychological concerns, results in a sense of commonality centered around substantive problems rather than methodology. This is a natural and probably desirable evolution for a maturing field.

Another facet, however, of the ongoing decrease in cohesiveness is, in terms of the analogy proposed earlier, the fact that one fraction of the party, while retaining its traditional association with it, has been in fact shifting in ideology. The traditional methodological position regarding the conventional status of models, and the issues of parsimony and explicitly derivable predictions, derives from the initial era of application of unquestionably simplifying models to simple phenomena or animal learning, and has been preserved in those content areas which deal with relatively 'microscopic' phenomena. In the more cognitive content areas such as concept learning and, to a lesser extent, verbal learning and memory, these priorities seem to be weakening, partly because of the overlap with the computer simulation work, but more crucially because the phenomena under study are of a nature accessible to introspection.

The introspective accessibility of the phenomena studied appears to create an entirely original set of questions and conflicts in connection with the use of mathematical models, both regarding the theoretical developments themselves and the criteria used to evaluate them. The main conflict stems from the fact that the introspective accessibility of the phenomenon encourages psychological realism and deterministic attitudes as it appears to yield an unequivocal criterion for what the 'true' process is. This feature may account for the drift in the concept-identification area outlined before. If the subject is conceived of as consciously entertaining hypotheses, it is tempting to hope that eventually the complete sequence of these will be tracked down, in the same perspective as Simon and Newell's ultimate aim to account for the problem behavior graph of a subject. The suggestion is not as strong in the case of memory and verbal learning models: the subject's introspective reports about the successive encodings of a stimulus-response pair or the content of his buffer at a given time would undoubtedly be sensed to be less trustworthy than a subject's report about which hypothesis he is making concerning a complex classification rule; hence the more resistant black-box status of these notions and the difference in the state of the two respective areas. Incidentally, the same feature may partly account for the traditional difference in philosophical outlook between computer simulation and mathematical psychology, as these two respective fields originated at what might be characterized (questionably but suggestively) as the two opposite ends of some complexity continuum.

Relatedly, regarding criteria for evaluation, the theories in the cognitive area are more vulnerable to criticisms referring to the realism of simplifying assumptions and to the accuracy of the quantitative accounts. This is in part desirable, insofar as these are healthy concerns and factors of progress. However, the resulting state of affairs is that the status of theories and the criteria according to which they are evaluated come to be different for different domains of application, and to that extent it requires at least a passing comment.

If the retina could talk, it probably would tell us how much off the mark our neurophysiological models for vision are. If the marble drawn so often from the urn by the statistician could talk, it probably would tell us how close we were to picking up its red neighbor and how foolish it is, therefore, to attach any significance to its being black in our statistical theorizing. Fortunately for the neurophysiologist and the statistician, introspective reports are not available in those fields to censor the probabilistic models. Two questions then arise. First, should our basic philosophy about the status of models be altered by our having a privileged view through introspection of the phenomenon we are modeling? Second, do introspective reports indeed constitute privileged information in the sense of giving us 'direct' access to the underlying mechanism? Regarding the latter question, a preliminary remark is that the emphasis on introspective evidence indicates a surreptitious return to phenomenology. If it were acknowledged as such and if models were aimed at accounting for introspective data, the status of these would be entirely clear. In the behavioristic framework in which we are operating, however, the question is different, as the data to be accounted for are overt responses, and introspection is informally used as a way of breaking into the traditional black box. The conflict between this informal practice and the orthodox methodological positions is obvious, and it seems to me that answering these two questions is one of the most urgent needs faced by the mathemathical approach to cognitive phenomena.

ACKNOWLEDGMENTS

This chapter was prepared while the author was at The Rockefeller University, partially supported by grant GM16735 from NIGMS, and partially by the Fonds National de la Recherche Scientifique (Belgium). I am grateful to J. Townsend and R. Millward for careful reading and constructive comments on an earlier draft of this chapter.

REFERENCES

Bourne, L. E., & Restle, F. Mathematical theory of concept identification. *Psychological Review*, 1959, **66**, 278–298.

Cotton, J. W. A sequence-specific concept identification model: Infra-structure for the Bower and Trabasso theory. *Journal of Mathematical Psychology*, 1971, **8**, 333–369.

Falmagne, R. Construction of a hypothesis model for concept identification. *Journal of Mathematical Psychology*, 1970, **7**, 60–96.

Falmagne, R. Conjoint analysis of two concept identification tasks. *Acta Psychologica*, 1971, **35**, 286–297.

Falmagne, R. Memory process in concept identification. *Journal of Experimental Psychology*, 1972, **92**, 33–42.

Feigenbaum, E. A. The simulation of verbal learning behavior. In E. A. Feigenbaum and J. Feldman (Eds.), *Computers and thought*. New York: McGraw-Hill, 1963.

Gibson, J. J., & Gibson, E. J. Perceptual learning: Differentiation or enrichment? *Psychological Review*, 1955, **62**, 36.

Gregg, L. W., & Simon, H. A. Process models and stochastic theories of simple concept formation. *Journal of Mathematical Psychology*, 1967, **4**, 246–276.

Hintzman, D. L. Explorations with a discrimination net model for paired-associate learning. *Journal of Mathematical Psychology*, 1968, **5**, 123–162.

Hull, C. L. Quantitative aspects of the evolution of concepts. *Psychological Monographs*, 1920, Whole No. 123.

Minsky, M. L. *Semantic information processing*. Cambridge: M.I.T. Press, 1968.

Watanabe, S. *Knowing and guessing*. New York: Wiley, 1969.

Foundations of
Stimulus Sampling Theory

W. K. Estes

ROCKEFELLER UNIVERSITY

Patrick Suppes

STANFORD UNIVERSITY

INTRODUCTION

Stimulus sampling models have enjoyed increasingly wide application in learning theory. Although the representation of a stimulus situation as a set of elements is a familiar aspect, at a verbal level, of the classical identical-elements conception of transfer (Thorndike, 1914), this notion was apparently first formalized in a theory developed to account for the effects of repetition in the acquisition process (Estes, 1950). Natural extensions of this theory have led to interpretations of discrimination, generalization, temporal processes, and even motivational phenomena. New developments reported during the past year include interpretations of stimulus encoding in memory (Bower, 1972), the partial reinforcement effect (Koteskey, 1972), and aspects of communication systems (Estes, 1971). At a more abstract level, Suppes (1969) has demonstrated that finite automata can be given representations within stimulus sampling theory. Thus we may anticipate efforts to deal with the still more challenging problem of extending the theory to interpret the acquisition of language.

The development of stimulus sampling theory has proceeded on a piecemeal basis, instigated and directed largely by empirical considerations.[1] Consequently it is not surprising that the literature includes many variations even in the treatment of simple learning. Always it is assumed that the subject in a learning experiment samples a population of stimuli, or 'cues,' on each trial, that his probability of making a given response depends on the proportion of sampled stimuli that are 'conditioned,' or 'connected,' to the response, and that the connections between stimuli and response change as a result of reinforcement and nonreinforcement during learning. However, some investigators have assumed independent sampling of stimulus elements on the part of the subject; some have assumed that the sample size is fixed; some have used a 'fluid model' in which the distinction does not appear. For the most part, in earlier work it was always assumed that both population and sample are large; consequently differences among the varying treatments were glossed over by 'large numbers' approximations. More recently, the advantage of dealing with sampling models as finite Markov processes has been recognized and the consequences of different assumptions about the sampling process have begun to come to view (Kemeny & Snell, 1957; Suppes & Atkinson, 1960).

An article (Estes, 1959b) organizing many of the results obtained in the mathematical aspects of stimulus sampling theory to date has clarified the differences among the particular variants and at the same time has brought out the need for a systematic treatment of the subject.

In this report we give some of the principal results of our analysis of the foundations of stimulus sampling models. The investigation has been conducted in the same spirit as our treatment of linear models (Estes & Suppes, 1959a). It has proved to be a more extensive enterprise, however, and more of the results are new from a psychological viewpoint. The novelty arises primarily from the generality of our methods, not from any intentional introduction of novel concepts or hypotheses. Where we define new concepts or state new assumptions, it is only for the purpose of making explicit distinctions that have not been made in previous work. One of our objectives has been to discover just what assumptions are necessary to justify the various results, learning functions, asymptotic predictions, etc., that are generally accepted as belonging to stimulus sampling theory.

The axioms for stimulus sampling presented in this chapter make explicit the independence of path properties and the trial invariance that have been tacitly assumed in nearly all contemporary theories. Concerning the nature of the sampling process, these axioms are less restrictive than those of any one extant theory; they suffice to generate as special cases both the independent sampling model and the fixed sample-size model.

---

[1] For an introduction to the literature, both psychological and mathematical, on stimulus sampling theory, and for extensive bibliographies, the reader is referred to Atkinson and Estes (1963), Bush and Estes (1959), Estes (1959a, 1972), and Neimark and Estes (1967).

The two principal sources of variation in stimulation are sharply distinguished in our analysis. As in the various published formulations of statistical learning theory, the total population of stimuli ever available during a given experiment is represented by a set S of stimulus elements, or 'cues.' The subset of cues that are available for sampling on a particular trial will be designated the *presentation set*, denoted by the letter T (with superscripts if needed to distinguish among two or more different presentation sets). Ordinarily the different presentation sets defined for a given experiment correspond to stimuli whose probabilities are under the control of the experimenter, as under a classical discrimination procedure. However, the probabilities of presentation sets may also vary with time, as in fluctuation models for retention, spacing effects, and other time-dependent phenomena. The subset of cues that affect the subject's behavior on a particular trial will be designated the *sample*, denoted s. The probability of a particular sample given the presentation set is assumed to be fixed for a given subject and experimental situation and, in particular, does not vary during the course of learning. Owing to this property, it might be expected that changes in the conditioned status of conditioned elements from trial to trial might be represented as transitions among states of a Markov chain. This is indeed the case, fortunately for calculational purposes, under certain circumstances; not always, however, for the probabilities of presentation sets and reinforcing events may, in general, depend upon outcomes of any number of preceding trials. One of our general results is a theorem prescribing the way in which, for any given experimental routine, states may be defined so as to permit interpretation of the process as a finite Markov chain.

The basic differences between stimulus sampling models and linear models can be explicated in terms of the sample space underlying each. To characterize a single trial in a stimulus sampling model, we require six items of information: the way in which the stimulus population is partitioned into subsets of elements conditioned (C) to the various possible responses; the presentation set (T); the sample (s); the response made by the subject (A); the experimenter-defined outcome, reward, punishment, etc. (O); and the reinforcing event (E). An experiment comprises a sequence of such trials; therefore, the sample space must contain a point corresponding to each possible sequence.

In the linear model of Bush and Mosteller (1955), a trial is characterized by only two of these items, A and O, both of which are observable; a third class of events is provided for, but does not actually enter into any applications of the Bush and Mosteller model that have appeared to date.

The linear model investigated by Estes and Suppes (1959a) requires three items of information to specify a trial: A, O, and E. The first two are, again, observable responses and experimenter-defined outcomes, but the third, E, is a purely hypothetical 'reinforcing event' that represents the conditioning

.effect of the trial outcome. Event E_i is said to have occurred when the outcome of a trial is such as to increase the probability of the response A_i in the presence of the given stimulus (provided, of course, that this probability is not already at its maximum value). Strictly speaking, an item corresponding to the presentation set T should appear in the linear models, but it has been possible conveniently to suppress it because the linear models have been developed primarily for the case of simple learning in which the same presentation set occurs on all trials. The learning axioms of linear models prescribe linear transformations of response probabilities; the parameters of the 'linear operators' applied on any trial depend, in general, on the response and the outcome of the trial but otherwise have no interpretation in terms of more primitive notions. The learning axioms of stimulus sampling models prescribe how the conditioned status of stimuli in the trial sample changes. Given the reinforcing event of a trial, the changes prescribed by these axioms are strictly deterministic in character. Linear transformations of response probability occur in certain cases of stimulus sampling models, but they are theorems rather than axioms; also, they differ from those of the linear models in that they do not describe changes in response probability for individual subjects.

It has commonly been assumed by investigators in this area that a linear model may be regarded as the limiting form to which a stimulus sampling model converges as the number of stimuli goes to infinity. The main basis for this assumption is the fact that in some cases recursive expressions for response probabilities derived from stimulus sampling models reduce to linear functions in the limit as $N \rightarrow \infty$ (N being the number of elements in the stimulus population S). Also, Kemeny and Snell (1957) showed that, for the noncontingent case of simple learning, the asymptotic distribution of response probabilities for an independent-sampling model agrees in the limit with that of the linear model. The first proof that, for large N, stimulus sampling models converge uniformly over trials to linear models was given in our original report (Estes & Suppes, 1959b). A different proof by a shorter and more elegant method, but under rather restrictive assumptions on the reinforcement schedule, has recently been given by Norman (1972, p. 206).

In this chapter we have omitted most of the theorems included in our original report, including the basic theorem on convergence of stimulus sampling models to linear models. We have retained the detailed development of the axiomatic foundations, and we have illustrated its usefulness by proving in essentially full generality the basic Markov theorem for stimulus sampling models. We hope that our detailed discussion of various complex reinforcement schedules whose contingencies extend over several trials will be suggestive of further experiments.

The excellent mathematical treatment of Norman (1972) mentioned above is restricted to reinforcement schedules whose contingencies do not extend back beyond the trial on which the reinforcement occurs. The kind of theoretical application to finite automata developed in Suppes (1969) already requires that the reinforcement on a given trial be partially dependent on the response on the preceding trial. Additional work in this direction seems likely. The general Markov theorem given here provides a foundation for such work.

FORMAL STATEMENT OF THEORY

Primitive and Defined Notions

The theory is based on five primitive notions, each of which has a simple psychological interpretation. The first notion is the set S of *stimuli*. It is to be emphasized from the beginning that in general the set S is not directly observable. The second and third primitive notions are, respectively, the number r of *responses* available and the number t of possible trial *outcomes*. In most experiments, r and t are completely determined by the experimenter.

The fourth primitive notion is the sample space X. Each element x of the sample space represents a possible experiment, that is, an infinite sequence of trials. In the present theory, each trial may be described by an ordered sextuple $\langle C, T, s, i, j, k \rangle$, where C = the *conditioning* function; T = the subset of stimuli *presented* to the subject on that trial; s = the *sampled* subset of T; i = the *response* made on that trial by the subject, $(1 \leq i \leq r)$; j = the *outcome* of the trial, $(0 \leq j \leq t)$; and k = the *reinforcing* event occurring on that trial, $(0 \leq k \leq r)$.

Our fifth primitive notion is a probability measure P on the Borel field $\mathcal{B}(x)$ of cylinder sets of X.[2] All probabilities must be defined in terms of the measure P.

We want to make a number of remarks about this sextuple description of a trial. Neither the conditioning function C nor the sampled set s is ordinarily observable; on the other hand, the response i and the outcome j are directly observable by the experimenter. The situation is more complicated for the presentation set T of stimuli. For the analysis of simple learning, we identify T and S (i.e., $T = S$). In the case of discrimination learning, the set T will vary from trial to trial; its complete observability on a given trial depends on the exact character of the discrimination experiment. We return to this point later. The r responses associated with a sample space X are mutually exclusive and exhaustive. The component j on any trial is to be interpreted as the operationally defined outcome of a trial, e.g., the reward, omission of reward,

---

[2] For a discussion of the meaning and intuitive significance of cylinder sets and the Borel field $\mathcal{B}(X)$, see Estes and Suppes (1959a).

unconditioned stimulus, or knowledge of results. Ordinarily, as already re-marked, the outcome is under the control of the experimenter, and always the outcome is observable by the experimenter. The component k, customarily referred to as a 'reinforcing event,' will determine which one of the three learning axioms (see following section) is to be applied on the trial. We shall follow the usual notational convention that the kth reinforcing event ($1 \leq k \leq r$) corresponds to the learning axiom which prescribes reinforce-ment of (an increase in probability of) the kth response, and that the inter-pretation of $k = 0$ is that no response was reinforced on the trial. Frequently, but not always, there is a one-to-one correspondence between outcomes and reinforcing events; when this is the case, it is customary in the literature to ignore the distinction between experimentally defined outcomes and rein-forcing events and to speak of the latter as though they were experimental operations (see, e.g., Bush & Mosteller, 1955; Estes, 1959b; Estes & Suppes, 1959a). In general, however, the number t of observable outcomes may be either smaller or larger than the number of reinforcing events. It is a conse-quence of our axioms that the probability of a reinforcing event depends only on the response and the outcome of the given trial.

The conditioning function C is defined over the set of first r positive inte-gers, and C_i (i.e., the value of the function C for the argument i) is the subset of S *conditioned, or connected*, to response i on the given trial.[3] A conditioning function partitions the set S of stimuli, assigning thereby each element of S to exactly one response.[4] Thus if $r = 2$ and

$$S = \{a, b, c\},$$

then a possible C is

$$C_1 = \{a, b\},$$
$$C_2 = \{c\}.$$

To summarize, the sample space X consists of all possible sequences of trials consisting of sextuples $\langle C, T, s, i, j, k \rangle$. We call X the *sample space rela-tive to S, r, and t*. It should also be mentioned that the order of events in the sextuple representation $\langle C, T, s, i, j, k \rangle$ reflects the assumption that this is the temporal order of events on each trial. In other words, the temporal order on any trial is (state of conditioning at beginning of trial) $\rightarrow$ (presenta-tion of stimuli) $\rightarrow$ (sampling of stimuli) $\rightarrow$ (response) $\rightarrow$ (outcome) $\rightarrow$ (rein-forcing event) $\rightarrow$ (state of conditioning at beginning of new trial).

---

[3] We use 'conditioned' and 'connected' as synonyms.
[4] More formally, we may define C as a conditioning function if, and only if,

   (i) C is a function whose domain is the set of first r positive integers,
   (ii) $\cup_i C_i = S$,
   (iii) if $i \neq i'$ then $C_i \cap C_{i'} = 0$.

It is also convenient to define the notion of a *sampling function* s_*. The domain of s_* is the set of responses, i.e., the first r positive integers; then s_i is the subset of S sampled and conditioned to response i on the trial which has sampling function s_*, and of course $s = \bigcup_i s_i$ is the total sample on that trial.[5] For example, if $r = 2$, $S = \{a, b, c\}$, $C_1 = \{b\}$, $C_2 = \{a, c\}$, and $s = \{a, b\}$, then $s_1 = \{b\}$ and $s_2 = \{a\}$; and the function s_* is the set of ordered couples $\{(1, b), (2, a)\}$. Given a sextuple $\langle C, T, s, i, j, k \rangle$ then s_* is uniquely determined by C and s, for each $s_i = C_i \cap s$.

We turn now to a number of defined notions. The first definitions are of certain important subsets, i.e., events, of the sample space X. First, $A_{i,n}$ is the event: *response i on trial n* (i.e., the set of all possible experimental realizations (elements of X) having i as the response component on the nth trial). Similarly, $O_{j,n}$ is the event: *outcome j on trial n*; and $E_{k,n}$ is the event: *reinforcement k on trial n*. (Informally, we have referred to k as a 'reinforcing event,' but from the standpoint of the sample space X it is $E_{k,n}$ that is an event, i.e., a subset of X. The point is a minor technical one and should cause no confusion.)

By attaching a subscript n to a presentation set T, we denote as T_n the set of experimental realizations that have T as the presentation set on trial n, and similarly for other sets or functions constructed from the set S of stimuli. Thus, for instance, $s_{i,n}$ is the set of all elements of X having s_i as the subset of S sampled and connected to response i on trial n. Or, as another example, suppose that in a simple discrimination experiment with $r = 2$ and $S = \{a, b, c\}$, the experimenter makes the subset $T = \{a, b\}$ available for sampling on trials when sequence A_1 is to be reinforced and $T' = \{b, c\}$ available when A_2 is to be reinforced. Then T_n would be the event that subset $\{a, b\}$ is available for sampling on trial n and T'_n the event that subset $\{b, c\}$ is available for sampling on trial n. Ordinarily the two conditions are equiprobable, so we would have $P(T_n) = P(T'_n) = \frac{1}{2}$.

It is also necessary to have a notation for the *number* of elements conditioned to a given response on trial n, the number of elements sampled, etc. In general, if A is any set, we designate the cardinality of A by $N(A)$. Following usage in learning theory, we let $N = N(S)$. Moreover, $N(s_n)$ is the set of all sequences x in X that on the nth trial have exactly $N(s)$ sampled stimulus elements. In like fashion we use the notation $N(T)$, $N(T_n)$, $N(C_i)$, $N(C_{i,n})$, $N(s_i)$, $N(s_{i,n})$. The distinction between $N(s)$ and $N(s_n)$, and so forth, needs explicit emphasis. $N(s)$ is an integer standing for the finite number of elements

---

[5] From a mathematical standpoint it would perhaps be simpler and more natural to let s be the sampling function and let s_* be the sampled subset, but two arguments weigh against this notation. First, the notation for the sampled subset is used more frequently than that for the sampling function. Second, usage in the literature is strongly on the side of the notation s for the sampled subset.

in s, a subset of S. In contrast, $N(s_n)$ is an infinite set of sample space points. Finally, we note that we continually use

$$T, T', T'', \ldots \quad \text{for presentation sets of stimuli,}$$
$$C, C', C'', \ldots \quad \text{for conditioning functions,}$$
$$s, s', s'', \ldots \quad \text{for sampled sets of stimuli.}$$

General Axioms

Our general axioms for stimulus sampling theory of learning divide naturally into two classes. First there are deterministic axioms that are concerned wholly with the sample space X itself independent of any probability considerations. They may be regarded as *learning* axioms since they deal with deterministic changes from one trial to the next.

The second class consists of the probabilistic axioms, involving the probability measure P. This class is naturally partitioned into three *sampling* axioms, three *response* axioms, two *reinforcement* axioms, and one *presentation* axiom. The reinforcement and presentation axioms make explicit a restriction on applicability of the model to situations in which probabilities of stimulus presentations and trial outcomes are set by a person (normally the experimenter) or environmental agency that has no direct access to the subject's internal state. It may be of interest to consider learning situations in which stimulus presentations or trial outcomes are under the control of the subject (other than by conditionalization on his responses), but these cases would not be interpretable within the class of stimulus sampling models here defined. Our axioms require the notion of an *experimenter's partition*, already introduced in Estes and Suppes (1959a). Here we shall give only a verbal, somewhat loose definition of such a partition.

An experimenter's partition $H(n)$ for trial n, with elements $\eta, \eta', \eta'', \ldots$, is a partition of the sample space X such that each element η of $H(n)$ is defined only in terms of events $T_{n'}, A_{i,n''}, O_{j,n'''}$, with $1 \leq n', n'' \leq n$ and $1 \leq n''' < n$. In the following axioms that are concerned with 'independence of path' assumptions, there is continual reference to n- or $(n-1)$-dimensional cylinder sets, which are simply sets defined in terms of possible trial outcomes through trial n or $n-1$, respectively. And it should be clear that the elements of an experimenter's partition $H(n)$ are simply special sorts of n-dimensional cylinder sets.

Formally, we say that a quintuple $\mathfrak{X} = \langle S, r, t, X, P \rangle$ *is a* STIMULUS SAMPLING MODEL *if the following five groups of axioms are satisfied.*

Learning axioms.   The three learning axioms describe how the conditioning of stimuli changes from trial to trial as a function of reinforcement and sampling.

For every conditioning function C, every sampled subset s, and every integer k, for $0 \leq k \leq r$, there is a unique conditioning function C' such that for every n the following three axioms are satisfied.

L1. The occurrence of a given conditioning function C, a given reinforcement E_k, and a given sample s on trial n imply the occurrence of a unique conditioning function C' on trial $n + 1$.

$$C_n \cap E_{k,n} \cap s_n \subseteq C'_{n+1}.$$

L2. If reinforcement occurs, i.e., $k \neq 0$, all stimuli sampled become conditioned to the reinforced response.

$$C'_k = C_k \cup s,$$

and

$$C'_j = C_j \sim s_j \quad for\ j \neq k.$$

L3. If no reinforcement occurs, i.e., $k = 0$, then there is no change in the state of conditioning.

$$C' = C.$$

Sampling axioms.

S1. The probability of a given sample is independent of the trial number.
If $P(T_m) > 0$ and $P(T_n) > 0$ then

$$P(s_m \mid T_m) = P(s_n \mid T_n).$$

S2. Samples of equal size are sampled equally often.
If $s \cup s' \subseteq T$ and $N(s) = N(s')$ and $P(T_n) > 0$ then

$$P(s_n \mid T_n) = P(s'_n \mid T_n).$$

S3. Sampling on any trial is independent of events on previous trials.
If W_{n-1} is an $n - 1$ cylinder set and $Y \subseteq W_{n-1} \cap C_n$ and $P(Y \cap T_n) > 0$ then

$$P(s_n \mid T_n \cap Y) = P(s_n \mid T_n).$$

Response axioms.

R1. The probability of any response A_i is the ratio of sampled elements connected to A_i to the total number of sampled elements.
If $s \neq 0$ and $P(s_{*_n}) > 0$ then

$$P(A_{i,n} \mid s_{*_n}) = \frac{N(s_i)}{N(s)}.$$

R2. If no stimulus elements are sampled on a trial, the probability of response A_i is equal to some number which does not depend on the conditioning function but may depend on the trial number.
If $s = 0$ and $P(s_n) > 0$ then there is a number $\rho_{i,n}$ such that

$$P(A_{i,n} \mid s_n) = \rho_{i,n}.$$

R3. Given the sample on trial n, no additional information about events of previous trials affects the conditional probability of any response A_i.
If W_{n-1} is an $n - 1$ cylinder set and $Y \subseteq W_{n-1} \cap C_n \cap T_n$ and $P(Y \cap s_{*_n}) > 0$ then

$$P(A_{i,n} \mid s_{*_n} \cap Y) = P(A_{i,n} \mid s_{*_n}).$$

Reinforcement axioms.

E1. The probability of an outcome event depends only on previous observables, namely, preceding presentation sets of stimuli, preceding responses, and preceding outcomes.
There is an experimenter's partition $H(n)$ such that if W_{n-1} is any $n - 1$ cylinder set, $Y \subseteq W_{n-1} \cap C_n \cap s_n$, η is in $H(n)$, and $P(Y \cap \eta) > 0$ then

$$P(O_{j,n} \mid Y \cap \eta) = P(O_{j,n} \mid \eta).$$

E2. The probability of a reinforcing event depends only on the response $A_{i,n}$ and the outcome $O_{j,n}$ of the same trial.
If W_{n-1} is an $n - 1$ cylinder set and $Y \subseteq W_{n-1} \cap C_n \cap T_n \cap s_n$ and $P(Y \cap A_{i,n} \cap O_{j,n}) > 0$, then

$$P(E_{k,n} \mid Y \cap A_{i,n} \cap O_{j,n}) = P(E_{k,n} \mid A_{i,n} \cap O_{j,n}).$$

Presentation axiom.

P1. The probability of a stimulus presentation set depends only on previous observables.
There is an experimenter's partition $H(n - 1)$ such that if W_{n-1} is any $n - 1$ cylinder set, $Y \subseteq W_{n-1} \cap C_n$, η is in $H(n - 1)$ and $P(Y \cap \eta) > 0$, then

$$P(T_n \mid Y \cap \eta) = P(T_n \mid \eta).$$

Preliminary Theorems

In this section we give some theorems needed for the general Markov theorem that is the subject of the following section.

We first state an independence-of-path result for conditional probability of a response. The gist of it is that if we are given the presentation set T and the set of conditioned stimuli C_i, then no further knowledge about conditioning of stimuli to other responses or about events on past trials will affect the probability of response i. (In Theorem 1 and hereafter the intersection symbol is suppressed and juxtaposition is used to denote intersection in the interest of simplifying notation. Thus we write $T_n C_{i,n} Y$ instead of $T_n \cap C_{i,n} \cap Y$, etc.)

THEOREM 1. *If* W_{n-1} *is an* $n - 1$ *cylinder set,* $Y \subseteq W_{n-1} C_n$, *and* $P(T_n C_{i,n} Y) > 0$, *then*

$$P(A_{i,n} \mid T_n C_{i,n} Y) = P(A_{i,n} \mid T_n C_{i,n}).$$

It may be noted that as a special case of the theorem just stated we have

$$P(A_{i,n} \mid T_n C_n) = P(A_{i,n} \mid T_n C_{i,n}),$$

provided $P(T_n C_n) > 0$.

We next give expressions for the probability of arriving at any given conditioned subset C_i' given the reinforcing event, presentation set, and conditioning function (or merely the conditioned subset C_i) on the preceding trial. The first of these expressions refers to the change in the subset of elements connected to a given response on a trial when that response is reinforced.

THEOREM 2. *If* $P(E_{i,n} T_n C_{i,n}) > 0$, *then*

$$P(C_{i,n+1}' \mid E_{i,n} T_n C_{i,n}) = \sum_s \frac{P(E_{i,n} \mid s_n T_n C_{i,n})}{P(E_{i,n} \mid T_n C_{i,n})} P(s_n \mid T_n),$$

where the summation runs over all s *such that* $s \cup C_i = C_i'$ *and* $s = T$.
Proof: It is easily seen that

$$P(C_{i,n+1}' E_{i,n} T_n C_{i,n}) = P(C_{i,n+1}' E_{i,n} \cup_s s_n T_n C_{i,n})$$

$$= \sum_s P(E_{i,n} s_n T_n C_{i,n}).$$

Then, making the appropriate conditionalizations, the desired result is obtained where $C_{i,n}$ is eliminated from $P(s_n \mid T_n C_{i,n})$ by appropriate use of the sampling axioms.

One might have expected that this basic expression for the change in the conditioning function on a reinforced trial would involve only the factor representing probability of a particular type of sample and not also the factors representing probabilities of the reinforcing event. However, it is possible for the reinforcing event to depend on the response made by the subject on the given trial, and this in turn depends on the nature of the sampled subset of stimuli. Thus information about the reinforcing event of trial n may convey information about the stimulus sample. Under some particular reinforcement schedules, e.g., the classical discrimination paradigm or simple noncontingent reinforcement, the factors involving $E_{i,n}$ cancel out.

The next two theorems deal similarly with the change in the subset of elements connected to a given response on trials when some alternative response is reinforced or when the neutral event E_0 occurs, respectively. The proofs follow that of Theorem 2 closely and are thus omitted.

THEOREM 3. *If $k \neq 0$ and $k \neq i$ and $P(E_{k,n}T_nC_{i,n}) > 0$, then*

$$P(C'_{i,n+1} \mid E_{k,n}T_nC_{i,n}) = \sum_s \frac{P(E_{k,n} \mid s_nT_nC_{i,n})P(s_n \mid T_n)}{P(E_{k,n} \mid T_nC_{i,n})},$$

where the summation now runs over all samples s such that $s \subseteq T$ and $s_i \cup C'_i = C_i$.

THEOREM 4. *If $P(E_{0,n}T_nC_{i,n}) > 0$, then*

$$P(C'_{i,n+1} \mid E_{0,n}T_nC_{i,n}) = \begin{cases} 1, & if \ C'_i = C_i, \\ 0, & otherwise. \end{cases}$$

MARKOV CHAIN PROPERTY

With a substantial number of independence-of-path theorems now established, we turn to the proof of what is probably the most important general theorem of stimulus sampling theory, namely, that under very broad conditions an appropriately chosen sequence of events is a Markov chain. The significance of this theorem lies in the fact that the mathematical theory of finite state Markov chains is simpler and more complete than that of nearly any other class of stochastic processes.[6]

In principle, response probabilities can always be computed, given the probabilities of the states of the chain. Except when the number of states is very small, it is usually impractical to give explicit formulas for response probabilities as functions of n, but in many experimentally important cases, asymptotic response probabilities turn out to have simple, closed expressions in terms of the asymptotic state probabilities.

---

[6] We define a Markov *chain* to be a Markov process whose transition probabilities are independent of n.

Some Examples

Before turning to formal developments, we want to describe intuitively in somewhat more detail the character of the results in this section and to give a sketch of some examples that show that the results are in a certain sense the best possible. By this we mean that the definition of state in the Markov chain cannot be essentially simplified without destroying the Markovian character of the process.

A result much used in the experimental literature is that the sequence $\langle C_1, C_2, \ldots, C_n, \ldots \rangle$ of conditioning random variables that take possible conditioning functions as their values forms a Markov chain for simple non-contingent and contingent reinforcement schedules. Superficially it might be thought that the sequence of events (or random variables) that forms a Markov chain would be quite different in discrimination and simple learning experiments. However, as we shall see, this difference is not critical at all. The crucial question is always, how many trials back do the probability dependencies in the reinforcement and presentation schedules extend?

Double contingent reinforcement with constant presentation set.   For example, let us first consider one of the most direct generalizations, within simple learning, of the simple contingent case, namely, the double contingent case for which the probability of an outcome or reinforcement on trial n depends on the responses of that trial and the previous trial. For the double contingent case the sequence of conditioning random variables $\langle C_1, C_2, \ldots, C_n, \ldots \rangle$ is not a Markov chain. Now it might be thought that this is not surprising, but that if we define the states as pairs $C_{n-1}C_n$ of conditioning functions, reflecting the fact that the contingency extends over two trials, then the sequence $\langle C_1C_2, C_2C_3, \ldots, C_{n-1}C_n, \ldots \rangle$ would be a Markov chain. However, this conclusion is not true except under very special restrictions. Consider, for example, the following model. The set S of stimuli has exactly one element that is sampled with probability $\theta, 0 < \theta < 1$, on every trial. To show that we do not have a Markov chain we need to show that for some n, C, C', C'', C''',

$$P(C''_{n+2}C''_{n+1} \mid C''_{n+1}C'_nC_{n-1}) \neq P(C'''_{n+2}C''_{n+1} \mid C''_{n+1}C'_n). \tag{1}$$

If we take $r = t = 2$,

$$P(E_{k,n} \mid O_{k,n}) = 1,$$
$$P(O_{1,n} \mid A_{j,n}A_{j'n-1}) = \pi_{j'j}$$

and $n = 2$, then it is tedious and lengthy, but not difficult, to establish Equation 1. Rather than give this computation, we believe it will be more instruc-

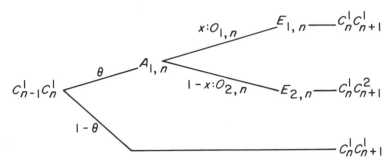

FIGURE 1.
The tree of paths leading from the pair $C_{n-1}^1 C_n^1$ terminating on trial n to the possible new pairs terminating on trial $n + 1$.

tive to show what goes wrong when we attempt to draw one of the trees for a Markov chain with the states being the pairs $C_{n-1}C_n$ of conditioning functions.

Using the notation C_n^i to indicate that the single stimulus is conditioned to response A_i on trial n, we can diagram the paths leading from the pair $C_{n-1}^1 C_n^1$ terminating on trial n to the possible new pairs terminating on trial $n + 1$ as shown in Figure 1. The construction of the tree is standard and requires little explanation.

The difficulty with the tree is that we do not have as part of it the responses on trial $n - 1$, and thus we are not able to indicate the probabilities x and $1 - x$ of outcomes $O_{1,n}$ and $O_{2,n}$ in the appropriate branches. This problem suggests as the second possibility a tree that retains the same definition of state but includes the responses on trial $n - 1$ among the branching possibilities.

In the case of this second tree, the difficulty is that the probability of an A_1 response on trial $n - 1$ is disturbed by the knowledge that the conditioning state on trial n is C^1. Without this knowledge, the probability of an A_1 response on trial $n - 1$ given C_{n-1}^1 is simply $\theta + (1 - \theta)\rho$, where ρ is the fixed probability of an A_1 response when no sample is drawn. With this additional information we cannot compute the probability of $A_{1,n-1}$ without also considering the reinforcement on trial $n - 1$, which immediately requires knowledge of the response on trial $n - 2$, and thereby invalidates the Markovian character of the tree. An appropriate definition of state for this double contingent case of reinforcement is the response on trial $n - 1$ and the conditioning function on trial n. A typical tree is shown in Figure 2. Because the probabilities of the various branches are independent of n, the trial number subscripts have been dropped.

The critical thing in defining the states of the Markov chain is to include all those events on which the reinforcement probabilities depend, as well as the conditioning function on the given trial. Before proceeding to the general

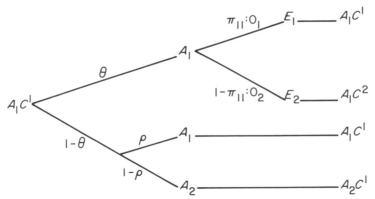

FIGURE 2.
A typical tree for the double contingent case of reinforcement.

theory, we give some additional examples. In all these examples we assume the same possible conditioning function and the same sampling condition as in the double contingent instance just discussed.

Noncontingent, Markov reinforcement schedule with constant presentation set.   Let

$$P(O_{i,n+1} \mid O_{j,n}) = \pi_{ji}$$

be the transition probabilities of a one-stage Markov chain in the trial outcomes. Then the appropriate definition of a state in the Markov learning process is the reinforcement on trial $n - 1$ and the conditioning function on trial n.

Noncontingent presentation and contingent reinforcement with lag.   Let T^m, $m = 1, 2$, be the two presentation sets of stimuli, and let the reinforcement schedule be defined by

$$P(O_{j,n} \mid T_n^m, A_{i,n-1}) = \pi_{imj}.$$

The Markov chain then has eight states $A_i C^j T^m$ for $i, j, m = 1, 2$; and it should be clear from the previous examples how to construct the tree with each state, and thereby the transition matrix of the process, once we specify noncontingent probabilities for T^1 and T^2, say, τ_1 and τ_2.

Contingent presentation and contingent reinforcement.   To show that it is not sufficient just to consider the past dependence of the reinforcement schedule, a simple discrimination setup will suffice, where the reinforcement is dependent on the presentation sets and where the probability of a presentation set itself depends on the response on the preceding trial. That is, $P(O_{j,n} \mid T_n^m) =$

π_{mj} and $P(T_n^m \mid A_{i,n-1}) = \tau_{im}$. For this situation, we may take as the states of the Markov process $A_i C^j$, for $i, j = 1, 2$. In this particular instance we may also take as states the conditioning functions and the presentation sets, i.e., $C^j T^m$. However, to simplify the statement of general results we shall restrict ourselves to states which have the conditioning function as the last event.

Experimenter's Schedule

We turn now to the general theory. We shall mean by an *experimenter's schedule* the set of conditional probabilities that determine the schedule of outcome events and the schedule of presentation sets. By virtue of Reinforcement Axiom E1 and Presentation Axiom P1 this dependence is restricted to preceding outcome events, responses, and presentation sets. We say that an experimenter's schedule has *finite character* $\mathcal{K}$ if there is a collection of finite sequences $\mathcal{K} = \{(X_1^{\ell_1}, \ldots, X_M^{\ell_M})\}$ with each $X_i^{\ell_i}$ an O_j, an A_i, or a T^m and such that, for each n,

$$P(O_{j,n} \mid A_{i,n} T_n^m K_{n-1} W_{n-1}) = P(O_{j,n} \mid A_{i,n} T_n^m K_{n-1}) \tag{2}$$

and

$$P(T_n^{m'} \mid K_{n-1} W_{n-1}) = P(T_n^{m'} \mid K_{n-1}) \tag{3}$$

for any response A_i, presentation set T^m, sequence K in $\mathcal{K}$, and W_{n-1} and $n-1$ cylinder set such that $P(A_{i,n} T_n^m K_{n-1} W_{n-1}) > 0$ for Equation 2 and $P(K_{n-1} W_{n-1}) > 0$ for Equation 3. The notation K_{n-1} denotes a sequence belonging to $\mathcal{K}$ that terminates on trial O_{n-1}. For example, if $\mathcal{K} = \{(O_1^1, A_1^1), (O_1^1, A_2^1), (O_2^1, A_1^1), (O_2^1, A_2^1)\}$ and $K = (O_1^1, A_2^1)$, then K_{n-1} is the event $O_{1,n-1} A_{2,n-1}$. The superscript ℓ_i indicates the lag behind trial n. Thus $\ell_i = 2$ refers to an event on trial $n - 2$. A more elaborate and explicit definition and notation could be used, but the sense of the present notation should be clear, and it is adequate for our purposes. We do need to add the provision that for any n the probabilities of the event sequences K_{n-1} for all K in $\mathcal{K}$ add to one, in order for the conditional probabilities of presentation and reinforcement to be completely fixed. Moreover, it is also understood from the definition of *finite character* that the conditional probabilities of Equations 2 and 3 are independent of n.

Unfortunately, the sets $C_n K_{n-1}$, when K is in $\mathcal{K}$ and C is a conditioning function, cannot by themselves serve as the states of the Markov chain when the dependencies in the experimenter's schedule extend back more than one trial, as is illustrated by the example of *contingent reinforcement with lag 2 and constant presentation set*. Because this is a case of simple learning, that is, the full set S of stimuli is presented on each trial, the experimenter's schedule is defined by the conditional probabilities of reinforcement, which here are:

$$P(O_{j,n} \mid A_{i,n-2}) = \pi_{ij}.$$

What is not determined is the new state to which any branch leads, for the response on trial $n - 1$ is not known. The method of remedying the situation in this special case is also the one that works in general, namely, to add the responses on trial $n - 1$ and take as the states of the process the events $C_n A_{i,n-1} A_{i',n-2}$.

For the general theory we need a notation for this extension of the finite character $\mathcal{K}$ of the experimeter's schedule. Let $K = (X_1^{\ell_1}, \ldots, X_M^{\ell_M})$. Then K^* is the enlarged sequence that for each $\ell_i > 1$ adds the events $X_i^1, \ldots, X_i^{\ell_i - 1}$. For example, if $K = (O_j^2, A_i^3)$ then $K^* = (O_{j'}^1, O_j^2, A_{i'}^1, A_{i''}^2, A_i^3)$, and the events $C_n O_{j',n-1} A_{i'',n-1} O_{j,n-2} A_{i',n-2} A_{i,n-3}$ form the states of the Markov process. Or, in the example just considered, $K = (A_i^2)$ and $K^* = (A_i^1, A_i^2)$.

General Markov Theorem

Before stating and proving the general Markov theorem, it will be convenient first to show that the transition probabilities of the events $C_n K_{n-1}^*$ are independent of n, for this result may then be used to show that the Markov process is indeed a Markov chain. Moreover, we may show independence of n by explicitly computing the transition probabilities and thereby providing a general method for obtaining the transition matrix of the Markov chain. To avoid onerous notation we take a slightly restricted family $\mathcal{K}$ of events in the statement of the theorem. (The proof is given in Estes & Suppes, 1959b.)

THEOREM 5. *If*

(i) $\mathcal{K} = \{(O_{j_1}^1, A_{i_1}^1, T^{1,m_1}, O_{j_2}^2, A_{i_2}^2, T^{2,m_2}, \ldots, O_{j_\nu}^\nu, A_{i_\nu}^\nu, T^{\nu,m_\nu})\}$,

(ii) $P(O_{j,n} \mid A_{i,n} T_n^m O_{j_1,n-1} A_{i_1,n-1} T_{n-1}^{m_1} \cdots O_{j_\nu,n-\nu} A_{i_\nu,n-\nu} T_{n-\nu}^{m_\nu})$

     $= \pi(j, i, m, j_1, i_1, m_1, \ldots, j_\nu, i_\nu, m_\nu)$,

(iii) $P(T_n^m \mid O_{j_1,n-1} A_{i_1,n-1} T_{n-1}^{m_1}, \ldots, O_{j_\nu,n-\nu} A_{i_\nu,n-\nu} T_{n-\nu}^{m_\nu})$

     $= \tau(m, j_1, i_1, m_1, \ldots, j_\nu, i_\nu, m_\nu)$,

(iv) $P(E_{k,n} \mid O_{j,n} A_{i,n}) = c_{ijk}$,

then

(a) $P(C_n K_{n-1}^* \mid C_{n-1}' K_{n-2}'^*) = \sum_k \sum_s c_{ij_1k} \dfrac{N(s \cap C_i')}{N(s)} P(s \mid T^{m_1})$

     $\cdot \pi(j_1, i_1, m_1, j_2, i_2, m_2, \ldots, j_\nu, i_\nu, m_\nu, j_{\nu+1}, i_{\nu+1}, m_{\nu+1})$

     $\cdot \tau(m_1, j_2, i_2, m_2, \ldots, j_{\nu+1}, i_{\nu+1}, m_{\nu+1})$

where $\sum\limits_s$ is over all samples s such that $C_k' = C_k \cup s_k$ and, for $\ell \neq k$, $s_\ell \cup C_\ell' = C_\ell$, provided if s is empty $N(s \cap C_i')/N(s)$ is replaced by $\rho_{i,n}$ and

$$K_{n-1}^* K_{n-2}'^* = O_{j_1,n-1} A_{i_1,n-1} T_{n-1}^{m_1}$$
$$\cdots O_{j_\nu,n-\nu} A_{i_\nu,n-\nu} T_{n-\nu}^{m_\nu} O_{j_{\nu+1},n-\nu-1} A_{i_{\nu+1},n-\nu-1} T_{n-\nu-1}^{m_{\nu+1}};$$

(b) $P(C_n K_{n-1}^* \mid C_{n-1}' K_{n-2}'^*) = 0$ provided $K_{n-1}^* K_{n-2}'^* = 0$.

For convenient statement of the general Markov theorem we may define for each n the random variable K_n^* that takes as its values the events $C_n K_{n-1}^*$ with K in $\mathcal{K}$ and C a possible conditioning function.

THEOREM 6. (*General Markov Theorem*). *If a stimulus sampling model has an experimenter's schedule of finite character $\mathcal{K}$, then the sequence of random variables $\langle K_1^*, K_2^* \ldots K_n^*, \ldots \rangle$ is a finite-state Markov chain.*

Proof: To simplify notation, we shall prove only a special case of the theorem, but the method of proof required is exactly that needed for the general case, and it will be perfectly apparent how to extend the proof in a routine manner. Let

$$\mathcal{K} = \{(O_j^1, T^{1,m}, A_i^2)\};$$

that is, the experimenter's schedule is determined by the conditional probabilities

$$P(O_{j,n} \mid O_{j',n-1} T_{n-1}^m A_{i,n-2}) = \pi(j, j', m, i) \tag{4}$$

and

$$P(T_n^{m'} \mid O_{j',n-1} T_{n-1}^m A_{i,n-2}) = \tau(m', j', m, i) \tag{5}$$

for $0 \leq j$, $j' \leq t$, $1 \leq m$, $m' \leq M$, $1 \leq i \leq r$, where M is the total number of presentation sets.

To establish the theorem for this special case we need to extend K to K^* and prove that—for every n, j, j', m, m', i, i', and i'', every pair of conditioning functions C and C', and every $n - 2$ cylinder set W_{n-2} which is an intersection of $C_{n'}' K_{n'-1}'^*$ sets with $n' < n - 1$ such that $P(C_{n-1}' K_{n-1}'^* W_{n-2}) > 0$—we have

$$P(C_n K_{n-1}^* \mid C_{n-1}' K_{n-2}'^* W_{n-2}) = P(C_n K_{n-1}^* \mid C_{n-1}' K_{n-2}'^*), \tag{6}$$

where

$$C_n K_{n-1}^* = C_n O_{j,n-1} A_{i,n-1} T_{n-1}^m A_{i',n-2} \tag{7}$$

and

$$C_{n-1}' K_{n-2}'^* = C_{n-1}' O_{j',n-2} A_{i',n-2} T_{n-2}^{m'} A_{i'',n-3}. \tag{8}$$

Now by elementary probability theory

$$P(C_n K_{n-1}^* \mid C_{n-1}' K_{n-2}'^* W_{n-2})$$
$$= \frac{\sum\limits_k P(C_n E_{k,n-1} O_{j,n-1} A_{i,n-1} T_{n-1}^m C_{n-1}' O_{j',n-2} A_{i',n-2} T_{n-2}^{m'} A_{i'',n-3} W_{n-2})}{P(C_{n-1}' K_{n-2}'^* W_{n-2})}. \tag{9}$$

In analyzing the various conditional probabilities obtained from the resulting expression, let us use Y for the set of remaining events that are not needed on the basis of independence-of-path results already established and that occur before the event whose conditional probability is being considered. Thus in Equation 10 below,

$$Y = O_{j,n-1}A_{i,n-1}T^m_{n-1}O_{j',n-2}A_{i',n-2}T^{m'}_{n-2}A_{i'',n-3}W_{n-2}.$$

In the first place, by virtue of Theorems 2 through 4, we have

$$P(C_n \mid E_{k,n-1}T^m_{n-1}C'_{n-1}Y) = P(C_n \mid E_{k,n-1}T^m_{n-1}C'_{n-1}). \qquad (10)$$

Second, on the basis of Reinforcement Axiom E2,

$$P(E_{k,n-1} \mid O_{j,n-1}A_{i,n-1}Y) = P(E_{k,n-1} \mid O_{j,n-1}A_{i,n-1}). \qquad (11)$$

Third, because of the experimenter's schedule assumption of Equation 4,

$$P(O_{j,n-1} \mid O_{j',n-2}T^{m'}_{n-2}A_{i'',n-3}Y) = P(O_{j,n-1} \mid O_{j',n-2}T^{m'}_{n-2}A_{i'',n-3}). \qquad (12)$$

Fourth, in view of Theorem 1,

$$P(A_{i,n-1} \mid T^m_{n-1}C'_{n-1}Y) = P(A_{i,n-1} \mid T^m_{n-1}C'_{n-1}). \qquad (13)$$

Fifth, because of the experimenter's schedule assumption of Equation 5,

$$P(T^m_{n-1} \mid O_{j',n-2}T^{m'}_{n-2}A_{i'',n-3}Y) = P(T^m_{n-1} \mid O_{j',n-2}T^{m'}_{n-2}A_{i'',n-3}). \qquad (14)$$

None of the conditional probabilities in Equations 10 through 14 depend on W_{n-2}, and thus we may infer at once from Equations 9 through 14 that Equation 6 holds, the desired result. Moreover, it follows at once from Theorem 5 that the probabilities in Equations 10 through 14 are independent of n, which establishes the chain character of the process. **Q.E.D.**

As an immediate corollary of this theorem we have the result, already mentioned, which is much used, explicitly or implicitly, in the experimental literature. In the statement of the corollary we use C_n for the conditioning random variable whose values are possible conditioning functions.

COROLLARY. *If the conditional probabilities on trial n of the experimenter's schedule depend only on occurrences of events on trial n, then the sequence of conditioning random variables $\langle C_1, C_2, \ldots, C_n, \ldots \rangle$ is a finite-state Markov chain.*

We may, by similar methods, which rely on additional 'independence-of-path' theorems, prove a general Markov theorem for the case when the conditioning functions C_n are simplified to the functions

$$N(C_n) = N(C_{1,n}) \cap N(C_{2,n}) \cap \cdots \cap N(C_{r,n}),$$

which simply indicate the *number* of stimuli conditioned to each response, provided the presentation set is constant over trials. Let us define for each n the random variable L_n^* which takes as its values the events $N(C_n)K_{n-1}^*$ with K in $\mathcal{K}$ and C a possible conditioning function. We omit proof of the following theorem.

THEOREM 7.   *If a stimulus sampling model has an experimenter's schedule of finite character* $\mathcal{K}$, *and if S is the presentation set on all trials, then the sequence of random variables* $\langle L_1^*, L_2^*, \ldots, L_n^*, \ldots \rangle$ *is a finite-state Markov chain.*

ACKNOWLEDGMENTS

This chapter is a revised and shortened version of a longer technical report (Estes & Suppes, 1959b). The original research was supported by the Office of Naval Research under contract NR 171-034 with Stanford University. Work on the present revised version has been partially supported by the National Science Foundation under grant NSFGJ-443X to Stanford. We are indebted to David Rogosa for a number of useful comments on this revised version.

REFERENCES

Atkinson, R. C., & Estes, W. K. Stimulus sampling theory. In R. D. Luce, R. R. Bush, and E. Galanter (Eds.), *Handbook of mathematical psychology*. Vol. II. New York: Wiley, 1963. Pp. 121–268.

Bower, G. H. Stimulus-sampling theory of coding variability. In A. W. Melton and E. Martin (Eds.), *Coding process in human memory*. Washington, D.C.: Winston, 1972.

Bush, R. R., & Estes, W. K. (Eds.). *Studies in mathematical learning theory*. Stanford: Stanford University Press, 1959.

Bush, R. R., & Mosteller, F. *Stochastic models for learning*. New York: Wiley, 1955.

Estes, W. K. Toward a statistical theory of learning. *Psychological Review*, 1950, **57**, 94–107.

Estes, W. K. Component and pattern models with Markovian interpretations. In R. R. Bush and W. K. Estes (Eds.), *Studies in mathematical learning theory*. Stanford: Stanford University Press, 1959. (a)

Estes, W. K. The statistical approach to learning theory. In S. Koch (Ed.), *Psychology: A study of a science*. New York: McGraw-Hill, 1959. (b)

Estes, W. K. Learning and memory. In E. F. Beckenbach and C. B. Tompkins (Eds.), *Concepts of communication*. New York: Wiley, 1971.

Estes, W. K. Research and theory on the learning of probabilities. *Journal of the American Statistical Association*, 1972, **67**, 81–102.

Estes, W. K., & Suppes, P. Foundations of linear models. In R. R. Bush and W. K.

Estes (Eds.), *Studies in mathematical learning theory.* Stanford, Calif.: Stanford University Press, 1959. (a)

Estes, W. K., & Suppes, P. *Foundations of statistical learning theory, II. The stimulus sampling model.* Technical Report No. 26. Stanford, Calif.: Institute for Mathematical Studies in the Social Sciences, Stanford University, 1959. (b)

Kemeny, J. G., & Snell, J. L. Markov learning processes in learning theory. *Psychometrika*, 1957, **22**, 221–230.

Koteskey, R. L. A stimulus-sampling model of the partial reinforcement effect. *Psychological Review*, 1972, **79**, 161–171.

Neimark, E. D., & Estes, W. K. *Stimulus sampling theory.* San Francisco: Holden-Day, 1967.

Norman, M. F. *Markov processes and learning models.* New York: Academic Press, 1972.

Suppes, P. Stimulus response theory of finite automata. *Journal of Mathematical Psychology*, 1969, **6**, 327–355.

Suppes, P., & Atkinson, R. C. *Markov learning models for multiperson interactions.* Stanford: Stanford University Press, 1960.

Thorndike, E. L. *The psychology of learning.* New York: Teachers College, 1914.

Effects of Overtraining, Problem Shifts, and Probabilistic Reinforcement in Discrimination Learning: Predictions of an Attentional Model

M. Frank Norman

UNIVERSITY OF PENNSYLVANIA

1. INTRODUCTION

This chapter is concerned with a model for discrimination learning that incorporates interacting perceptual- and response-learning processes. The subject learns to pay attention to the relevant stimulus dimension. Simultaneously, he learns to bias his responses toward the correct value or cue along that dimension.

The concept of selective attention to a stimulus dimension has only received full respectability within experimental psychology over the last two decades. The phenomenon that implicates an attentional mechanism most directly is this: intradimensional shifts are generally learned more easily than extradimensional shifts (Estes, 1970, pp. 169–170). In the first case, the subject is shifted to a new problem with the same relevant and irrelevant dimensions (e.g., shape and color of geometrical forms), while the relevant and irrelevant dimensions are interchanged in extradimensional shifts. Specific response transfer can be eliminated in both paradigms by introducing new cues (e.g., square and cross in place of circle and triangle) on both dimensions. Thus the advantage of the intradimensional shift must be due to transfer of attention to the previously relevant dimension into the second phase of the experiment.

The prediction of the relative difficulty of these two shifts is so straight-forward that it may be regarded as following from 'attention theory' rather than from any particular 'two-process model.' However, one need not look far in the literature on discrimination learning to find important phenomena of sufficient subtlety that careful analysis is greatly facilitated by a precise model. Two of these are the relative difficulty of extradimensional and reversal shifts, and the effect of overtraining on reversal. In a reversal shift, the relevant and irrelevant dimensions remain the same, as do the cues on these dimensions, but the correct and incorrect cues (on the relevant dimension) are interchanged.

Overtraining sometimes facilitates reversal (the overlearning reversal effect or ORE) and sometimes retards it (Mackintosh, 1969). Children learn reversal more quickly than extradimensional shift (Campione, 1971), but Kelleher's (1956) rats learned extradimensional shift more easily. As we see in Sections 8 and 9, any of these results can be explained by suitable choice of the parameter values in the model considered. For example, the relative rates of perceptual and response learning must be chosen appropriately. These choices make good sense psychologically, and yield testable predictions for other experiments.

Reward is perfectly correlated with one cue on the relevant dimension in all of the preceding experimental paradigms. Other experiments have used probabilistic reinforcement, with attendant imperfect correlation. For example, in a brightness discrimination with position irrelevant, black might be correct with probability π, $\frac{1}{2} < \pi < 1$, while white is correct on the remaining trials. On such schedules, subjects' asymptotic proportions of black choices almost always fall between π and 1, and values in the upper part of this range are common in experiments with animals, even when response correction is allowed after errors. The upper limit 1, which represents optimal behavior, is approached under noncorrection procedures (Sutherland & Mackintosh, 1971, pp. 405–409).

In summary, performance in these experiments ranges from fairly efficient to very efficient. We see in Section 10 that these levels of efficiency are consistent with the model, provided that correct responses produce more perceptual and response learning than incorrect ones. This imposes a heavy constraint on the model's parameters. However, this constraint is consistent with those imposed by shift and overtraining studies.

The scope and power of attentional concepts are generally appreciated in psychology today, but our understanding of these ideas lacks depth and precision. It is very difficult to form a clear idea of the possibilities inherent in two-process conceptions of discrimination learning without specifying a mathematical model and exploring the effects of variations in its parameters. These are my objectives in this chapter.

2. EXPERIMENTS

It is often easiest to understand an abstract psychological model within the context of a specific experiment. I describe two typical experiments in this section: learning of a brightness discrimination by a rat in a *jumping stand*, and learning of a color discrimination by a child in a modified *Wisconsin General Test Apparatus* (WGTA). Discussion of the model in later sections is cast primarily in the terminology of a jumping stand, and secondarily in that of WGTA. The reader should have no difficulty transposing the discussion to other settings.

(1) *Jumping stand.* (See Sutherland & Mackintosh, 1971, Fig. 2.1, p. 25). On each trial, the rat must jump from a central platform to a right- or left-hand ledge. Above each ledge is a window in which a stimulus card is displayed. One card is black, the other is white, and the black card appears on the left on a random 50 percent of trials. Behind the window is a platform with a tray of food. One of the cards, say the black one, can be pushed aside permitting access to food. The window containing the white card is always locked.

(2) *WGTA.* (See Zeaman & House, 1963, Fig. 5-1, p. 160.) The child moves one of two stimulus objects on a tray before him in order to expose a shallow well. On half the trials, the objects are a red triangle and a green circle; on the remaining trials, they are a red circle and a green triangle. Each object appears equally often on the child's left and right. There is a piece of candy under the red object, but nothing under the green one.

In either of these experiments, response *correction* may be permitted. Thus a child who makes an error can move the other object and obtain candy. In a noncorrection procedure, no such second choice is allowed.

Probabilistic reinforcement. In these examples, reward is perfectly correlated with one cue on the relevant dimension. This is *consistent reinforcement*. In probabilistic reinforcement experiments, this correlation is imperfect. I have already mentioned the possibility that reward might be associated with one cue on a proportion π of the trials and with the other cue on the same dimension on the remaining trials. This is called *noncontingent reinforcement*, in recognition of the fact that the correct cue on any trial is determined by the experimenter, without regard to the subject's response.

Consider an experiment of this type in a jumping stand, and let π_B and π_W be the probabilities that black (B) and white (W) responses are correct:

$$\pi_B = P(B \text{ correct}), \quad \pi_W = P(W \text{ correct}).$$

Then

$$\pi_B = 1 - \pi_W = \pi. \tag{1}$$

In noncorrection experiments, there is no need to unlock exactly one window on each trial. Thus π_B and π_W can be varied independently. These parameters determine a *probabilistic reinforcement schedule*. In addition to noncontingent schedules, which satisfy Equation 1, we will be interested in *symmetric schedules*, defined by

$$\pi_B = \pi_W = \zeta. \tag{2}$$

Under such a schedule, brightness and position are both irrelevant (i.e., useless) dimensions. *Extinction* is the special case where no response is ever rewarded ($\zeta = 0$). The only probabilistic reinforcement schedule that we exclude at the onset is the one on which all responses are correct ($\zeta = 1$). In other words, *it is always assumed that*

$$\pi_B < 1 \quad or \quad \pi_W < 1. \tag{3}$$

For any number p, let $p' = 1 - p$. The quantity

$$\ell = \pi_W' / (\pi_W' + \pi_B') \tag{4}$$

is associated with probability matching, in the sense that $P(B) = \ell$ is equivalent to

$$P(B) = P(\text{reinforcement of B}). \tag{5}$$

"Reinforcement of B" means that the rat jumps to an unlocked black window or a locked white window, hence

$$P(\text{reinf. of B}) = P(B)\pi_B + (1 - P(B))\pi_W'.$$

It follows that

$$
\begin{aligned}
P(\text{reinf. of B}) - P(B) &= -P(B)\pi_B' + (1 - P(B))\pi_W' \\
&= \pi_W' - P(B)(\pi_W' + \pi_B') \\
&= (\pi_W' + \pi_B')(\ell - P(B)).
\end{aligned}
$$

By Equation 3, $\pi_W' + \pi_B' > 0$, so $P(B) = \ell$ is equivalent to Equation 5, as claimed. For noncontingent schedules this equivalence is trivial, since

$$P(\text{reinf. of B}) = \pi = \ell.$$

Note that consistent reinforcement of black is the special case of probabilistic reinforcement defined by $\pi_B = 1$ and $\pi_W = 0$.

3. THE MODEL

The model treated in this chapter was proposed by Zeaman and House (1963) and Lovejoy (1966). I call it the *Zeaman-House-Lovejoy* or *ZHL model*. Some special features of the formulations in these two papers will be noted after the model has been described in the context of a jumping-stand experiment with probabilistic reinforcement.

On any trial, the rat attends to brightness (br) or to position (po), but not to both. His probability of attending to brightness is denoted v:

$$v = P(\text{br}).$$

If he attends to brightness, he chooses black (B) rather than white (W) with conditional probability y:

$$y = P(\text{B} \mid \text{br}).$$

If he attends to position, he chooses B with probability 0.5. The variables v and y or, equivalently, the composite variable

$$x = (v, y),$$

determines the subject's 'state of learning' on any trial. Given x, the probability of B is

$$P(\text{B} \mid x) = yv + 2^{-1}v', \tag{6}$$

where

$$v' = 1 - v.$$

I now describe how v and y change on each trial. This depends on what the subject attends to, what response he makes, and whether this response is correct (C) or incorrect (I). The variable y changes only when the subject attends to brightness. It increases after a correct B or an incorrect W and decreases otherwise. The quantity v increases when the subject attends to brightness and is correct, or attends to position and is incorrect. On other trials it decreases.

These changes are effected by linear transformations. Thus if the subject attends to brightness, jumps to B, and is rewarded,

$$\Delta y = \theta_1 y'$$

for some $0 < \theta_1 < 1$. The increment in y is a proportion θ_1 of the maximum possible increment $y' = 1 - y$. Similarly,

$$\Delta y = -\theta_2 y$$

TABLE 1
Events, associated transformations,
and probabilities for the ZHL model

Event	Δv	Δy	Probability
brBC	$\varphi_1 v'$	$\theta_1 y'$	$vy\pi_B$
brBI	$-\varphi_2 v$	$-\theta_2 y$	$vy\pi'_B$
brWC	$\varphi_1 v'$	$-\theta_1 y$	$vy'\pi_W$
brWI	$-\varphi_2 v$	$\theta_2 y'$	$vy'\pi'_W$
poBC	$-\varphi_3 v$	0	$v'\pi_B/2$
poBI	$\varphi_4 v'$	0	$v'\pi'_B/2$
poWC	$-\varphi_3 v$	0	$v'\pi_W/2$
poWI	$\varphi_4 v'$	0	$v'\pi'_W/2$

if he attends to brightness, jumps to B, and is not rewarded. Table 1 lists the
values of Δv and Δy corresponding to the eight possible combinations of
attention, choice, and outcome. Any such combination is called an 'event.'
Probabilities of these events are also listed.

The fact that there are four φ_is in Table 1 instead of eight, and two θ_js
instead of four, reflects an assumption of black-white symmetry. Thus brBC
and brWC have identical effects on v. Also, brBC has the same effect on
$y = P(B)$ $[\Delta y = \theta_1(1 - y)]$ that brWC has on $y' = P(W)$ $[\Delta y' = \theta_1(1 - y')]$.
It is assumed throughout the chapter that

$$0 < \varphi_i < 1 \quad and \quad 0 < \theta_j < 1 \tag{7}$$

for all i and j. The occurrence of near-optimal performance under probabilistic
reinforcement points to very small values of the nonreward parameters φ_2, φ_4,
and θ_2 for noncorrection procedures. The exclusion of zero values of these
parameters represents the most notable loss of generality in Equation 7.

I turn now to the relationship of the present formulation to its predecessors.
Zeaman and House (1963) were interested in discrimination learning by
retarded children. The model they described could handle an arbitrary
number of stimulus dimensions. I restrict attention to the case of only two
dimensions, because it appears to be much more tractable mathematically
than the general case. An important feature of the Zeaman-House formulation is that it specifies a learning process for the probability z of choosing
left, given attention to position, and thus describes the laterality as well as
the brightness of a subject's choice. In particular, it can predict certain types
of 'position habits.' [1] However, since the black card appears on the left and

---

[1] If a rat is switched from a problem with left correct to one with black correct, the model
predicts better performance when black is on the left than when it is on the right. Graf and
Tighe (1971), who observed an analogous difference in an experiment with turtles, thought
it was at variance with attention theory.

right equally often, $P(B)$ does not depend on z, and the model can be 'reduced' to the form given in Table 1.

Zeaman and House assumed that $\varphi_1 = \varphi_2 = \varphi_3 = \varphi_4$ and $\theta_1 = \theta_2$. A number of implications of this extremely restrictive condition are presented in Section 7.

Lovejoy (1966) was concerned with the ORE in rats. Some of his work is reviewed in Section 9. My description of his model differs significantly from his in only one respect. He avoids restriction to experiments with a single irrelevant dimension by simply not specifying what the subject is doing when he is not attending to the relevant dimension. In effect, multidimensional problems are reduced to two dimensions by lumping together all irrelevant dimensions. This approach to multidimensional problems is not compatible with that of Zeaman and House.

How can the ZHL model be applied to the WGTA experiment with its two irrelevant dimensions, form and position? In the discussion of shifts in Section 8, we simply ignore position, on the assumption that pretraining and instructions have suppressed it within the child's attentional repertoire. An alternative suggested by Lovejoy's formulation is to describe the focus of attention as 'color' or 'something else.'

I now introduce some notations and note some simple equalities that are needed in subsequent sections. Let V_n, Y_n, and X_n be the values of v, y, and $x = (v, y)$ on trial n, where $n = 0, 1, 2, \ldots$. Clearly V_n and Y_n are random variables, and X_n is a random vector. Let

$$v_n = E(V_n) \quad \text{and} \quad y_n = E(Y_n)$$

be the expectations of V_n and Y_n. A subscript n on br, po, B, W, C, or I indicates an occurrence on trial n. For example, B_n means 'the rat jumps to black on trial n.' Clearly $v_n = P(\text{br}_n)$, and, by Equation 6,[2]

$$P(B_n) = E(V_n Y_n) + 2^{-1}v_n'. \tag{8}$$

Similarly,

$$P(W_n) = E(V_n Y_n') + 2^{-1}v_n'. \tag{9}$$

4. REGULARITY AND ABSORPTION

It is easy to see that a subject's state of learning, X_n, on trial n summarizes all information about preceding trials that is relevant to predicting future

---

[2] Here we use the fact that, for an arbitrary event B an an arbitrary random vector X, $P(B) = E(P(B|X))$. Similarly, for an essentially arbitrary random variable Y, $E(Y) = E(E(Y|X))$ (Brunk, 1965, p. 94). These basic relations are used in the sequel without further comment.

behavior. Hence this stochastic process is Markovian. Let $K^{(n)}(x, \cdot)$ be the distribution of X_n when $X_0 = x$:

$$K^{(n)}(x, A) = P(X_n \in A \mid X_0 = x).$$

Under the assumptions of Equations 3 and 7, the Markov process X_n is *regular*. This means that, as $n \longrightarrow \infty$, $K^{(n)}(x, \cdot)$ converges (weakly) to a distribution $K^\infty(\cdot)$ that does not depend on x. In particular, the limits

$$v_\infty = \lim v_n,$$

$$y_\infty = \lim y_n,$$

$$E(V_\infty Y_\infty) = \lim E(V_n Y_n),$$

$$P(B_\infty) = \lim P(B_n)$$

exist and do not vary with x. In each case, convergence occurs at a geometric rate.

To proceed further it is necessary to note whether the process X_n has any absorbing states. It is easy to show that $(1, 1)$ is absorbing if and only if $\pi_B = 1$, that $(1, 0)$ is absorbing if and only if $\pi_W = 1$, and that no other states are absorbing. Equation 3 excludes the case $\pi_W = \pi_B = 1$ of two absorbing states, which is incompatible with regularity.[3]

(a) Suppose that $\pi_B < 1$ and $\pi_W < 1$, so that there are no absorbing states. In this case, $0 < P(B_\infty) < 1$. Let $\bar{B}_{I,J}$ be a single subject's proportion of Bs in the J-trial block beginning with an arbitrary trial I. Then

$$\bar{B}_{I,J} \longrightarrow P(B_\infty) \tag{10}$$

with probability one or almost surely (a.s.) as $J \longrightarrow \infty$. In particular, *a subject's asymptotic proportion of jumps to* B *does not depend on his initial perceptual or response biases, or on the idiosyncrasies of his training.* These idiosyncrasies, such as the particular sequence of rewards and nonrewards experienced by the subject, reflect the inherent randomness of the model.

The quantity

$$\rho_j = \lim_{n \to \infty} [P(B_n \text{ and } B_{n+j}) - P(B_n)P(B_{n+j})]$$

is a measure of the asymptotic dependence between responses j trials apart. Let

$$\sigma^2 = \rho_0 + 2 \sum_{j=1}^{\infty} \rho_j.$$

The law of large numbers in Equation 10 is complemented by the following central limit theorem: $\sigma^2 > 0$, and $\bar{B}_{I,J}$ is asymptotically normally distributed

---

[3] If $(1, i)$ is absorbing, and $X_0 = (1, i)$, then $y_\infty = i$. Hence, if both $(1, 1)$ and $(1, 0)$ are absorbing, y_∞ depends on X_0, and X_n is not regular.

with mean $P(B_\infty)$ and variance σ^2/J as $J \longrightarrow \infty$. The quantity σ^2 can be estimated from a single subject's data by standard methods, and this estimate can be used in conjunction with the central limit theorem to make inferences about $P(B_\infty)$ (see Norman, 1971). For example, we can test the hypothesis that $P(B_\infty)$ equals the probability matching asymptote ℓ or some other specified value.

(b) Suppose that $\pi_B = 1$ and $\pi_W < 1$. Then $(1, 1)$ is the only absorbing state, and X_n is an *absorbing process*. This means that $V_n \longrightarrow 1$ and $Y_n \longrightarrow 1$ a.s. Clearly $P(W_\infty) = 0$. Furthermore

$$\#W = \text{total number of Ws over all trials}$$

is finite a.s. and $E(\#W) < \infty$, regardless of the distribution of X_0. Similarly $P(po_\infty) = 0$, $\#po < \infty$ a.s., and $E(\#po) < \infty$.

Thus, when B is always correct but W is not, the rat eventually stops making both overt and perceptual errors (Ws and pos). This highly intuitive prediction is embarrassingly difficult to derive rigorously. It is of greater mathematical than empirical interest.

(c) The case $\pi_B < 1$ and $\pi_W = 1$ parallels (b).

Comments.[4]   Norman (1972, Ch. 16) treats the ZHL model with consistent reinforcement. By generalizing arguments in that chapter, it can be shown that the ZHL model with probabilistic reinforcement is *distance diminishing*, and that X_n is a *regular compact Markov process*. Such models and processes are studied at great length in Part I of the same volume. Most of the results in this section follow easily from this general theory. In particular, the bulk of the material under (a) follows from theorems in Chapter 5 via the Corollary to Theorem 6.1.1 (p. 99). We note that the same approach yields analogous properties of uniprocess linear models with no absorbing states (see Norman, 1972, pp. 180–181).

5. CHANGES IN v_n AND y_n

Table 1 describes the changes in the random variables V_n and Y_n that result from various events on trial n. For later computations, we shall need the following formulas for changes in their expectations v_n and y_n:

$$\Delta y_n = E(V_n Q(Y_n)), \tag{11}$$

$$\Delta v_n = E(H(V_n, Y_n)), \tag{12}$$

---

[4] Most proofs and comments in lieu of proofs are given at ends of sections. All such material can be skipped without loss of continuity.

where

$$Q(y) = \delta yy' + \theta_2(y'\pi'_W - y\pi'_B),$$
$$\delta = (\theta_1 - \theta_2)(\pi_B - \pi_W), \tag{13}$$

$$H(v, y) = v[\varphi_1 v'(y\pi_B + y'\pi_W) - \varphi_2 v(y\pi'_B + y'\pi'_W)] + v'[-\varphi_3 v 2^{-1}(\pi_B + \pi_W) + \varphi_4 v' 2^{-1}(\pi'_B + \pi'_W)]. \tag{14}$$

Proof. We begin by computing $E(\Delta Y_n \mid X_n = x)$. Weighting the values of Δy in the first four rows of Table 1 by their probabilities of occurrence we obtain

$$E(\Delta Y_n \mid X_n = x) = \theta_1 y' vy\pi_B - \theta_2 y v y\pi'_B - \theta_1 y v y'\pi_W + \theta_2 y' v y'\pi'_W$$
$$= v[\theta_1(\pi_B - \pi_W)yy' + \theta_2(y'^2\pi'_W - y^2\pi'_B)]. \tag{15}$$

Now $y^2 = y - yy'$ and $y'^2 = y' - yy'$, hence

$$y'^2\pi'_W - y^2\pi'_B = (\pi'_B - \pi'_W)yy' + y'\pi'_W - y\pi'_B$$
$$= -(\pi_B - \pi_W)yy' + y'\pi'_W - y\pi'_B.$$

Substitution of the latter expression into Equation 15 yields

$$E(\Delta Y_n \mid X_n = x) = vQ(y).$$

Taking expectations on both sides, we obtain

$$E(\Delta Y_n) = E(V_n Q(Y_n)),$$

and Equation 11 follows on noting that $\Delta y_n = E(\Delta Y_n)$.

Similarly, to establish Equation 12 one verifies that

$$E(\Delta V_n \mid X_n = x) = H(v, y).$$

6. SYMMETRIC SCHEDULES

This section considers schedules with $\pi_B = \pi_W = \zeta < 1$. If we take $Y_0 = \frac{1}{2}$, then all parameters of the model (learning rate, schedule, and initial bias) incorporate B – W symmetry, so we must have $P(B_n) = P(W_n)$ and $y_n = y'_n$; i.e., $P(B_n) = y_n = \frac{1}{2}$. This yields

$$P(B_\infty) = y_\infty = \frac{1}{2} \tag{16}$$

on letting $n \longrightarrow \infty$. However, as noted in the last section, $P(B_\infty)$ and y_∞ do not depend on the initial values of v and y. Consequently, Equation 16 holds whether or not $Y_0 = \frac{1}{2}$.

The standard extinction paradigm is the special case $\zeta = 0$. However, according to the model any symmetric schedule leads to 'choice extinction,' in the sense that the subject's proportion of Bs over a long block of trials will approach $\frac{1}{2}$.

Let

$$\#_J B = \text{number of Bs over trials } 0 \text{ to } J - 1,$$

and let $\#_J W$ be the analogous quantity for W. If the subject starts the current phase of the experiment with a brightness preference, $\#_J B - \#_J W$ provides a measure of the resulting excess or deficiency in B choices over J trials.

THEOREM 1. *As $J \longrightarrow \infty$,*

$$E(\#_J B - \#_J W) \longrightarrow (y_0 - 2^{-1})/\theta_2 \zeta'. \tag{17}$$

It is remarkable that the right-hand side of Equation 17 depends on only one of six learning-rate parameters, and does not depend on v_0.

Our main interest in this theorem is its implication for the effect of over-training on subsequent extinction. If B is consistently reinforced in the preceding phase of the experiment, the final value of $E(Y)$ is an increasing function of the number of trials administered. This final value of $E(Y)$ is the initial value for extinction, denoted y_0 in Equation 17. Thus y_0 is increased by overtraining. Suppose that the number J of extinction trials is sufficiently large that the two sides of Equation 17 can be treated as equal. Then $E(\#_J B - \#_J W)$ is increased by overtraining. Thus the model predicts that overtraining with B correct tends to increase the excess of B choices in a large number of extinction trials. In other words, *overtraining increases resistance to extinction.* Data supporting this conclusion, but using number of trials to a criterion of extinction as the dependent variable, have been reported by Mackintosh (1963). It is perhaps surprising that this prediction holds for all values of the model's parameters, even those that yield an ORE.

Proof. Since $\delta = 0$, Equation 13 yields

$$Q(y) = \theta_2 \zeta'(y' - y).$$

Thus, by Equation 11,

$$\Delta y_n = \theta_2 \zeta' E(V_n(Y_n' - Y_n)).$$

Subtracting Equation 8 from Equation 9 we get

$$P(W_n) - P(B_n) = E(V_n(Y_n' - Y_n)),$$

so

$$\Delta y_n = \theta_2 \zeta'[P(W_n) - P(B_n)].$$

Summation over $0 \leq n \leq J - 1$ yields

$$y_J - y_0 = \theta_2 \zeta' \left[\sum_{n=0}^{J-1} P(W_n) - \sum_{n=0}^{J-1} P(B_n) \right]$$
$$= \theta_2 \zeta' [E(\#_J W) - E(\#_J B)]$$
$$= \theta_2 \zeta' E(\#_J W - \#_J B).$$

The theorem follows on noting that the left-hand side converges to $2^{-1} - y_0$ as $J \longrightarrow \infty$.

7. THE CASE OF ONLY TWO LEARNING RATES

Following Zeaman and House (1963) it is assumed in this section that there are only two learning-rate parameters: one for attentional learning and one for response learning. In other words,

$$\varphi_i = \varphi \quad \text{and} \quad \theta_j = \theta \tag{18}$$

for all i and j. Under this assumption it is possible to calculate $P(B_\infty)$. When $\pi_B = 1$, so that $P(B_\infty) = 1$, there is a simple formula for $E(\#W)$.

Theorem 2 relates $P(B_\infty)$ to the probability matching asymptote ℓ (see Eq. 4).

THEOREM 2. $P(B_\infty) = \ell \left[\dfrac{1 + 2\ell'}{1 + 4\ell\ell'} \right].$

It is easily shown that the bracketed ratio is less than 1, so that $P(B_\infty) < \ell$, for $\frac{1}{2} < \ell < 1$. Thus, *under the assumption of Equation 18, the ZHL model predicts that $P(B_\infty)$ will undershoot the probability matching asymptote.* Zeaman and House (1963, pp. 206, 210) obtained some examples of undershooting in simulations of the multidimensional version their of model. The prediction of undershooting is at variance with the results of numerous simultaneous visual discrimination experiments on animals. Surprisingly, there do not seem to be any reports of comparable experiments on human subjects. In Section 10 we see that the model predicts more efficient performance for other parameter values.

Theorem 3, which assumes Equation 18, gives the only explicit formula for $E(\#W)$ that is presently known.

THEOREM 3.   *If $\pi_B = 1$ and $\pi_W < 1$,*

$$\pi'_W E(\#W) = \varphi^{-1} v'_0 + 2\theta^{-1} y'_0. \tag{19}$$

This equation is the basis for our comparison of shifts in Section 8 and our study of overtraining in Section 9.

Proofs.   Since $\delta = 0$ in Equation 13,

$$Q(y) = \theta(y' \pi'_W - y \pi'_B),$$

and Equation 11 yields

$$\theta^{-1}\Delta y_n = E(V_n(Y'_n\pi'_{\mathrm{W}} - Y_n\pi'_{\mathrm{B}})). \tag{20}$$

According to Equation 14,

$$\varphi^{-1}H(v, y) = v[v'(y\pi_{\mathrm{B}} + y'\pi_{\mathrm{W}}) - v(y\pi'_{\mathrm{B}} + y'\pi'_{\mathrm{W}})]$$
$$+ v'[-v2^{-1}(\pi_{\mathrm{B}} + \pi_{\mathrm{W}}) + v'2^{-1}(\pi'_{\mathrm{B}} + \pi'_{\mathrm{W}})].$$

Noting that

$$y\pi_{\mathrm{B}} + y'\pi_{\mathrm{W}} = 1 - (y\pi'_{\mathrm{B}} + y'\pi'_{\mathrm{W}})$$

and

$$2^{-1}(\pi_{\mathrm{B}} + \pi_{\mathrm{W}}) = 1 - 2^{-1}(\pi'_{\mathrm{B}} + \pi'_{\mathrm{W}}),$$

we obtain

$$\varphi^{-1}H(v, y) = v[v' - (y\pi'_{\mathrm{B}} + y'\pi'_{\mathrm{W}})]$$
$$+ v'[-v + 2^{-1}(\pi'_{\mathrm{B}} + \pi'_{\mathrm{W}})]$$
$$= v'2^{-1}(\pi'_{\mathrm{B}} + \pi'_{\mathrm{W}}) - v(y\pi'_{\mathrm{B}} + y'\pi'_{\mathrm{W}}).$$

Thus, by Equation 12,

$$\varphi^{-1}\Delta v_n = v'_n 2^{-1}(\pi'_{\mathrm{B}} + \pi'_{\mathrm{W}}) - E(V_n(Y_n\pi'_{\mathrm{B}} + Y'_n\pi'_{\mathrm{W}})). \tag{21}$$

When $\pi_{\mathrm{B}} = 1$, multiplication of Equation 20 by two and addition of Equation 21 yields

$$\varphi^{-1}\Delta v_n + 2\theta^{-1}\Delta y_n = v'_n 2^{-1}\pi'_{\mathrm{W}} + E(V_n Y'_n)\pi'_{\mathrm{W}}$$
$$= \pi'_{\mathrm{W}}P(W_n).$$

Theorem 3 follows when this equality is summed over $n \geq 0$.

In the remainder of the section, π_{B} is unrestricted. Since

$$Y'_n\pi'_{\mathrm{W}} - Y_n\pi'_{\mathrm{B}} = (\pi'_{\mathrm{W}} + \pi'_{\mathrm{B}})(\ell - Y_n),$$

Equation 20 can be rewritten

$$\theta^{-1}\Delta y_n = (\pi'_{\mathrm{W}} + \pi'_{\mathrm{B}})[\ell v_n - E(V_n Y_n)].$$

Letting $n \longrightarrow \infty$, we obtain

$$E(V_\infty Y_\infty) = \ell v_\infty, \tag{22}$$

and, subtracting this from v_∞,

$$E(V_\infty Y'_\infty) = \ell' v_\infty. \tag{23}$$

Dividing Equation 21 by $\pi'_{\mathrm{B}} + \pi'_{\mathrm{W}}$ and letting $n \longrightarrow \infty$, we find that

$$0 = 2^{-1}v'_\infty - E(V_\infty Y_\infty)\ell' - E(V_\infty Y'_\infty)\ell.$$

In view of Equations 22 and 23,

$$0 = 2^{-1}v'_\infty - 2\ell\ell'v_\infty.$$

Hence

$$v_\infty = (1 + 4\ell\ell')^{-1},$$

and, using Equation 22 once again,

$$E(V_\infty Y_\infty) = \ell(1 + 4\ell\ell')^{-1}.$$

The proof of Theorem 2 is concluded by combining these equations with the limiting form of Equation 8.

8.   SHIFTS

In recognition of the huge number of shift studies on children, I present the results concerning comparisons between shifts in this context. Consider, then, an experiment in the WGTA with stimuli varying along the dimensions of color, form, and position (see part 2 of Sec. 2). I assume that the subject is ignoring position, and, consequently, I have nothing further to say about this dimension. Suppose that, after reaching a strict criterion in Phase 1 of the experiment, *all subjects are shifted to a problem with form (triangle or circle) irrelevant, color (red or green) relevant, and red correct.* Assuming that there are only two learning rates, substituting green for W in Equation 19, and noting that $\pi_{\text{green}} = 0$, we obtain the basic formula

$$E(\#\text{green}) = \varphi^{-1}v'_0 + 2\theta^{-1}y'_0. \tag{24}$$

Here v is the probability of attending to color (rather than form), and y is the probability of choosing red, given attention to color:

$$v = P(\text{color}), \quad y = P(\text{red} \mid \text{color}).$$

The quantities v_0 and y_0 are expected values of v and y on the initial trial of Phase 2.

The type of shift is defined by the stimulus and reinforcement conditions in Phase 1. For reversal (R), the same stimuli were used in Phase 1, color was relevant, but green was correct. As a first approximation, we shall assume that the child attends to color and chooses green with probability 1 at the beginning of Phase 2. Thus $v_0 = 1$ and $y_0 = 0$.

The intradimensional (I) shift also had color relevant in Phase 1, hence $v_0 = 1$. However there were different cues on both dimensions: e.g., blue and yellow, cross and square. Assuming no color generalization between phases, $y_0 = \frac{1}{2}$.

We want to compare both R and I to extradimensional (E) shift, in which form was relevant and color irrelevant in Phase 1. Thus $v_0 = 0$ and $y_0 = \frac{1}{2}$. In order to control for stimulus novelty in comparisons with R and I, it is desirable to retain Phase 1 cues in the first case and to introduce new cues in the second case. However the values of v_0 and y_0 are not sensitive to this variation in experimental procedure.

Values of v_0 and y_0 for the three shifts are summarized in Table 2, along with the corresponding expected number of errors from Equation 24.

TABLE 2
Values of v_0, y_0, and
$E(\#\text{green})$ for three shifts

	v_0	y_0	$E(\#\text{green})$
R	1	0	$2\theta^{-1}$
E	0	1/2	$\varphi^{-1} + \theta^{-1}$
I	1	1/2	θ^{-1}

Denoting $E(\#\text{green})$ for R, E, and I by R*, E*, and I*, we note the following inequalities:

$$I^* < E^*, \tag{25}$$

$$E^* < R^* \quad \text{if } \varphi > \theta, \tag{26}$$

$$E^* > R^* \quad \text{if } \varphi < \theta. \tag{27}$$

As indicated in Section 1, one expects any attentional model to predict that I is easier than E. Thus the first inequality is not surprising. The second and third inequalities show that the relative difficulty of E and R is controlled by the relative rates of attentional and response learning. When response learning is faster, R is easier. Because R requires more response learning than E, this prediction is intuitively satisfying.

This comparison of I, E, and R would be of far greater interest if it did not presuppose only two learning rates. An important task for the future is to see how Equations 25, 26, and 27 must be modified in the general case.

The values of v_0 and y_0 in Table 2 are only approximations. To see this, note that they would not allow the effect of overtraining in Phase 1 to be taken into account. (An alternative viewpoint is that they presuppose substantial overtraining.) The treatment of the effect of overtraining on reversal in part 1 of the next section makes use of a more refined analysis of the values of v and y at the beginning of Phase 2.

9. THE OVERLEARNING REVERSAL EFFECT

The ZHL model will predict the ORE only when the values of its parameters ensure that perceptual learning profits more than response learning suffers as a result of overtraining. This condition can be met if the perceptual learning rates φ_i are smaller than the response-learning rates θ_j, or if these rates are of equal magnitude and V_0 is not too large. The influence of learning rates on overtraining is considered in part 1, the influence of V_0 in part 2. By taking account of both of these factors, Mackintosh (1969) was able to give a very comprehensive account of the experimental literature on the ORE in rats. This tour de force is discussed in part 3.

Throughout the section we consider a brightness discrimination in a jumping stand. Black is correct in Phase 1, white in Phase 2.

(1) *The influence of φ/θ.* Assume that there are only two learning rates, and suppose that

$$V_0 < 1 \quad \text{and} \quad Y_0 < 1 \tag{28}$$

a.s., where V_0 is the probability of attending to brightness on the initial trial of Phase 1, and Y_0 is the corresponding probability of choosing black, given attention to brightness. Let T_n be the expected total number of errors after a reversal on trial n, given V_n and Y_n. Applying Theorem 3 to reversal, we obtain

$$T_n = \varphi^{-1}V_n' + 2\theta^{-1}Y_n. \tag{29}$$

Note the appearance of Y_n rather than Y_n' on the right-hand side.

THEOREM 4. *If $\varphi < \theta$, T_n decreases for n sufficiently large. If $\varphi > \theta$, T_n increases for n sufficiently large.*

The statements of the theorem hold a.s. The first statement means that there is a (random) trial N beyond which each additional trial of training leads to fewer expected errors. This is a form of ORE. The magnitude of N surely depends on V_0 and Y_0 as well as φ and θ.

An earlier analytical study of the ORE dealt with $E(T_n)$ and was limited to small φ and θ. It found that $E(T_n)$ decreases over certain intervals $0 \ll N_1 < n < N_2$ for $\varphi/\theta < 3$, and increases for $\varphi/\theta > 3$ (Norman, 1972, Theorem 16.3.1). Though the 'critical value' of φ/θ is different from that in Theorem 4, the qualitative conclusion is the same: the ZHL model predicts the ORE for 'small' values of φ/θ but not for 'large' values.

Referring back to Equation 27, we see that the condition $\varphi < \theta$ under which the ORE is predicted is precisely the same as that under which reversal is easier than extradimensional shift. In the present experimental context, this means that an extradimensional shift from position to brightness should be more difficult than black-white reversal when and only when overtraining facilitates black-white reversal. One would like to know to what extent this prediction holds up when the unrealistic restriction of Equation 18 is dropped.

The proof of Theorem 4 is given at the end of the section.

(2) *The influence of V_0.* Lovejoy (1966) simulated the model in Table 1 with

$$\varphi_1 = \varphi_3 = \theta_1 = 0.07,$$
$$\varphi_2 = \varphi_4 = \theta_2 = 0.01.$$

These two values correspond to correct and incorrect responses, respectively. A variety of experimental findings, such as efficient performance on probabilistic schedules, require that the second value be smaller than the first. No stat-rats had initial response biases ($Y_0 = \frac{1}{2}$). For some, the relevant dimension was very obvious initially ($V_0 = 1$); for others it was not ($V_0 = 0.5$). Nonovertrained stat-rats were reversed after meeting a criterion of 15 consecutive correct responses. Overtrained animals had 150 additional trials between criterion and reversal. Sixty stat-rats were run under each combination of amount of training and initial obviousness. Table 3 gives the mean number of trials to criterion in reversal for each group.

TABLE 3
Trials to criterion in reversal
in Lovejoy's simulation

	V_0	
	0.5	1.0
Nonovertrained	108.3	81.1
Overtrained	86.1	96.6

Differences between overtrained and nonovertrained animals were significant at the 2 percent level according to t tests within each column. The directions of these differences show that there is an ORE when $V_0 = 0.5$, but that overtraining hinders reversal when the relevant dimension is so obvious that it consistently attracts attention at the beginning of the experiment. Lovejoy (1966) showed that salience of the relevant dimension is also a crucial determinant of the effect of overtraining in experiments with real rats.

(3) *The joint influence of φ_i, θ_j, and V_0.* Mackintosh (1969) surveyed the experimental literature on overtraining and reversal in rats and concluded that, with few exceptions, the ORE occurred when and only when two conditions were met: the discrimination to be learned was fairly difficult and correct responses received large rewards. He also reported three new experiments whose results confirmed this generalization. The difficulty of a discrimination is a function of two variables: salience of the relevant and irrelevant dimensions (e.g., position is undoubtedly more obvious than brightness for naive rats) and distance between cues on the relevant dimension (e.g., a dark grey–light grey discrimination is more difficult than a black-white discrimination).

Mackintosh varied V_0 and θ_1 in the ZHL model to take account of problem difficulty and reward magnitude. As in Lovejoy's study, a larger value of V_0 corresponded to an easier problem. In addition, a larger value of θ_1 (which controls response learning after correct responses) was used to reflect a larger reward. Mackintosh simulated the model with the following parameter values:

$$Y_0 = 0.5;$$

$$V_0 = \begin{cases} 0.9, & \text{(easy problem)}, \\ 0.5, & \text{(hard problem)}; \end{cases}$$

$$\varphi_2 = \varphi_4 = \theta_2 = 0.01;$$

$$\varphi_1 = \varphi_3 = 0.10;$$

$$\theta_1 = \begin{cases} 0.10, & \text{(large reward)}, \\ 0.05, & \text{(small reward)}. \end{cases}$$

A group of 25 stat-rats was run under each combination of V_0 and θ_1 values. Each stat-rat was reversed twice, once with criterion values of V_n and Y_n and once with values obtained after 100 overtraining trials. The numbers of trials to criterion in reversal for each group, with and without overtraining, are presented in Mackintosh's Figure 2. Only the group that learned a hard problem with a large reward ($V_0 = 0.5$, $\theta_1 = 0.10$) showed an ORE.

I conclude that most experimental results relating the ORE to problem difficulty and reward magnitude can be interpreted within the framework of the ZHL model.

Proof of Theorem 4. We saw in part b of Section 4 that $\#W < \infty$ and $\#\text{po} < \infty$ a.s. Let L be the trial after the last occurrence of either W or po. (If $\#W = \#\text{po} = 0$, let $L = 0$.) Then $n \geq L$ implies $\text{br}_n B_n C_n$, so that, according to Table 1,

$$\begin{aligned} \Delta V_n &= \varphi V_n', \\ \Delta Y_n &= \theta Y_n'. \end{aligned} \tag{30}$$

It follows from Equation 30 that

$$V'_n = (1 - \varphi)^{n-L}V'_L = (1 - \varphi)^n V^*,$$

where

$$V^* = (1 - \varphi)^{-L}V'_L.$$

Substituting $(1 - \varphi)^n V^*$ for V'_n in Equation 30, we obtain

$$\Delta V_n = \varphi(1 - \varphi)^n V^*. \tag{31}$$

Since, by Equation 7, $\varphi < 1$, Equation 28 implies that $V'_j > 0$ for all $j \geq 0$. Hence $V'_L > 0$, and $V^* > 0$. Similarly,

$$\Delta Y_n = \theta(1 - \theta)^n Y^*, \tag{32}$$

where

$$Y^* = (1 - \theta)^{-L}Y'_L > 0.$$

Differencing Equation 29 and applying Equations 31 and 32, we obtain

$$\Delta T_n = -\varphi^{-1}\Delta V_n + 2\theta^{-1}\Delta Y_n$$
$$= -(1 - \varphi)^n V^* + 2(1 - \theta)^n Y^*$$

for $n \geq L$. Thus $\Delta T_n < 0$ for n sufficiently large if $\varphi < \theta$, and $\Delta T_n > 0$ for n sufficiently large if $\varphi > \theta$.

10. APPROXIMATING $P(B_\infty)$

In this section I describe an approximation to $P(B_\infty)$ that is valid when the learning-rate parameters φ_i and θ_j are small so that learning is slow. If $\pi_B = 1$ and $\pi_W < 1$, as in part b of Section 4, then $P(B_\infty) = 1$; if $\pi_B < 1$ and $\pi_W = 1$, then $P(B_\infty) = 0$. Thus we can restrict our attention to the case where $\pi_B < 1$ and $\pi_W < 1$.

Letting $n \longrightarrow \infty$ in Equations 11, 12, and 8, we obtain

$$0 = E(V_\infty Q(Y_\infty)), \tag{33}$$
$$0 = E(H(V_\infty, Y_\infty)), \tag{34}$$
$$P(B_\infty) = E(V_\infty Y_\infty) + 2^{-1}v'_\infty. \tag{35}$$

If the asymptotic variances var (V_∞) and var (Y_∞) were zero, these equations would yield

$$0 = v_\infty Q(y_\infty),$$
$$0 = H(v_\infty, y_\infty),$$
$$P(B_\infty) = v_\infty y_\infty + 2^{-1}v'_\infty.$$

The first two equations could be solved for v_∞ and y_∞, and these could be substituted into the third to obtain $P(B_\infty)$. In fact, var (V_∞) and var (Y_∞) are not zero, but they are small when φ_i and θ_j are small. Thus we expect this procedure to yield approximations to v_∞, y_∞, and $P(B_\infty)$ that become more and more accurate as φ_i and θ_j approach 0.

Let us denote these approximations by v^*, y^*, and $P(B)^*$. The first two are defined to be the solutions of

$$v^*Q(y^*) = 0, \tag{36}$$

$$H(v^*, y^*) = 0, \tag{37}$$

such that $0 \leq v^*, y^* \leq 1$. The third is defined by

$$P(B)^* = v^*y^* + 2^{-1}(1 - v^*).$$

It can be shown that Equations 36 and 37 have unique solutions with $0 \leq v^*$, $y^* \leq 1$, and that, in fact, $0 < v^*, y^* < 1$. These solutions are quite easy to calculate. First, the quadratic equation

$$Q(y^*) = 0 \tag{38}$$

is solved for y^*; then the quadratic Equation 37 is solved for v^*.

Equations 37 and 38 are equivalent to $q(y^*) = 0$ and $h(v^*, y^*) = 0$, where q and h are obtained from Q and H by dividing by one of the learning-rate parameters, say θ_1. This has the effect of replacing all φ_is and θ_js in Equations 13 and 14 by the corresponding ratios φ_i/θ_1 and θ_j/θ_1. It follows that v^* and y^* depend only on ratios of learning-rate parameters, not on their absolute values. This suggests that we hold these ratios fixed as the learning-rate parameters approach zero.

THEOREM 5.   *Suppose that the φ_is and θ_js approach 0 in such a way that their ratios remain constant. Then*

$$\text{var } (V_\infty) \longrightarrow 0, \quad \text{var } (Y_\infty) \longrightarrow 0,$$

$$v_\infty \longrightarrow v^*, \quad y_\infty \longrightarrow y^*,$$

and

$$P(B_\infty) \longrightarrow P(B)^*. \tag{39}$$

Thus $P(B)^*$ will be a good approximation to $P(B_\infty)$ when learning is slow. Table 4 illustrates the variation of $P(B)^*$ with reinforcement frequency and learning-rate parameters. The schedules are noncontingent ($\pi_B = \pi'_w = \pi$). As in Lovejoy's simulations (see part 2 of Sec. 9), it is assumed that

TABLE 4
$P(B)^*$ as a function of θ_1/θ_2 and π

θ_1/θ_2	π				
	0.50	0.60	0.70	0.80	0.90
1.0	0.50	0.55	0.61	0.68	0.79
2.5	0.50	0.59	0.68	0.79	0.90
5.0	0.50	0.64	0.77	0.88	0.95
10.0	0.50	0.73	0.87	0.93	0.97
20.0	0.50	0.83	0.93	0.97	0.99

$\varphi_1 = \varphi_3 = \theta_1$ and $\varphi_2 = \varphi_4 = \theta_2$. These triples of parameters correspond to reward and nonreward, respectively. Under these conditions, $P(B)^*$ depends only on π and θ_1/θ_2. The entries in the first column and first row of Table 4 are values of $P(B_\infty)$ as well as $P(B)^*$. More generally, $P(B_\infty) = P(B)^*$ if $\pi_B = \pi_W$ or if $\varphi_i = \varphi$ and $\theta_j = \theta$.

The most interesting feature of Table 4 is the steady increase of $P(B)^*$ for $\pi \geq 0.6$ as reward becomes more effective relative to nonreward. For $\theta_1/\theta_2 = 5$, $P(B)^*$ is slightly above π; for $\theta_1/\theta_2 = 20$ and $\pi \geq 0.7$, it is close to 1. When θ_1 and θ_2 are both small (and thus all φ_i are also small), $P(B_\infty)$ should behave similarly in view of Equation 39. Therefore the ZHL model predicts efficient performance (i.e., large $P(B_\infty)$) when learning is slow and reward is substantially more effective than nonreward.

It seems likely that small values of θ_2 will ensure fairly efficient performance even when θ_1 is not small.

Comments. Recall that K^∞ is the asymptotic joint distribution of V_n and Y_n as $n \longrightarrow \infty$ (see Sec. 4). As φ_i and θ_j approach zero in such a way that their ratios remain fixed, the distribution K^∞ approaches normality. A proof of this fact and of Theorem 5 can be constructed along the lines of the proof of Theorem 10.1.1(i) of Norman (1972). This represents an extension of the latter proof from one-process to two-process models.

Analogous results for the distribution of (V_n, Y_n) (n finite) are contained in Theorem 8.1.1 of Norman (1972). The approximations to v_n and y_n given by part (B) of that theorem are defined by a certain differential equation. The expected operator approximations considered by Zeaman and House (1963, pp. 173–175) are defined by analogous difference equations. A slight variant of the proof of Theorem 8.1.1(B) establishes the validity of expected operator approximations when φ_i and θ_j are small.

11. SOME RELATED MODELS

All-or-none learning.   According to the first line of Table 1, the effect of attending to brightness, choosing black, and being correct on trial n is

$$\Delta V_n = \varphi_1 V_n' \quad \text{and} \quad \Delta Y_n = \theta_1 Y_n'.$$

Alternatively, we might assume that $V_{n+1} = 1$ if attentional conditioning is effective, $V_{n+1} = V_n$ if it is not effective, $Y_{n+1} = 1$ if response conditioning is effective, and $Y_{n+1} = Y_n$ if it is not effective. It remains to specify the probabilities of various combinations of effectiveness of conditioning in the two processes. The simplest possible assumptions are complete dependence and complete independence. In the first case, conditioning is either effective for both processes or ineffective for both processes, and these two events have probabilities c_1 and $1 - c_1$. In the second case, effective attentional conditioning has probability c_1, effective response conditioning has probability d_1, and these events occur simultaneously with probability $c_1 d_1$.

When comparable changes are made throughout Table 1, we obtain an all-or-none analog of the ZHL model. This all-or-none model might be of some interest in connection with experiments on human subjects. Though one expects it to be more mathematically tractable than the ZHL model, nothing is known about its predictions, except when effective conditioning occurs with probability 1. In that case, it reduces to the ZHL model with $\varphi_i = \theta_j = 1$.

Successive discrimination.   This chapter has focused on a model for simultaneous discrimination, in which both cues on the relevant dimension (e.g., black and white) are present on each trial. In successive discrimination, only one cue is present on each trial. Thus, for a brightness discrimination in a jumping stand, the stimulus cards are either both white or both black. Right might be correct in the former case, left in the latter. Bush (1965) developed some ideas of L. B. Wyckoff, Jr., into a two-process model for successive discrimination that has much in common with the ZHL model. According to Bush's model, there is a probability v of observing the brightness cue, there are probabilities y_B and y_W of choosing right on black and white trials given the observing response, and there is a probability z of choosing right when the brightness cue is not observed. These probabilities undergo linear transformations on each trial. Some predictions of this model are described by Norman (1972, Sec. 17.2). The model's empirical adequacy has not been investigated.

An analogous all-or-none model was formulated somewhat earlier by Atkinson (1961). He applied it to an experiment in which college students could make overt observing responses as well as discrimination responses. Reinforcement was probabilistic. The model predicted asymptotic frequencies of both types of responses quite accurately.

12. CONCLUDING REMARKS

Though we have not systematically reviewed the experimental literature relevant to the ZHL model, we have seen that it is in qualitative agreement with data from a surprisingly wide variety of experiments. It has been claimed that multiple-cue learning in experiments with redundant relevant dimensions is inconsistent with 'one-look' models like the ZHL model; however, Shepp, Kemler, and Anderson (1972) have recently shown that this is not the case. This finding suggests that phenomena that appear damaging to these models must be interpreted with great care. Two such phenomena are errorless incidental learning (see Sutherland & Mackintosh, 1971, pp. 37–38; Shepp et al., 1972, pp. 326–327) and the tendency of rats to break position habits by choosing the correct visual cue (see Lovejoy, 1968, pp. 22, 45–46).

The ZHL model represents an extreme theoretical position, which doubt-less has serious empirical limitations, but the nature of these limitations is not yet clearly understood. One reason for this is the lack of information concerning the quantitative accuracy of the model's predictions. No one has systematically estimated the model's parameters and compared its predictions with a variety of statistics from a suitable experiment. Only in this way can it be determined, for example, to what extent the magnitude and fine structure of position habits are compatible with the ZHL model. It would seem that the model has given a sufficiently accurate qualitative account of discrimination learning to merit the additional labor of quantitative testing.

REFERENCES

Atkinson, R. C. The observing response in discrimination learning. *Journal of Experimental Psychology*, 1961, **62**, 253–262.
Brunk, H. D. *An introduction to mathematical statistics.* (2nd ed.) Waltham, Mass.: Blaisdell, 1965.
Bush, R. R. Identification learning. In R. D. Luce, R. R. Bush, and E. Galanter (Eds.), *Handbook of mathematical psychology.* Vol. III. New York: Wiley, 1965.
Campione, J. C. The performance of preschool children on reversal and two types of extradimensional shifts. *Journal of Experimental Child Psychology*, 1971, **11**, 480–490.
Estes, W. K. *Learning theory and mental development.* New York: Academic Press, 1970.

Graf, V., & Tighe, T. Subproblem analysis of discrimination shift learning in the turtle (*Chrysemys picta picta*). *Psychonomic Science*, 1971, **25**, 257–259.

Kelleher, R. T. Discrimination learning as a function of reversal and nonreversal shifts. *Journal of Experimental Psychology*, 1956, **51**, 379–384.

Lovejoy, E. Analysis of the overlearning reversal effect. *Psychological Review*, 1966, **73**, 87–103.

Lovejoy, E. *Attention in discrimination learning.* San Francisco: Holden-Day, 1968.

Mackintosh, N. J. Extinction of a discrimination habit as a function of overtraining. *Journal of Comparative and Physiological Psychology*, 1963, **56**, 842–847.

Mackintosh, N. J. Further analysis of the overtraining reversal effect. *Journal of Comparative and Physiological Psychology Monograph*, 1969, **67**, 1–18.

Norman, M. F. Statistical inference with dependent observations: Extensions of classical procedures. *Journal of Mathematical Psychology*, 1971, **8**, 444–451.

Norman, M. F. *Markov processes and learning models.* New York: Academic Press, 1972.

Shepp, B. E., Kemler, D. G., & Anderson, D. R. Selective attention and the breadth of learning: An extension of the one-look model. *Psychological Review*, 1972, **79**, 317–328.

Sutherland, N. S., & Mackintosh, N. J. *Mechanisms of animal discrimination learning.* New York: Academic Press, 1971.

Zeaman, D., & House, B. J. The role of attention in retardate discrimination learning. In N. R. Ellis (Ed.), *Handbook of mental deficiency.* New York: McGraw-Hill, 1963.

Strength/Resistance
Theory of the Dynamics
of Memory Storage

Wayne A. Wickelgren
UNIVERSITY OF OREGON

The theory described in this chapter attempts to characterize the dynamics of storage in memory from the end of the learning period to the time of retrieval. In addition, it is necessary to make some nondynamic assumptions concerning elemental retrieval processes, in order to test the theory of storage dynamics.

This chapter deals with such theoretical questions as the following. First, how many memory traces are there with different storage dynamics? The theory described here is a two-trace theory (short-term memory and long-term memory), and arguments will be given to support this choice of exactly two, dynamically different memory traces.

Second, what kinds of variables should be chosen to represent the properties of memory traces in storage? The present theory characterizes a short-term memory trace (short trace) by a single real-valued property, its strength. The theory characterizes a long-term memory trace (long trace) by two real-valued properties, its strength and its resistance. Only trace strengths influence the probability of correct recognition or recall at any given retention interval. However, the resistance of a long trace affects its susceptibility to subsequent decay, interference, or disruption due to a variety of causes. No arguments will be advanced to try to prove that existing evidence requires characterization of memory traces by continuous variables, rather than a small number of states. This issue has proved so complex that very likely the issue can only be 'settled' by determining which approach yields the simplest general theory of memory.

Third, how are the increments to memory contributed by multiple learning trials integrated with one another? The present theory assumes that trace strengths contributed by multiple learning trials simply add, and that the resistance of the long trace is determined entirely by the resistance of the first increment. Relearning and retention following relearning are also discussed as a natural extension of the problem of multiple learning trials.

Fourth, what is the form of the strength-retention function for the short and long traces? Determining the form of the strength-retention function means determining the way in which the rate of forgetting depends upon the level of strength and the time since the end of learning. Currently available evidence favors the assumption that the short trace decays exponentially $(s = \lambda e^{-\beta t})$ and very strongly favors the assumption of an 'exponential power' decay $(\ell = \lambda e^{-\psi t^{1-\gamma}})$ for the long trace.

Fifth, what are the storage-interference properties of both short and long traces? Neither the short trace nor the long trace shows a 'pure' time-decay function. The rates of decay are influenced by the nature of the conditions that obtain during the retention interval, but the exact nature of the storage-interference properties differs for the short and long traces.

Sixth, how are accidental and experimentally produced retrograde amnesia related to the theory?

Seventh, how valid are the retrieval assumptions made concerning 'yes-no' recognition-memory tasks? The strength-resistance theory assumes that in 'yes-no' recognition-memory tasks, a subject responds 'yes' if and only if the total strength of the relevant trace exceeds a criterion. The central property of this criterion decision rule is the assumption that it is only the total trace associated with the single test item that is judged in recognition memory. No 'competition' among several different memory traces is necessarily involved in the 'yes-no' recognition-memory task. Evidence for this assumption of 'independence from irrelevant strengths' is discussed. The effects of context on retrieval and the assumption that noise in retrieval and acquisition of memory strengths are normally distributed are briefly discussed.

Eighth, what is the relation between different retrieval tasks? The retrieval tasks to be compared are 'yes-no' recognition memory, multiple-choice recognition memory, recall from small populations of response alternatives, recall from large populations of response alternatives, and recency judgments. Although specific retrieval assumptions are formulated for each of these retrieval tasks, relatively little evidence is available to support the validity of these assumptions, except in the case of 'yes-no' recognition memory.

It is also important to take note of the limitations in the scope of the present theory. The theory is concerned with all aspects of the dynamics of the storage phase in memory and with a limited characterization of elementary retrieval processes. The theory is not concerned with the dynamics of acquisition (learning) nor with the dynamics of the retrieval phase. That is to say, the theory does not attempt to develop time functions for the initial establishment of memory traces during the study period, nor does it attempt to develop time functions for the accessing of memory traces during retrieval.

Furthermore, the theory does not attempt to account for many of the more complex combinations of retrieval processes that must be occurring in such tasks as ordered recall of a long list of events or even recognition and recall of a single item, where considerable time is allowed for the recognition or recall and subjects are permitted to generate and test a variety of alternative hypotheses. In short, the retrieval theory is far from being a complete theory of all aspects of retrieval.

Nothing is said in the current theory about the coding aspects of memory. The modalities of memory, associative or nonassociative character of storage in any modality, the nature of representation of any event within a modality, etc., are all memory-coding phenomena that are outside the scope of the present theory. Finally, along the same line, the theory is not concerned with characterizing the logical nature of what is stored in our memory. That is to say, this theory does not characterize the types of concepts, facts, principles, etc., by which human beings encode their knowledge of the world.

Finally, the theory is concerned with (associative) conceptual memory, not (nonassociative) sensory, adaptational, fatigue, or physical types of memories. In particular, the theory is not concerned with the nonassociative type of memory involved in visual or other sensory very short term memory, such as persistence of vision or audition, or afterimages.

It might be worth mentioning that recognition memory for 'single' items such as words, letters, and digits are just as much tests of associative memory as tests of the recognition or recall of paired associates. In 'single' item recognition memory, one is deciding whether that item appeared earlier in the experimental session or on some trial of the session. One is not deciding whether he has ever encountered the item before in his life, in virtually all cases experimentally investigated. In all likelihood, subjects are making judgments based on the associations between the items and some encoding of the experimental context. However, except for the assertion that both single-item recognition memory and paired-associate recognition memory should be incorporated within the same theory of memory dynamics, no more explicit characterization of the nature of encoding in either case is incorporated in the present theory.

THEORY

This section is divided into two parts. The first part presents the definitions and assumptions concerning the dynamics of memory traces. The second part presents the additional definitions and assumptions relevant to the retrieval of memory traces in 'yes-no' recognition, multiple-choice recognition, recall, and recency memory tasks. Each part contains an introductory verbal description of the theory, followed by the definitions and a formal description and discussion of the axioms of the theory and their principal consequences.

Dynamics

The theory of memory-storage dynamics described in this section is a slightly modified combination of the short-term-memory theory presented in Wickelgren (1970) and the long-term-memory theory presented in Wickelgren (1972). The theory assumes that there are two types of associative memory traces with different dynamics: the short trace and the long trace. Each trace is characterized by a real-valued *strength* that determines recognition and recall probabilities. In addition, long traces are characterized by a second real-valued quantity, *resistance*. Greater strength implies greater probability of correct recognition or recall (in general), and greater resistance implies less susceptibility to disruption by time, interference, and certain noxious agents (e.g., concussion, electroconvulsive shock, and some drugs).

Because learning (acquisition) must probably be assumed to be somewhat variable, even under controlled experimental conditions, initial strengths of memory traces are characterized by real-valued random variables assumed to have normal distributions (under certain controlled experimental conditions). In the retrieval section of the theory, there are additional assumptions concerning normally distributed noise introduced during retrieval of both strengths and resistances. However, it is assumed that the noise (variability) contributed by the storage phase is negligible in comparison with the noise contributed by the learning and retrieval phases. If this assumption is correct, then one can essentially lump acquisition and retrieval noise together and ignore it throughout the storage phase. Thus, one can have essentially a real-variable theory of memory dynamics, without the necessity of getting involved in stochastic processes. In the present theory, learning variability and retrieval variability simply sum and do not affect the basic form of the retention function.

Short-term memory is assumed to be formed essentially simultaneously with perception (within fractions of a sec) and to decay exponentially with a time constant varying from a few seconds to perhaps 10 seconds, in the absence of conscious rehearsal. Even when there is no conscious rehearsal, there is assumed to be an (unconscious) trace-maintenance process that retards the decay of the short trace. This trace-maintenance process is assumed to be insensitive to storage load (the sum of short-trace strengths), at least up to the memory span. However, the maintenance process is sensitive to the rate of forming new short traces for events during the retention interval. Although short-term memory is associative and subject to associative interference effects in retrieval via recall tests, the rate of decay of short traces in storage is assumed to be unaffected by the similarity of new events to previously stored events within the same modality.

Currently, the long trace is also assumed to be formed simultaneously with perception. That is to say, the present assumption is that there is no need to separate an acquisition and a consolidation phase in the establishment of long traces. However, although the strength of the long trace is assumed to be formed at the time of perception or very shortly thereafter, the resistance of this trace is extremely low immediately after its formation. When resistance is low, the long trace is easily destroyed by interference, head injury, and possibly other causes. The resistance of a long trace is assumed to increase monotonically with time since learning. Thus, the older a long trace is, the more difficult it is to destroy or partially degrade the trace. Note that this theory of 'consolidation-type effects' (such as retrograde amnesia) does not require the long trace to be unavailable for use in recognition or recall tests for some period of time following learning. The trace can be available to mediate recall and recognition judgments, but still be in a state of extreme susceptibility to disruption. Furthermore, in congruence with the clinically observed range of human retrograde amnesias, the increase in trace resistance is assumed to be continuing (at a decelerating rate) for the lifetime of the memory.

When there are multiple learning trials separated by some appreciable period of time, the last learning trial is assumed to add an increment to the decaying strength established by previous learning trials. This assumption holds for both short and long traces. However, in the case of long-term memory, an additional assumption must be made concerning the resistance of the long trace. Currently, the theory assumes that the resistance of the entire trace (the sum of the increments contributed by all learning trials) is determined entirely by the time since the first learning trial. That is to say, each new increment to learning is entered with a resistance that increases proportionally to the time since the first learning trial for the item.

Definitions. Let s be the strength of the short trace. Let ℓ be the strength of the long trace.

Let ϕ be the decay force constant for the short trace, $\phi > 0$. Let ρ be the trace-maintenance parameter for the short trace, $1 > \rho > 0$.

Let r be the resistance of the long trace. Let f be the force of decay acting on the long trace.

Let π be the similarity of the material currently being learned to the material involved in some previously formed trace (decay-force parameter for the long trace).

Let μ be the rate of growth of long-trace resistance.

Let t be the retention interval (time from the end of the study period to the retention test).

Let α be the degree of learning in short-term memory: the short strength at $t = 0$, $\alpha \sim N[\bar{\alpha}, \sigma_\alpha]$. (That is, α is normally distributed with mean $\bar{\alpha}$ and standard deviation σ_α.)

Let λ be the degree of learning in long-term memory: the long strength at $t = 0$, $\lambda \sim N[\bar{\lambda}, \sigma_\lambda]$.

Axioms.

(A1) $\dfrac{ds}{dt} = -(1 - \rho)\phi s, \quad 0 \le \rho \le 1.$

(A2) A short-trace maintenance process determines ρ. This maintenance process operates in a limited-capacity relation with learning or other processing in the same modality.

Axioms 1 and 2 assert that the decay of the short trace is proportional to its strength. That is to say, short traces decay exponentially. In addition, the rate of decay of short-term memory is assumed to be influenced by the effectiveness of operation of a hypothetical short-trace maintenance process. This trace-maintenance process operates to reduce the rate of decay of short-term memory below some hypothetical maximum-decay rate (ϕ), which would obtain if the constant short-trace decay force were not balanced to some extent by the maintenance process. Trace maintenance is assumed to be unaffected by storage load, that is to say, the number or total strength of traces in short-term memory. However, the trace-maintenance process is assumed to utilize some of the same neural machinery as is involved in learning or other processing in the same modality. Thus, when an individual is learning new material, his short-trace maintenance process will operate less effectively, increasing the rate of decay for previously acquired short traces.

To some extent this is assumed to be a modality-specific limited-capacity mechanism, so that the maintenance process operates more effectively when the interpolated information processing is in a modality different from that in which the traces are stored. This implies a certain degree of similarity dependence to the storage-interference processes in short-term memory, but it is assumed that, within a modality, there is no further dependence upon the 'fine grain' similarity of interpolated learning to original learning. Thus, for example, in the retention of verbal material during interpolated verbal learning, the phonetic or semantic similarity of the interpolated material to the original material should be irrelevant. However, listening to tones or looking at pictures during the retention interval should allow the short-trace maintenance process to operate more effectively for verbal short traces, producing a comparatively low decay rate in this case.

(A3) $\dfrac{d\ell}{dt} = -\dfrac{f}{r} = -\dfrac{\pi\ell}{\mu t^{\gamma}}.$

(A4) $\mu = \mu_0(1 - e^{-\lambda}).$

Axiom 3 expresses the principal assumptions concerning the basic form of the strength-retention function for the long trace as formed by a single learning trial. The rate of decay of the long trace is determined by the ratio of two abstract quantities: the force of decay acting on the trace and the resistance of the trace. The force of decay is assumed to be interference from learning occurring during the retention interval. The magnitude of this force is jointly determined on the one hand by the similarity of interpolated learning to original learning (π), and on the other hand by the remaining strength of the long trace (ℓ). Thus the theory assumes that the decay of long traces is not a passive temporal process, but rather is due to storage interference resulting from new learning. Furthermore, the degree of storage interference is proportional to the similarity between the traces currently being established and the previously learned trace. Underlying the abstract assumption of similarity-dependent storage interference may be the intuitive structural assumption that similar traces involve strengthening associations to internal representatives that are somewhat overlapping. If internal representatives have limited connection capacity, then a very likely mechanism for living within this limited capacity would be one that strengthens a new association to an internal representative and weakens all previously established associations to that internal representative.

Making storage interference proportional to trace strength provides a natural vehicle for keeping all trace strengths nonnegative. At the same time, it is reasonable to suppose that total trace strength is made up of many 'molecular' components, with each component being equally subject to the storage-interference force. Such a process requires that the total force on a trace be considered proportional to the strength of the trace.

The resistance of a trace is assumed to increase monotonically as a power function of its age. The exponent of the power function (γ) is assumed to be a universal constant for all subjects, all materials, and all conditions. This constant is currently assumed to be in the vicinity of $\gamma = 0.75$. The increasing resistance of a memory trace makes it increasingly less vulnerable to storage interference.

If the rate of growth of trace resistance (μ) is relatively constant for all traces that were originally learned above some minimum criterion of strength, then the resistance of all such memories provides information about the relative time of occurrence of different past events for which one has established memory traces. If the resistance of a memory trace is a retrievable property of that trace, then recency judgments might be based on this resistance property. Thus, in addition to expressing the increasing invulnerability of memory traces of increasing age, the concept of resistance might also provide a mechanism for at least one type of 'biological clock.' Using trace resistance as a biological clock to make relative recency judgments for different events will be reliable only if the rate of increase of trace resistance for different events is close to being a constant. However, the rate of growth of trace resistance must depend to some extent on the strength of the initial trace established during the learning period. Otherwise, traces that had zero degree of initial learning would be hypothesized to have the same growth of trace resistance initiated for them as traces established with substantial initial degrees of learning. It seems absurd to imagine that a trace would have a substantial degree of resistance when it had never been learned in the first place or had been learned only at a very, very low level. Thus, one probably must assume that μ is in some way a function of the initial degree of learning in long-term memory (λ). A reasonable choice for such a function, that would satisfy all the constraints previously mentioned, would be to have μ exponentially approach a limit (μ_0) with increasing λ. This is precisely the assumption stated in Axiom 4 concerning the relationship between the rate of growth of trace resistance and the level of acquisition in long-term memory.

Note, however, that Axiom 4 provides only a very limited degree of coupling from trace strength to trace resistance, compared with the much more extensive coupling provided in Axiom 3 from trace resistance to trace strength. At all delays, the resistance of the trace affects the rate of change of long-trace strength, but only the initial strength of the long trace influences the growth of trace resistance. The retrieval assumptions specify that only strength determines recall and recognition judgments and that, under some circumstances, only resistance determines recency judgments. Such a theory produces the anomalous (and probably absurd) prediction that subjects could judge normally the recency of an event that they had completely forgotten, provided that it was initially well learned but had been subjected to extensive storage interference. There are other reasons for thinking that an extensive coupling from trace strength to trace resistance may be needed in some future formulation of this theory, and Axiom 4 should only be viewed as a first step in this direction.

One might note that the rate of decay of the short trace as expressed in Axiom 1 could be considered to result from a force applied to the short trace divided by the resistance to this force provided by the short-term memory trace-maintenance process. This formulation is somewhat clumsier than that expressed in Axiom 1, but it does highlight the systematic differences in the assumptions concerning basic trace dynamics for storage in short- and long-term memory. In both cases, the force on the trace is proportional to trace strength. However, the force on the long trace is proportional to the similarity of interpolated learning to original learning, while the force on the short trace is independent of such similarity. The resistance of the long trace is assumed to grow monotonically with its age. By contrast, the resistance of the short trace is in no way dependent upon its age. Rather, the resistance of the short trace depends on the effectiveness with which the short-trace maintenance process operates in conjunction with any requirements for new learning or processing during the retention interval. In the present formulation, resistance is not really a property of the short trace in the same way that resistance is a property of the long trace. If one formulates the decay or storage dynamics for short-term memory in terms of forces and resistances, resistance is a property of the short-term memory *system*, not of each individual trace. This provides another reason, besides simplicity, for not formulating Axioms 1 and 3 in a parallel manner.

Besides the invariance assumptions already mentioned in previous paragraphs, there is one more invariance assumption that is implicitly contained in Axioms 1 through 4 and that bears explicit mention. The decay in storage for both short and long traces is assumed to be independent of the number of previously established traces (the storage load). Thus, proactive interference is assumed to affect learning and/or retrieval, not storage, of memory traces. The contrary view of proactive interference proposed by Posner and Konick (1966) as the 'acid bath' theory of proactive interference in short-term memory has recently been disconfirmed by Hawkins, Pardo, and Cox (1972). In agreement with this result, neither the number of previously learned memory traces nor the similarity of these traces one to another is assumed to affect the subsequent decay of either short or long traces.

(A5) The short- and long-strength increments from multiple learning trials are additive.

(A6) The resistance of a long trace transfers completely to subsequent increments.

The first four axioms describe the storage dynamics for traces established by a single learning trial. When the same event occurs on several different learning trials separated by intervening mental processing (e.g., other learning or test trials), then some assumptions must be made concerning the integration of learning across the multiple learning trials.

Axiom 5 makes what is probably the simplest assertion concerning the combination of trace strengths established by multiple learning trials, namely, that these strengths are strictly additive. It should be noted that this is not equivalent to the assertion that all that a second, or third, or later learning trial does is to increment the strength established by the first learning trial. Axiom 5 asserts that subsequent learning trials do increment the originally established strengths, but it is quite likely that other traces different from the trace established on the first learning trial may also be established on subsequent learning trials. For example, on the second learning trial, a subject may establish a memory trace that this item or pair of items has been presented twice in the experiment. Nothing in Axiom 5 should be interpreted to detract from this very likely possibility.

In the case of short traces, Axiom 5 is sufficient to describe completely the interaction of multiple learning trials. However in the case of long traces, it is necessary to make some assumption concerning the resistance either of the entire memory trace or of each increment to the memory trace contributed by any of the learning trials. Probably the most natural assumption would be that each learning trial contributes its own increment to trace strength and has its own resistance (determined by the time since that particular learning trial). However, there are two simpler alternative assumptions that are extreme in opposite directions. One extreme assumption would be that the resistance of a long trace is determined by the time since the *last* learning trial. According to this assumption, multiple learning trials increase the degree of learning, but each new learning trial resets the trace resistance value back to zero. Finally, the extreme assumption incorporated in Axiom 6 is that there is a single resistance for the entire trace, and it is the resistance determined by the *first* learning trial. That is to say, each additional learning trial contributes an increment to the strength of the long trace and that increment automatically acquires the resistance of the previously established long trace. Clearly, such an assumption provides a natural advantage for spaced over massed practice, in terms of the rate of forgetting following the last learning trial, when a fixed number of learning trials has been employed in both instances (not necessarily when learning to a criterion).

Theorems.   The most basic equation to derive from the axioms of storage dynamics is the form of the strength-retention function for both short and long traces, under constant conditions during the retention interval. A strength-retention function specifies the value of strength as a function of time since the end of learning. Under constant conditions during the storage period, the forms of the strength-retention functions for both short and long traces are quite simple.

Axiom 1 specifies that the short trace decays according to a simple exponential:

$$s = \alpha e^{-\beta t}, \quad \text{where } \beta = (1 - \rho)\phi. \tag{1}$$

The acquisition parameter (α) specifies the initial degree of learning established after either a single learning trial or a series of learning trials. The decay-rate parameter (β) depends on the degree to which the trace-maintenance process can operate during the retention interval but, if the operation of the trace-maintenance process is constant over time, then the β parameter is constant for different delays since learning. Thus, the form of the short-term-memory strength-retention function should be linear on a semilog plot (log strength plotted against linear time): $\log s = \log \alpha - \beta t$.

The form of the long-term strength-retention function, as specified by Axiom 3, is only slightly more complicated, being an 'exponential power' function:

$$\ell = \lambda e^{-\psi t^{1-\gamma}}, \quad \text{where } \psi = \frac{\pi}{\mu(1-\gamma)} \tag{2}$$

$$\ell = \lambda e^{-\psi t^{0.25}}, \quad \text{if } \gamma = 0.75. \tag{3}$$

The acquisition parameter λ specifies the initial degree of learning in long-term memory established either by a single learning trial or at the end of a series of learning trials. The decay-rate parameter (ψ) is directly proportional to the similarity of interpolated learning to original learning and inversely proportional to the rate of growth of trace resistance multiplied by $(1 - \gamma)$, where γ is the exponent of growth of trace resistance. Assuming that the exponent of the growth of trace resistance is a universal constant (in the vicinity of 0.75, as specified in Eq. 3), then the decay rate of long-term memory is simply determined by the similarity of original to interpolated learning divided by the rate of growth of trace resistance. The form of the long-term strength-retention function as specified in Equation 2 should be linear on a plot of log strength against time to the $(1 - \gamma)$th power. If γ equals 0.75, then the form of long-term strength-retention function should be linear on a plot of log strength against the 0.25 power of time.

The long-term strength-retention functions specified in Equations 2 or 3 are a specific quantitative formulation of Jost's Second Law (in Hovland, 1951, p. 649) that the rate of forgetting is constantly decreasing with increasing age of the memory trace. According to the present theory, the absolute loss of trace strength per unit time is decreasing for two reasons: (a) because strength is decreasing and the force of decay is proportional to memory strength, and (b) because resistance to decay is increasing with time since learning.

Retrieval

The theory of memory retrieval described in this section is equivalent to the theory described by Norman and Wickelgren (1969), Wickelgren and Norman (1966), and Wickelgren (1968a) for recognition memory, multiple choice, and recall from a small population of alternatives. However, this section deviates from these previous strength theories in opting for a high-threshold rule for recall from a large population of alternatives (following Bahrick, 1965); it also extends previous strength-theory formulations to provide a theory of the retrieval-decision processes involved in certain nonassociative recency judgments. The statistical decision theory used in this analysis of memory retrieval is in the tradition of Thurstonian Scaling and Signal Detection Theory (see Green & Swets, 1966), and the analysis of recall from a large number of alternatives follows Bahrick (1965).

Definitions.   Let d be the total strength of the short and long traces, $d = s + \ell$.
   Let c_i be the criterion for a response more extreme than i, $c \sim N[\bar{c}, \sigma_c]$.
   Let k be the recall threshold, $k \sim N[\bar{k}, \sigma_k]$.

Axioms.

(A7)   Only the sum of short and long traces ($d = s + \ell$) can be retrieved.

The meaning of Axiom 7 is that it is impossible for subjects to separately judge the strength of short and long traces for any purpose. Thus, according to Axiom 7 it would be impossible for subjects to judge the recency of an item by the strength of the short trace alone, ignoring a substantial long-trace component. Also, according to Axiom 7, it would be impossible for subjects to judge whether an item had appeared in the last list by judging only the short component. Both short- and long-component strengths must be retrieved as a sum as input to any judgment process based on trace strength. According to Axiom 7, in order for an experiment to be concerned solely with short-term memory, it must normally be necessary for the long traces of both correct and incorrect items for the last trial to be equal. In this case, the difference between the strengths for correct and incorrect items would tap only short-term memory.

(A8)   In recognition, a subject chooses a response more extreme than i, iff the total strength of the bidirectional trace exceeds a criterion: $(d - c_i) \geq 0$.   (Criterion Decision Rule.)

Axiom 8 specifies that recognition-memory judgments use the criterion decision rule, according to which a subject responds 'yes' to a test item, iff the total (short and long) strength of a memory trace for that item exceeds the criterion for a 'yes' response. In addition, when subjects are asked to employ confidence judgments, in addition to their 'yes-no' responses, the responses are considered to be ordered on a continuum from the most confident 'yes' to the least confident 'yes' and the least confident 'no' to the most confident 'no.' Each response in this rating scale is assumed to be defined by criteria (c_i), which are ordered in the obvious way on the strength dimension, paralleling the ordering of the responses in the rating scale.

Probably the most critical component of the criterion decision rule for recognition memory is the assumption that only a single memory trace for the test item needs to be judged in an elementary recognition-memory task. According to this decision rule, the strengths of all other items in memory are irrelevant to recognition-memory judgments, since they play no role in the recognition-memory retrieval-decision process. Obviously, this does not have to be true for all 'real life' recognition-memory judgments. Subjects can and frequently do recall a number of additional events or contextual cues to assist them in making their recognition-memory judgments. Such recognition-memory judgments are considered to be 'complex.' Axiom 8 asserts that there exists an elementary recognition-memory judgment process that follows the simple criterion decision rule. It is of course an open experimental question whether one can control recognition-memory judgments to follow a simple criterion decision rule, even if such an elementary process does exist.

The term 'bidirectional' simply means that both forward and backward associations are included.

(A9)   In multiple-choice recognition memory or recall from a small population of alternatives, a subject chooses the alternative with the maximum total strength of the bidirectional trace: max $\{d_j - c_j\}$. (Maximum Decision Rule.)

The maximum decision rule for multiple-choice recognition and recall from a small population of alternatives is probably the most natural assumption for these retrieval processes. When one has a choice among a number of alternatives, it seems reasonable (within continuous strength theory) to make that choice be the one with the maximum strength in memory. The only other property of Axiom 9 is that a response bias (c_j) is assumed to be attached to every alternative response (j) in addition to the memory strength (d_j) associated with that response. However, one assumes that in a variety of situations these response biases are approximately equal, or else that pooling across different types of responses permits one to ignore effects of response bias.

(A10)   In recall from a large population of alternatives, the subject chooses an alternative only if the total strength of its unidirectional trace exceeds the recall threshold, $d - k \geq 0$. (High-threshold Decision Rule.)

Basically, Axiom 10 applies to situations where it seems unreasonable to imagine the subject could in any way compare the strengths of all the possible alternatives in the recall task. Such situations include prominently those in which the set of response alternatives might be any word in a subject's vocabulary. The term 'unidirectional' means that only the forward association can contribute to recall from a large population.

At present, the theory is deliberately vague concerning the transition region between a small population of alternatives and a large population of alternatives. Presumably, the resolution of this issue will have something to do with limitations on a subject's ability to maintain a response set. To the extent that a subject can maintain a small set of responses in a readily available state, recall would be assumed to follow the maximum decision rule. To the extent that a subject cannot maintain the entire relevant set of possible response alternatives, recall would be assumed to follow the high-threshold decision rule.

(A11)   In nonassociative recency judgments, a subject chooses a response more extreme than i, iff $(r - c_i) \geq 0$.

Axiom 11 asserts that subjects can retrieve trace resistance for the purpose of determining how long ago the event occurred that established the memory trace. Traces with high resistance are judged to have been established a long time ago. The thrust of this axiom is that we can have a direct feeling regarding the recency of different events. Clearly this process must be assumed to have considerable noise involved in it, because our ability to determine whether an event occurred one hour ago or an hour and fifteen minutes ago is rather poor.

Furthermore, many recency judgments are based directly or indirectly on associations to time (including calendar) concepts. Thus, we often determine how long ago an event occurred by looking at our watch at the time some event occurred and later remembering that time by association. Very long-term recency judgments, on the order of years, are undoubtedly based largely on direct or indirect associations to time concepts. Thus, we remember how long ago it was that some event took place because we remember the context in which it occurred including some context that is associated to a more or less definite date. However, there are frequently situations in which it seems that there is no possibility of determining recency by direct or indirect associations to time concepts, and yet we are able to make judgments of recency that are considerably in excess of chance (even though these judgments may be terribly poor in relation to what can be achieved by examining a tape-recorder type of memory). Because it seems necessary to postulate trace resistance in order to account for a variety of other phenomena, it is parsimonious to assume that the same trace resistance is judged in these 'nonassociative' recency judgments. Because recencies fall on a single-ordered rating scale, the most natural decision assumption is the criterion decision rule.

Theorems. The most important theorem derived from the retrieval assumptions concerns the form of the operating characteristic for recognition memory:

$$z[P(\text{yes} \mid d)] = \frac{\sigma}{\sigma_d} z[P(\text{yes} \mid 0)] + \frac{d}{\sigma_d}. \tag{4}$$

Equation 4 specifies that the z transform (tails normal deviate transform) of a recognition-memory rating probability for an item with memory strength d is a linear function of the z transform of the corresponding recognition probability for a condition with memory strength zero. The slope of this function on normal-normal probability coordinates (z coordinates) is $m = \sigma/\sigma_d$, where σ is the standard deviation of the strength distribution for the condition with zero mean strength and σ_d is the standard deviation for the strength distribution with mean strength d.

The x and y intercepts (d_x and d_y) of this linear function provide estimates of the mean difference between the strength distributions in units of the standard deviation of either the zero mean-strength distribution or the strength distribution whose mean equals d, namely, $d_y = d/\sigma_d$, $d_x = d/\sigma$. The x intercept (d_x) is generally referred to in signal detection theory as d'.

In determining strength-retention functions, it is important to measure strengths at all different delays using the same unit, usually the standard deviation of the zero mean-strength condition (new items). This would indicate plotting the condition at each different delay vs the new-item condition and choosing the x intercept (d_x) from all such operating characteristics. Although d_x is usually the unbiased estimate of the strength differences one wishes to measure, d_x usually has high variance because slope is quite variable. A considerably lower variance, but biased, estimate is provided by determining the intersection of the operating characteristic with the negative diagonal and looking up this point in the tables of Elliott (1964). This estimate of total strength difference d is $d_s = d/\frac{1}{2}(\sigma_d + \sigma)$. Derivation of the form of the operating characteristic and equations for the slope and intercept parameters can be found in Green and Swets (1966), Wickelgren and Norman (1966), and Wickelgren (1968a).

When one has a large number of different operating characteristics obtained from the same subject at different delays since learning, it is possible to obtain an estimate of d for each condition which has both the unbiased property of d_x and the low-variance property of d_s. To achieve this estimate (d_a), we assume that the variance of the strength distribution of new items is σ^2 and the variance of the strength distribution for old items tested t sec after learning is $[\sigma^2 + \sigma_0^2 f^2(t)]$, where $f(t)$ is the strength-retention function for the decay of the total memory trace. In general, this assumption states that the variance in the strength of old items contains a fixed component common to the variance in the strength of new items (perhaps due largely to retrieval noise) plus a variable component which is proportional to the magnitude of the mean strength (perhaps largely due to acquisition noise).

From the above formulation of the relationship between the means and variances of strength distributions, it is possible to derive rather simple equations that permit low variance and unbiased estimates of d over a set of operating characteristics. Let d_a be the new (unbiased and low-variance) estimate of d_x.

$$d_a = \frac{d_s}{1 - Kd_s^2}, \quad \text{where } K = \frac{(1 - m)}{(1 + m)} \cdot \frac{1}{d_s^2} \text{ and } m = \frac{1 - Kd_s^2}{1 + Kd_s^2}.$$

In practice, one determines values of slope (m) and d_s for each of the operating characteristics in the set being considered and determines the average value of K for the set of operating characteristics. Then one can convert the low-variance estimate d_s for each operating characteristic into an unbiased and low-variance estimate d_a by means of the previously specified formula.

In addition, whenever one has but one point on an operating characteristic, making it impossible to determine d_s in the usual way, it is possible to estimate d_s and then d_a for that one-point operating characteristic by means of the following equation: $z_d = m(d_a + z_0)$ where z_d is the z transform of the probability for the (old item) strength distribution with mean d, and z_0 is the z transform of the probability for the (new item) strength distribution with mean zero. This equation involves two unknowns, m and d_a, but the equation can be converted into an equation involving the two variables d_s and K:

$$\frac{d_s}{1 + Kd_s^2} + \frac{1 - Kd_s^2}{1 + Kd_s^2} z_0 - z_d = 0.$$

Since one will already have determined the value of K from the set of operating characteristics that have two or more points each, the above equation involves only one unknown, d_s. The above equation can be solved by numerical methods for the value d_s, which can then be converted into d_a using preceding formulas.

Provided that certain simplifying assumptions are valid, it is possible to determine estimates of strength differences (d) from probabilities of correct choice in multiple-choice experiments and recall from a small population of alternatives. The assumptions involved in this process and the method of deriving such strength estimates are discussed in detail in Norman and Wickelgren (1969) and Wickelgren (1968a). Earlier equivalent formulations of multiple-choice decision processes in a psychophysical context are discussed in Green and Swets (1966) and Swets (1964).

Estimates of d can be derived from probabilities of correct recall from a large number of alternatives, provided two parameters are estimated: k and K. The parameter k is the distance of the recall threshold from the mean of the strength distribution for new items in units of the standard deviation for new items. The parameter K expresses the relationship between a slope (m) and d_s, as specified earlier. If one has run recognition-memory experiments using the same materials, contexts, and conditions as were used for recall memory, then the value of K derived from the recognition experiments might well be used in the analysis of the recall data. If not, then K will have to be an estimated parameter for the recall data, just as k must necessarily be. Presumably, the value of k will be somewhere between 1.5 and 4 standard deviations above the mean of the strength distribution for new items.

The scaling of recency and the determination of degrees of discriminability between different recency distributions is accomplished in the same way as for recognition memory.

PHENOMENA

Dynamics

Exponential decay of the short trace.   The earliest success of strength theory was the obtaining of exponential decay in certain short-term memory tasks (Wickelgren & Norman, 1966). The type of task in which exponential decay of the short trace is consistently observed includes 'two-phase' tasks in which subjects are given a list of items to remember, followed by a probe item that may be a cue for a recognition judgment of that item or for recall of the succeeding item in the previous list. Besides Wickelgren and Norman (1966), the most extensive and definitive test of the exponential decay hypothesis for short-term memory is found in a study of recognition memory for single letters at different rates of presentation from one letter per sec up to four letters per sec (Wickelgren, 1970).

An example of the excellent fit provided by the exponential decay hypothesis to the data for all three rates of presentation used in this latter study is shown in Figure 1. The results shown in Figure 1 are averaged across all six subjects who participated in this experiment. To avoid the possibility of distorting the form of the retention function via the averaging process, the logs of the strengths for each subject at each rate of presentation were averaged, rather than averaging the strength values themselves or pooling the choice data across all subjects, etc.

In addition, there is a monotonic (approximately linear) relation between the decay rate and the presentation rate. This relation can be derived from a relatively simple quantitative formulation of Axiom 2, which concerns the short-trace maintenance process (see Wickelgren, 1970). The hypothesized short-trace maintenance process is discussed in more detail in the following section concerned with storage interference in short-term memory.

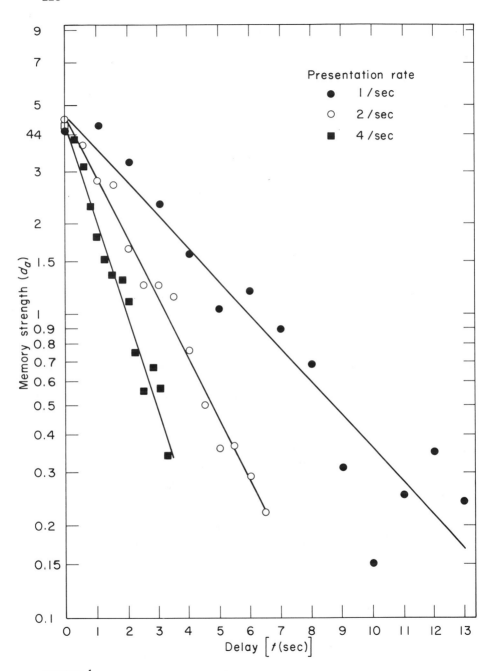

FIGURE 1.
Average strength retention functions on a semilog plot for probe recognition of single letters presented at rates from 1 letter/sec to 4 letters/sec. The straight line represents the best-fitting exponential decay function.

The excellent fit of the exponential decay hypothesis contrasts sharply with the very systematic deviation (shown in Fig. 2 for these same short-term retention data) from the exponential power retention function ($\ell = \lambda e^{-\psi t'^{-\gamma}}$) found by Wickelgren (1972) to provide a good fit to long-term retention data. In addition to these two studies, several other two-phase recognition-memory studies also provide somewhat noisier support for the hypothesis of exponential decay (Wickelgren, 1967, 1968b; Wickelgren & Norman, 1971). Finally, Norman (1966) found approximately the same decay process in two-phase probe-recall tasks as in two-phase probe-recognition tasks.

Unfortunately, at present, the confirmation of exponential decay of the short trace is confined exclusively to two-phase paradigms. The other paradigm that is suitable for assessing the strength retention function for the short trace—namely, the three-phase paradigm used originally by Brown (1958) and Peterson and Peterson (1959)—has consistently yielded strength-retention functions that deviate from simple exponential decay. This deviation is considered by almost everyone to result from the presence of a long-trace component in addition to the short-trace component in these tasks. Wickelgren (1969) and Wickelgren and Berian (1971) provided some support for this hypothesis by finding that when the long component was subtracted from the total memory trace, in three-phase tasks involving both memory for pitch and memory for verbal materials, then the remaining (short?) component can be well fit by an exponential decay. Nevertheless, the paradigm-invariance of the exponential decay of the short trace requires extensive further demonstration.

However, it should be noted that the present theory well explains why the three-phase paradigms that have been used should have exhibited a long component, whereas the two-phase memory paradigms previously discussed did not. The reason derives directly from retrieval Axiom 7 that only the sum of short and long traces can be judged, in combination with observations regarding the frequency of repeating the same item across different trials in the experiment. All of the two-phase studies that are well fit by exponential decay involve a small population of items from which the selection occurs for the list on each trial, with rather little time elapsing between the occurrences of the same item from one trial to the next. Assume that the traces for all trials are strengthened associations from some set of cues (concepts, representatives, etc.) that are approximately identical over a long sequence of trials to the item (letter, digit, etc.) representatives. For example, a concept such as 'presented on this trial' is potentially common to all trials. Under such circumstances the long traces for correct and incorrect items on a given trial must be approximately equal, because long traces from previous trials will not have decayed very much. Because the measure of strength (d) is an interval scale measuring strength differences between correct and incorrect items, only the short component will be present in these two-phase paradigms.

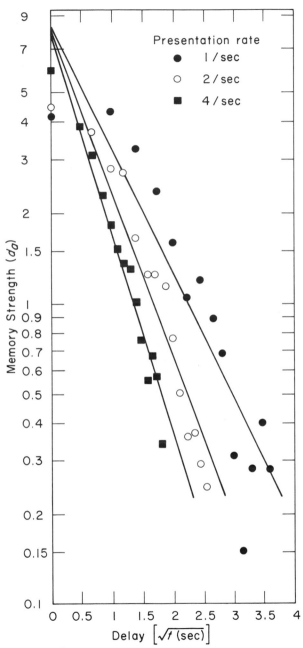

FIGURE 2.
Same data as in Figure 1 on a plot of log d_a vs $t^{0.5}$, the type of plot which is approximately linear for the long trace.

By contrast, in all of the three-phase experiments that have demonstrated substantial long components, the frequency of repeating the same item from trial to trial is very much lower than in the two-phase experiments. Obviously, further experiments should be done to show that it is the frequency of repeating the same item that accounts for the difference, not the different paradigms.

Storage interference in short-term memory.   Bower and Bostrom (1968) and Wickelgren (1967) have shown that storage interference produced by subsequent learning is independent of the similarity of this subsequent learning to original learning in short-term memory. This conclusion derives from the finding that the ability to correctly recognize a previously presented A–B pair in contrast to a nonpresented A–D pair is identical whether interpolated learning included an A–C pair or consisted entirely of X–C pairs. Of course, interpolated A–C learning causes more retrieval interference than does X–C learning on a recall test of short-term memory to the probe A. However, on a recognition test this difference disappears, indicating that the effect of the interpolated A–C learning is entirely on retrieval and not on storage. This contrasts sharply with results discussed in a subsequent section, which indicate that storage interference (as measured by recognition tests) is similarity-dependent in long-term memory.

However, the lack of similarity-dependent storage interference for the short trace should not lead one to conclude that storage in short-term memory is characterized by a passive temporal-decay process with storage interference playing no role. The short trace is characterized by its own particular type of similarity-independent storage interference. Although the 'fine grain' (A–B, A–C) similarity of interpolated to original learning seems to be unimportant in short-term memory, a grosser similarity of the modality employed in original and interpolated tasks is important to the rate of decay of the short trace. Reitman (1969) has shown that retention over a 15 sec interval (presumably including some short-trace component) is substantially superior when the interpolated task consists of detection of tones in white noise, compared to an interpolated task that consists of detection of a target verbal item against a background of nontarget verbal items. Reitman argues that conscious rehearsal was eliminated from all of her conditions and, if it was, the results argue for the modality dependence of an unconscious trace-maintenance process as specified in the present theory. Despite Reitman's moderately strong case for the absence of rehearsal in her task, caution must be exercised in the interpretation of these findings. Nevertheless, whether the trace-maintenance process in this case was conscious or unconscious, the results argue that similarity of modality for interpolated vs original material does play a critical role in the short-trace storage process.

In addition to the effects of gross modality similarity between original and interpolated learning, storage in short-term memory is affected by the amount and the difficulty of information-processing activity in the retention interval, whether the interpolated activity involves learning or not. Marcer (1968) has shown that recall of a CCC trigram becomes poorer the faster subjects perform a simple subtraction task (counting backwards by threes or fours from a three-digit number) during the retention interval. Posner and Rossman (1965), Posner and Konick (1966) and Merikle (1968) have all shown that more difficult interpolated information-processing tasks produce poorer recall. All of these experiments employed the Brown-Peterson three-phase design, but Wickelgren (1970) showed that increased rate of presentation of items in a two-phase probe-recognition design increased the rate of forgetting for any item in the list. These studies demonstrate that forgetting in short-term memory does not simply depend upon the time delay, but is influenced by the nature of interpolated activity during retention interval.

However, Wickelgren (1970) also demonstrated that the storage interference in short-term memory is not a simple 'knockout' process, where each interpolated item substitutes for some item previously presented in a buffer store of limited capacity. That is to say, amount of forgetting was not directly proportional to the number of interpolated items. Rather, forgetting was intermediate between what would be expected from a pure time-decay process and what would be expected from a pure item-interference process. Similar tendencies also exist in the probe-recall data of Waugh and Norman (1965) and Norman (1966), though the effects were smaller in the recall studies, presumably due to complicating effects of retrieval interference in the recall tasks.

There has been some suggestion that the requirement of *learning* interpolated material increases the rate of decay for the short trace, compared with doing other types of information processing during the retention interval. The strongest evidence for this is the faster decay rates observed with the two-phase probe tasks (where interpolated material is being learned), compared with the three-phase tasks (where the interpolated material has virtually never required learning). However the probable presence of a substantial long-trace component in all of these previous three-phase tasks makes it impossible to conclude anything definite with respect to the effects of interpolated learning vs nonlearning tasks on the short-trace decay rate. In addition, there might also be some other 'paradigm' difference.

All in all, some assumption of a short-trace maintenance process seems necessary to account for the effects of the modality and difficulty of the interpolated tasks in short-term retention. However, more experimental work is obviously needed to determine the specific nature of this hypothetical short-trace maintenance process and the conditions that affect its operation. Hopefully, the theory can be strengthened in some simple ways in order to capture more of the details of this short-trace maintenance process.

Exponential power decay of the long trace. Wickelgren (1972) studied retention intervals from 1 min to over 2 years using both continuous recognition and study-test recognition-memory paradigms under a variety of experimental conditions for a variety of types of verbal material. This study found that a single (long-term) memory trace with the exponential power form specified in Equation 2 provided a good fit to retention functions from delays of 1 min to delays of over 2 years. Wickelgren (1972) found the good fit with $\gamma = 0.5$, but noted that the optimal assumed exponent of growth of trace resistance (γ) was probably somewhat greater than 0.5. Subsequent work on a greater variety and range of experiments indicates that the correct value of the growth of trace resistance is probably closer to $\gamma = 0.75$. The exact value of the exponent is not determined at present because any exponent in the region of $\gamma = 0.5$ to 0.8 appears to provide a reasonably good fit to the data. However, the basic exponential power decay form for the long trace is rather well established by comparison with a variety of alternative simple hypotheses regarding the form of the long-term strength-retention function. Alternative hypotheses ruled out by Wickelgren (1972) were linear decay ($\ell = \lambda - \psi t$), exponential decay ($\ell = \lambda e^{-\psi t}$), logarithmic decay ($\ell = \lambda - \psi \log t$), and power function decay ($\ell = \lambda t^{-\psi}$).

Retrograde amnesia. Following severe head injury of the concussion variety, human beings frequently cannot remember events that occurred for some time prior to the injury. Clinical studies of retrograde amnesia indicate that this memory loss is temporally defined rather than being defined on the basis of trace strength, trace importance, personal-impersonal, etc. (Russell, 1959; Whitty, 1962). In retrograde amnesia following concussion, it is the most recent memories that are lost, not the strongest nor the weakest, nor the most or the least important, or personal vs general factual memory, etc. The period of time over which the RA extends appears to be almost continuously variable, from RAs that extend over only a few seconds prior to the injury to RAs that extend over periods of many minutes, hours, days, weeks, months, years, or even tens of years. The overwhelmingly predominant tendency is for short RAs of only a few seconds or tens of seconds, but the existence of RAs of almost any length led Russell (1959) to argue that something about the character of the memory trace is continually changing over the entire lifetime of the memory.

Precisely this type of continuous change is postulated in the strength-resistance theory of memory. Furthermore, because trace strength is not the basis for the selectivity observed in retrograde amnesia, some property other than trace strength must be postulated to be continually changing over the lifetime of the memory. The increasing trace resistance that appears to be necessary in order to account for the form of the long strength-retention function provides precisely the type of memory property needed to explain the clinical phenomenon of retrograde amnesia. According to this hypothesis, the same property of the memory trace that makes it more resistant to normal forces of forgetting also makes it more resistant to loss in retrograde amnesia due to concussion.

It should be observed that retrograde amnesia is frequently only a temporary phenomenon, with substantial recovery of the memory occurring over a period of time following the injury. As the memory recovers, it appears to recover in a temporally defined manner as well, so that the oldest memories are recovered first, followed by the next oldest, and then the next oldest, . . . , up to the most recent. Frequently there is a residual amnesia of a few seconds or minutes that is never cleared up, but occasionally the residual amnesia extends for an even longer period of time. Similar temporally defined and shrinking retrograde amnesias have been found following electroconvulsive shock in humans (Williams, 1966).

Studies of retrograde amnesia in animals following electroconvulsive shock, anaesthetics, anoxia, convulsant drugs, hypothermia, concussion, spreading depression of the cortex, local brain stimulation, etc., have found retrograde amnesias in animals that are also temporally defined in a somewhat similar manner to that found for human beings (Weiskrantz, 1966). Just as in the case of retrograde amnesia in human beings, the period of time covered by the amnesia appears to be quite variable over the different conditions studied, ranging from a few seconds up to several hours or even days. Superficially, this can be taken to provide support for a long trace that is continually increasing in resistance over its lifetime. However, because the variability and extent of RA in animals under these various conditions is not well understood, it would be premature to draw any firm conclusion on this matter at the present time.

The present theory does not account in any way for the conditions under which the retrograde amnesia should be temporary or permanent, but it does account for the basic temporally defined character of this retrograde amnesia and the recovery therefrom. The accounting for retrograde amnesia is largely qualitative in comparison to the accounting for the form of the long-trace retention function. However, it should be noted that a function specifying that resistance approaches a limit will fail to fit the retrograde amnesia data, just as it will fail to fit the data from normal long-term retention. The increase in the resistance property of the long trace must be assumed to be going on continuously from the moment of formation (or within a few seconds or tens of seconds thereafter) to the lifetime of the memory (possibly years or tens of years).

Hemispheric Conflict and the Forgetting
of Lateralized Engrams

Recently, Goldowitz, Burešova and Bureš (1973) have developed a hemi-spheric conflict technique for studying the nature of the long-term retention function in animals. The technique involves training animals to make one of two choices on one day with one hemisphere under spreading depression. Then at various retention intervals, the relative strengths of both traces are assessed with both hemispheres functioning normally in the choice situation. The results of their study indicate that habits learned on two different days cannot be equated at all retention intervals by the same relative numbers of initial learning trials for the two conflicting habits. Rather, as the retention interval increases, equal relative habit strength on the retention tests requires less and less difference in the initial degree of learning of the two habits.

This is precisely what one expects from the present strength-resistance theory, because memory traces have a type of temporal encoding ('know their age'). According to the present theory, the retention functions for habits learned on different days will intersect at progressively longer delays, the smaller the initial difference in degree of learning. (Of course, the initially learned habit must have had a greater degree of learning than the subse-quently learned habit if there is to be any crossing of the retention functions.) The qualitative convergence of theoretical conclusions from such method-ologically disparate studies as human verbal memory and choice memory in rats is quite satisfying. However, because of the use of a different dependent variable, it is not possible at the present time to determine whether or not there is precise quantitative agreement between the animal and human studies.

Similarity-Dependent Storage Interference
in Long-Term Memory

As discussed in Wickelgren (1972), over a dozen studies use recognition tests that demonstrate that increasing the 'fine grain' similarity of interpolated to original learning increases the storage interference produced by the inter-polated learning. For example, AB–AC, AB–CB, or AB–AB$_r$ interpolated learning designs produce greater retroactive interference than does an AB–CD design. In contrast to the 15 or more positive confirmations of this law, there are no published contradictions to it known to me. Thus, we may regard similarity-dependent storage interference of the long trace as extremely well established.

Spacing of Multiple Learning Trials

It is widely believed to be well established that forgetting following spaced learning trials (distributed practice) is slower than forgetting following massed learning trials (massed practice). In actual fact, numerous experiments by Underwood and his colleagues have frequently failed to find this superiority in retention following distributed vs massed practice.

Surprisingly enough, the failures to obtain superior retention following distributed practice are as confirming of the present theory as are the successes in achieving superior retention following distributed practice. The reason for this is that the failures to obtain superior retention following distributed practice (e.g., Underwood & Richardson, 1955) have always used learning to a criterion, with the frequent result that the total time between the first and last learning trials was not much different for the massed and distributed practice conditions. Under these circumstances, the present theory would not expect any difference between massed and distributed practice in the rate of forgetting following the last learning trial. The general lack of any consistent difference under these conditions actually supports the present theory.

By contrast, the successful examples, where distributed practice produces significantly slower forgetting than massed practice (e.g., Keppel, 1964), have generally employed a fixed number of learning trials and, in the case of the Keppel experiment, an extremely long spacing between some of the trials (e.g., an entire day). Creating a vast difference between the time of the first and last learning trials is precisely what the present theory requires in order to exhibit a large difference in the rate of forgetting following the last learning trial.

These results provide largely qualitative support for the present theory, but one experiment described in Wickelgren (1972) did provide a very limited degree of quantitative support for Axiom 6 that the resistance of long traces transfers completely to subsequent increments (making the resistance determined entirely by the time since the first learning trial).

Further implications of this theory for the comparison of retention following learning trials with different types of spacing need to be investigated. For instance, the present theory asserts that two massed learning sessions separated by a long interval would be equivalent in retention properties to a series of learning trials that were evenly spaced throughout the entire period from first to last learning trials, provided that the time between the first and last learning trials was equated. Rates of forgetting in the two cases should be identical, though it might be necessary to vary the number of learning trials in the two instances in order to achieve equal degrees of learning.

Relearning. According to the present theory, retention following relearning of previously learned material should be characterized by a slower rate of decay than that following original learning or the learning of comparable new material, no matter how much time has elapsed since original learning and no matter how little memory strength remains. The reason for this is that resistance continues to increase while strength decreases during retention interval. At the time of relearning, according to Axiom 6, the resistance of the original trace transfers completely to the increments during relearning. To my knowledge, there is no available evidence concerning retention functions following relearning. However, speed of relearning is invariably faster than original learning or comparable new learning, even under conditions where recall or recognition performance is extremely low (see Nelson, 1971). Furthermore, Nelson (1971) found that savings in relearning was the same for items that were recognized as for items that were not recognized in a retention test prior to the relearning. This suggests that some other factor besides strength is influencing the relearning performance. The resistance property postulated by the present theory could serve this function, under the assumption that forgetting between learning trials is a significant factor retarding original learning but not relearning (because of high resistance).

Some of the probable differences between relearning and original learning can probably be explained by virtue of the trace-resistance property. However, it seems likely that when relevant data become available concerning relearning and retention following relearning it will be necessary to make some modification of the present theory in the direction of postulating a greater coupling from strength to resistance, in addition to the presently postulated coupling from resistance to strength. Undoubtedly, as strength decreases to a very low level, resistance does not continue to increase and may even begin to decrease. It seems counterintuitive to imagine that a memory which has been largely forgotten should be characterized by slower forgetting following relearning, the longer one waits after the memory has been essentially forgotten. However, since my intuition is not based on any relevant data, the theory may turn out to be right and my intuition to be wrong.

Evidence for two traces. Many classes of evidence that have been alleged to support a two-trace theory of memory as opposed to a single-trace theory of memory are not at all convincing (see Gruneberg, 1970). As Gruneberg emphasizes, the rapid forgetting characteristically observed during the first few seconds of a retention interval does not imply that the memory trace decaying over that period of time is different from the memory trace decaying over retention intervals from minutes to hours to days to years. It has already been repeatedly pointed out that long-term-memory traces are continually decreasing in their rate of forgetting on any absolute scale (Jost's Second Law). Furthermore, the difference between the rate of decay at retention intervals of minutes vs retention intervals of years (both considered to depend only on the long trace) is greater than the difference in decay rate of retention intervals of seconds (considered to depend on the short trace) and retention intervals of minutes or tens of minutes. From a strictly *qualitative* point of view, the extremely rapid forgetting at short retention intervals is consistent with comparable findings for long-term memory at all different comparisons of shorter vs longer retention intervals. Arguments that derive from the rapid forgetting property of the short trace are also not definitive.

However, there are at least three classes of evidence available at present that strongly support the assumption of two dynamically different memory traces, rather than a single memory trace.

First, I have consistently found that the long-trace retention function, which works well for delays greater than a minute (recent evidence indicates that it works well down to a delay of about 20 sec), will not work when extrapolated down to retention intervals within the first 20 sec following learning. In order to fit strength-retention functions quantitatively within the first 20 sec following learning, it appears to be necessary to assume a short-trace component in addition to the long-trace component. However, it must be emphasized that there are an infinity of possible quantitative theories, and it would be very premature to contend that no single-trace theory of simple form could handle all strength-retention functions from zero sec delays to the lifetime of the memory trace. Nevertheless, the fact that these retention functions can be accounted for by a simple two-trace theory constitutes support for the two-trace theory until such time as someone can demonstrate a plausible single-trace theory that also accounts for this data.

Second, perhaps the single most convincing qualitative evidence for the distinction between short- and long-term memory is the difference in the storage-interference properties of the two traces. As has already been pointed out, experiments considered to be tapping primarily the short trace have demonstrated that storage interference is independent of the fine-grain similarity of interpolated to original learning. By contrast, storage interference for the long trace is similarity dependent. The similarity independence of storage interference in short-term memory requires considerable further replication, but if it continues to be obtained, this is probably definitive qualitative evidence for a distinction between short and long traces.

Third, the existence of certain patients (with bilateral mesial temporal and hippocampal lesions) who have severe deficits in the ability to consolidate new long-term memory, but relatively little impairment in the ability to establish new short-term memories, is an impressive piece of evidence in support of the two-trace theory (Scoville & Milner, 1957; Milner, 1966; Wickelgren, 1968b). Recently, a reverse impairment of auditory verbal short-term memory with no impairment of long-term memory has been observed by Warrington and Shallice (1969) and Warrington, Logue, and Pratt (1971) in several different patients. In this latter case, however, the memory impairment seems to be specific to the verbal modality, not a global impairment of all short-term memory (e.g., short-term memory is normal for visually presented material).

Retrieval

Independence from irrelevant associations. As pointed out in the theory section, perhaps the most important component of the criterion decision rule for recognition memory is the assumption that only a single strength needs to be judged to determine a recognition rating response. Thus, if a subject is to judge whether an A–B pair was presented in a previous list, he is assumed to judge only the strength of the A–B association, without being influenced by the strengths of any 'competing' A–C association. One way to test this is to determine whether strengthening an A–C association has any effect on the ability to distinguish a correct A–B association from an incorrect A–D association. The results of two published experiments on recognition in short-term memory support the assumption of independence from irrelevant association (Bower & Bostrom, 1968; Wickelgren, 1967).

As previously mentioned, for A–B recognition to be equally good following A–C interpolated learning as following C–D interpolated learning, storage interference in short-term memory must be similarity independent, in addition to independence from irrelevant associations holding during retrieval via the recognition test. Thus, the same studies are simultaneously evidence for both phenomena. The fact that the same findings are not observed for long-term memory is attributed to the presence of similarity-dependent storage interference in the case of the long trace, not to any lack of independence from irrelevant associations in retrieval. However, this is obviously a matter of comparative plausibility, not logical necessity. It is the independence from irrelevant associations that largely forms the factual basis for the assertion that recognition is a more direct test of the strength of memory traces in storage than is recall. Recall is obviously subject to retrieval interference effects in the form of specific A–B, A–C response competition, which the previously cited results indicate did not affect recognition.

To conclude from the above that recognition tests are free of all possible retrieval interference factors and directly indicate loss in storage would be premature. I have conducted some unpublished studies on the effects of changing background context on recall and recognition that indicate that contextual change is much less important in the case of recognition memory than in the case of recall memory. In some cases, contextual change may have no effect at all on memory assesed by recognition tests.

However, in other situations, DaPolito, Barker, and Wiant (1971), Light and Carter-Sobell (1970), and Tulving and Thomson (1971) have all shown that changes in associative context from learning to retrieval can have a significant effect on recognition-memory performance. If the probability of spontaneously occurring contextual change alters systematically with delay since learning, then this may be influencing the form of the retention function in addition to, or instead of, other causes of forgetting observed on recognition-memory tests. Alternatively, effects of contextual change in recognition memory under these conditions may simply serve to multiply the memory trace by the same constant at all delays (in which case it would be absorbed in the acquisition parameters). Resolution of the problem concerning 'spontaneous' contextual changes in the forgetting observed by recognition-memory tests is an important theoretical issue in the interpretation and evaluation of strength-resistance theory.

Normally distributed noise.   Probably one of the least important assumptions of the present theory is that the noise involved in the acquisition and retrieval processes is normally distributed. The assumption that the noise in acquisition and retrieval is normally distributed can be assessed by determining the fit of operating characteristics to straight lines on normal-normal probability coordinates. Determining the goodness of fit for operating characteristics generated by the rating method in recognition memory can now be done quite precisely using the method of maximum likelihood as described by Dorfman and Alf (1969). To my knowledge, this has not yet been done for recognition-memory data. When it is done, I would not be surprised to see that, in at least some cases, the assumption of normally distributed noise could be rejected.

What has been done is to determine by 'eyeball' methods that the normal distribution assumption is at least approximately accurate. There are at least two interesting, theoretically predicted exceptions to this statement (Norman & Wickelgren, 1965; Wickelgren, 1969), but in general the assumption has proved quite satisfactory. Because the level of accuracy aspired to by the present theory of memory dynamics is about 1.5 significant figures, all that really needs to hold is that the strength distributions are unimodal. As long as the strength distributions are unimodal, a characterization by the best-fitting normal approximation will undoubtedly be adequate. The only danger in using normal approximations where they may not be strictly valid comes from using the tails of the distributions. It is dangerous to use a single operating characteristic to determine a d_s difference greater than four standard deviation units. In cases where one wishes to assess differences in means of strength distributions that exceed four standard deviation units, it is desirable to construct discriminability scales, using the method suggested by Creelman (1967). In this method, one compares condition 1 with condition 2 and condition 2 with condition 3 in order to derive the discriminability difference between condition 1 and condition 3. In using this method, it is important to keep in mind that slopes must be taken into account, so that all strength discriminability values are scaled in terms of the same unit standard deviation.

Relation between different retrieval tasks. For some reason, Tanner and Swets (1954), in their original paper introducing signal-detection theory to psychology, considered that the prediction from one type of decision task to another was an essential initial criterion for the evaluation of statistical decision theory. Comparison from 'yes-no' to multiple-choice (forced choice) or recall paradigms is riddled with theoretically uninteresting complications (for a discussion of these, see Wickelgren, 1968a). Thus, it is probably fortunate that the application of statistical decision theory to the study of recognition memory has largely ignored this problem of predicting across different retrieval-decision tasks.

There have been a few attempts, and surprisingly enough they have been relatively successful. Green and Moses (1966) showed that the ds derived from 'yes-no' recognition-memory performance could be used to predict two-alternative multiple-choice recognition-memory performance, and Kintsch (1968) showed that the statistical decision assumptions made successful predictions across 'yes-no,' two-, four-, and eight-alternative multiple-choice paradigms. Norman and Wickelgren (1969) were not quite so successful in making predictions across 'yes-no' recognition, multiple-choice recognition, and recall tasks, but all that was necessary to achieve successful prediction was the estimation of an additional parameter relating the retrieval noise for 'yes-no' recognition to the retrieval noise for multiple choice and recall. Frankly, because of all the complications discussed in Wickelgren (1968a), I have little confidence that much has been demonstrated by these few attempts to predict absolute levels of performance across different retrieval-decision tasks.

A more promising approach is probably to compare the forms and rates of retention functions obtained with different retrieval-decision tasks. Because of the greater simplicity of the criterion decision rule for recognition memory than any of the other decision rules, recognition memory has been used to determine almost all of the retention functions obtained in previous research designed to test strength theories of memory. This made good sense as an initial strategy, but it is probably now time to begin studying retention functions by recall and multiple choice. One early study of verbal short-term memory by Norman (1966) found that the form and rate of decay for the short trace was approximately the same whether probe recall or probe recognition was used. Extensive work on this problem needs to be done to confirm both the retrieval-decision rules for multiple choice and recall and also to confirm the assumption that the same dynamical types of memory traces are tapped by multiple-choice and recall memory tasks as are tapped by 'yes-no' recognition-memory tasks.

Recency judgments. Wickelgren (1972) has shown that the discriminability of the recencies of two memory traces is a negatively accelerated, monotonically increasing function of the time delay between the two memory traces. In that experiment, the function could not be well fit by a power function with an exponent similar to that used in fitting the strength-retention functions for recognition memory. However, certain flaws in the design of that recency-memory experiment may have led to precisely the type of small, consistent deviation from a power-function increase in recency discriminability that was observed. Thus, it would be premature to reject the extremely attractive possibility that the same property of the memory trace underlies recency judgments and the increased resistance to forgetting.

ACKNOWLEDGMENT

This work was supported by grant MH 17958 from NIMH.

REFERENCES

Bahrick, H. P. The ebb of retention. *Psychological Review*, 1965, **72**, 60–73.

Bower, G. H., & Bostrom, A. Absence of within-list PI and RI in short-term recognition memory. *Psychonomic Science*, 1968, **10**, 211–212.

Brown, J. Some tests of the decay theory of immediate memory. *Quarterly Journal of Experimental Psychology*, 1958, **10**, 12–21.

Creelman, C. D. Empirical detectability scales without the jnd. *Perceptual and Motor Skills*, 1967, **24**, 1079–1084.

DaPolito, F., Barker, D., & Wiant, J. Context in semantic information retrieval. *Psychonomic Science*, 1971, **24**, 180–182.

Dorfman, D. D., & Alf, E., Jr. Maximum-likelihood estimation of parameters of signal-detection theory and determination of confidence intervals—rating-method data. *Journal of Mathematical Psychology*, 1969, **6**, 487–496.

Elliott, P. B. Tables of d'. In J. A. Swets (Ed.), *Signal detection and recognition by human observers*. New York: Wiley, 1964.

Goldowitz, D., Burešova, O., & Bureš, J. Forgetting of lateralized engrams studied by interhemispheric conflict in rats. *Behavioral Biology*, 1973, **8**, 183–192.

Green, D. M., & Moses, F. L. On the equivalence of two recognition measures of short-term memory. *Psychological Bulletin*, 1966, **66**, 228–234.

Green, D. M., & Swets, J. A. *Signal detection theory and psychophysics*. New York: Wiley, 1966.

Gruneberg, M. M. A dichotomous theory of memory—unproved and unprovable? *Acta Psychologica*, 1970, **34**, 489–496.

Hawkins, H. L., Pardo, V. J., & Cox, R. D. Proactive interference in short-term recognition: Trace interaction or competition? *Journal of Experimental Psychology*, 1972, **92**, 43–48.

Hovland, C. I. Human learning and retention. In S. S. Stevens (Ed.), *Handbook of experimental psychology*. New York: Wiley, 1951.

Keppel, G. Facilitation in short- and long-term retention of paired associates following distributed practice in learning. *Journal of Verbal Learning and Verbal Behavior*, 1964, **3**, 91–111.

Kintsch, W. An experimental analysis of single stimulus tests and multiple-choice tests of recognition memory. *Journal of Experimental Psychology*, 1968, **76**, 1–6.

Light, L. L., & Carter-Sobell, L. Effects of changed semantic context on recognition memory. *Journal of Verbal Learning and Verbal Behavior*, 1970, **9**, 1–11.

Marcer, D. Subtraction as interpolated activity in short-term retention. *Psychonomic Science*, 1968, **11**, 359.

Merikle, P. M. Unit size and interpolated-task difficulty as determinants of short-term retention. *Journal of Experimental Psychology*, 1968, **77**, 370–375.

Milner, B. Amnesia following operation on the temporal lobes. In C. W. M. Whitty and O. L. Zangwill (Eds.), *Amnesia*. London: Butterworths, 1966.

Nelson, T. O. Recognition and savings in long-term memory: Related or independent? *Proceedings of the 79th Annual Convention of the American Psychological Association*, 1971, 15–16.

Norman, D. A. Acquisition and retention in short-term memory. *Journal of Experimental Psychology*, 1966, **72**, 369–381.

Norman, D. A., & Wickelgren, W. A. Short-term recognition memory for single digits and pairs of digits. *Journal of Experimental Psychology*, 1965, **70**, 479–489.

Norman, D. A., & Wickelgren, W. A. Strength theory of decision rules and latency in retrieval from short-term memory. *Journal of Mathematical Psychology*, 1969, **6**, 192–208.

Peterson, L. R., & Peterson, M. J. Short-term retention of individual verbal items. *Journal of Experimental Psychology*, 1959, **58**, 193–198.

Posner, M. I., & Konick, A. F. On the role of interference in short-term retention. *Journal of Experimental Psychology*, 1966, **72**, 221–231.

Posner, M. I., & Rossman, E. The effect of size and location of informational transforms upon short-term retention. *Journal of Experimental Psychology*, 1965, **70**, 496–505.

Reitman, J. S. B. *Short-term verbal retention with interpolated verbal and non-verbal signal detection*. Ann Arbor: Mental Health Research Institute Communication #262 and Information Processing Working Paper #14, University of Michigan, 1969.

Russell, W. R. *Brain · memory · learning*. Oxford: Oxford University Press, 1959.

Scoville, W. B., & Milner, B. Loss of recent memory after bilateral hippocampal lesions. *Journal of Neurology, Neurosurgery and Psychiatry*, 1957, **20**, 11–21.

Swets, J. A. (Ed.) *Signal detection and recognition by human observers*. New York: Wiley, 1964.

Tanner, W. P., Jr., & Swets, J. A. A decision-making theory of visual detection. *Psychological Review*, 1954, **61**, 401–409.

Tulving, E., & Thomson, D. M. Retrieval processes in recognition memory: Effects of associative context. *Journal of Experimental Psychology*, 1971, **87**, 116–124.

Underwood, B. J., & Richardson, J. Studies of distributed practice: XIIL interlist interference and the retention of serial nonsense lists. *Journal of Experimental Psychology*, 1955, **50**, 39–46.

Warrington, E. K., Logue, V., & Pratt, R. T. C. The anatomical localisation of selective impairment of auditory verbal short-term memory. *Neuropsychologia*, 1971, **9**, 377–387.

Warrington, E. K., & Shallice, T. The selective impairment of auditory verbal short-term memory. *Brain*, 1969, **92**, 885–896.

Waugh, N. C., & Norman, D. A. Primary memory. *Psychological Review*, 1965, **72**, 89–104.

Weiskrantz, L. Experimental studies of amnesia. In C. W. M. Whitty and O. L. Zangwill (Eds.), *Amnesia*. London: Butterworths, 1966.

Whitty, C. W. M. The neurological basis of memory. *Modern Trends in Neurology*, 1962, **3**, 314–335.

Wickelgren, W. A. Exponential decay and independence from irrelevant associations in short-term recognition memory for serial order. *Journal of Experimental Psychology*, 1967, **73**, 165–171.

Wickelgren, W. A. Unidimensional strength theory and component analysis of noise in absolute and comparative judgments. *Journal of Mathematical Psychology*, 1968, **5**, 102–122. (a)

Wickelgren, W. A. Sparing of short-term memory in an amnesic patient: Implications for strength theory of memory. *Neuropsychologia*, 1968, **6**, 235–244. (b)

Wickelgren, W. A. Associative strength theory of recognition memory for pitch. *Journal of Mathematical Psychology*, 1969, **6**, 13–61.

Wickelgren, W. A. Time, interference, and rate of presentation in short-term recognition memory for items. *Journal of Mathematical Psychology*, 1970, **7**, 219–235.

Wickelgren, W. A. Trace resistance and the decay of long-term memory. *Journal of Mathematical Psychology*, 1972, **9**, 418–455.

Wickelgren, W. A., & Berian, K. M. Dual trace theory and the consolidation of long-term memory. *Journal of Mathematical Psychology*, 1971, **8**, 404–417.

Wickelgren, W. A., & Norman, D. A. Strength models and serial position in short-term recognition memory. *Journal of Mathematical Psychology*, 1966, **3**, 316–347.

Wickelgren, W. A., & Norman, D. A. Invariance of forgetting rate with number of repetitions in verbal short-term recognition memory. *Psychonomic Science*, 1971, **22**, 363–364.

Williams, M. Memory disorders associated with electronconvulsive therapy. In C. W. M. Whitty and O. L. Zangwill (Eds.), *Amnesia*. London: Butterworths, 1966.

Search and Decision Processes in Recognition Memory

Richard C. Atkinson
STANFORD UNIVERSITY

James F. Juola
UNIVERSITY OF KANSAS

INTRODUCTION

In this chapter we develop and evaluate a mathematical model for a series of experiments on recognition memory. The model is extremely simple, incorporating only those assumptions necessary for treatment of the phenomena under analysis. It should be noted, however, that the model is a special case of a more general theory of memory (Atkinson & Shiffrin, 1968, 1971); thus its evaluation has implications not only for the experiments examined here, but also for the theory of which it is a special case.

Before discussing the model and the relevant experiments, it will be useful to provide a brief review of the general theory. The theory views memory as a dynamic and interactive system; the main components of the memory system and paths of information flow are diagrammed in Figure 1. Stimuli impinge on the system via the *sensory register*, and the system in turn acts upon its environment through the *response generator*. Within the system itself, a distinction is made between the *memory storage network*, in which information is recorded, and *control processes* that govern the flow and sequencing of information. The memory storage network is composed of the *sensory register*, a *short-term store* (STS), and a *long-term store* (LTS). The sensory register analyzes and transforms the input from the sensory system

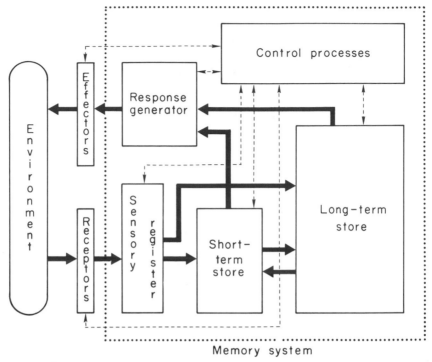

FIGURE 1.
A flowchart of the memory system. Solid lines indicate paths of information transfer. Dashed lines indicate connections that permit comparison of information arrays residing in different parts of the system; they also indicate paths along which control signals may be sent which modulate information transfer, activate rehearsal mechanisms, set decision criteria, alter biases of sensory channels, initiate the response generator, etc.

and briefly retains this information while it is selectively read into one of the memory stores. The STS is a working memory of limited capacity from which information decays fairly rapidly unless it is maintained by control processes such as imagery or rehearsal. The contents of STS may be thought of as the 'current state of consciousness' for the subject. The LTS is a large and essentially permanent memory bank; information once recorded in this store does not decay, but its availability for further processing depends upon the effectiveness of retrieval processes. In the figure, STS and LTS are depicted as two separate boxes, but this is not meant to imply neurologically separate systems; it is quite possible that STS is simply the active phase of neural processes quiescent in LTS. The control processes regulate the transfer of information from one store to another, and the sequencing of operations within each memory store. These processes are labile strategies adopted by the subject in response to environmental and task conditions. They include selective attention, rehearsal, coding, selection of retrieval cues, and all types of decision strategies.

Although the model developed in this paper is a special case of the theory represented in Figure 1, it also can be interpreted as consistent with a number of other theories.[1] It is possible to theorize about components of the memory process without making commitments on all aspects of a theory of memory. Component problems can be isolated experimentally and local models developed. Work of this sort eventually leads to modification of the general theory, but a close connection between local models and the general theory is not required at every stage of research.

The term 'recognition memory' covers a wide variety of phenomena in which the subject attempts to decide whether or not a given object or event has been experienced previously (Kintsch, 1970a, 1970b; McCormack, 1972). It is a common process in everyday life and one that is readily subject to experimentation. In the recognition task that we have been investigating, the subject must decide whether or not a given test stimulus is a member of a predefined set of target items. For any set S of stimuli, a subset S_1 is defined that is of size d. Stimuli in S_1 will be referred to as *target items;* subset S_0 is the complement of S_1 with respect to S, and its members will be called *distractor items.* The experimental task involves a long series of discrete trials with a stimulus from S presented on each trial. To each presentation the subject makes either an A_1 or A_0 response, indicating that he judges the stimulus to be a target or distractor item, respectively.

The target sets in our experiments involve fairly long lists of words (sometimes as many as 60 words) that are thoroughly memorized by the subject prior to the test session. During the test session individual words are presented, and the subject's task is to respond as rapidly as possible, indicating whether or not the test word is a member of the target set. Errors are infrequent, and the principal data are response latencies (i.e., the time between the onset of the test word and the subject's response). The length of the target list and other features of the experimental procedure prevent the subject from rehearsing the list during the course of the test session, thus requiring that the subject access LTS in order to make a decision about each test word.

In some respects this task is similar to that studied by Sternberg (1966) and others. In the Sternberg task, a small number of items (e.g., 1 to 6 digits) are presented at the start of each trial, making up the target set for the trial. The test item is then presented, and the subject makes an A_1 response if the item is a member of that trial's target set, or an A_0 otherwise. In the Sternberg task the subject does not need to master the target set, for it is small and can be maintained in STS while needed. This type of short-term recognition experi-

---

[1] See, for example, a collection of papers concerning models of memory edited by Norman (1970).

ment differs then from our long-term studies in terms of the size and mastery of the target set. The data from the two types of studies are similar in many respects, but there are some striking differences. In both types of studies, response latency is an increasing linear function of the size of the target set; however, the slope of the function is about 5 msec per item in the long-term studies, compared with about 35 msec in the short-term studies. Other points of comparison will be considered later.

From a variety of long-term recognition studies we have achieved a better understanding of how information is represented in memory and how it is retrieved and processed in making response decisions. A model based on this work is formally developed in the next section. First, however, a more intuitive account is given.

Consider the case in which the target set consists of a long list of words that the subject has thoroughly memorized prior to the test session. The initial problems are to postulate mechanisms by which this information is used to distinguish target words from distractors. It is assumed that every word in the subject's language has associated with it a particular long-term memory location that we refer to as a node in the lexical store (Miller, 1969; Rubenstein, Garfield, & Millikan, 1970). When a word is presented for test, the sensory input is encoded and mapped onto the appropriate node. This process is essential in identifying or naming the test stimulus as well as in retrieving other information that is associated with the item. Figure 2 shows a representation of a single node in the lexical store (panel A), along with an example of an associative network by which various nodes are interconnected (panel B). Each node is a functional unit representing a single word or concept (such as the relational concepts 'to the left of,' 'above,' or concepts dealing with size and shape). A variety of nodes and their associations in the lexicon is necessary in accounting for language use and other symbolic behavior (Schank, 1972), but for our purposes we need only consider nodes that correspond to potential test words.

At each node is stored an array of codes. The input codes represent the end results of the encoding processes that operate on the auditory, pictorial, or graphemic information in the sensory register. These codes serve as means to access the appropriate node in the lexicon. Internal codes are alternative representations of the stimulus word that can be used to locate the item if it is stored elsewhere in memory. The internal codes can be of various types; they may be abstract pictorial or auditory images, a list of semantic-syntactic markers, predicate relations, etc. Information recorded in memory involves an array of internal codes, and the same object or event may be represented by different codes depending on the memory store involved and related information. Finally, output codes, when entered into the response generator, permit the subject to produce the word in various forms (oral, written, etc.). The property of lexical nodes that allows transformation from one code to

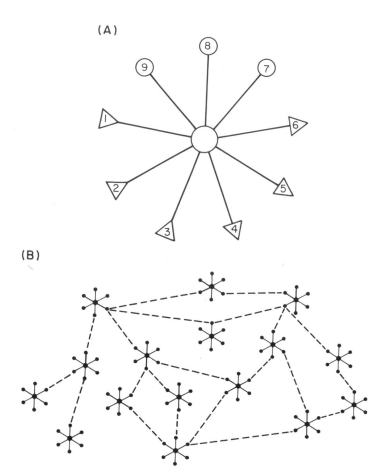

FIGURE 2.
A schematic representation of the lexical store. Panel (A) illustrates a hypothetical node in the lexicon with associated input codes [(1) auditory, (2) pictorial, (3) graphemic], output codes [(4) written, (5) spoken, (6) imaged], and internal codes [(7) acoustical code for STS, (8) imaginal code for LTS, (9) verbal code for LTS]. Panel (B) illustrates a subset of nodes in the lexicon, with dashed lines indicating codes that are shared by more than one lexical node. For example, depending on an individual's experience, the nodes for mare and stallion could share a common internal code; if this code is used (along with others) to represent a particular episode, then information about the horse's sex will not be recorded in memory.

another has proved useful in other theories of memory, most notably in the logogen system of Morton (1969, 1970).

It is possible that information stored at the node representing the test word could lead directly to the decision to make an A_1 or A_0 response. This would be the case if, for example, each node corresponding to a target word has associated with it a marker or list tag that could be retrieved when the item is tested (Anderson & Bower, 1972). We take the alternative view, however, that information contained in the lexical store is relatively isolated from those parts of the memory system that record the occurrence of particular events, experiences, and thought processes. The lexical store contains the set of symbols used in the information-handling process, and the various codes associated with each symbol; these codes are the language in which experiences are recorded, but the actual record is elsewhere in memory. Thus, memorizing a list of words involves extracting appropriate codes from the lexicon and organizing these codes into an array to be recorded in a partition of LTS separate from the lexical store. There is no direct link between a word's node in the lexicon and its representation in the memory structure for the word list; to establish that a word is a member of the memorized list involves extracting an appropriate code from the word's lexical node and scanning it against the list for a possible match.

Thus, LTS is viewed as being partitioned into a lexical store and what we call the event-knowledge store (E/K store). As noted above, the lexical store maintains a set of symbols and codes that can be used by the subject to represent knowledge and the occurrence of particular events. When the subject is confronted with new information, he represents it in the form of an array of internal codes, and if it is to be retained on a long-term basis, that array is recorded in the E/K store.[2] Our representation of words resembles the model proposed by Kintsch (1970b), but differs from his model regarding the representation of a memorized list. Kintsch assumes that acquisition of a list involves increasing the familiarity or strength of an item in the lexical store. Although we agree with Kintsch up to this point, we also propose that the code or codes of a word in the lexical store are copied and placed in the E/K store. The organization of these codes in the E/K store, as suggested by Herrmann (1972), will depend on the particular study procedure used in acquisition (e.g., serial order, an arbitrary pairing of words, or clustering by a common meaning such as category membership). The division of LTS into

---

[2] In order to simplify the presentation, a sharp distinction has been made between the lexical store and the E/K store. The distinction is satisfactory for the experiments treated in this chapter. However, in general, we view LTS as a graded set of memories; those described here as lexical nodes represent one extreme, while event memories represent the opposite extreme. The lexical store evolves over a lifetime; by analysis of past memories the individual develops new codes that make the storage of future events more economical. Thus one's history of experiences determines the codes available in the lexical system and, in turn, the ability to store different types of information (Atkinson & Wescourt, 1974).

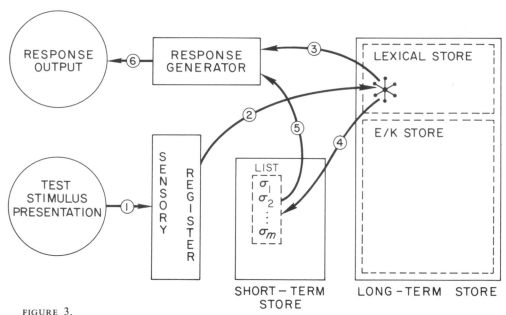

A schematic representation of the search and decision processes in long-term recognition memory. A test stimulus is presented (1) and then encoded and matched to the node in the lexicon (2). The familiarity index associated with the node may lead to an immediate decision (3) and in turn generate a response (6). Otherwise an extended search of the stored target list is initiated (4), which eventually leads to a decision (5) and a subsequent response (6). Path (1), (2), (3), (6) results in a faster response than path (1), (2), (4), (5), (6), and the response that is independent of target-set size.

a lexical store and an E/K store is similar to the distinction made by Tulving (1972) between semantic and episodic memory. In Tulving's taxonomy, the lexical store would be classified as semantic memory. The E/K store, however, might be classified by Tulving as either semantic memory or episodic memory, depending on the type of information in the E/K store. To Tulving, one's memory for a list learned in a psychology experiment constitutes an episodic memory, but the knowledge one learns in a chemistry course (such as the periodic table of elements) constitutes a semantic memory. It is maintained here that both kinds of information are held in the E/K store and are treated by the memory system in essentially the same manner (Atkinson & Wescourt, 1974).

Figure 3 presents a summary of the processes involved in recognition memory for words that are members of a list stored in long-term memory. When the test word is presented, it is encoded into an input code that allows direct access to the appropriate node in the lexical store. Although the node does not contain a tag or marker indicating list membership, it will be assumed that by accessing the node the subject can arrive at an index of the test word's *familiarity*. The familiarity value for any node is a function of the time since that node was last accessed relative to the number of times the node had been accessed in the past. Infrequently occurring words receive a large increase in familiarity after a single test, whereas the test of a frequent word results in only a small increase in its familiarity. The familiarity value for any word is assumed to regress to its base value as a function of time since the last access of the node.[3]

In recognition experiments of the type described above, the familiarity value of a word sometimes can be a fairly reliable indicator of list membership. It will be assumed that, when the subject finds a very high familiarity value at the lexical node of the test word, he outputs an immediate A_1 response; if he finds a very low familiarity value, he outputs an immediate A_0. If the familiarity value is intermediate (neither low nor high), the subject extracts an appropriate code for the test word and scans it against the target list in the E/K store. If the scan yields a match, an A_1 is made; otherwise A_0. The recognition process sketched out above is similar to that proposed by Mandler, Pearlstone, and Koopmans (1969). In the next section, these ideas are quantified and tested against data involving both error probabilities and response latencies.

A MODEL FOR RECOGNITION

Several special cases of the model to be considered here have been presented elsewhere (Atkinson & Juola, 1973; Juola, Fischler, Wood, & Atkinson, 1971; Atkinson, Herrmann, & Wescourt, 1974). These papers may be consulted for further intuitions about the model, as well as for applications to a variety of experimental tasks.

It is assumed that each node in the lexicon has associated with it a familiarity measure that can be regarded as a value on a continuous scale. The familiarity values for target items are assumed to have a mean that is higher than the mean for distractors, although the two distributions may overlap. In many recognition studies (e.g., Shepard & Teghtsoonian, 1961), the target set is not well learned and involves stimuli that have received only a single study presentation. Under these conditions the familiarity value of the test

---

[3] Familiarity as used here is not specific to particular events. It can be viewed as a reverberatory activity that dissipates over time. Whenever a node is accessed, it is set in motion. The amount of reverberation and its time course depend on the prior reverberation of the node and the reverberatory activity at neighboring nodes (Schvaneveldt & Meyer, 1973). When a node is accessed, the system can gauge the current reverberatory level of that node and use the measure as an item of information.

stimulus leads directly to the decision to make an A_1 or A_0 response; that is, the subject has a single criterion along the familiarity continuum that serves as a decision point for making a response. Familiarity values above the criterion lead to an A_1 response, whereas those below the criterion lead to an A_0 response (Banks, 1970; Kintsch, 1967, 1970a, 1970b; Parks, 1966; Shepard, 1967).

The studies that we consider differ from most recognition experiments in that the target stimuli are members of a well-memorized list. In this case, it is assumed that the subject can use the familiarity value to make an A_1 or A_0 response as soon as the appropriate lexical node is accessed, or can delay the response until a search of the E/K store has confirmed the presence or absence of the test item in the target set. These processes are shown in the flowchart of Figure 4. When a test stimulus is presented, the subject accesses the appropriate lexical node and obtains a familiarity value. This value is then used in the decision either to output an immediate A_1 or A_0 response (if the familiarity is very high or very low, respectively) or to execute a search of the E/K store before responding (if it is of an intermediate value).

A schematic representation of the decision process is shown in Figure 5. Here the distributions of familiarity values associated with a distractor item and a target item are plotted along the familiarity continuum (x). If the initial familiarity value is above a high criterion (c_1) or below a low criterion (c_0), the subject outputs a fast A_1 or A_0 response, respectively. If the familiarity value is between c_0 and c_1, the subject searches the E/K store before responding; this search guarantees that the subject will make a correct response, but it takes time in proportion to the length of the target list.

On the nth presentation of a given item in a test sequence, there is a density function reflecting the probability that the item will generate a particular familiarity value x; the density function will be denoted $\phi_{1,n}(x)$ for target items and $\phi_{0,n}(x)$ for distractor items. The two functions have mean values $\mu_{1,n}$ and $\mu_{0,n}$, respectively. Note that the subscript n refers to the number of times the item has been tested, and not to the trial number of the experiment. The effect of repeating specific target or distractor items in the test sequence is assumed to increase the mean familiarity value for these stimuli. This is illustrated in Figure 6 where $\mu_{1,n}$ and $\mu_{0,n}$ shown in the bottom panel ($n > 1$) have both been shifted to the right of their initial values $\mu_{1,1}$ and $\mu_{0,1}$ shown in the top panel. The effect of shifting up the mean familiarity values is to change the probability that the presentation of an item will result in a search of the E/K store.

We can now write equations for the probabilities that the subject will make a correct response to target and distractor items. As shown in Figure 5, it is assumed that the subject will make an error if the familiarity value of a target word is below c_0, or if the familiarity of a distractor is above c_1. In all

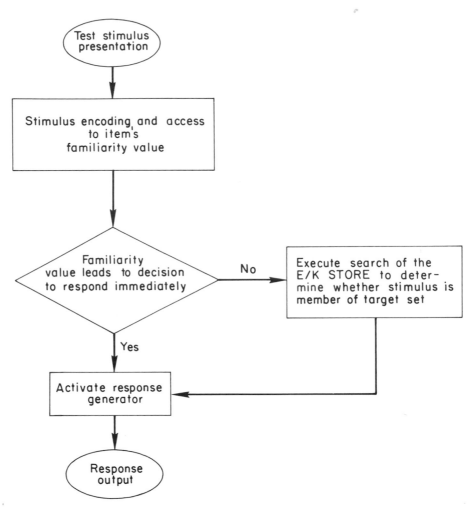

FIGURE 4.
Flowchart representing the memory and decision stages involved in recognition.

other cases, the subject will make a correct response. Thus the probability of a correct response to a target word presented for the nth time is the integral of $\phi_{1,n}(x)$ from c_0 to ∞:

$$P(A_1 \mid S_{1,n}) = \int_{c_0}^{\infty} \phi_{1,n}(x)\, dx = 1 - \Phi_{1,n}(c_0). \tag{1}$$

Similarly, the probability of a correct response to a distractor presented for the nth time is the integral of $\phi_{0,n}(x)$ from $-\infty$ to c_1:

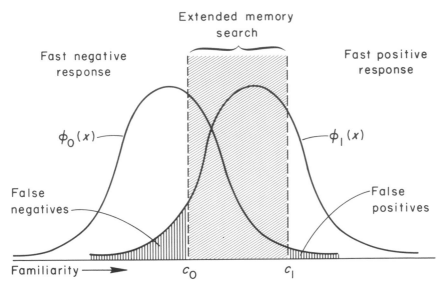

Extended memory search

Fast negative response

Fast positive response

$\phi_0(x)$

$\phi_1(x)$

False negatives

False positives

Familiarity

c_0

c_1

FIGURE 5.
Distributions of familiarity values for distractor items, $\phi_0(x)$, and target items, $\phi_1(x)$.

$$P(A_0 \mid S_{0,n}) = \int_{-\infty}^{c_1} \phi_{0,n}(x)\ dx = \Phi_{0,n}(c_1). \tag{2}$$

Note that $\Phi(\cdot)$ designates the distribution function associated with the density function $\phi(x)$.

In deriving response latencies, we assume that the processes involved in encoding the test stimulus, retrieving information about the stimulus from memory, making a decision about which response to choose, and emitting a response can be represented as successive and independent stages. These stages are diagrammed in the flowchart in Figure 7. When the test stimulus is presented, the first stages involve encoding the item, accessing the appropriate node in the lexical store, and retrieving a familiarity value x. The times required to execute these stages are combined and represented by the quantity ℓ in Figure 7. The next stage is to arrive at a recognition decision on the basis of x; the decision time depends on the value of x relative to c_0 and c_1, and is given by the function $v(x)$. If $x < c_0$, a negative decision is made; if $x > c_1$, a positive decision is made. If $c_0 \leq x \leq c_1$, a search of the E/K store is required. The time for this search is assumed to be a function of d, the size of the target set; namely, $\kappa + \theta_i(d)$. In this equation, κ denotes the time to extract an appropriate search code from the lexical node and initiate the scan of the target list; $\theta_i(d)$ is the time to execute the scan and depends upon d and upon whether the test item is a target ($i = 1$) or a distractor ($i = 0$).

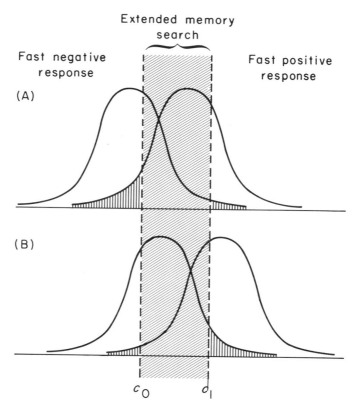

<small>FIGURE 6.</small>
Distributions of familiarity values for distractor items and target items that have not been tested (Panel A), and that have had at least one prior test (Panel B).

The final stage is to output a response once the decision has been made, the response time being r_0 for an A_0 response and r_1 for an A_1 response.[4] The quantities ℓ, $v(x)$, κ, $\theta_i(d)$, and r_i are expected values for the times necessary to execute each stage. If assumptions are made about the forms of the distributions associated with these expected values, then expressions for all moments of the latency data can be derived. Their derivation is complicated under some conditions of the model, but under others it simply involves a probabilistic mixture of two distributions; that is, the times resulting from

---

[4] The successive and independent stages of the process, as represented by the blocks in Figure 7, should be regarded as an approximation to the true state of affairs (Egeth, Marcus, & Bevan, 1972). Psychological and physiological considerations make it doubtful that the phenomena considered here are composed of truly independent stages, but stage models tend to be mathematically tractable, and thus are useful analytic tools.

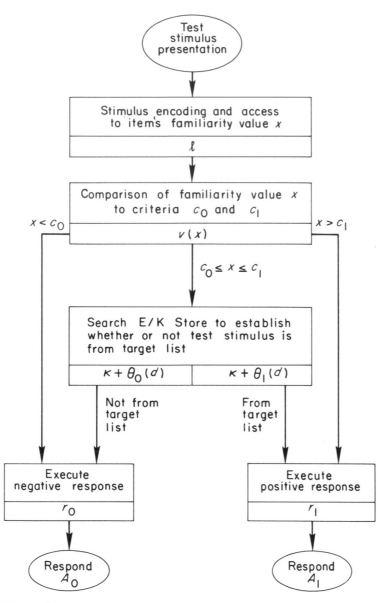

FIGURE 7.
Flowchart representing memory search and decision stages of recognition. The bottom entry in each box represents the time required to complete that stage.

fast responses based on the familiarity value alone and times resulting from slow responses based on the outcome of the extended memory search. In this chapter, however, we only make assumptions about the expected value for each stage, thereby restricting the analysis to mean response data.

We let $t(A_i \mid S_{j,n})$ denote the expected time for an A_i response to the nth presentation of a particular stimulus drawn from set S_j $(i, j = 0, 1)$. Expressions can be derived from these quantities by weighting the times associated with each stage by the probability that the stage occurs during processing. Thus, for example, the time to make an A_1 response to the nth presentation of a given target item (S_1) is simply the time required to execute a response based on the familiarity value alone plus the time to execute a response based on a search of the E/K store, each weighted by their respective probabilities. If x is the familiarity value, then the time for a fast A_1 response is $\ell + v(x) + r_1$; if, however, a search of the E/K store is made, then response time is $\ell + v(x) + \kappa + \theta_1(d) + r_1$. The weighting probabilities must take account of the fact that we are concerned with the time for an A_1 response, conditional on its being correct. The probability of a fast A_1 response, conditional on the fact that it is correct, is the integral of $\phi_{1,n}(x)$ from c_1 to ∞, divided by the probability of a correct A_1 response (the integral of $\phi_{1,n}(x)$ from c_0 to ∞). Similarly, the probability of a slow A_1 response, conditional on the fact that it is correct, is the integral $\phi_{1,n}(x)$ from c_0 to c_1, divided by the integral of $\phi_{1,n}(x)$ from c_0 to ∞. Thus the expected time for an A_1 response to the nth presentation of a particular target item is

$$\left[\int_{c_1}^{\infty} [\ell + v(x) + r_1]\phi_{1,n}(x)\, dx\right]\left[\int_{c_0}^{\infty} \phi_{1,n}(x)\, dx\right]^{-1}$$
$$+ \left[\int_{c_0}^{c_1} [\ell + v(x) + \kappa + \theta_1(d) + r_1]\phi_{1,n}(x)\, dx\right]\left[\int_{c_0}^{\infty} \phi_{1,n}(x)\, dx\right]^{-1}.$$

Note that ℓ and r_1 may be removed from under the integral. Doing this and rearranging terms yields

$$t(A_1 \mid S_{1,n}) = \ell + r_1 + \left[\int_{c_1}^{\infty} v(x)\phi_{1,n}(x)\, dx\right.$$
$$\left. + \int_{c_0}^{c_1} [\kappa + \theta_1(d) + v(x)]\phi_{1,n}(x)\, dx\right]\left[1 - \Phi_{1,n}(c_0)\right]^{-1} \cdot (3)$$

where again $\Phi(\cdot)$ denotes the distribution function associated with the density function $\phi(x)$. Similarly,

$$t(A_0 \mid S_{0,n}) = \ell + r_0 + \left[\int_{-\infty}^{c_0} v(x)\phi_{0,n}(x)\, dx\right.$$
$$\left. + \int_{c_0}^{c_1} [\kappa + \theta_0(d) + v(x)]\phi_{0,n}(x)\, dx\right]\left[\Phi_{0,n}(c_1)\right]^{-1}; (4)$$
$$t(A_0 \mid S_{1,n}) = \ell + r_0 + \left[\int_{-\infty}^{c_0} v(x)\phi_{1,n}(x)\, dx\right]\left[\Phi_{1,n}(c_0)\right]^{-1}; \quad (5)$$

$$t(A_1 \mid S_{0,n}) = \ell + r_1 + \left[\int_{c_1}^{\infty} v(x)\phi_{0,n}(x)\, dx \right]\left[1 - \Phi_{0,n}(c_1) \right]^{-1}. \tag{6}$$

Equations 3 and 4 are the expected times for correct responses, and Equations 5 and 6 are expected times for incorrect responses, to target and distractor items, respectively.

In fitting the model to data, we assume that $\phi_{i,n}(x)$ is normally distributed with unit variance for all values of i and n. Thus, the presentation of an item causes the distribution to be shifted up without changing its form or variance.[5] No assumptions are made about how $\mu_{i,n}$ changes with n. Several assumptions seem reasonable on an a priori basis; rather than select among them, we bypass the issue by estimating $\mu_{i,n}$ from the data for each value of n. This approach is practical because the range on n is small for the experiments considered here.

It should be remarked that the criteria c_0 and c_1 are set by the subject. In the initial stages of an experiment, they would vary as the subject adjusted to the task, but it is assumed that in time they would stabilize at fixed values. Again, no theory is given of how c_0 and c_1 vary over initial trials, and thus data for the early stages of an experiment are not treated.

Yet another simplifying assumption should be mentioned at this point. Equations 1 and 2 indicate that errors are determined by the values of $\mu_{i,n}$, c_0, and c_1. In the experiments examined in this chapter, there is no evidence to suggest that error rates vary as a function of d, the size of the target list. Thus, in treating data we assume that $\mu_{i,n}$, c_0, and c_1 are independent of d. Experimental procedures can be devised where this assumption would be violated (see Atkinson & Juola, 1973), but for the studies discussed here it is warranted.

What remains to be specified are the functions $v(x)$ and $\theta_i(d)$. It is assumed that $v(x)$ takes the following form:[6]

$$v(x) = \begin{cases} \rho e^{-(x-c_1)\beta}, & \text{for } x > c_1, \\ \rho, & \text{for } c_0 \le x \le c_1, \\ \rho e^{-(c_0-x)\beta}, & \text{for } x < c_0. \end{cases} \tag{7}$$

Figure 8 presents a graph of the equation. If the familiarity value x is far above the upper criterion or far below the lower criterion, the decision time approaches zero; for values close to the criteria, the decision time approaches ρ. A special case of interest is when $\beta = 0$; namely,

$$v(x) = \rho. \tag{8}$$

---

[5] The assumption that only the mean and not the form of the distribution changes is made primarily to simplify the mathematics. Other assumptions, such as those considered by Suppes (1960) for a different problem, seem equally plausible and should be investigated in formulating a more general model of familiarity change.

[6] The $v(x)$ function proposed here is similar to one investigated by Thomas (1971) for a signal-detection task.

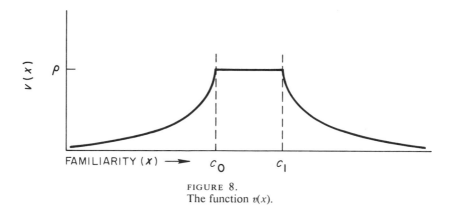

FIGURE 8.
The function $v(x)$.

In this case, the time to evaluate the familiarity value is constant regardless of its relation to c_1 and c_0.

The quantity $\theta_i(d)$ represents the time to search the E/K store, and is assumed to be a linear function of target-set size. For the most general case we assume that search times on positive and negative trials vary independently; that is,

$$\theta_1(d) = \alpha d, \tag{9a}$$

$$\theta_0(d) = \alpha' d. \tag{9b}$$

As a special case of Equation 9, it is possible that the search times are identical for target and distractor items:

$$\theta_1(d) = \theta_0(d) = \alpha d. \tag{10}$$

Alternatively, it might be that the length of the memory search is shorter on positive trials than on negative trials. This situation would occur if the target items are stored as a list structure, and portions of the list are retrieved and scanned as the subject seeks a match for the test stimulus. When a match is obtained, the search ends; otherwise all the memory locations are checked. The time for this process is

$$\theta_1(d) = \alpha[(d + 1)/2], \tag{11a}$$

$$\theta_0(d) = \alpha d. \tag{11b}$$

The memory-search processes described by Equations 10 and 11 correspond to the exhaustive and self-terminating cases of the serial scanning model proposed by Sternberg (1966, 1969b). While Sternberg's models have proved to be extremely valuable in interpreting data from a variety of memory-search experiments, good fits between the models and data do not require that the underlying psychological process be serial in nature. There are alternative models, including parallel scanning models, that are mathe-matically equivalent to those proposed by Sternberg and yield the same predictions as Equations 10 and 11 (Atkinson, Holmgren, & Juola, 1969; Murdock, 1971; Townsend, 1971; Shevell & Atkinson, 1974). Thus, the use of the above equations to specify the time to search the E/K store does not commit us to either a serial or parallel interpretation.

EFFECTS OF TARGET-LIST LENGTH
AND TEST REPETITIONS

The first experiment we consider was designed primarily to replicate two earlier experiments, as well as to provide a large data base with which to test the model. Juola et al. (1971) demonstrated that recognition time is a straight-line function of the number of items in a large (10 to 26 items) target set: as the number of items in the target set increased, response latency increased linearly for both positive and negative trials. A second experiment (Fischler & Juola, 1971) showed that response latency depends on whether or not the test stimulus has been presented previously. The response latency for a repeated target item was more than 100 msec less than the latency for a target on its first presentation. For a distractor, repetitions increased latency, with reponse time being about 50 msec greater for a repeated distractor than for one receiving its first presentation.

Our study also included repeated tests of target and distractor items, and three target-list lengths were used. Groups of 24 subjects each were given lists of either 16, 24, or 32 words. Each list was constructed by randomly selecting d words from a pool of 48 common, one-syllable nouns. The words remaining in the pool after each list had been selected were used as the distractor set (S_0) to accompany that target set (S_1). Each subject was given a list about 24 hours before the experimental session, and instructed to memo-rize it in serial order.

At the start of the test session, each subject successfully completed a written serial recall of the target list. The subject was then seated in front of a tachistoscope, in which the test words were presented one at a time. To each presentation the subject made either an A_1 or A_0 response by depressing one of two telegraph keys with his right forefinger. The experimental procedure was identical to that of Fischler and Juola (1971).

The test sequence consisted of 80 consecutive trials that were divided into four blocks. For Block I, four target words and four distractors were ran-domly selected from S_1 and S_0, respectively. For Block II, the eight Block I words were repeated, and four new targets and four new distractors were also shown. Block III included all the words presented in Block II with eight new words added (four targets and four distractors). Finally, Block IV included all the words of Block III and eight new words (the remaining unused target and distractor items). Order of presentation within blocks was randomized.

With this method of presentation, 16 target words and 16 distractors were presented to each subject. The test words thus included all of S_1 for subjects with lists of 16 words. For the other groups, the 16 target words tested were either the first or last 16 words in the 24-word lists, or they were the first, middle, or last 16 in the 32-word lists. It should be pointed out that the specific part of the target list that was tested during the experimental session had no effect on response times or error rates. Thus, no further distinction on which part of the target list was tested is made between groups of subjects. The lack of any effects due to the list part that was tested is not surprising when it is noted that in several previous experiments (Atkinson & Juola, 1973; Fischler & Juola, 1971; Juola et al., 1971) no effects were observed due to the serial position of the target word, that is, positive response latencies plotted against the target words' serial position yielded a flat function. The overall effect of list length on latency is also uninfluenced by the testing scheme used; the magnitude of the list-length effect observed in this study is the same as in studies where all items of each list are tested (Juola et al., 1971). The procedure used here has the nice feature that the test sequence is the same for all groups, the only difference among groups being the length of the list memorized prior to the test session. The subjects who memorized the longer lists were not told that only part of the list would be used, and in the debriefing session at the end of the experiment no one commented on the fact that some items were not tested.

The mean latencies for correct responses are presented in Figure 9; the data are from the last two trial blocks only (Blocks III and IV). The effects shown in Figure 9 were also obtained in Trial Blocks I and II; however, response times were somewhat greater on these trials, presumably due to practice effects. The data from Blocks III and IV were very similar and will be regarded as representing asymptotic performance. In another paper (Atkinson & Juola, 1973), we used the model to make predictions about all the data, including practice effects, for a similar experiment, but here we are concerned only with the data presented in Figure 9. As shown in Figure 9, means were obtained separately for A_1 and A_0 responses to test words that were presented for the first, second, third, and fourth times ($n = 1, 2, 3,$ or 4). Because, within blocks, the presentation number was randomly ordered, the effects shown in Figure 9 are attributable only to the prior number of times the test word had been presented. In general, the results closely replicate the findings of earlier studies. By comparing the mean latencies as the presentation number increases from one to four in Figure 9, it can be seen that the targets and distractors yield opposite effects. Repetitions decrease response latencies for targets, and increase latencies for distractors. The line

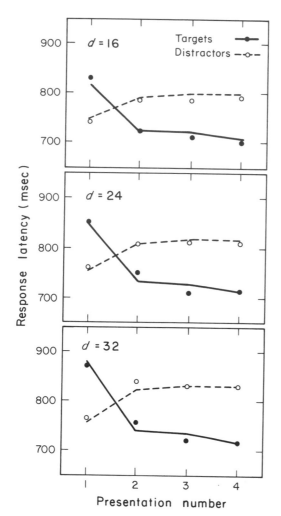

FIGURE 9.
Correct response latencies as functions of presentation number for target and distractors for three list-length (*d*) conditions: the top panel presents data for *d* = 16, the middle panel for *d* = 24, and the bottom panel for *d* = 32. The broken lines fitted to the data represent theoretical predictions.

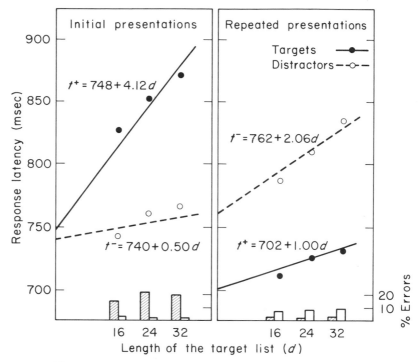

FIGURE 10.
Correct response latencies and error percentages as functions of target-list length; the data represent a weighted average of response latencies from Trial Blocks III and IV. The left panel presents data for initial presentations of target and distractor words, and the right panel presents the data for repeated presentations. Incorrect responses to target words are indicated by the shaded bars, and errors to distractors by the open bars. The straight lines fitted to the data represent theoretical predictions.

segments fitted to the data were generated from the model and are discussed later.

The data from Figure 9 are replotted in Figure 10 so that mean response latencies are presented as functions of target-list length. The left panel includes the data for items receiving their first presentations ($n = 1$), whereas the right panel presents the average data for repeated presentations ($n = 2, 3,$ and 4) weighted by the number of observations for each value of n. Again the effects of repetitions are evident; repetitions decrease latency on positive trials by more than 100 msec, whereas repetitions increase negative latencies by about 50 msec, on the average. Similarly, repeated tests decreased errors to target words (shaded bars along the lower axis), and repetitions increased errors to distractors (open bars). The linear functions fitted to the data in Figure 10 are discussed later.

The number of target words affected response latency, with mean latency being an approximately linear function of target size. By way of contrast, note that error rates do not increase with the number of target words, but are relatively constant across the three list lengths. Further, an examination of error latencies showed that there was no effect of list length on the speed of an incorrect response.

Perhaps most interesting, however, is the interaction between target-set size and the effects of repetitions. For target words, repetitions decrease the size of the list-length effect; that is, the slope of the function relating mean response latency to target-list length is less for repeated targets than for initially presented targets. The opposite is true for distractors; repeating distractors increases the slope of the latency function.

A discussion of these results is postponed until the end of the next section. We first demonstrate how parameters can be estimated and the model fitted to data.

THEORETICAL ANALYSIS OF THE LIST-LENGTH EXPERIMENT

There are several approaches that can be taken to estimate parameters. The method used here is not the most efficient, but it has the merit of being quite simple. It involves using the error probabilities to estimate the $\mu_{i,n}$s. The estimates of the $\mu_{i,n}$s are then substituted into the latency equations and treated as fixed values. The remaining parameters are estimated by selecting them so that the differences between observed and predicted latencies are minimized.[7]

Table 1 presents observed error probabilities for target and distractor items. These probabilities were obtained by averaging over the three list-length conditions, because there were no significant differences in error rates across

TABLE 1
Observed error probabilities
for targets and distractors

	$P(A_0 \mid S_{1,n})$	$P(A_1 \mid S_{0,n})$
$n = 1$	0.171	0.005
$n = 2$	0.016	0.039
$n = 3$	0.014	0.049
$n = 4$	0.007	0.049

[7] There are methods that permit simultaneous estimates of all parameters, but practical limitations make them unfeasible except in special cases (see Atkinson & Juola, 1973).

groups. We use these data and Equations 1 and 2 to estimate the $\mu_{i,n}$s. For example, $P(A_0 \mid S_{1,1}) = \Phi_{1,1}(c_0)$ from Equation 1, and the observed value for this probability is 0.171 from Table 1. Consulting a normal probability table, $\mu_{1,1} = c_0 + 0.95$ in order for the error rate to be 0.171. Similarly $\mu_{1,2} = c_0 + 2.14$, $\mu_{1,3} = c_0 + 2.20$, and $\mu_{1,4} = c_0 + 2.46$, using the remaining error data in the first column of Table 1. Proceeding in the same way, using Equation 2 and the error data in the second column of the table, we obtain $\mu_{0,1} = c_1 - 2.58$, $\mu_{0,2} = c_1 - 1.76$, $\mu_{0,3} = c_1 - 1.66$, and $\mu_{0,4} = c_1 - 1.66$. Thus the observed error probabilities fix the estimates of $\mu_{1,n}$ in terms of c_0, whereas $\mu_{0,n}$ is in terms of c_1. It can be shown that the theoretical predictions for error probabilities and latencies do not depend on the absolute values of c_0 and c_1, but only on their difference. Thus, one or the other can be set at an arbitrary value. For simplicity, we let $c_0 = 0$; note that no matter what value is selected for c_1, the error data will be fit perfectly. By setting c_0 equal to zero and by assuming unit variance for the ϕ-distributions, we have in essence defined the zero point and measurement unit for the familiarity scale.

With $c_0 = 0$ and the $\mu_{i,n}$s restricted by the error data, the remaining parameters can be estimated from the latency data. Six special cases of the general model are used to fit the latency data. As indicated in Table 2, the cases differ

TABLE 2
Six models defined in terms of the functions $v(x)$ and $\theta_i(d)$

$v(x)$ $\diagdown$ $\theta_i(d)$	Equation 9	Equation 10	Equation 11
Equation 8	Model I c_1 $(\ell + \rho + r_1)$ r κ α α'	Model II c_1 $(\ell + \rho + r_1)$ r κ α	Model III c_1 $(\ell + \rho + r_1)$ r κ α
Equation 7	Model IV c_1 $(\ell + r_1)$ r κ ρ β α α'	Model V c_1 $(\ell + r_1)$ r κ ρ β α	Model VI c_1 $(\ell + r_1)$ r κ ρ β α

Note: $r = r_0 - r_1$.

in how the functions $v(x)$ and $\theta_i(d)$ are defined. Equations 7 and 8 define two versions of $v(x)$, and Equations 9, 10, and 11 define three versions of $\theta_i(d)$. Listed in Table 2 are the parameters that must be estimated for each case; the parameter r is simply the difference between r_0 and r_1. The parameters grouped in parentheses cannot be individually identified—that is, the predictions of the model depend only on the sum of these parameters, which means that they cannot be estimated separately.[8] Note that the pair of models in each column of Table 2 are equivalent if $\beta = 0$; thus the lower model in a column must predict the data better than the one above it unless β is estimated to be zero. Similarly, Model I reduces to Model II and Model IV to V if $\alpha = \alpha'$; Model I must be better than II and Model IV better than V unless the estimates of α and α' are identical.

Our method of parameter estimation involves the 24 data points in Figure 9. Parameter estimates are selected that minimize the sum of the squared deviations (weighted by the number of observations) between the data points and theoretical predictions. Specifically, we define the root mean square deviation (RMSD) between observed and predicted values as follows:

$$\text{RMSD} = \left[(1/N) \sum_{i=1}^{24} n_i(t_{p,i} - t_{o,i})^2\right]^{1/2}, \tag{12}$$

where N = the total number of observations; i = an index over the 24 data points shown in Figure 9; n_i = the number of observations determining data point i; $t_{p,i}$ = predicted response latency for data point i; and $t_{o,i}$ = observed response latency for data point i.

For each of the six models, the function defined in Equation 12 is to be minimized with respect to the parameter set given in Table 2. We have not attempted to carry out the minimization analytically, for it appears to be an impossible task; rather a computer was programmed to conduct a systematic search of the parameter space for each model until a minimum was obtained.[9] The minimum RMSDs obtained are shown in Table 3, along with the number of parameters estimated in the computer search for each model. Models III and VI clearly yield the poorest fit and can be eliminated from contention. The fact that Models I and II are about equally good—as are Models IV and V—indicates that separate estimates of α and α' do not substantially improve the goodness of fit. The conclusion to be drawn from this observation is that the time to search the E/K store is approximately the same for both targets and distractors. Note also that Models I and IV are about equally good, as are Models II and V, suggesting that the more complicated $v(x)$ functions

---

[8] Proof of this remark is straightforward and is not given here. Note that for Models I, II, and III the parameter ρ is not identifiable but is lumped in the quantity $(\ell + \rho + r_1)$, whereas for Models IV, V, and VI ρ is identifiable and only $(\ell + r_1)$ is lumped.

[9] For a discussion of such search procedures, see Wilde (1964).

TABLE 3
Minimum RMSDs obtained in computer search

Model	Minimum RMSD	Number of parameters estimated
I	9.93	6
II	9.94	5
III	10.89	5
IV	9.86	8
V	9.92	7
VI	10.34	7

yield little improvement over the constant function. Add to these observations the fact that Model II with only five parameters produces virtually as good a fit as does Model IV with eight parameters.

In view of the preceding considerations, Model II is our preferred choice among the six models. Table 4 presents the parameter estimates for Model II;

TABLE 4
Parameter estimates
for Model II

Parameter	Estimate
c_1	1.02
$(\ell + \rho + r_1)$	687 msec
r	44 msec
κ	137 msec
α	9.9 msec

Note: $r = r_0 - r_1$.

the predicted response times from this model are shown in Figure 9 as connected lines. The straight lines shown in Figure 10 are the predicted functions based on Model II for initial presentations (left panel) and repeated presentations (right panel). The fits displayed in Figure 10 could be improved upon somewhat, but it should be kept in mind that they were obtained by using parameter estimates based on a different breakdown of the data (i.e., that shown in Fig. 9).[10]

---

[10] Similarity factors not represented in the model could contribute to the list-length effects displayed in Figures 9 and 10. As the target set increases in size, the probability that any given distractor will be similar to a target item also increases. Visual (or graphemic) similarity could affect the speed with which the appropriate lexical node is accessed, leading to

The latency of an error response should be fast according to the theory, because errors can occur only if the subject responds before the extended memory search is made. The data support this prediction, and they accord well with the values predicted by Model II. Specifically, the latency of an error is close to the predicted value of $\ell + \rho + r_0 = 731$ msec for an S_1 item, and close to $\ell + \rho + r_1 = 687$ msec for an S_0 item. Furthermore, as predicted by the model, the observed error latencies do not appear to be influenced by the length of the target list.

A verbal interpretation of the results in terms of Model II reads as follows. When a target item is presented for the first time, the probability that a search of the E/K store will occur before a response is made exceeds the probability that a fast positive response will be emitted on the basis of the item's familiarity value alone. The opposite is true for initial presentations of distractors: most trials result in fast negative responses. Thus, the mean latency is longer for initial presentations of targets than for initial presentations of distractors, and the list-length effect is greater for targets than for distractors (because list-length effects depend only upon the search of the E/K store). The effect of repeated tests of words is to increase the familiarities of both targets and distractors. This results in an increased latency for responses to distractors, and a decrease in latency to targets; the magnitudes of the list-length effects are observed to change concomitantly.[11]

APPLICATION OF THE MODEL
TO RELATED EXPERIMENTS

Other experiments have been conducted to test various features of the theory. One such study involved target sets in which any specific word was included

---

confusions of identification. Direct evidence of this possibility is reported by Juola et al. (1971), who showed, among other things, that distractor words graphically *very* similar to target items were responded to more slowly. In this experiment, no estimate can be made of the contribution of similarity to the overall set-size effect. However, results from several long-term recognition studies indicate that both semantic and graphemic similarity cause increased error rates as well as increased response latencies (Atkinson & Juola, 1973; Juola et al., 1971). Because there were no differences in error rates among the three groups, it is unlikely that a significant proportion of the list-length effects is attributable to similarity factors.

[11] Variables other than those represented in the model influence familiarity. Of particular importance is the effect of the number of intervening trials between successive tests on a given item. Lag effects in response latency have been observed, with the magnitude of the effect decreasing with lag for both target and distractor items (Fischler & Juola, 1971; Juola et al., 1971). This phenomenon would be accounted for in the theory by assuming that the familiarity of an item increases immediately after presentation and then gradually declines over trials. To develop this idea mathematically would complicate the model. By design, lags were relatively constant for the data treated here and need not be represented explicitly in the model.

once, twice, or three times in the list memorized prior to the experimental session. If the number of occurrences of a word in the target list affects its familiarity value, then both error rate and latency should be less for multiply represented items than for items appearing only once in the list. If, however, the word's familiarity is unaffected by repetitions in the study list, then the error rate should be the same for all target items; further, any latency effects would have to be due to a faster search of the E/K store for an item multiply represented in the target list compared with one appearing only once. The results showed that error rate and response latency were less for items that occurred two or three times in the list than for items included only once. Model II was used to generate fits to the data, assuming that the expected familiarity value of a target word is an increasing function of the number of times it was included in the target list; the search of the E/K store was postulated to take the same time for all items. The model provided an excellent fit to the data (Atkinson & Juola, 1973).

Other experiments have demonstrated the importance of semantic properties of words in determining the familiarity value of an item. Juola et al. (1971) reported that if synonyms of target words were used as distractors both response latencies and error rates increased over the values obtained for semantically unrelated distractors. Another experiment (Atkinson & Juola, 1973) provided target sets arranged into a tree structure to reflect the semantic hierarchy from which the words were taken. During the test session target words were selected either from a 'dense' portion of the hierarchy (one of four nodes on a branch with up to four exemplar words under each node) or from a 'sparse' portion (one of two nodes with only two exemplar words under each node). The data showed that mean latencies for positive responses were less for targets from dense portions of the tree than for targets from the sparsely represented regions. The results from these two experiments indicate that the expected familiarity value of a word can be increased by testing semantically related words.

An experiment by Juola (1973) was designed to test the importance of stimulus-encoding factors in determining an item's familiarity value. The subjects memorized a list of 48 common nouns and then were tested with either words or simple outline drawings of the objects named by the words. Both words and pictures were presented as targets and distractors, and all items were tested twice. Of interest was the nature of the repetition effects when the second test of an item was either identical in form (e.g., 'CAT' followed by 'CAT') or different (e.g., 'CAT' followed by a picture of a cat). Repetition of the same pictorial form resulted in a faster encoding time; repetition (whether in the same or a different form) also increased the familiarity value of the items. The relative importance of these two effects was estimated by comparing mean latencies for repeated targets and distractors for the case in which the exact form of the stimulus was preserved on both tests with the case in which different forms of the item were presented on successive tests. The results showed that subjects were faster on trials in which repeated items were presented in the same form (word or picture) as they had been shown on the first presentation. This was true for distractors as well as for target items. However, there were no significant differences in the error rates for items that were tested with the same or different stimulus forms on successive presentations. These results indicate that the familiarity value of an item is relatively independent of the form of the stimulus at the time of test. However, the form of the stimulus does have an effect on encoding time.

RECOGNITION MEMORY FOR ITEMS IN SHORT-TERM STORE

The theory presented in the previous sections was originally formulated to deal with recognition experiments involving large target sets stored in LTS. It is possible, however, to extend the model to the case in which the target set consists of a small number of items in STS. The results from experiments using small memory sets have generally shown that response latencies are linear, increasing functions of the number of target items, with roughly equal slopes for positive and negative responses. A model used to account for these findings is the serial scanning process proposed by Sternberg (1966, 1969a, 1969b). According to Sternberg's model, the subject encodes the test stimulus into a form that is comparable to the internal representations of the target items stored in STS. The encoded test item is scanned in serial fashion against each of the memory items, and then a decision is made about whether or not a match was obtained. The model predicts that latency will be a linear function of memory-set size, with both positive and negative responses having the same slope but possibly different intercepts.

Whereas the Sternberg model has proved adequate in explaining the results from many short-term recognition experiments, there are reports in the literature of systematic discrepancies between data and the model's predictions. It is not possible to review these results here (see Nickerson, 1970), but variations from the model have involved departures from linearity in the functions relating response latencies to target-set size, differences in slopes between the functions obtained for positive and negative responses (including cases in which the slope for positive responses is significantly greater than that for negatives), serial position effects in the latencies of positive responses, and trial-to-trial dependencies. These findings have led some authors (Baddeley & Ecob, 1970; Corballis, Kirby, & Miller, 1972) to propose alternative models for short-term recognition memory, suggesting that response decisions might be based solely on the test item's memory strength. Strength models usually assume that there is a single criterion along the strength continuum; values above this criterion lead to positive responses. In addition, the decision time is assumed to be greater for values near the criterion, and both the criterion itself and the mean strength value of the target items are assumed to decrease as the number of targets increases.

It is our view that the test item's familiarity value (which in some sense is comparable to a strength notion) may play the same role in the short-term case as it does in long-term recognition studies. List-length effects are still to be explained in terms of a scan of the target set, but on occasion this search may be bypassed if the test item's familiarity is very high or very low; as in the long-term case, the probability of bypassing the target-set search will depend upon the reliability of the familiarity measure in generating correct responses.

The probability of bypassing the target-set search should be minimal in experiments using a small pool of items from which targets and distractors are to be drawn on each trial, as in the Sternberg (1966) study, which involved only the digits 0 to 9. The reason is that, during an experimental session, all items in the stimulus pool receive repeated presentations, and the resulting high familiarity values become less and less useful in distinguishing targets from distractors; thus a search of the target set will be made on most trials, resulting in large list-length effects. Support for this view comes from a study by Rothstein and Morin (1972), who reported much larger slopes for the response-time function in a short-term scanning task when the stimuli were selected from a small pool (10 words) than when selected, without replacement, from a very large pool of words. For the small item pool, we assume that repeated presentation increases the familiarity of all items to a uniformly high level, thereby reducing its usefulness as a basis for responding. Thus, the probability of executing a target-set search should be maximal, causing the slope of the response-time functions to take on its maximum value.

Figure 11 presents a flow diagram of the processes involved in recognition memory for items stored in STS. As in the case for target sets stored in the E/K store (Fig. 3), the test item is first encoded and the appropriate node in the lexical store is accessed, leading to the retrieval of a familiarity value for the item. If the familiarity value is very high or very low, the subject outputs a fast response that is independent of memory-set size. For intermediate familiarity values, the subject retrieves an internal code for use in scanning STS. Thus far, the processes proposed for short-term recognition are identical with those of the long-term case. However, the internal code used to search STS may not be the same as that used in the long-term memory search. For example, Klatzky, Juola, and Atkinson (1971) provided evidence that alternative codes for the same test item can be generated and compared with either verbal or spatial representations of target-set items. After retrieval of the appropriate internal code, a search of the target list stored in STS is

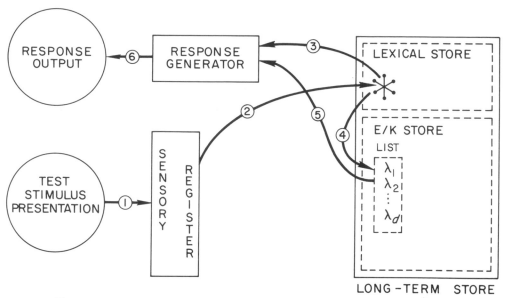

FIGURE 11.
A schematic representation of the search and decision processes in a short-term recognition memory study. A test stimulus is presented (1) and then matched to a node in the lexical store (2). The familiarity value associated with the node may lead to an immediate decision (3) and response output (6). Otherwise, a search code is extracted and scanned against the target list in STS (4), which leads to a decision (5) and subsequent response. Path (1), (2), (3), (6) results in a faster response than Path (1), (2), (4), (5), (6), and the response is independent of the size of the ST set.

executed, and a response based on the outcome of this scan is then made.

An unpublished study conducted by Charles Darley and Phipps Arabie at Stanford University was designed to assess the effects of item familiarity in a short-term memory task. The familiarity values of distractor items were manipulated to determine if this variable would affect the slopes and intercepts of the function relating latency to target-set size. On each of a long series of trials, a target set of from two to five words was presented auditorally, followed by the visual presentation of a single test word. The words used in the target sets were different on every trial of the experiment; that is, a word once used in a target set was never used in any other target set. On half the trials a word from the current target set was presented for test; these trials will be designated P trials to indicate that a 'positive response' is correct. On the other half of the trials, a distractor (a word not in the current target set) was presented for test; these trials will be called N trials because a 'negative response' is correct. The distractor words were of three types: new words never presented before in the experiment (denoted N_1, because the word was presented for the first time); words that had been presented for the first time

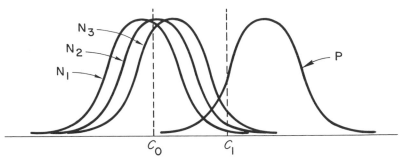

FIGURE 12.
Distributions of familiarity values for the three types of distractor items (N_1, N_2, N_3) and for target items (P).

in the experiment as distractors on the immediately preceding trial (denoted N_2, because the word was now being presented for the second time); and words that had been presented for the first time both as a member of the memory set and as a positive test stimulus on the immediately preceding trial (denoted N_3, because the word was now being presented for the third time). Thus there were four types of test items (N_1, N_2, N_3, P), and we assume that different degrees of familiarity are associated with each.

Figure 12 presents a schematic representation of the four familiarity distributions. The density functions associated with the test word on an N_1, N_2, N_3, or P trial are denoted $\phi(x; N_1)$, $\phi(x; N_2)$, $\phi(x; N_3)$, or $\phi(x; P)$, respectively; as in the previous application, these functions are assumed to be normally distributed with unit variance. Their expected values are denoted μ_{N_1}, μ_{N_2}, μ_{N_3}, and μ_P. The quantity μ_P should be largest because the test word on a P trial is a member of the current trial target set and should be very familiar; μ_{N_1} should be smallest because N_1 words are completely new; and μ_{N_2} and μ_{N_3} should be intermediate because N_2 and N_3 words appeared on the prior trial. The probabilities of errors for the four trial types are determined by the areas of the familiarity distributions above c_1 for distractors, and below c_0 for targets; that is,

$$P(\text{Error} \mid N_i) = \int_{c_1}^{\infty} \phi(x; N_i)\, dx, \quad \text{for } i = 1, 2, 3; \tag{13}$$

$$P(\text{Error} \mid P) = \int_{-\infty}^{c_0} \phi(x; P)\, dx. \tag{14}$$

Let us now derive expressions for reaction times in this situation. For simplicity, only Model II of the preceding section is considered. To obtain equations for response latencies, it is necessary to sum the time for the encoding and familiarity-retrieval process (time ℓ), the time for a fast response decision based on the familiarity value alone (time ρ) weighted by its probability, the time for a search of the memory list in STS (time $\kappa + \alpha m$, with m defined as the size of the short-term target set) also weighted by its probability, and the time for response output (r_0 and r_1 for negative and positive responses, respectively). Thus, the expected time for a correct response is

$$t(N_i) = \ell + r_0$$
$$+ \left[\int_{-\infty}^{c_0} \rho\phi(x; N_i)\, dx + \int_{c_0}^{c_1} (\rho + \kappa + \alpha m)\phi(x; N_i)\, dx \right] \left[\int_{-\infty}^{c_1} \phi(x; N_i)\, dx \right]^{-1}$$

$$(15)$$

for $i = 1, 2, 3$; and

$$t(P) = \ell + r_1$$
$$+ \left[\int_{c_1}^{\infty} \rho\phi(x; P)\, dx + \int_{c_0}^{c_1} (\rho + \kappa + \alpha m)\phi(x; P)\, dx \right] \left[\int_{c_0}^{\infty} \phi(x; P)\, dx \right]^{-1}.$$

$$(16)$$

The expression $t(N_i)$ gives the time to respond correctly to an N_i item, whereas $t(P)$ gives the time for a correct response to a P item. The preceding expressions can be written more simply if we define

$$s_i' = \left[\int_{c_0}^{c_1} \phi(x; N_i)\, dx \right] \left[\int_{-\infty}^{c_1} \phi(x; N_i)\, dx \right]^{-1}, \quad \text{for } i = 1, 2, 3; \quad (17)$$

$$s = \left[\int_{c_0}^{c_1} \phi(x; P)\, dx \right] \left[\int_{c_0}^{\infty} \phi(x; P)\, dx \right]^{-1}. \quad (18)$$

Then

$$t(N_i) = [\ell + \rho + r_0] + s_i'[\kappa + \alpha m], \quad \text{for } i = 1, 2, 3; \quad (19)$$
$$t(P) = [\ell + \rho + r_1] + s[\kappa + \alpha m]. \quad (20)$$

The quantities s_i' and s are determined by the familiarity distributions and c_1 and c_0 and are not influenced by m. Thus $t(N_i)$ and $t(P)$ plotted as functions of m yield straight lines with slopes $\alpha s_i'$ and αs, respectively.

The latency data from the experiment are presented in Figure 13. Note that latency increases with memory-set size and is ordered such that P is fastest, and N_1, N_2, and N_3 are progressively slower. To fit the model to these data, we proceed in the same way as we did for the long-term experiment. The observed probabilities of an error on N_1, N_2, and N_3 trials were 0.008, 0.018, and 0.058, respectively. Using these error probabilities and Equation 13 yields the following relations: $\mu_{N_1} = c_1 - 2.41$; $\mu_{N_2} = c_1 - 2.10$; $\mu_{N_3} = c_1 - 1.56$. The probability of an error on a P trial was 0.028; using Equation 13 yields $\mu_P = c_0 + 1.91$. Setting c_0 equal to zero leaves the following five parameters to be estimated from the latency data: c_1, $(\ell + \rho + r_1)$, r, κ, α, where r is again defined as $r_0 - r_1$. An RMSD function equivalent to the one

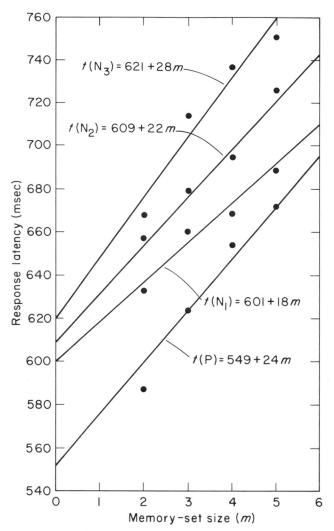

FIGURE 13.
Correct response latencies as a function of the size of the memory set. The straight lines fitted to the data represent theoretical predictions.

presented in Equation 12 was specified for the 16 data points in Figure 13, and a computer was programmed to search the parameter space for a minimum.

Table 5 presents the parameter estimates, and the theoretical predictions are graphed as straight lines in Figure 13. In carrying out these fits, 9 parameters were estimated from the data; however, there are 4 error probabilities and 16 latency measures to account for. Thus 9 of 20 degrees of freedom

TABLE 5
Parameter estimates for the
short-term memory study

Parameter	Estimate
c_1	2.52
$(\ell + \rho + r_1)$	499 msec
r	64 msec
κ	70 msec
α	33.9 msec

Note: $r = r_0 - r_1$.

were used in the estimation process, leaving 11 against which to evaluate the goodness of fit.

The results in Figure 13 indicate that the familiarity value of the distractor item has a large effect, with the slopes and intercepts of the negative functions increasing with their expected familiarity values. These effects are captured by the model, which generally does a satisfactory job of fitting the data. The predicted slope of the $t(P)$ function is 24 msec, whereas the predicted slopes for $t(N_1)$, $t(N_2)$, and $t(N_3)$ go from 18 msec to 22 msec to 28 msec, respectively. If the subject ignored the familiarity measure and made a search of the memory list on every trial, then all four functions would have a slope equal to α, which was estimated to be 33.9 msec.[12]

The results shown in Figure 13 support the proposition that familiarity effects play a role in short-term memory scanning experiments. Further, these effects can be accounted for with the same model that was developed for long-term recognition studies. However, examination of the parameter estimates for the short- and long-term cases indicates that the time constants for the two processes are not the same (see Tables 4 and 5). For example, the time to initiate the extended search, κ, is 70 msec in the short-term study compared with 137 msec in the long-term study. In contrast, the search rate, α, is 33.9 msec in the short-term case and only 9.9 msec in the long-term case. Thus, the search is initiated more rapidly in the short-term case, but the search rate is faster in the long-term case. We will not pursue these comparisons here, but will return to them later.

In the next section the model is generalized to an experiment in which target items were stored in either STS or LTS, or in both. For this case, the theory must be elaborated to account for such possibilities as sequential or simultaneous search of the two memory stores and changes in the decision

---

[12] Similar fits were carried out using Model I, which involved estimating both α and α'. The estimate of α' was somewhat below that of α, but the goodness of fit was only slightly improved over that obtained for Model II, using one less parameter.

criteria, depending on whether the test item is potentially a member of a list stored in LTS, in STS, or in both.

AN EXPERIMENT INVOLVING BOTH
LONG- AND SHORT-TERM TARGET SETS

Experiments by Wescourt and Atkinson (1972) and Mohs, Wescourt, and Atkinson (1973) were designed to compare results for the cases in which the subject maintained target sets in LTS, in STS, or in both. Figure 14 presents a flow diagram for the case in which the test stimulus could be a member of a target set in either store. When the test stimulus is presented, it is encoded and the appropriate lexical node is accessed. If the familiarity value associated with that node is above the high criterion or below the low criterion, a fast response is emitted. If familiarity is of an intermediate value, the subject executes an extended search of the two memory stores. Again, it is likely that the internal representations of items in STS and the E/K store are different;

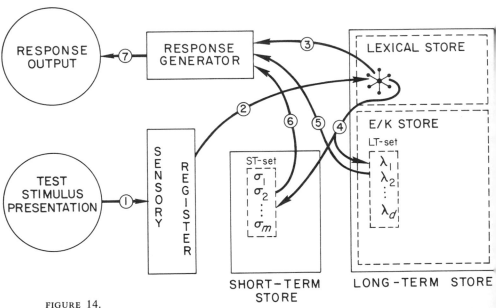

FIGURE 14.

A schematic representation for the case where part of the target set is in STS and part is in LTS. A test item is presented (1) and then matched to its node in the lexical store (2). The familiarity index of the node may lead to an immediate decision (3) and response output (7). Otherwise, an ST code and an LT code are extracted for the lexical node, and then used to search STS and LTS (4). A decision about the test item is eventually made based on the search of LTS (5) or of STS (6), and a response is output (7).

thus, different codes of the test item must be extracted from the test item's lexical node before this search can begin. The search continues until a match is obtained or until both sets are searched without finding a match, and then the appropriate response is made.

In the study considered here, two types of trial blocks were used. For one type, designated the S Block, the target set consisted of only short-term items (ST set). For the other, the M Block, the target set involved a 'mix' of both an ST set and an LT set. The ST set is distinguished from the LT set in two ways:

(1)   The ST set was presented on each trial before the onset of the test stimulus; it always involved a new set of words never before used in the experiment. On the other hand, the LT set was thoroughly memorized the day before the first test session and used throughout the experiment.
(2)   The ST set contained a small number of words (1 to 4), which could readily be maintained in short-term memory without taxing its capacity. The LT set consisted of a list of 30 words (memorized in serial order) stored in long-term memory.

The subjects were tested in three consecutive daily sessions (the data from the first day are not included in the results reported here). Each session was divided into M and S Blocks. On each trial of an M Block, 0 to 4 words (ST set) were presented prior to the onset of the test word. On positive trials, the test word was selected from either the LT set or the ST set if the ST set was nonempty (load condition); or the test word was selected from the LT set if there were no ST items (no-load condition). On negative trials, the test word was not in either the ST or LT set and had never been used before in the experiment. On each trial of the S Block, an ST set of from 1 to 4 words was presented prior to the onset of the test stimulus; on positive trials a word from the ST set was presented for test, and on negative trials a word never used before was presented.

Trials in the S Block are like those in a short-term memory-scanning experiment and are referred to as S trials. The no-load trials of the M Block correspond to those in a long-term recognition task such as the one reported earlier in this chapter; because tests involve only the long-term target set, these trials are called L trials. The load trials of the M Block require the subject to evaluate a test word against both an ST set and the LT set, and they are called M trials. Thus, S trials involve a pure test of short-term memory, L trials a pure test of long-term memory, and M trials involve a mix of both short- and long-term memories.[13] Figure 15 illustrates the various trial types.

---

[13] Studies of this sort have been reported by Forrin and Morin (1969) and Doll (1971). However, they have employed very small LT sets, and there is the possibility that the subject could enter the entire LT set into short-term memory on some or all of the trials. Thus a complete separation of the long- and short-term searches might not have been achieved.

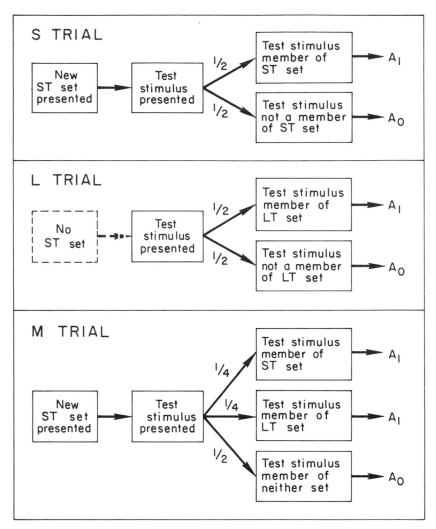

FIGURE 15.
Diagram representing the three types of trials. In all blocks, distractors involve words never presented before in the experiment.

Figure 16 presents the mean latencies of correct responses for the various trial types. The straight lines fitted to the data represent theoretical predictions and are discussed later. In discussing these results, it is useful to adopt the notation defined in Table 6. In all cases these measures refer to the latency of a correct response. The subscript on t indicates the trial type (S, L, or M); the P in parentheses indicates that a positive response was correct (i.e., a

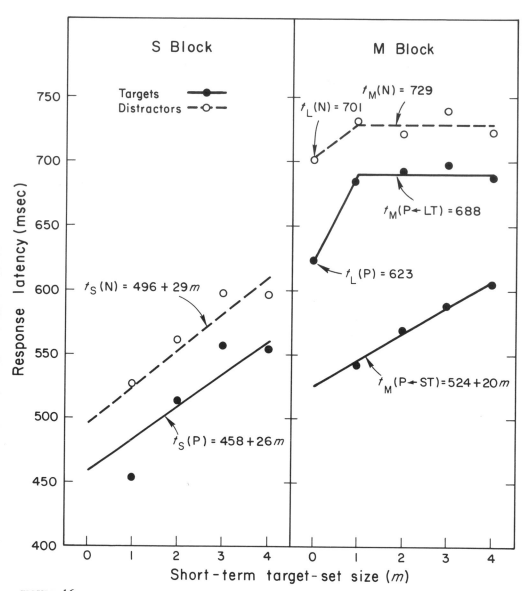

FIGURE 16.
Mean response latencies as functions of ST-set size (*m*) for the S Block (left panel) and the M Block (right panel). The linear functions fitted to the data are explained in the text.

TABLE 6
Definition of notation

Notation	Definition
$t_S(P)$	Time for a positive response on an S trial
$t_S(N)$	Time for a negative response on an S trial
$t_L(P)$	Time for a positive response on an L trial
$t_L(N)$	Time for a negative response on an L trial
$t_M(P \longleftarrow ST)$	Time for a positive response to a test item from the ST set on an M trial
$t_M(P \longleftarrow LT)$	Time for a positive response to a test item from the LT set on an M trial
$t_M(N)$	Time for a negative response on an M trial.

target item was presented for test), whereas N indicates that a negative response was correct (i.e., a distractor was presented for test).

Inspection of Figure 16 shows that the observed values for $t_S(P)$, $t_S(N)$, and $t_M(P \longleftarrow ST)$ are all increasing functions of m, the size of the ST set. In contrast, neither $t_M(P \longleftarrow LT)$ nor $t_M(N)$ appears to be systematically influenced by the size of the ST set. The presence or absence of an ST set in the M Block, however, does have an effect, as is evident by comparing responses on L trials with comparable ones on M trials. Specifically, note that the four observed values for $t_M(P \longleftarrow LT)$ are well above $t_L(P)$, and that the four $t_M(N)$ values are above $t_L(N)$.

The model to be tested against these data assumes that the extended searches are executed separately in STS and in the E/K store. The questions to be asked involve the notion of whether the two memory stores are searched sequentially or simultaneously. Figure 17 presents several flowcharts that represent the differences between serial and parallel searches of STS and the E/K store. The diagram in Figure 17(A) represents the sequence of events on an S trial and corresponds to the short-term recognition model presented

FIGURE 17. (*facing page*)
Flowcharts representing models for processing strategies in searching the memory stores. The model for S trials is shown in Panel A; arrows (1) and (2) represent fast responses based on familiarity alone, whereas (4) and (5) represent responses after a search of STS has occurred. The model for L trials is shown in Panel B and has the same interpretation as Panel A except that the search involves the E/K store. Two alternative models for M trials are presented in the bottom two panels. Panel C presents a parallel search. As before (1) and (2) indicate fast responses based on familiarity; (3) and (4) indicate that the searches of STS and the E/K store are done simultaneously. If the test item is found in the ST set (5) or in the LT set (7), a positive response is made; if the item is not found in the ST set (6) the subject has to wait for a similar outcome from the search of the LT set (8) before a negative response can be made. In Panel D, a sequential search model is presented for M trials. The arrows (1) and (2) represent fast responses based on familiarity. When a search is required, the ST set is examined first (3). If a match is found, a positive response is made (4); if not, the LT set is searched (5). When the LT-set search is complete, either a positive (6) or negative response (7) is output.

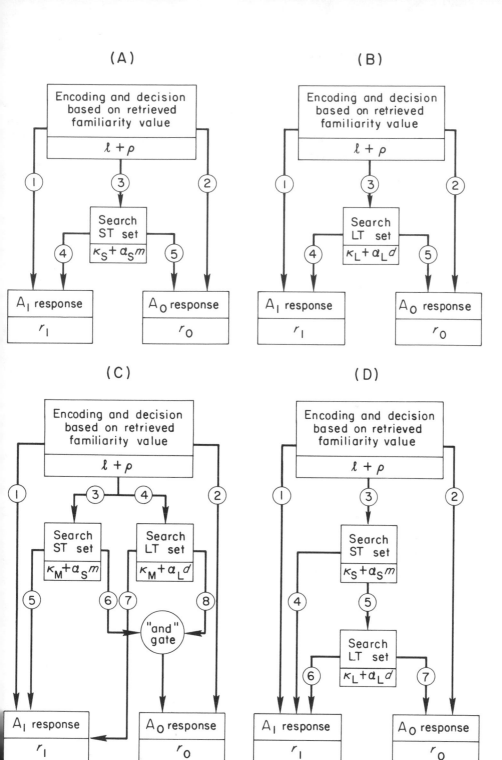

in the preceding section. It assumes that initially the subject makes a familiarity estimate of the test item, and on this basis he outputs a fast positive or negative response if its value is above the high criterion or below the low criterion, respectively. Otherwise, the subject delays his response until a search of STS has been made, the length of this search being a linear function of m (the size of the ST set). Figure 17(B) represents the stages involved on an L trial. Again, the subject can output a fast negative or positive response based on familiarity alone. Otherwise he initiates a search of the E/K store before responding; the time for this search is a linear function of d (the size of the LT set).[14]

For M trials there are at least two search strategies that suggest themselves. First, it is possible that the subject might search both STS and the E/K store simultaneously, outputting a response when the test item is found or when both stores have been searched exhaustively without finding the target. This strategy is represented in Figure 17(C). Alternatively, it is possible that the two memory stores are searched sequentially. Because response time is less to a test item from the ST set than to one from the LT set, we assume that STS is searched first, as shown in Figure 17(D). For both of these M-trial strategies, a fast response will be emitted before a search of either store is made if the retrieved familiarity value is above the high criterion or below the low criterion.

Examination of the data in Figure 16 indicates that the sequential model of Figure 17(D) can be rejected. In this model, the search of the E/K store cannot begin until the STS scan has been completed. Because the length of the STS search depends on the size of the ST set, the beginning of the search of the E/K store and, in turn, $t_M(P \longleftarrow LT)$ and $t_M(N)$ should increase as the ST set increases. The data in Figure 16 indicate that this is not the case; both $t_M(P \longleftarrow LT)$ and $t_M(N)$ appear to be independent of ST-set size. However, these data are compatible with a parallel search model of the type shown in Figure 17(C), if it is assumed that the rate of search in the E/K store is independent of the number of ST items. In order to make a detailed analysis of the models shown in Figure 17, we must derive theoretical equations and fit them to the data.

THEORETICAL PREDICTIONS FOR THE STS–LTS INTERACTION STUDY

The decision stage of the general model, as represented in Figure 5, must be adapted to account for the experimental conditions of the experiment. It is necessary to allow for differences in the decision process, depending on

---

[14] Throughout this chapter, d is used to denote the size of a long-term target set and m to denote the size of a short-term target set.

whether the test item is potentially located in STS only, in the E/K store only, or in both. These differences may be included in the model either by allowing the means of the familiarity distributions to vary as a function of the trial type, or by allowing the decision criteria to change. For the present analysis, we assume that the means of the familiarity distributions are constant over all conditions. This seems to be the most parsimonious assumption; familiarity should be a property of the test stimulus, but the subject could be expected to adjust his decision criteria differently depending on whether it is an S trial, an L trial, or an M trial. Three familiarity distributions are specified: one associated with a test item drawn from the ST set; another for a test item from the LT set; and the third for a distractor item. These distributions are assumed to be unit-normal, with cumulative distribution functions $\Phi_S(\cdot)$, $\Phi_L(\cdot)$, and $\Phi_D(\cdot)$, respectively. The means of the distributions are designated μ_S, μ_L, and μ_D, and they are assumed to be fixed for the data analyzed in this chapter. The reasons for fixing the means are the following: distractor items and ST items appear only once during the experiment, and thus repetition effects on familiarity are not a factor; for the LT items, we treat data only after these items have had several prior tests, and their familiarity should be close to an asymptotic level.

Figure 18 presents a diagram of the familiarity distributions as they apply on S, L, and M trials. Note that the mean for each distribution is placed at the same point on the familiarity scale, no matter what type of trial is involved. Differences in the decision process arise because the subject can set his criteria at different values in anticipation of an S, L, or M trial. This possibility is indicated in Figure 18. The low and high criterion values are denoted as $c_{0,S}$ and $c_{1,S}$ for S trials; as $c_{0,L}$ and $c_{1,L}$ for L trials; and as $c_{0,M}$ and $c_{1,M}$ for M trials. How the subject sets the criteria depends on the trade-off he is willing to accept between speed and accuracy; the nature of the trade-off, of course, varies as a function of the trial type.

Notation comparable to that in Table 6 is used to denote error probabilities. For example, $E_S(P)$ denotes the probability of an error on an S trial for which the correct response was positive. This probability is the tail of the ST distribution to the left of $c_{0,S}$ in Figure 18. Table 7 presents theoretical expressions for the various types of errors.

As before, it is possible to derive equations for response latencies by weighting each stage of the process by the probability that it occurs, and then summing over stages. On every trial the test stimulus must be encoded and the appropriate node in the lexical store accessed; time for this stage is ℓ and is assumed to be the same for all trial types. Next, the subject must make a decision based on the retrieved familiarity value; using Model II, we assume that this decision time is ρ and also is independent of the trial type. If a fast positive or negative response is called for, based on the familiarity value, it will be executed with time r_1 or r_0, respectively.

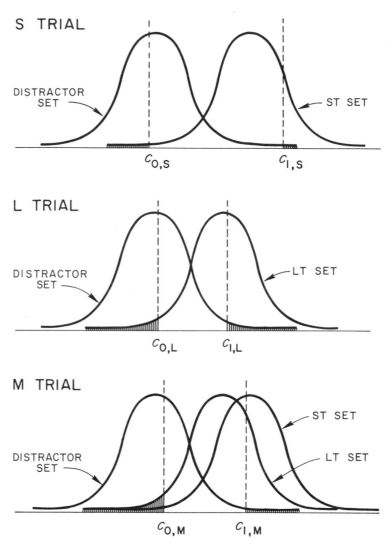

FIGURE 18.
Distributions of familiarity values for the three trial types.

When the familiarity value falls between the two criterion values, a search of the stored target list or lists is required. The nature of this search depends on the trial type because different internal codes may be used and different memory stores scanned. Three classes are to be considered.

S trials. An ST code is extracted from the test item's lexical node and then is scanned against the target set in STS; the time to extract the code

TABLE 7
Theoretical expressions for the probabilities of seven types of errors

S trials	L trials	M trials
$E_S(P) = \Phi_S(c_{0,S})$	$E_L(P) = \Phi_L(c_{0,L})$	$E_M(P \leftarrow ST) = \Phi_S(c_{0,M})$
$E_S(N) = 1 - \Phi_D(c_{1,S})$	$E_L(N) = 1 - \Phi_D(c_{1,L})$	$E_M(P \leftarrow LT) = \Phi_L(c_{0,M})$
		$E_M(N) = 1 - \Phi_D(c_{1,M})$

is denoted as κ_S, and then time $m \cdot \alpha_S$ is required to scan the m items in the ST set.[15]

L trials. An LT code is extracted from the lexical node, which takes time κ_L, and then is scanned against the d items in the LT set, which takes time $d \cdot \alpha_L$ (d in the experiment is 30).

M trials. Both an ST code and an LT code are extracted from the node, and each is scanned against the appropriate list. The extraction of the two codes takes time κ_M, and the respective scans take times $m \cdot \alpha_S$ and $d \cdot \alpha_L$. (Thus, a positive response to an ST or LT item takes time $m \cdot \alpha_S$ or $d \cdot \alpha_L$, respectively; a negative response takes time $d \cdot \alpha_L$ because both lists must be scanned, and the time is determined by the slowest scan which always involves the LT set.)

Whichever of these three cases applies, a positive or negative response—once a decision has been made—requires time r_1 or r_0, respectively.[16]

In terms of these assumptions, we can derive expressions for the latency of a correct response for each of the trial types. The derivation is similar to that for Equations 15 and 16, and only the results are presented:

$$t_S(P) = (\ell + \rho + r_1) + s_S(\kappa_S + m\alpha_S); \tag{21a}$$

$$t_S(N) = (\ell + \rho + r_0) + s_S'(\kappa_S + m\alpha_S); \tag{21b}$$

$$t_L(P) = (\ell + \rho + r_1) + s_L(\kappa_L + d\alpha_L); \tag{22a}$$

---

[15] The parameters κ and α are used here in the same way as in earlier accounts of the theory. The subscript indicates that κ depends on the code(s) to be extracted, and α on the memory store to be scanned.

[16] It is assumed that α_L is independent of the size of the ST set, and that any differences in scanning the LT set on L trials and on M trials is due to κ_L and κ_M, respectively. Independent support for this assumption comes from a study that replicated the M-Block trial sequence, except for the fact that all targets were drawn from the LT set. Subjects had to maintain a set of items in STS (that varied from 0 to 4 words); however, they knew that the test would involve either an LT item or a distractor. Under these conditions the latency of a positive response to an LT item and the latency of a negative response to a distractor were both constant as the ST-set size varied from 0 to 4 (i.e., no change in latency occurred when an ST set was or was not present). In this experiment the scan of the LT set was determined by α_L and κ_L on all trials; the parameter κ_M was not required because only the LT code had to be extracted from the lexical node on both L trials and M trials.

$$t_L(N) = (\ell + \rho + r_0) + s'_L(\kappa_L + d\alpha_L); \tag{22b}$$

$$t_M(P \longleftarrow ST) = (\ell + \rho + r_1) + s_{M,S}(\kappa_M + m\alpha_S); \tag{23a}$$

$$t_M(P \longleftarrow LT) = (\ell + \rho + r_1) + s_{M,L}(\kappa_M + d\alpha_L); \tag{23b}$$

$$t_M(N) = (\ell + \rho + r_0) + s'_M(\kappa_M + d\alpha_L). \tag{23c}$$

The s functions in these equations represent the probability of an extended search conditional on the occurrence of a correct response; they are comparable to those in Equations 17 and 18 and are given in Table 8.

TABLE 8
Probability of an extended memory search
conditional on a correct response

s function	Theoretical expressions
s_S	$[\Phi_S(c_{1,S}) - \Phi_S(c_{0,S})][1 - \Phi_S(c_{0,S})]^{-1}$
s'_S	$[\Phi_D(c_{1,S}) - \Phi_D(c_{0,S})][\Phi_D(c_{1,S})]^{-1}$
s_L	$[\Phi_L(c_{1,L}) - \Phi_L(c_{0,L})][1 - \Phi_L(c_{0,L})]^{-1}$
s'_L	$[\Phi_D(c_{1,L}) - \Phi_D(c_{0,L})][\Phi_D(c_{1,L})]^{-1}$
$s_{M,S}$	$[\Phi_S(c_{1,M}) - \Phi_S(c_{0,M})][1 - \Phi_S(c_{0,M})]^{-1}$
$s_{M,L}$	$[\Phi_L(c_{1,M}) - \Phi_L(c_{0,M})][1 - \Phi_L(c_{0,M})]^{-1}$
s'_M	$[\Phi_D(c_{1,M}) - \Phi_D(c_{0,M})][\Phi_D(c_{1,M})]^{-1}$

In fitting the model to the data, we used a procedure somewhat different from the one employed in the previous experiments. An RMSD function comparable to that given in Equation 12 was defined, but it was composed of two components that were weighted and summed. The first component involved deviations between the 7 observed and predicted error probabilities of Table 7, and the second component involved deviations between the 22 observed and predicted latencies given by Equations 21 through 23. Parameter estimates were then obtained by using a computer to search the parameter space and obtain values that minimized the RMSD function; in the search μ_D was arbitrarily set at zero. The parameter estimates are given in Table 9. Fifteen parameters were estimated from the data, but there are 7 error probabilities and 22 latency measures to be predicted; thus 15 of 29 degrees of freedom were used in parameter estimation, leaving 14 against which to judge the goodness of fits.

The theoretical fits for the latency data are presented as straight lines in Figure 16. The most deviant point is that for $t_S(P)$ when $m = 1$. This particular discrepancy is not unexpected in view of previous research (Juola & Atkinson, 1971); it appears that for a memory set of one item (in the pure

TABLE 9
Parameter estimates

Latency measures	Familiarity measures and decision criteria
$(\ell + \rho + r_1) = 408$ msec	$\mu_D = 0$
$r = 30$ msec	$\mu_L = 1.53$
$\kappa_S = 69$ msec	$\mu_S = 1.51$
$\kappa_L = 140$ msec	$c_{0,S} = -0.99$
$\kappa_M = 207$ msec	$c_{1,S} = 2.13$
$\alpha_S = 35.0$ msec	$c_{0,L} = -0.33$
$\alpha_L = 9.8$ msec	$c_{1,L} = 1.56$
	$c_{0,M} = -0.25$
	$c_{1,M} = 1.72$

Note: $r = r_0 - r_1$.

short-term case) a decision can be based on a direct comparison between a sensory image of the memory item and the sensory input for the test item. Thus, a different process is operative on these particular trials, leading to unusually fast response times. Otherwise, the fits displayed in Figure 16 are quite good, given the linear character of the predictions.[17] Also, the parameter estimates are ordered in the expected way. The estimate of κ_S is less than κ_L, as would be expected by comparing the κ values for the long-term and short-term recognition experiments given in Tables 4 and 5; κ_M is the largest of the group and should be since it involves extracting both an ST and LT code. There is close agreement between the estimate of κ_S in this study (69 msec) and in the short-term study (70 msec); similarly, the estimate of κ_L (140 msec) agrees with the corresponding estimate in the long-term study (137 msec). The α values are also ordered as expected, with a much slower search rate for the ST set than for the LT set. Note that the estimate of α_S (35.0 msec) is close to the α value estimated for the short-term study (33.9 msec), and that α_L (9.8 msec) is virtually identical to the α value estimated for the

---

[17] The curvilinear component in the data of the left panel of Figure 16 [excluding $t_S(P)$ for $m = 1$] was unexpected, because a study by Juola and Atkinson (1971), using a similar procedure but employing only S-type trials, yielded quite straight lines. (For a comparison of the two procedures, see Wescourt & Atkinson, 1973.) The model presented in this chapter can be generalized to yield curvilinear predictions. One possibility is that the subject adjusts his decision criteria as a function of the ST-set size; when the large memory set is presented, he anticipates a slow response and attempts to compensate by adjusting the criteria to generate more fast responses based on familiarity alone. Another possibility is that, under certain experimental conditions, the familiarity of the target items depends on their serial position in the study list (Burrows & Okada, 1971). This assumption would lead to serial position effects and could also account for the curvilinear effects noted here. For a discussion of these possibilities see Atkinson, Herrmann, and Wescourt (1974).

long-term study (9.9 msec). Differences in response keys and stimulus displays make it doubtful that $(\ell + \rho + r_1)$ or r should agree across the three studies reported in this chapter. The parameters that one might hope to be constant over experiments do indeed seem to be, providing some support for the model beyond the goodness-of-fit demonstration.

SUMMARY AND CONCLUSIONS

In this chapter we have considered a model for recognition memory. The model assumes that, when a test stimulus is presented, the subject accesses the lexical store and retrieves a familiarity value for the stimulus. Response decisions based only on this familiarity value can be made very quickly, but result in a relatively high error rate. If the familiarity value does not provide the subject with sufficient information to respond with confidence, a second search of a more extended type is executed. This latter search guarantees that the subject will arrive at a correct decision, but with a consequent increase in response latency. By adjusting the criteria for emitting responses based on familiarity versus those based on an extended memory search, the subject can achieve a stable level of performance, matching the speed and accuracy of responses to the demand characteristics of the experiment.

The model provides a tentative explanation for the results of several recognition-memory experiments. The memory search and decision stages proposed in the present chapter are indicative of possible mechanisms involved in recognition. We do not, however, believe that they provide a complete description of the processes involved; the comparisons of data with theoretical predictions are reported mainly to demonstrate that many features of our results can be described adequately by the model.

There are several additional observations, however, that suggest that the memory and decision components of the model correspond to processing stages of the subject. Introspective reports indicate that subjects might indeed output a rapid response based on tentative, but quickly retrieved, information about the test stimulus. Subjects report that they are sometimes able to respond almost immediately after the word is presented without 'knowing for sure' if the item is a target or not. The same subjects report that on other trials they recall portions of the memorized list before responding. The fact that subjects are always aware of their errors supports the general outline of the model; even if the initial familiarity of an item produces a decision to respond immediately, the search of the appropriate memory store continues and, when completed, permits the subject to confirm whether or not his response was correct.

Additional support for the model comes from its generality to a variety of experimental paradigms (for examples, see Atkinson & Juola, 1973). As reported here, the model can be used to predict response times in recognition tasks with target sets stored in LTS or STS, or in both. It can also handle results from other classes of recognition experiments, such as those employing the Shepard-Teghtsoonian paradigm (e.g., Hintzman, 1969; Okada, 1971). The differences in results from these various types of tasks can be explained in terms of the extended memory search stage; the likelihood that the subject delays his response and makes an extended search of memory is determined by the criteria he adopts to minimize errors while still insuring fast responses. Once the extended search is initiated, its exact nature depends on how the target set is stored in memory (Smith, 1968). If the target set is a well-ordered and thoroughly memorized list of words, the extended search will involve systematic comparisons between the test stimulus and the target items. On the other hand, the target set may be represented in memory as a list of critical attributes (Meyer, 1970). In this case, the extended search would involve checking features of the test stimulus against the attribute list (Neisser, 1967). The dependency of latency on target-set size then would be determined by the relationship between the number of attributes needed to unambiguously specify a target set and the set's size. Finally, target items may be weakly represented in memory (e.g., because they received only a single study presentation); then the extended search might be aimed at retrieving contextual information, with search time relatively independent of target-set size (Atkinson, Herrmann, & Wescourt, 1974; Atkinson & Wescourt, 1974).

These speculations about recognition memory and the nature of the specific task lead to certain testable hypotheses. If the subject adjusts his criteria to balance errors against response speed, different instructions could be used to alter the criteria. For example, if the target set is a well-memorized list of words, and the subject is instructed to make every effort to avoid errors, the appropriate strategy would be to always conduct the extended search before responding. Because the time necessary to complete this search depends on target-set size, both overall latency and list-length effects should increase. Alternatively, if response speed is emphasized in the instructions, the subject should respond primarily on the basis of familiarity. In this case, responses would be emitted without an extended search, and overall latency would decrease and there should be few, if any, list-length effects.

For the theory described in this chapter, the encoding process that permits access to the appropriate node in the lexical store is assumed to occur without error and at a rate independent of the size and make-up of the target set. For highly familiar and minimally confusable words, this assumption appears to be reasonable and is supported by our data. However, for many types of stimuli, increases in target-set size will lead to greater confusability and consequently to slower, as well as less accurate, responses (Juola et al., 1971). When this is the case, the explanation of the set-size effect given here will not be sufficient, for we have assumed that it is due entirely to the extended memory search. Analyses of set-size effects in the framework of this theory would be inappropriate if the experiment were not designed to minimize confusions among stimuli. The theory can be extended to encompass confusion effects by reformulating the encoding scheme and perhaps the extended search process. However, the result would be a cumbersome model with so many interacting processes that it would be of doubtful value as an analytic tool. Trying to account for stimulus confusability in a theory of recognition memory is too ambitious a project, given our current state of knowledge. Greater progress can be made by employing experimental paradigms specifically designed to study recognition memory and other paradigms specifically designed to study confusions among stimuli.

ACKNOWLEDGMENTS

This research was supported by grants from the National Institute of Mental Health (MH 21747) and the National Science Foundation (NSFGJ–443X3). The authors are indebted to J. C. Falmagne and D. J. Herrmann for comments and criticisms on an early draft of this paper.

REFERENCES

Anderson, J. R., & Bower, G. H. Recognition and retrieval processes in free recall. *Psychological Review*, 1972, **79**, 97–123.

Atkinson, R. C., Herrmann, D. J., & Wescourt, K. T. Search processes in recognition memory. In R. L. Solso (Ed.), *Theories in cognitive psychology: The Loyola symposium*. Potomac, Md.: Erlbaum Assoc., 1974.

Atkinson, R. C., Holmgren, J. E., & Juola, J. F. Processing time as influenced by the number of elements in a visual display. *Perception & Psychophysics*, 1969, **6**, 321–326.

Atkinson, R. C., & Juola, J. F. Factors influencing speed and accuracy of word recognition. In S. Kornblum (Ed.), *Fourth international symposium on attention and performance*. New York: Academic Press, 1973.

Atkinson, R. C., & Shiffrin, R. M. Human memory: A proposed system and its control processes. In K. W. Spence and J. T. Spence (Eds.), *The psychology of learning and motivation*. Vol. II. New York: Academic Press, 1968.

Atkinson, R. C., & Shiffrin, R. M. The control of short-term memory. *Scientific American*, 1971, **225**, 82–90.

Atkinson, R. C., & Wescourt, K. T. Some remarks on a theory of memory. In P. Rabbitt and S. Dornic (Eds.), *Fifth international symposium on attention and performance*. London: Academic Press, 1974.

Baddeley, A. D., & Ecob, J. R. *Reaction time and short-term memory: A trace strength alternative to the high-speed exhaustive scanning hypothesis*. Technical Report No. 13. San Diego: Center for Human Information Processing, University of California, 1970.

Banks, W. P. Signal detection theory and human memory. *Psychological Bulletin*, 1970, **74**, 81–99.

Burrows, D., & Okada, R. Serial position effects in high-speed memory search. *Perception & Psychophysics*, 1971, **10**, 305–308.

Corballis, M. C., Kirby, J., & Miller, A. Access to elements of a memorized list. *Journal of Experimental Psychology*, 1972, **94**, 185–190.

Doll, T. J. Motivation, reaction time, and the contents of active verbal memory. *Journal of Experimental Psychology*, 1971, **87**, 29–36.

Egeth, H., Marcus, N., & Bevan, W. Target-set and response-set interactions: Implications for models of human information processing. *Science*, 1972, **176**, 1447–1448.

Fischler, I., & Juola, J. F. Effects of repeated tests on recognition time for information in long-term memory. *Journal of Experimental Psychology*, 1971, **91**, 54–58.

Forrin, B., & Morin, R. E. Recognition time for items in short- and long-term memory. *Acta Psychologica*, 1969, **30**, 126–141.

Herrmann, D. J. The effects of organization in long-term memory on recognition latency. Unpublished doctoral dissertation, University of Delaware, 1972.

Hintzman, D. Recognition time: Effects of recency, frequency, and the spacing of repetitions. *Journal of Experimental Psychology*, 1969, **79**, 192–194.

Juola, J. F. Repetition and laterality effects on recognition memory for words and pictures. *Memory & Cognition*, 1973, **1**, 183–192.

Juola, J. F., & Atkinson, R. C. Memory scanning for words vs. categories. *Journal of Verbal Learning and Verbal Behavior*, 1971, **10**, 522–527.

Juola, J. F., Fischler, I., Wood, C. T., & Atkinson, R. C. Recognition time for information stored in long-term memory. *Perception & Psychophysics*, 1971, **10**, 8–14.

Kintsch, W. Memory and decision aspects of recognition learning. *Psychological Review*, 1967, **74**, 496–504.

Kintsch, W. *Learning, memory, and conceptual processes.* New York: John Wiley, 1970. (a)

Kintsch, W. Models for free recall and recognition. In D. A. Norman (Ed.), *Models of human memory.* New York: Academic Press, 1970. (b)

Klatzky, R. L., Juola, J. F., & Atkinson, R. C. Test stimulus representation and experimental context effects in memory scanning. *Journal of Experimental Psychology*, 1971, **87**, 281–288.

Mandler, G., Pearlstone, F., & Koopmans, H. S. Effects of organization and semantic similarity on recall and recognition. *Journal of Verbal Learning and Verbal Behavior*, 1969, **8**, 410–423.

McCormack, P. D. Recognition memory: How complex a retrieval system. *Canadian Journal of Psychology*, 1972, **26**, 19–41.

Meyer, D. E. On the representation and retrieval of stored semantic information. *Cognitive Psychology*, 1970, **1**, 242–300.

Miller, G. A. The organization of lexical memory: Are word associations sufficient? In G. A. Talland and N. C. Waugh (Eds.), *The pathology of memory.* New York: Academic Press, 1969.

Mohs, R. C., Wescourt, K. T., & Atkinson, R. C. Effects of short-term memory contents on short- and long-term memory searches. *Memory & Cognition*, 1973, **1**, 443–448.

Morton, J. The interaction of information in word recognition. *Psychological Review*, 1969, **76**, 165–178.

Morton, J. A functional model for memory. In D. A. Norman (Ed.), *Models of human memory*. New York: Academic Press, 1970.

Murdock, B. B., Jr. A parallel-processing model for scanning. *Perception & Psychophysics*, 1971, **10**, 289–291.

Neisser, U. *Cognitive psychology*. New York: Appleton-Century-Crofts, 1967.

Nickerson, R. S. *Binary-classification reaction time: A review of some studies of human information-processing capabilities*. Technical Report No. 2004. Cambridge, Mass.: Bolt, Beranek, and Newman, 1970.

Norman, D. A. (Ed.) *Models of human memory*. New York: Academic Press, 1970.

Okada, R. Decision latencies in short-term recognition memory. *Journal of Experimental Psychology*, 1971, **90**, 27–32.

Parks, T. E. Signal-detectability theory of recognition-memory performance. *Psychological Review*, 1966, **73**, 44–58.

Rothstein, L. D., & Morin, R. E. The effects of size of the stimulus ensemble and the method of set size manipulation on recognition reaction time. Paper presented at the meetings of the Midwestern Psychological Association, Cleveland, Ohio, May 1972.

Rubenstein, H., Garfield, L., & Millikan, J. A. Homographic entries in the internal lexicon. *Journal of Verbal Learning and Verbal Behavior*, 1970, **9**, 487–492.

Schank, R. Conceptual dependency: A theory of natural language understanding. *Cognitive Psychology*, 1972, **3**, 552–631.

Schvaneveldt, R. W., & Meyer, D. E. Retrieval and comparison processes in semantic memory. In S. Kornblum (Ed.), *Fourth international symposium on attention and performance*. New York: Academic Press, 1973.

Shepard, R. N. Recognition memory for words, sentences, and pictures. *Journal of Verbal Learning and Verbal Behavior*, 1967, **6**, 156–163.

Shepard, R. N., & Teghtsoonian, M. Retention of information under conditions approaching a steady state. *Journal of Experimental Psychology*, 1961, **62**, 302–309.

Shevell, S., & Atkinson, R. C. A theoretical comparison of list scanning models. *Journal of Mathematical Psychology*, 1974, in press.

Smith, E. E. Choice reaction time: An analysis of the major theoretical positions. *Psychological Bulletin*, 1968, **69**, 72–110.

Sternberg, S. High-speed scanning in human memory. *Science*, 1966, **153**, 652–654.

Sternberg, S. The discovery of processing stages: Extensions of Dander's method. In W. G. Koster (Ed.), *Attention and performance II. Acta Psychologica*, 1969, **36**, 276–315. (a)

Sternberg, S. Memory scanning: Mental processes revealed by reaction-time experiments. *American Scientist*, 1969, **57**, 421–457. (b)

Suppes, P. Stimulus-sampling theory for a continuum of responses. In K. J. Arrow, S. Karlin, and P. Suppes (Eds.), *Mathematical methods in the social sciences*. Stanford, Calif.: Stanford University Press, 1960.

Thomas, E. A. C. Sufficient conditions for monotone hazard rate: An application to latency-probability curves. *Journal of Mathematical Psychology*, 1971, **8**, 303–332.

Townsend, J. T. A note on the identifiability of parallel and serial processes. *Perception & Psychophysics*, 1971, **10**, 161–163.

Tulving, E. Episodic and semantic memory. In E. Tulving and W. Donaldson (Eds.), *Organization of memory*. New York: Academic Press, 1972.

Wescourt, K., & Atkinson, R. C. Memory scanning for information in short- and long-term memory. *Journal of Experimental Psychology*, 1973, **98**, 95–101.

Wilde, D. J. *Optimum seeking methods*. Englewood Cliffs, N.J.: Prentice-Hall, 1964.

Index

(VOLUME I)